# DELIVERY OF PUBLIC SERVICES IN ASIAN COUNTRIES:
## Cases in Development Administration

**Edited by**

Suchitra Punyaratabandhu-Bhakdi

Purachai Piumsombun

Voradej Chandarasorn

Soonthorn Kerdkaew

Pisan Suriyamongkol

Kusumal Devahastin

LIBRARY
AMERICAN GRADUATE SCHOOL
OF INTERNATIONAL MANAGEMENT
GLENDALE, ARIZONA 85306

School of Public Administration

National Institute of Development Administration

*Cataloging in Publication Data*

Main entry under title:

Delivery of public services in Asian countries: cases
 in development administration

   Selected papers presented at the 11th EROPA Conference on
"Delivery of Public Services in National Development" held in Bangkok, 8-14 December 1985, co-sponsored by the School of Public Administration, NIDA and the EROPA.
   Includes bibliographical references and indexes.
   1. Public Administration—Asia—Congress. 2. Public administration—ASEAN countries—Congresses. I. Suchitra Punyaratabandhu-Bhakdi, et al., eds. II. National Institute of Development Administration. School of Public Administration. III. Eastern Regional Organization for Public Administration.
JA 35.5.E 2   354.5
ISBN 974-8161-37-4

*COPYRIGHT © 1986 by the National Institute of Development Administration*

All rights reserved. No part of this book may be reproduced in any form or by any means without permission in writing from the National Institute of Development Administration.

Thammasat University Press
Bangkok, Thailand

# Preface

In December 1985, the Eastern Regional Organization for Public Administration (EROPA) held its Eleventh General Assembly and Conference in Bangkok. The Assembly and Conference were hosted by the Royal Thai Government, which designated the National Institute of Development Administration as the institution in charge of conference arrangements and preparations.

This book consists of a selection of the papers that were presented at the Conference, with two new introductory and concluding chapters. Each chapter addresses some aspect of the Conference theme, "Delivery of Public Services in National Development: Problems, Solution Alternatives, and Structural Adjustments." Due to limitations of space, however, it was not possible to include a number of worthy Conference presentations. Selection of the papers that appear here was based in part on the desire to secure broad coverage of the major sectors of public service delivery, as well as those components of administrative systems that affect the delivery of public services; and in part on the extent to which different case studies were interrelated so as to provide a comparative perspective.

The Conference was made possible through generous grants from the Royal Thai Government and the Asian and Pacific Development Center. In preparation for the Conference, a separate Workshop for paper writers was held in advance under the sponsorship of the Asia Foundation. Most grateful acknowledgement is made here of their contributions. The Rector of the National Institute of Development Administration, Dr. Amara Raksasataya, also lent his gracious support and guidance.

A great many individuals and institutions contributed to the success of the Conference. They are too numerous to be mentioned here, but special recognition is due to: the Steering Committee, chaired by Dean Thongsri Kambhu; the Subcommittees, which took care of the Conference arrangements down to the last detail; and the faculty and staff of the Graduate School of Public Administration (NIDA), who tirelessly put in long hours of overtime. Faculty and staff from NIDA's Library and Information Center, English Language Program, and Audiovisual Center also gave most generously of their time and energy.

The EROPA Conference was attended by participants from a total of twenty-six countries, with papers submitted from: Guam, Hong Kong, India, Indonesia, Japan, Korea, Malaysia, Nepal, the Philippines, Singapore, Sri Lanka, and Thailand. Panel and Workshop proceedings during the Conference benefited from the lively discussions that took place. Discussants and moderators came from: the Asian Institute of Technology, Chulalongkorn University, the Civil Service Commission, Kasetsart Univerity, Mahidol University, the Ministry of Interior, the Office of the National Economic and Social Development Board, Ramkamhaeng University, Sukhothai Thammatiraj University, and Thammasat University. Faculty from NIDA's Schools of Development Economics, Business Administration, and Public Administration, as well as from the Research Center and English Language Program also served most ably as discussants and moderators. Special acknowledgment is due to all.

In preparing this volume for publication, the editors were most fortunate to obtain valuable comments and insights from Dr. Martin Landau, Institute of Governmental Studies and the Political Science Department, University of California at Berkeley, and from Dr. Uthai Laohavichien, Graduate School of Public Administration, National Institute of Development Administration, Bangkok. The editors gratefully acknowledge the inspired editorial assistance of Captain Sumaet Punyaratabandhu, who also provided the indexes that appear at the end of this book.

This volume should be viewed as an end product of the EROPA Conference. It was made possible through the efforts of all of the individuals and institutions named above, and through a publication grant from the Royal Thai Government. Any errors of omission or commission remain the sole responsibility, of course, of the editors.

# Contents

| | | |
|---|---|---|
| Preface | | iii |
| Introduction | | vii |
| Chapter 1 | Delivery of Public Services: Philosophical and Historical Antecedents<br>*The Editors* | 1 |
| Chapter 2 | Service Delivery System of the Agricultural Sector in Thailand: Alternatives and Structural Adjustments for Development<br>*Patom Manirojana* | 20 |
| Chapter 3 | Agricultural Service Delivery System in India<br>*B. M. Verma* | 50 |
| Chapter 4 | Structures for Health Service Delivery in the Philippines: The Case of the Primary Health Care Approach<br>*Victoria A. Bautista and Josie H. de Leon* | 76 |
| Chapter 5 | Delivery System of Public Health Services in Rural Areas: The Korean Case<br>*In-Joung Whang* | 104 |
| Chapter 6 | Urban Low Cost Housing in the ASEAN: A Comparative View<br>*Jürgen Rüland* | 130 |
| Chapter 7 | Delivery of Public Services in Urban Korea, with Special Reference to Shelter Problems<br>*Chung-Hyun Ro* | 158 |

| Chapter 8 | Strategies Management in the Delivery of an Effective Transportation System in Singapore<br>*Chee Meow Seah* | 175 |
| Chapter 9 | Toward Effective Delivery of Public Services at the Local Level: Restructuring of Local Government in Peninsular Malaysia<br>*Shamsuddin Kassim* | 202 |
| Chapter 10 | The Delivery of Services at Sub-District Level: The Concept of Service Centers in Nepal<br>*Khagendra Nath Sharma* | 219 |
| Chapter 11 | Toward Productivity and Excellence: A Comparative Analysis of the Public Personnel Systems in the ASEAN Countries<br>*Jon S.T. Quah* | 238 |
| Chapter 12 | Toward Effective Delivery of Public Services: An Analysis of the National Budgetary System and Reforms in Sri Lanka<br>*C. T. Elangasekere* | 273 |
| Chapter 13 | Delivery of Public Services: Framework for Policy Analysis and Strategy Recommendations<br>*The Editors* | 294 |

**List of Abbreviations** 313
**Index of Names** 315
**Index of Subjects** 319

# Introduction

Once upon a time, we had to rely upon our Western friends to teach us about the processes known as development administration. If that was the case some time ago, it is no longer so. For the past two decades (more or less), we have experienced at first hand and on a day-to-day basis the problems and the issues of development administration. As development administrators—whether practitioners or academics—we have been deeply involved in the search for solutions to our problems. Our commitment extends beyond mere professional or academic interest.

The eleven case studies that are presented here, whatever their imperfections, are grappling with the effort of what *to do*. They document the past development experience as well as ongoing processes in the developing countries in Asia. In this respect, they constitute a valuable source of descriptive case materials. Their empirical orientation supplies us with much-needed information regarding structures and processes of development administration in the region. From this empirical base we can then proceed to build an analytical framework to guide us in our search for solutions.

Chapter One gives a broad-based perspective by examining the historical and philosophical antecedents of the delivery of public services. Questions that ask whether a particular service *ought* to be provided, or what *ought* to be the scope and nature of public service delivery, call for answers that are basically, if not entirely, normative in character. The authors of Chapter One do not presume to supply the answers; their main purpose is to explain the genesis of current developments by describing their philosophical foundations and the related historical experiences. In this way, a better understanding of the present could be gained from understanding the past. In turn, knowing how and why we got to where we are today would hopefully affect prescriptions regarding future courses of action.

In Chapter Two, Patom Manirojana describes the institutional framework and institutional performance of the agricultural sector in Thailand. He identifies weaknesses in the structural, organizational, managerial, and procedural aspects of the delivery system. Chapter Three by B.M. Verma takes an historical approach in examining the development of the agricultural credit system in India. An account is given of policy shifts that have occurred over the past three decades.

Chapters Four and Five deal with delivery systems of public health services. In Chapter Four, Victoria Bautista and Josie H. de Leon focus on structural arrangements in the delivery of health services in the Philippines, problems that derive from current structures, and contextual variables that affect program implementation. Specifically, the Primary Health Care Approach, first instituted in 1980, is examined, with the Southern Tagalog Region serving as a case study of program implementation. In Chapter Five, In-Joung Whang provides a descriptive analysis of the Korean delivery system of public health care services in remote rural areas. He examines availability of health care services, patterns of health care utilization, and discusses issues such as private versus public services, community health care service, and management issues in the rural health delivery system of Korea.

The next three chapters deal with delivery systems in urban areas. A comparative perspective on delivery of urban low cost housing services in the ASEAN countries is provided by Jürgen Rüland (Chapter Six). Assessment is made of the impact of major low cost housing strategies on the living conditions of the poor, with special reference to the Philippines, Thailand, and Malaysia. In Chapter Seven, Chung-Hyun Ro examines urban housing policies and housing administration in Korea. A description is given of a research experiment for the improvement of a squatter settlement in Nankok-Dong, Seoul. Chapter Eight constitutes a case study of a quite different dimension of urban service delivery, namely, the transportation system. Chee Meow Seah discusses the policymaking process in Singapore with respect to transportation. His account focuses on the nature of decisionmaking in policy formulation and identifies contextual variables which constrain the choices available to policymakers.

Administrative structures significantly affect the quality and effectiveness of delivery of public services. Accordingly, two of our chapters consider institutional arrangements in the provision of services at the local level. In Chapter Nine, Shamsuddin Kassim describes the restructuring of local authorities in Peninsular Malaysia, analyzes problems arising from restructuring, and makes recommendations on how to solve the problems. K.N. Sharma discusses the concept of service centers set up under the multi-sectoral Integrated Rural Development Project in Nepal (Chapter Ten). The service centers are viewed as an important aspect of Nepal's Decentralization Act.

Personnel and budgeting are integral components of public service delivery systems. In recognition of this fact, two chapters in this book are devoted to these topics. Jon S.T. Quah, in Chapter Eleven, provides a comparative analysis of the public personnel systems in five ASEAN countries. In Chapter Twelve, C.T. Elangasekere describes the national budgeting system of Sri Lanka and links it to the delivery of public services.

Chapters Two through Twelve stand on their own merit as case studies of public service delivery in Asian countries. The intent of this book, however, is not only to provide in-depth analyses of specific problem contexts. More ambitiously, the aim of this book is to discern and extrapolate underlying trends with respect to public service delivery, and to make an assessment of what we have learned from the lessons of history, based on the individual case studies. Our final chapter, therefore, presents an analytical framework, based upon the case materials, that should be useful for policy analysis and identification of appropriate options. Sharing, as most Asian countries do, a related cultural heritage and historical background, as well as possessing in common many socioeconomic and political features, we would do well to engage in, and benefit from, learning transfers. The present volume constitutes a modest effort in that direction.

*Suchitra Punyaratabandhu-Bhakdi*
*Purachai Piumsombun*
*Voradej Chandarasorn*
*Soonthorn Kerdkaew*
*Pisan Suriyamongkol*
*Kusumal Devahastin*

School of Public Administration
National Institute of Development
   Administration
Bangkok, December 1986

# 1 Delivery of Public Services: Philosophical and Historical Antecedents

*The Editors*

In many developing countries today, it is taken as axiomatic that in order to achieve economic and social development goals, the state should arrange for the provision of a large variety of public services, ranging from, for example, national defense, maintenance of law and order, transportation and communications, to a host of services that bear the generic label of social services. In recent years, however, the limits to government and the limitations of government have become increasingly apparent. Faith in the efficacy of big government, so implicit in the development programs launched in the 1950s and early 1960s, has steadily eroded in light of events that have actually transpired. The promise of big government has not been fulfilled.

Yet the goal of achieving a more rapid development through planned change while ensuring, at the same time, a reasonable degree of social equity in improving the quality of life, has forced the public sector in the developing countries to take, of necessity, a lead role in chartering the course of national development. Nevertheless, governments in the Asian countries today are all too aware of the constraints imposed by limited resources and imperfect technologies, in management and administration as well as in other substantive areas.

In an effort to resolve their dilemma, governments have considered a number of strategies. Privatization of public enterprises and the contracting out of tasks to private sector organizations constitute two responses to the management problem. Both strategies assume that the private sector manages more efficiently than public agencies. In addition, privatization implies that the burden of shouldering the cost of services should be borne directly, and in full, by the consumer.

Other responses to the problem of resource scarcity and unwieldiness of highly centralized administrative systems have been to encourage grassroots participation, sometimes during plan or project formulation, but especially during the implementation phase, and also to deconcentrate and decentralize authority. Strategies such as grassroots participation and decentralization derive their justification on two separate grounds. The first is instrumental--that by decentralizing decisionmaking power to lower units of administration, and by involving popular participation, decisions will be arrived at that are more suited to the particular needs of a locality than are decisions made at a distance by unseen bureaucrats in the central administration. The second justification rests on normative grounds--that grassroots involvement and decentralized processes are "more democratic," and by implication somehow "better," than centralized, authoritarian or paternalistic styles of government.

It is the normative aspect of public service delivery which concerns us in this chapter. We are interested not only in questions regarding forms of administration, but also in questions pertaining to scope and nature of the public services to be supplied. How is it that certain kinds of services (e.g., social welfare) are provided most generously by the state in some countries, whereas in other countries those services are provided only minimally or sometimes not at all? These are nontrivial questions. The case studies that comprise the remainder of this book describe what is actually being done with respect to provision of public services in selected Asian countries. In so doing, they assert, by implication, that the particular activities described should legitimately be treated as public services. Or, some of the case studies reach the conclusion that certain programs should be removed from the domain of public services and the activities transferred over to the private sector. In either case, what we are presented with, implicitly in the first case, explicitly in the second, is a normative statement concerning which activities ought to be treated as public services, and which ought to be discontinued.

When prescriptions are based on normative judgments, the question is begged regarding the origins of the norms. This chapter adopts a historical perspective in outlining changes that have occurred in philosophical thought over the centuries with respect to the role and duties of government in the discharge and provision of public services. Both eastern and western philosophies are examined. In most, if not all, of the Asian countries today, modern governmental systems, especially in countries that were once under the colonial rule of the European powers, reflect rather obviously the influence of western thought. Yet it is equally obvious that western philosophies constitute no more than a surface overlay, that to understand properly the philosophical basis for societal norms governing provision of public services, one must also take into account the traditional, indigenous culture and philosophies of government. Where eastern and western precepts are congruent or complementary, norms become entrenched, permanent features of the system. But when eastern and western precepts turn out to be at variance with each other, then the status of derivative norms is much more tenuous. Policies that are based on one set of norms may meet with apathetic responses or even resistance from target groups who have been conditioned by another set of norms.

Norms are fashioned not only from philosophical tenets but also from the historical experience. In a later section of this chapter we shall examine the historical antecedents of the delivery of public services, with particular attention to the emergence of social services in Western Europe as a consequence of urbanization and the Industrial Revolution. We note that although the term "public service delivery" is of recent vintage, coined by the American federal government administration in the 1960s, the concept itself is as old as government.[1] As soon as there is sufficient institutional evolution and differentiation to enable one to speak of the government of a society, there are actions which, successful or not, are designed to carry the government's intentions into effect. In traditional societies, the objectives of public service delivery are simple, limited to such matters as preserving law and order and national defense. The institutions which deliver public services are likewise simple, relatively small, and often not comparatively differentiated from institutions with other purposes. As societies increase in size and complexity, as governments grow larger and take on more functions, the processes of public service delivery become more specialized, and the systems that provide the services become large, complex, and highly differentiated.

**Oriental Philosophies of Public Service Delivery**

The philosophies of public service delivery have their historical antecedents in ancient times. The heritage of most Asian countries is the heritage of India and China. In India, the conceptual basis for public services in political and legal terms is found, long before the Christian era, in some portions of the epic *Mahabharata,* which represents an attempt of Vedic Brahminism to adjust itself to the importation of Aryan culture. According to the *Mahabharata,* the primary function of the king or ruler is to protect the people and to punish wrongdoers; otherwise the strong will tyrannize the weak. The ideal-type king is viewed as created by God in order to protect all beings from the terror of anarchy.

Further obligations of the ruler are contained in the *Dharma-sastra,* systematized and codified by Manu, the well-known lawgiver of antiquity. According to Manu, the *dharma* is the only solid ground on which to base either individual or collective actions. A government derives its legitimacy from adherence to the principles of the *dharma.* Manu states:

> (Man) is both good and bad. It is the duty of the ideal state to create conditions and opportunities that will gradually help man overcome his ignorance, selfishness, and immoral tendencies, so that a harmonious community may evolve in which every individual can advance toward the supreme goal of spiritual freedom.[2]

Manu held, moreover, that since the people paid revenue for public safety and social services, the king did not own the state. Rather, the king's role was one of leader, protector, and provider of public services, ruling in accordance with the principles of the *dharma.* We note, in passing, that this Indian concept comes close to the Western idea of "no protection, no taxation." Furthermore, only a legitimate king is worthy of the scepter, which, in turn, destroys a tyrant or unrighteous ruler. In Suka's words,

> The king should behave in three different ways: like the (pleasant) autumn moon to the learned, like the (scorching) summer sun to the enemy, like the (moderate) spring sun to his subjects.[3]

Buddhism, originating in India in the fifth century B.C., was antithetical to Brahminic doctrines by advocating meditation as a means of attaining enlightenment. In addition to its ethical teachings, Buddhism also specifies the ten kingly duties or virtues. These are: charity or *dana;* high moral character or *sila;* self-sacrifice or *pariccaya;* integrity or *ajjava;* kindness or *maddava;* self-control or *tapa;* non-anger or *akkodha;* non-oppression or *avihimsa;* tolerance or *khanti;* and conformity to the law or *avirodhana.*

In the third century B.C., King Asoka the Great was converted to Buddhism. Enlightened by the teachings of the Buddha, the great warrior-king became renowned for his just and righteous rule. Peace treaties were concluded with neighboring states, and religious emissaries were sent abroad to disseminate the Buddha's teachings. The spread of Buddhism east and southeast of India meant also that Buddhist precepts of kingship, as embodied in the ten kingly virtues, were transplanted and took root in the countries that converted to Buddhism. By the fifth century A.D., Buddhism had taken three separate forms: Hinayana (Lesser Vehicle) or Theravada (Way of the Elders); Mahayana (Greater Vehicle); and Vajrayana or Lamaism. Hinayana Buddhism became well established in Sri Lanka, Burma, Thailand, Laos and Cambodia. Mahayana Buddhism gained popularity in Vietnam, China, Korea, and Japan; while Vajrayana Buddhism remained largely in the Himalayan states of Bhutan, Sikkim, Nepal, and Tibet.

At about the same time that Buddhism appeared in India, Kung-tzu founded the school of Confucius in China in the fifth century B.C.. Having in his lifetime witnessed oppression and persecution of the helpless and ignorant by unrighteous rulers, Kung-tzu was inspired to search for principles by which to legitimate kingship and good government. Confucian precepts teach that:

> A good society is based on the natural sympathy of men toward men. To make human relations peaceful and beneficial for all, all must practice genuine reciprocity in their social intercourse with others.[4]

This concept of reciprocity in social intercourse comes close to the Christian precept of doing "unto others as you would have others do unto you."

The Confucian school of thought regards the king or ruler as a man of virtue who harmoniously regulates both man and nature. Kung-tzu describes the relationship between ruler and ruled as that between wind and grass, meaning that the grass bows whenever the wind blows over it. But the analogy is not intended to imply mere subservience. The further interpretation can be made that when a king or ruler sets an example by performing his duties well, the public are to emulate him by carrying out their duties in like manner.

In the third century B.C., Meng-tzu, a student of Kung-tzu, founded the school of Mencius, which provides a more liberal interpretation of Confucian teaching. According to Mencius, if a ruler or government has no concern for the well-being of the people and possesses no paternal benevolence, then the people have the right to abolish that ruler or government. Heaven sees as the people see, and hears as the people hear. The metaphor that Mencius supplies is one in which the people are the water, and their ruler is the boat. Water keeps the boat afloat, but it can also sink the boat. In his advocacy of equal rights and liberty, universal education, free trade, and a simple tax system, Meng-tzu's ideas parallel the modern concept of liberal democracy.

Mencian concepts took hold rapidly--so much so that in 1946, Wang Gung-hsing, Chinese consul in New Orleans, could write:

> During the past two thousand years, China has more or less followed the political pattern woven by Mencius. ... The right to revolt not only made our rulers mindful of the interest of the people but also kept our nation politically virile and dynamic.[5]

Confucian and Mencian precepts found their way eastward to Japan, where the concepts of government and public service not only were adopted but also became one of the most concrete bases for the establishment of Japanese nationalism. The Japanese interpreted the legitimacy of their ruling dynasty as due to heaven. The Japanese emperor was the Son of Heaven who received his mandate to rule in accordance with benevolent principles. These principles corresponded to Confucian and Mencian precepts, with one notable exception: the Mencian right to revolt was never recognized either by the Japanese government or by the Japanese people. In fact, this right was considered as both inapplicable and positively harmful to the polity.

**Western Philosophies of Public Service Delivery**

While concepts of public service and governance in the Far East and South and Southeast Asia are largely the product of Hindu-Buddhist and Confucian-Mencian influences, Western concepts owe much to the legacy of Greece and Rome. We can trace the origins of public service delivery back to the city-state of Athens, more than two thousand years ago. As a unified community, the city-state was, of course, far different from the leviathan nation-state of the twentieth century.[6] Social classes in the Athenian city-state consisted of the citizen class, the resident-foreigner group, and the slave class. Citizens were all equal, and they *were* the state. In a word, the state existed for the citizens, not the converse. It was the function of the state to provide a minimum of economic welfare for its citizens. The state, thus,

> employed public works, defense projects, relief for the indigent, pensions for disabled veterans, business and price regulation, sharing of tribute and the spoils of war, religious festivals, and other devices to ensure a minimum standard of living for its people.[7]

Slaves, on the other hand, were owned mainly by the state and were employed as miners, mariners of the merchant fleet, policemen, executioners, jailers, maintenance men, and construction workers on public projects.[8] In terms of the public administration, citizens may be thought of as the rulers or public administrators, while slaves performed the indispensable function of delivering public services. M. Judd Harmon elaborates further:

> The Athenian "bureaucracy" on the lower levels was largely made up of state slaves who, over the years, acquired some real power by virtue of their knowledge of the functioning of the governmental agencies to which they were attached. Since elective positions held by the citizens were of short tenure, generally one year, the slave civil servant was able to guide and direct the citizen official who was not so well instructed in the intricacies of public administration.[9]

Deeply rooted in the city-state are the democratic political and social ideals of Athenian citizenship. The Greeks believed that state instrumentalism went hand-in-hand with the "service state." The state arises in the first place in answer to the demand for the satisfaction of reciprocal needs; a community organization is obviously best fitted to accomplish that end. Since some men perform a particular task better than others, they should perform only that task. Each person works at what he does best, and through organization, not only satisfies his own needs but also the needs of others for that service. The formation of classes in society is therefore simple: it aims to supply the community with the material necessities of life. Thus, the best state is that state which satisfies this need best; and the state which satisfies this need perfectly is *ipso facto* the perfect state.[10]

It is with respect to the means for achieving the perfect state that the Greek philosophers differed. Socrates held that this condition was to be attained through government by the "virtuous," and not through the Athenian democracy. The Socratic view is that in any society there exists a minority with greater intelligence and knowledge --and consequently, with more virtue --than is found in the majority of the populace. It follows from this premise that government by the many is government by the nonvirtuous, which is obviously unjust. Employing a similar definition of virtue, Plato also agrees with the view that the most virtuous people should be the rulers. He holds, moreover, that it is the task of the ruler to develop a virtuous people. This is to be accomplished through the delivery of educational services to the citizens, upon whom the welfare of the state depends. Failure to deliver such services will result in the loss of a considerable potential, which might otherwise be devoted to the achievement of the perfect state.

Aristotle takes a quite different position from either Socrates or Plato. In fact, his political philosophy, emphasizing as it does constitutionalism and the rule of law, is much closer to the Athenian democratic ideal. Aristotle criticizes Plato's advocacy of the rule of the elite or the philosopher-king and his abandonment of the rule of law. Acknowledging that there are no perfect (i.e., virtuous) men, Aristotle arrives at the conclusion that since no class has the right to be sovereign, the position of sovereignty must be accorded to the law. The rule of law, not of force, should govern men. Thus, though men may not be equal in all, or even some respects, in the good society they must be entitled to equal standing under the law.

The Aristotelian ideal of the good state begins with the rule of law which is directed toward promoting the good life of the individual. Priority is given to the inculcation of morality among the citizens, and subordination of material things to that end. The good state is never aggressive or imperialist. It is solely concerned with maintaining the peace and with bringing about internal improvements through provision of public services. Aristotle identifies six distinct areas in which the state should be involved: agriculture, arts and crafts, defense, land ownership, religion, and general government service.[11] The best state is one which can best help its citizens to achieve the good life. Aristotle concurs with Plato that education is the chief means by which to attain this ends. Thus his advocacy of a publicly supported educational system.

The teachings of Plato and Aristotle strongly influenced the philosophers of the Roman Empire. Polybius in the first century B.C. was the first to apply Aristotle's rule of law to governmental institutions and to propose a system of checks and balances, as it is known today.[12] It was Polybius' belief that such a system conduces to the preservation of individual freedom, and hence will best ensure perfect public service delivery.[13]

Roman legal theory also received its influence from Aristotle's rule of law. A system of law was established that rested upon principles of justice having universal applicability (the *jus gentium,* or law common to all peoples), with the emperor as the chief source of law. In fact, the Roman empire provided legal principles and the rudiments of an administrative structure that have carried over into modern times.

While Cicero held that men are all equal under the law, later Roman philosophers were to give a somewhat different emphasis to government. Seneca proposed the necessity of maintaining order, and advocated that government was best which could exercise the most efficient control. By the fourth century A.D., Augustine was to claim that the primary function of the state is the enforcement of law and order, not the securing and preservation of right.[14]

The philosophical debate over the role of government continued into the Middle Ages, the Renaissance, and into modern times. The medieval philosopher John of Salisbury proposed a model, considered by Cicero, of a commonwealth governed by a public authority and in accordance with the law. In this model, the ruler is not justified in seeking his own ends, but instead has an obligation to his subjects. It is the duty of the ruler to preserve peace and order, as well as to create the conditions of well-being which are necessary to the moral welfare of his people. A ruler must be obeyed if he complies with the law and with the divine will, for he is the steward of God. An attack upon a just ruler is an attack upon God and the Church. But if the ruler acts against the law and the divine will, the people have not only the right but the duty to remove him.[15]

St. Thomas Aquinas, writing in the thirteenth century, supports this political philosophy but also goes further by formulating the theory of law, arguing that legal means must be employed to remove the tyrant. Moreover, in the belief that legal measures alone cannot bring relief and prosperity to the people, Aquinas proposes a welfare state which would intervene directly in the lives and activities of its citizens in order to improve their condition.[16] To achieve this end, he suggests the securing of economic justice through currency control, price regulation, care for the poor, and such other measures as might be required.[17]

By contrast, the fifteenth century philosopher Niccolo Machiavelli did not occupy himself with framing plans for an ideal state. Men are self-seeking, so a ruler must understand them and act accordingly.

> A man who wishes to make a profession of goodness in everything must necessary come to grief among so many who are not good. Therefore it is necessary for a prince, who wishes to maintain himself, to learn how not to be good, and to use this knowledge and not use it, according to the necessity of the case.[18]

Rulers are admonished to secure their power by employing whatever tactics may be necessary. For Machiavelli, the (legitimate) state is one in which the ruler is voluntarily supported by the people. The chief task of a ruler is the achievement of unity, to which ends he must subordinate all others. The "liberty" which Machiavelli advocates for the people of a state is understood as security and freedom from oppression, rather than as any system of individual rights that are guaranteed by the state.[19] Most significantly, there is no substantial evidence in his writings that he was concerned with the welfare of the people.[20]

Countering Machiavelli a generation later, the French philosopher Jean Bodin declared that unity is desirable only as a means to an ends, not as an ends in itself. For Bodin, the ultimate purpose of the state is the securing of the mental and physical good of all persons. To achieve this, the state must provide defense, secure justice, and contribute to the economic welfare of the people. In addition, the state must assist the people to realize virtue; it must make it possible for them to lead moral lives, and must enhance intellectual values. In Bodin's view, to implement these intentions successfully, a centralized public service delivery system is required. Harmon points out:

> Diffusion of power was, to Bodin, one of the principal causes of the troubles he was attempting to overcome, and he was convinced that only the concentration of authority in a single agency could be effective.[21]

Later philosophers have only iterated one or the other positions already described. At one end of the spectrum there is Thomas Hobbes and his contract theory of the state, in which the view is propounded that the only purpose of the state is the maintenance of civil order. At the other extreme, there are philosophers such as Jeremy Bentham, for whom the best government is the one with the capacity to provide its citizens with the greatest happiness.[22]

**Growth of Public Services: A Historical Perspective**

Historical developments concerning the growth of public services did not quite parallel philosophical thought, either in the East or in the West. We examine, first, the growth of public services in the West, because public services as we know them today may in a real sense be viewed as outcomes of the Industrial Revolution and rising levels of urbanization that took place in Western Europe during the late eighteenth and nineteenth centuries.

Ernest Barker identifies three distinct periods in the history of state social services in Western Europe.[23] The first period is that prior to the Industrial Revolution. In the agrarian societies of England and Western Europe before the rise of industrialism, state-provided services were minimal, but already there existed various forms of poor relief. Based on acknowledgment of the principle of the right to life, poor relief constitutes the first form of social service performed by the state. In England, a system of poor relief, intended to provide work and housing for the indigent, came into being during the reign of the Tudors, in the latter half of the sixteenth century. By 1795, however, the system had degenerated into what critics at the time condemned as a "method of pauperization," because it consisted of allowances in aid of farm wages, which had the effect of actually depressing wage rates. The Poor Law Amendment Act of 1834 was designed to remedy the defects of the old system. Instead of being left to the justices of the peace, administration was transferred to elected boards serving groups of parishes, and these elected boards were in turn made accountable to a newly-created central administrative authority. This structure remained in place until 1929, when administration of public assistance was transferred to county councils and the councils of county boroughs.[24]

By contrast, the more economically prosperous France suffered relatively few problems of rural poverty or pauperism. Until the French Revolution of 1789, an informal system of poor relief existed, nevertheless, that was largely dependent upon the largesse of the Crown and the Catholic Church. The exceedingly wealthy Church maintained many charitable institutions, including hospitals and centers of outdoor relief. After the Revolution, however, the power and wealth of the Church were diminished. Poor relief was left largely to local authorities, although in 1871 the Third Republic enacted legislation that provided for "general assistance" to be administered by the departments. Assistance was provided, for example, to destitute children, to lunatics, and to those who were unable to work either from sickness or from old age. By and large, however, poor relief remained within the domain of local government, and reliance was placed also on voluntary contributions.[25]

In Prussia, and later in the unified Germany, poor relief was similarly a function of local government. Earlier, the Prussian kings had dealt with the problem of poverty by encouraging immigration into their dominions and by instituting corn depots as a mechanism to stabilize prices and control the cost of living.[26]

The second period in the development of social services occurs during the First Industrial Revolution, which is considered to have ended in the 1880s. Whereas the first period saw the rise of poor relief or public assistance services, the second was marked by the growth of health-related services and accompanying legislation. England provides a case illustration. As Barker notes:

> Men began to recognize that there was such a thing as the right to health, over and above the right to mere life which the old system of poor relief had recognized; and they drew the conclusion that, in order to guarantee this right, the State must perform the service of providing some decent minimum of general sanitation in the town, and of securing in the factory, the mining centre, and the industrial aggregation of every kind-the hours and the general conditions of labour which were necessary to the health and the physical well-being of the worker.[27]

The first Factory Act, passed in 1802, was followed by a number of successors, which provided for, among other things, factory inspections and maximum working hours. Similar provisions were extended to other classes of workers. The first Mines Regulation Act was instituted in 1842; transport workers were covered by the Merchant Shipping Act of 1876 and the Regulation of Railways Act of 1889. In 1848, the Public Health Act stipulated, for the first time, that private houses, as well as factories and workshops, should satisfy "a national minimum of sanitation."[28]

What distinguishes the second period in the provision of social services from the first is not only the extension of scope from poor relief to encompass factory legislation and public health, but, more significantly, the provision of certain kinds of social services is transformed from a moral obligation, to be undertaken or not as the case might be, into one guaranteed by law. This has the effect of subtly altering the old notions of social services as a form of charity, into one where charity plays little part. Philanthropy gives way to civic consciousness.

The growth of social services occurred, not unexpectedly, at different rates in the various European countries, depending on their degree of urbanization and industrialization. The third period began in Germany in the 1880s, its chief characteristic being the emergence of social insurance. With "the object of defeating the Socialists by making the State itself socialist," Bismarck promulgated legislation in 1883, 1884, and 1889, which successively insured workers against sickness, against the risk of accident, and against invalidity and old age.[29] Both workers and employers were to contribute to the insurance schemes, but in the last case, the state itself made contributions to pension funds. In 1911, a new scheme was introduced which provided old age pensions for workers after the age of 65.

The German model was soon adopted by other European countries, with England as the next to follow suit. The Workman's Compensation Act was passed in 1897, the Old Age Pensions Act (funded entirely by the state) in 1908, and the National Insurance Act in 1911. The latter provided for health insurance, but in addition, and quite importantly, it introduced unemployment insurance for specific industries. Earlier, in 1909, a Trade Boards Act had been passed which guaranteed a minimum wage to workers. France was slower to follow, but when she did, her legislative enactments were quite similar.[30]

Moreover, in 1903 England had introduced a Housing of the Working Classes Act, the predecessor of Housing Acts of later years, which ultimately was to go beyond the original intention of achieving a minimum standard of sanitation in dwellings, to pave the way for provision of what we know today as housing development and urban renewal programs. Thus, public housing as a policy area derived its initial impetus from the concern with problems of public health and sanitation.

Nowadays, public education occupies an important place in the area of public services, but this was not always the case. Until the eighteenth century, education was unquestioningly assumed to be a function of the Church, whose schools had the primary purpose of religious instruction and the production of potential recruits to clerical orders. Soon after 1720, however, the Protestant Frederick William I of Prussia was prompted by his religious principles to declare compulsory universal education, although initially the costs were borne entirely by parents and local communes. The state did not begin to contribute toward the cost of education until the late eighteenth century, when secondary and university education was placed under the control of a state department. Primary education remained, however, largely in the hands of the clergy. It was not until the period after 1815 that universal compulsory education, conducted by the state as a state service, became fully established. By the early twentieth century, primary education in Germany was free, and continuing education programs were beginning to be set up for working people.[31]

Developments in England and France lagged far behind those in Germany. In England, education remained a matter for the different religious denominations, Anglican and Nonconformist, supported by voluntary contributions. After the Reform Bill of 1832, however, state intervention and supervision slowly increased: by 1856 an Education Department had been created; in 1870, an Education Act was passed that provided for the formation of a system of state schools to be administered by local government school boards; in 1881, compulsory, free, elementary education was introduced; and in 1902, the state system of education was extended from primary schools to secondary schools.

The case of France was again somewhat different. Here, the evolution of education as a public service was marked by conflict between Church and State, in the period following the French Revolution. Although Napoleon had planned for a system of state education, his concord with the Catholic Church left primary education in the hands of the Church. It was not until the Third Republic that the education system was gradually made independent of Church control. In 1881 and 1882, laws were passed that made primary education both free and compulsory. The training of teachers was controlled by the state.

By 1904, members of religious congregations were barred from opening schools and were not allowed even to give religious instruction. Unlike the English case, where cooperation between Church and state continues even to the present time, in France, education became exclusively a service rendered by the state, with a highly centralized form of administration.

Thus, by World War I, most of the major elements of social service delivery systems were already firmly established in the European countries. The principle that the state should not only guarantee the right to life, but should also guarantee the rights to health and to decent standards of subsistence had become deeply entrenched. The growth in the scope and complexity of social services in the period following the two World Wars up to the present time should properly be viewed as a continuation of patterns that were fixed by the early part of the twentieth century.

If we have dwelled at some length on the origins of public services, it is because we wish to make the point that developments in the West were based on a quite different set of historical circumstances than those of Asian countries. Social services in the West should be seen as a direct outcome of industrialization and urbanization, when informal systems of welfare became unable to cope with the magnitude of demands placed upon them. Moreover, the growth of the trades union movement resulted in the presence of an active and articulate interest group, ever ready to voice its demands. The provision of public education, on the other hand, was largely a result of the state wresting control away from the Church.

Despite fundamental similarities in the underlying philosophies of East and West, the development of public services in Asia took a rather different turn. In the agrarian, peasant societies of South and Southeast Asia and the Far East, the function of poor relief and other social services was largely performed by the existing village social structure, and especially by the extended family and kinship system. In the East, as in the West, religious institutions provided the chief centers of learning. The primary role of the state was to maintain law and order, dispense justice, and defend territorial jurisdictions.

The spread of colonialism to South and Southeast Asia in the late eighteenth and nineteenth centuries was to have the effect of completely disrupting the existing order. Although the experience of each country has been somewhat different, Clark D. Neher summarizes several common consequences of colonial rule. They are: the formation of separate nation-states with fixed geographical boundaries; the growth of economic structures; the creation of a dual economy, with urban dwellers participating in a money economy, leaving the rural citizenry to remain dependent on subsistence agriculture; and most importantly, the rise of nationalism as an outcome of the colonialist conception of the nation-state.[32]

If the colonial rulers undertook public works and social service programs, it was mainly from economic considerations, rather than out of humanitarian principles. In Southeast Asia, for example, according to Brian Harrison, the "construction of roads and railways was primarily designed to assist production for export," while "(m)edical and other social services were financed out of a part of the revenues resulting from economic expansion."[33] Even the educational systems that the colonial rulers established were "generally designed at first to meet the requirements of economic expansion."[34] Schools were established that offered instruction in English (or French), and colleges and universities founded in accordance with Western models.

Two countries that were never colonized were Japan and Thailand, but even they felt compelled, in the interest of survival, to modernize following westernized models. In order to remain secure from Western domination, and with the objective of abolishing extraterritoriality, both Japan and Thailand conducted sweeping administrative reforms in the late nineteenth century and early part of the twentieth century.

In brief, however, we may conclude that if in the West, the growth of public services was largely a function of industrialization and urbanization, in the East, it was largely to serve the purposes of the colonialist economic system. That same system which introduced a money economy also deliberately fostered the creation of primate cities and the establishment of a dual economy. The beneficiaries of public services were the very small minority of the population living in the cities. The majority who inhabited the rural areas continued to lead a subsistence life in much the same manner as they had traditionally led.

World War II and its aftermath was to change all this. While the foundations of public service systems in the West were laid in the latter part of the nineteenth century, it was not until the end of World War II that public services in most Asian countries became an important component of public sector activities. The impetus was generated both internally and externally. Internally, the rise of nationalism was accompanied by the desire on the part of the new political order to effectuate economic and social change, and to lift the peasant masses from their condition of subsistence-level poverty. The new intellectual leadership, Western trained and educated for the most part, were, as Neher points out, "(s)teeped in the environment of Western technology" and influenced by Western ideals and principles.[35] "Development" that comprehended provision of public services became the self-proclaimed goal of government. Indeed, in the absence of a well-developed private sector, only the state possessed, or was in a position to mobilize, the resources necessary to undertake the task of development.

External conditions favored, and in fact guided the direction of, development efforts. John Maynard Keynes' *General Theory of Employment, Interest and Money* had provided the theoretical justification for government intervention in order to break up economic stagnation, and had profoundly influenced the shaping of Roosevelt's New Deal in the post-Depression years. The success of the New Deal in America was, in turn, to inspire post-War Administrations to export New Deal-type programs both to nations devastated by the War and to the Third World. The philosophy of the American Founding Fathers, as embodied in the Jeffersonian view that government is best when it governs least, was supplanted, in the 1950s and 1960s, by the perception that state intervention was necessary in order to bring about social and economic change, to ensure the well-being of all citizens.

In the heyday of foreign assistance, the developing countries were destined to be recipients not only of the "massive export" of American tools and technologies of public administration, but they were also unavoidably influenced by American value orientations, which, as William J. Siffin notes in retrospect, "did not necessarily fit the circumstances to which they were being transferred."[36] Siffin points out that administrative structures and procedures, established for the implementation of development programs, were based on Western assumptions about bureaucratic norms as well as assumptions about the character of the task environment many of which, in the event, turned out to be ungrounded. The growth of public services in the developing countries of Asia cannot be regarded as a response to purely indigenous demand. Rather, it was influenced in no small measure by prevailing Western, and in particular American value orientations, both in respect to program content and in respect to modes and structures for implementation.

## Conclusion

If this chapter has fulfilled its purpose, it suggests the following conclusions. First, while both eastern and western philosophies hold that the state has a moral obligation to look after the welfare of its citizens, there are fundamental differences in interpretation of what is actually entailed. Eastern philosophies have tended to emphasize kingly virtues: the ideal type is one of benevolent paternalism, where the monarch is a just and righteous ruler, ever mindful of the well-being of his subjects. Western philosophies, by contrast, are far more specific as regards scope of action of the state, although sharply divergent views exist as to what this ought to be, ranging from the Hobbesian view of minimalist intervention to Aristotelian advocacy of the state's responsibility for promoting the good life. Moreover, eastern philosophies would reject outright the Machiavellian notion that political power can be divorced from moral and social considerations. According to oriental schools of thought, political power is not an ends in itself. Rather, it is a means to protect and serve the society at large.

Second, granted the existence of philosophies which provide the value orientations for governments, if we examine the growth of public services, it appears that states begin to extend their role when two conditions are met. The first condition has to do with the incapacity of the existing social system to handle problems pertaining to the general welfare, so that responsibility devolves, by default as it were, upon the state. The second condition, which we have not mentioned directly, but which may be inferred from the account given in the preceding pages, concerns the presence of sufficient capital formation to underwrite public services. Where there is sufficient capital formation, as in the case of the industrialized countries, or where capital is made available through foreign assistance loans and grants, the state may choose to expand the scope of public services. This is obviously not an option in the case of subsistence level economies.

If, given current economic realities, many of the developing countries in Asia today are considering a diminished role for the state in regard to provision of public services--or an altered role in which increased responsibility is assigned to the private sector--they would do well to make careful assessment of where they stand with respect to each of the two conditions we have described. Clearly, the policy choices will vary for each public service area.

## NOTES

1. James W. Fesler, *Public Administration: Theory and Practice* (Englewood Cliffs, New Jersey: Prentice-Hall, 1980), p. 248.

2. C.A. Moore (ed.), *The Indian Mind: Essentials of Indian Philosophy and Culture* (Honolulu: East-West Center Press, 1967), p. 275.

3. *Ibid.*, p. 282.

4. H.G. Callis, *China: Confucian and Communist* (New York: Henry Holt & Co., 1959), p. 117. For additional reading, see, for example, C.A. Moore (ed.), *The Chinese Mind: Essentials of Chinese Philosophy and Culture* (Honolulu: East-West Center Press, 1967).

5. Wang Gung-hsing, "Mencius, Founder of Chinese Democracy," in *The Chinese Mind* (New York: John Day, 1946), p. 30. See also, A.F. Verwilgen, *Mencius: The Man and His Ideas* (New York: St. John's University Press, 1967). An account of the influence of Confucian and Mencian thought in Japan is given in C.A. Moore (ed.), *The Japanese Mind: Essentials of Japanese Philosophy and Culture* (Tokyo: Charles E. Tuttle, 1967). See also, Edwin O. Reischauer, *Japan: The Story of a Nation* (Tokyo: Charles E. Tuttle, 1981). For a general perspective, see P.H. Clyde and B.F. Beers, *The Far East* (Tokyo: Prentice-Hall, 1966).

6. Gustave Gtotz, *The Greek City and Its Institutions* (New York: Alfred Knopf, 1930).

7. Alfred Zimmern, *The Greek Commonwealth,* 5th rev. ed. (Fair Lawn, N.J.: Oxford University Press, 1931), pp. 413-414.

8. Gtotz, *op. cit.,* p. 260.

9. M. Judd Harmon, *Political Thought: From Plato to Present* (New York: McGraw-Hill, 1964), p. 15.

10. *Ibid.,* p. 34.

11. See, for example, A.E. Taylor, *Socrates: The Man and His Thought* (Garden City, N. Y.: Anchor Books, Doubleday, 1954) and Harmon, *op. cit.,* pp. 29-74. For original sources, see *The Republic of Plato* (F.M. Cornford translation) (Fair Lawn, N.J.: Oxford University Press, 1945) and *The Politics of Aristotle* (Ernest Barker translation) (Fair Lawn, N.J.: Oxford University Press, 1946).

12. Harmon, *op. cit.,* p. 82.

13. *Ibid.,* p. 82.

14. *Ibid.,* pp. 84-102.

15. *Ibid.*, pp. 120-123.
16. *Ibid.*, pp. 123-126.
17. Thomas J. Cook, *History of Political Philosophy from Plato to Burke* (Englewood Cliffs, N.J.: Prentice-Hall, 1936), p. 224, cited in *ibid.*, p. 126.
18. Machiavelli, *The Prince* (translated by Luigi Ricci and revised by E.R.P. Vincent) (Fair Lawn, N.J.: Oxford University Press, 1935), chapt. 15.
19. See Harmon, *op. cit.*, p. 168.
20. See *ibid.*, p. 170.
21. *Ibid.*, p. 211.
22. Thomas Hobbes, *Leviathan* (New York: E.P. Dutton, 1914), chapt. 18, and Jeremy Bentham, *An Introduction to the Principles of Morals and Legislation* (New York: Hafner, 1948), chapt. 1. For additional philosophers, see also, for example, Peter Laslett (ed.), *John Locke: Two Treatises of Government* (New York: Cambridge University Press, 1960).
23. Ernest Barker, *The Development of Public Services in Western Europe, 1660-1930* (Hamden, Conn.: Archon Books, 1966).
24. *Ibid.*, pp. 70-71.
25. *Ibid.*, pp. 71-72.
26. *Ibid.*, pp. 72.
27. *Ibid.*, p. 73.
28. *Ibid.*, p. 74.
29. *Ibid.*, pp. 74-75.
30. *Ibid.*, pp. 76-77.
31. The development of state education in the European countries is described in *ibid.*, chapter 5.
32. Clark D. Neher, *Politics in Southeast Asia* (Cambridge, Mass.: Schenkman, 1981), pp. 16-19.
33. Brian Harrison, *Southeast Asia: A Short History,* 2nd ed. (London: Macmillan, 1964), p. 227.
34. *Ibid.*, p. 227.
35. Neher, *op. cit.*, p. 19.
36. William J. Siffin, "Two Decades of Public Administration in Developing Countries," in James W. Fesler (ed.), *American Public Administration: Patterns of the Past* (Washington, D.C.: the American Society for Public Administration, 1982), p. 182.

# 2 The Service Delivery System of the Agricultural Sector in Thailand : Alternatives and Structural Adjustments for Development

*Patom Manirojana**

The agricultural sector usually assumes a significant role in the economy of most less developed countries. In geographical terms, the sector normally embraces a vast rural area in the countryside with a large number of remote, fragmented, and scattered small communities. Typical to a majority of rural areas and communities, as observed and documented by several scholars, is the prevalence of the so-called "vicious circle" of poverty, sickness, and illiteracy. Consequently, in terms of development strategy, rural people cannot be taken for granted as constituting a sufficiently qualified and prepared work force ready to assume or take part in development activities right away. Hence the fact that most agricultural development efforts have to be preceded or accompanied by community development-type strategies or mechanisms. It should be noted in this context that the basic aim of development projects to alleviate the hardships of rural people is not for purely welfare purposes. Rather, development projects are formulated and executed for the specific purpose of helping people to help themselves.

Apart from the fact that the territorial jurisdiction of the agricultural sector is so vast and target rural communities are widely dispersed, it must also be recognized that the issues and activities involved in the sector are numerous and widely varied, ranging from resource-based issues of land, forestry, and water, to commodity-based features such as livestock, fisheries, lumbering, and crops. Each commodity or crop can be further subdivided into a more detailed classification scheme. Moreover, each sub-sector or commodity normally involves regular procedures or cycles of production, transformation, and marketing, either for domestic consumers or for export.

---

*National Institute of Development Administration, Bangkok, Thailand.

A major difficulty of agricultural development is that the production-marketing cycle of every crop or commodity tends to possess more or less unique characteristics. The problems of some specific crops or commodities (such as rice, sugar, and cassava in the Thai context) can be considered as unique in terms of production technology, input supplies, post-harvesting services, agro-industry, or the nature of the market. It has been evident that the policies, measures, or mechanisms designed to cope with each commodity are not transferable or interchangeable. The highly segmented nature of the sector therefore calls for a large-scale, sophisticated, and complicated service delivery system.

This chapter proposes to conceptualize, describe, and analyze the Thai agricultural sector in terms of the service delivery model. Since the scope of the sector is so large that a consideration of any service alone is unlikely to reflect and represent the image of the entire sector, an attempt will be made to scrutinize the structure and functions of the sector in general in an effort to assess the overall sectoral performance. Subsequently, a recommendation concerning alternative structural or procedural arrangements will be proposed.

**Service Delivery System Concepts**

A service or set of services rendered in any community is a function of system demands and actions taken by an authoritative organ to satisfy them. Conceptually speaking, a service delivery system involves two major parties: providers and recipients. However, the extent and nature of interaction between these parties depends to a considerable extent on the service to be delivered, the nature of the delivery system, as well as the set-up and magnitude of the service providers and receivers themselves.

Basically, the structure and function of the service delivery model is clearly visible if reference is made to a simplistic delivery system of a single service from an individual provider to an individual receiver. Such factors as the multiplicity of the providing and receiving agents, the scale and number of services, the distance and fragmentation of providers and recipients contribute to the complexity of the delivery system.

Greater complexity is to be found in a mixed economy where both the public and private sectors are entitled to have some share in developmental efforts. With a relatively broad range of choices, a government in the mixed economy usually enjoys considerable discretion in directing the course of actions either to the right, the left, or the middle of the road.

The extent to which governments assume public duties and responsibilities varies from place to place depending on such factors as political orientation and culture, social and economic systems, historical practices, the strength or weakness of the private sector, the orientation of dominant political parties, the nature or type of services, etc. Even in the same system, ideas and practices may be modified from time to time. For instance, a campaign for nationalization and consolidation of private enterprise can be actively launched by one regime only to be rejected and replaced by a "privatization" policy in a subsequent regime.[1]

Although the total picture of service delivered in the context of any sectoral development is very complicated, the basic and most familiar pattern is a set of public services rendered directly by governmental agencies to the private sector. In addition, the delivery of some other functions may be performed by joint venture between public and private enterprise. Some developmental functions may even be conducted by non-governmental organizations or private organizations. Under certain circumstances, in fact, the government agencies themselves become the recipients of services delivered by other agencies or even non-governmental organizations. The channels and directions of such service delivery are depicted in Figure 1.

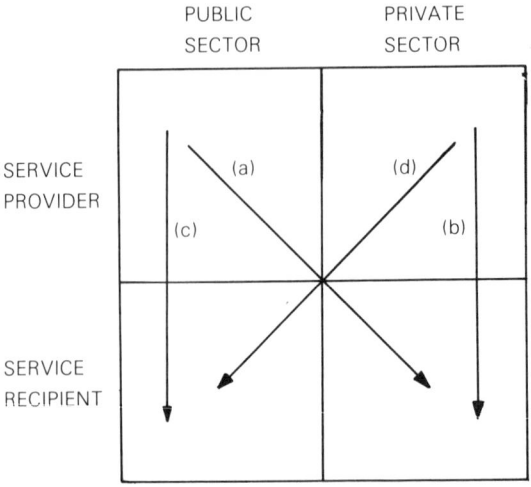

**Figure 1**  Pattern of Relationship Between Public and Private Sector in Service Delivery

The scope of examination of public services in this chapter will concentrate on the role of public agencies in Thailand as providers rather than recipients of services. However, one point that should be made clear is that the Thai government, despite a pervasive belief in the philosophy of big government, should not be mistaken as the sole service delivery agent in Thai society. Private corporations, non-governmental organizations, and even poorly organized farmers' organizations are quite able to fulfill the function of service delivery. Caiden has observed that, "When governments assume responsibility for a new activity, they have various options open to them. They may contract it out to other social institutions, undertake it within the public bureaucracy, or join with other organizations in some form of joint delivery."[2] He points out that public service delivery can be handled by combinations of seven different systems, namely, voluntary organizations, the market place, external suppliers, other domestic governments, public enterprises, private contractors, and third sector organizations.[3]

In the particular context of the sectoral development of agriculture, it should be noted that contemporary perspectives no longer view the role of farmers as merely a means to achieve the ultimate end of agricultural growth. Rather, the goals of agricultural development are set in light of the broader perspective of rural development or overall development. For instance, Earl Kulp views the objectives of agricultural development as," ... the system of concern to us in the whole complex of basic analytical concepts, policy, strategy, tactics, institutions, and procedures for providing all the necessary services that will induce and enable peasants to modernize, to overcome their technical and commercial backwardness, or, ... to change from peasant to farmer."[4]

With regard to the service delivery system, it is appropriate to briefly look into the service or package of services under study. When the study is of a service delivery system in which the unit of analysis is large, if no special emphasis is given to any particular service, the list of major services rendered in the system is surveyed and outlined. Bollens and Schmandt in their analysis of the delivery of services in metropolitan areas, for instance, prepare a list of 15 urban services regularly found in the unit of analysis.[5] In the case of the agricultural sector, our unit of reference in this study, Kulp proposes an interesting analytical framework by distinguishing 'core services' from 'peripheral services.' Core services in the agricultural sector include extension, supply, marketing, and credit. Peripheral services fall into two major categories: (1) engineering (including soil surveys, irrigation, and tractor hire); (2) protection, including spraying and innoculating animals.[6] Overall, a list of 10 functions is given, which include: technology, marketing, supply, transport, incentives, extension, credit, group action, land development, and planning.[7]

In order to clearly delineate and appreciate how these multiple services are delivered to the highly fragmented recipients or clients in the agricultural sector, an examination has to be made of the overall administrative system within which the services are initiated, decided, processed, implemented, integrated, and evaluated.

In general, a national administrative system is basically a network of central ministries which handle overall policy guidelines, plans, and technical services. These ministries also coordinate services to be integrated and implemented by multiple tiers of territorial or spatial organizations at regional, provincial, district, township, and village levels. In addition, as earlier mentioned, private organizations, non-governmental organizations, and people's organizations also participate in the delivery of services. An example of the relationship between agriculture-related services and responsible institutions is given in Table 1.

**Table 1** Agricultural Development Services and Related Institutions

| Services | Institutions |
| --- | --- |
| Technology | research departments of ministries, agribusiness, agricultural faculties |
| Marketing | cooperatives, local merchants, agribusinesses, marketing boards |
| Supply | cooperatives, local merchants, agribusinesses, public enterprise |
| Transport | national and local public work agencies, local authorities, railroads, shipping firms |
| Incentives | governmental price support agencies, established markets, community social structures |
| Extension | extension services, community development service, cooperatives, agribusinesses, voluntary associations |
| Credit | banks, cooperatives, agribusinesses, money-lenders |
| Group action | cooperatives, extension, community development agencies, existing social structures |
| Land development | irrigation departments, agricultural engineering services, land cooperatives, settlement authorities |
| Planning | ministry of agriculture, planning commissions, regional development authorities, interagency committees, local associations |

Source : Earl M. Kulp, *Designing and Managing Basic Agricultural Programs* (Bloomington, Ind. : International Development Institute, 1977), p. 16.

It should be noted that public services in subsistence rural areas are designed not just to serve the general or occupational needs of the people. Rather, the services may have to tackle rural problems at a very fundamental level. Productivity, for instance, may be desirable in the long run, but in the short run more basic needs must first be met. Projects that identify the "basic minimum needs" of farmers should probably be assigned high priority.

As for the more modernized commercial sector, the nature of public services is quite different. Because members of the modernized sector are generally far better off than their rural counterparts in terms of living standards, competence, skills, resources, organization, and managerial and technical know-how, the services for this more affluent sector will be of either the regulative or promotional type. The roles of middlemen, businessmen, bankers, or manufacturers vis-a-vis the farmers will be regulated in order to prevent the former from taking excessive advantage of the underprivileged rural sector.

With regard to the rural agricultural sector, George Gant has summarized governmental roles required to regulate, promote, and serve this sector as follows:

> It is not only the production and the delivery of the inputs for modern agricultural production and the skill of the farmer but also the supporting infrastructure which must be provided to complete the system and make possible the result of greatly increased productivity. This infrastructure of support assumes first of all the stability assured by the maintenance of law and order and the provision of essential public services. More specifically required by the agricultural operation are storage facilities for the harvest and practicable systems to protect, preserve, and subsequently process and market the harvested grains. Roads and vehicles adequate to the purpose of transporting farm produce must be provided. Maintenance, service, and repair facilities are needed for the buildings, roads, and machines involved in the agricultural enterprise. These massive inputs, their production and delivery, and the supporting infrastructure, must all be available and in place in reasonably effective relationship to make possible the increase in agricultural productivity...[8]

In short, the delivery of services in the agricultural sector is a complicated network of relationships. Several institutions exclusively or jointly deliver a number of services to countless clients with diversified backgrounds and needs located all over the country. This situation poses a challenge for both scholars and professional managers attempting to study, manage, or propose structural change.

## The Thai Agricultural Sector in Perspective : Concepts, Activities, and Distinguishing Characteristics

An agricultural sector can basically be conceptualized in terms of a resource-based framework consisting of three principal resources: land, forest, and water. Forest areas have to be strongly guarded and properly managed to ensure an adequate supply of water, flood control, a balanced climate and ecosystem, natural beauty, as well as commercial or economic utilization. Water resources should also be well planned and managed for a variety of purposes: transportation, energy, fisheries, consumption, and especially, for agricultural use.

Excluding forests and hilly areas, an agricultural sector may be viewed in spatial terms as dealing essentially with the management of land outside the densely populated urban areas. However, provided that there is nothing wrong with the quality of the soil, the degree to which any area is productive depends directly on access to water resources. Accordingly, this becomes a major criterion for a classification of agricultural areas into irrigated and rainfed areas. This classification scheme has formed the basis of two economic categories : a progressive sector corresponding to irrigated areas, and a subsistence (or poverty-stricken) sector, corresponding to rainfed areas.

The agricultural sector can be viewed as consisting of several sub-sectors. For instance, the Ministry of Agriculture and Cooperatives in Thailand embraces five groups of activities in its jurisdiction, namely: livestock, fisheries, forestry, irrigation, and cropping. For the purposes of this study, however, the scope will be confined mainly to the last sub-sector, i.e., cropping.

To general observers, the agricultural sector appears to consist of farmers, their activities, and products generated on their farms. This view, however, does not represent the entire picture of the sector in functional or procedural terms. Farming or cropping in fact constitutes only the initial phase of a long process or cycle of agriculture-related activities. In the modern economy, only a minimum of farm products are set aside for consumption on the farm. Most of the produce has to undergo a long journey involving either processing, manufacturing, or simply handling before transportation or shipment to domestic or overseas consumers.

Viewed in this light, agriculture involves numerous activities undertaken by non-farm personnel or parties once the products leave the farm gate. A flow chart of the process of agricultural products is shown in Figure 2.

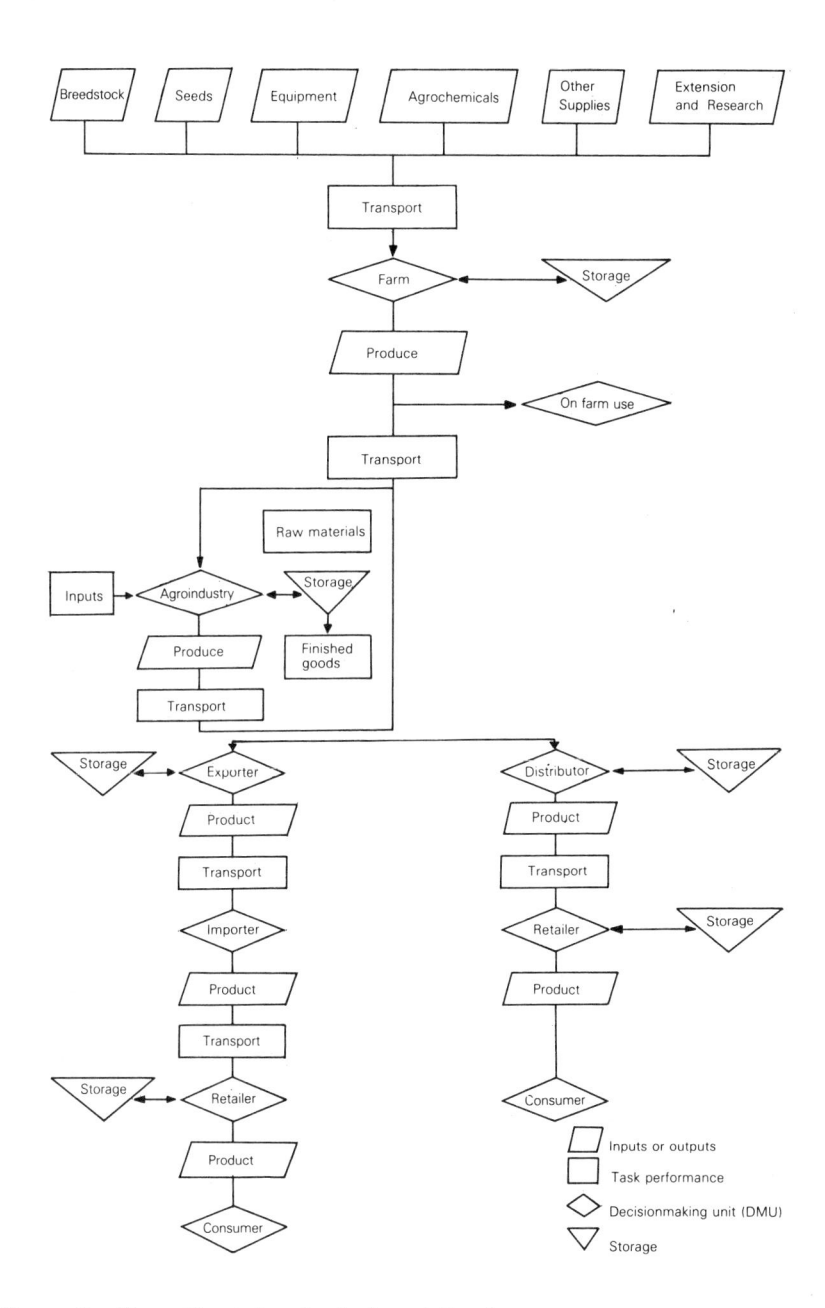

**Figure 2**  Flow Chart for Agricultural Products

Source : Adapted from James E. Austin, *Agroindustrial Project Analysis* (Baltimore : the Johns Hopkins University Press, 1981), p. 16.

Thus, the agricultural sector cannot be adequately defined only in geographical terms (i.e., rural areas) or only in functional terms (e.g., farming and cropping). The sector involves participants and activities in the more modernized commercial sub-sector as well as members of the less-developed rural sub-sector. It is therefore convenient to identify active parties involved in the process of agricultural development as consisting of farmers, middlemen, consumers, and the government.

The agricultural sector in Thailand has long played a principal role in the economy. Agricultural products, despite a gradually decreasing proportion over the past 20 years, are still considered a leading sector of the economy, contributing to approximately 25% of GDP. Moreover, the 15 million people in agriculture still constitute about 70% of the entire labor force. The number would be even higher if employment in agriculture-related activities such as transportation, wholesaling, retailing, and the export sector were taken into account.

In particular, the greatly diversified cropping pattern has resulted in a situation which constitutes a vast improvement over the traditional reliance on a small number of major crops. Many crops are produced primarily for domestic consumption, with some surplus for export (such as paddy, sugar cane, tobacco, mung beans, peanuts, jute, and fruits). Moreover, the production of some crops is export-oriented in nature (e.g., cassava, maize, rubber), while some crops serve as import substitutes (e.g., cotton, soy beans, castor beans).[9]

Agricultural development in Thailand has enjoyed a satisfactory rate of growth over the past two decades in comparison with the rest of the world. Prospects are no longer as favorable as before, however, because the extensive growth in the past through the expansion of cropping areas has been at the expense of forest resources, whose rapid depletion has now reached a critical point. Thus, the future growth of the Thai agricultural sector depends on intensive strategies, i.e., the optimal utilization of existing land resources.

Intensive agricultural development is very difficult and costly. The government has, for instance, regularly invested heavily in the construction of irrigation systems. In fiscal year 1986, the budget of the Royal Irrigation Department amounted to over 50% of the entire budget of the Ministry of Agriculture and Cooperatives. And yet, the proportion of the irrigated area relative to total cultivated areas is discouraging. Of the 147 million *rai* under cultivation, the irrigated portion amounts to only 16 million *rai*.[10] Consequently, the non-irrigated area has become a target for a newly formulated rural development package initiated, coordinated, administered, and evaluated at the national level.[11]

It should be noted that agricultural development has not been evenly distributed all over the country. The current Thai agricultural sector (as well as the overall economy) evidences all the properties of "dualism": two different levels of development. This characteristic feature is more apparent in spatial or geographical terms, where agricultural areas are sub-categorized into the progressive, irrigated zone and the non-progressive, rain fed zone.[12]

These two different categories of agricultural areas experience different sets of problems. Villages and farms in the rain fed areas are numerous, scattered, and remote. Their major problems center around the availability, accessibility, and affordability of goods and services to ameliorate their disadvantages and hardships. The problems of the more progressive areas lie in the under-utilization of resources in which heavy investments have earlier been made.

There are, moreover, problems common to both areas, i.e., those of low prices and the marketing systems of agricultural products. Farmers who grow a variety of crops usually keep on investing in the same agricultural products without discerning the market situation. Once their products fail to be absorbed by the already saturated market (domestic or international), the issue then is transformed into a political one as the government is heavily pressured to reduce the agricultural surplus through market intervention measures. Among the major crops that have been over-produced are rice, sugar, and tapioca. The Ministry of Industry, the Ministry of Commerce, as well as the Cabinet have to tackle this kind of problem almost every year.[13]

**The Institutional Framework and Agriculture-Related Services in Thailand**

As mentioned earlier, the services delivered in the agricultural sector are provided on a regular basis by private entrepreneurs, non-government organizations (local merchants, agri-businesses, agro-industries, commercial banks, money lenders, etc.), as well as by public agencies. Usually, government agencies concentrate on services that are common goods or that are public investments, such as land development, irrigation, extension services, and planning. Also, government agencies may participate in providing supply, credit, group action, transport, incentives, and technology. Private sector institutions may share responsibilities in some or many of the above services. Private businesses tend to do exceptionally well in the area of marketing services.

Overall, the structural-functional framework of service delivery systems in Thai agriculture tends to follow the pattern outlined above. As the focus of the study is, however, confined to service deliveries primarily undertaken by public sector institutions, the public institutional framework in Thailand dealing with the agriculture-related service delivery system will therefore be described and analyzed. Initially, however, the overall structural arrangement of public institutions at all levels in the country will be briefly examined.

As depicted in Figure 3, the structural arrangement of the Thai public administrative system consists of three major sub-systems: central administration (with some territorial field administration), provincial administration, and semi-autonomous local authorities.

*The Central Administration.* The Thai central administration consists of 14 ministries organized mainly on a functional basis of which the Ministry of Agriculture and Cooperatives constitutes a part. Other ministries are: Defense; Interior; Education; Public Health; Industry; Commerce; Science, Technology, and Energy; Foreign Affairs; Communications; University Affairs; Justice; Finance; and the Office of the Prime Minister. With the exception of the Ministry of Defense, the ministries are divided into departments which are subdivided into divisions. In 1982, the total number of departments and divisions in all ministries except for the Ministry of Defense was 121 and 1,373, respectively.[14]

Overall, the central administration serves as headquarters of the entire national administrative system. In principle, the central administration is responsible for such strategic matters as nationwide policy planning, devising programs and projects, allocating resources, integrating and coordinating the execution of plans, conducting technical activities, and providing technical assistance to the field agencies.

The findings of several studies indicate that departments usually enjoy a highly stable, powerful, and exclusive status with a strong sense of departmentalization. Each department is entitled to draw up and manage its own budget, personnel, and projects. Moreover, many departments have field units in the countryside which perform a variety of functions such as undertaking technical studies, providing technical advice, coordinating, monitoring, supervising, and evaluating·departmental plans and projects. In many instances, these field units of the central departments are directly involved in the management and operation of public service deliveries to clients in the localities.[15]

At ministerial level, projects initiated and proposed by the departments are loosely screened by the permanent secretary of each ministry, whose small office is inadequately equipped, funded, and manned relative to the workload generated by the various departments under his jurisdiction.

The Agricultural Sector in Thailand    31

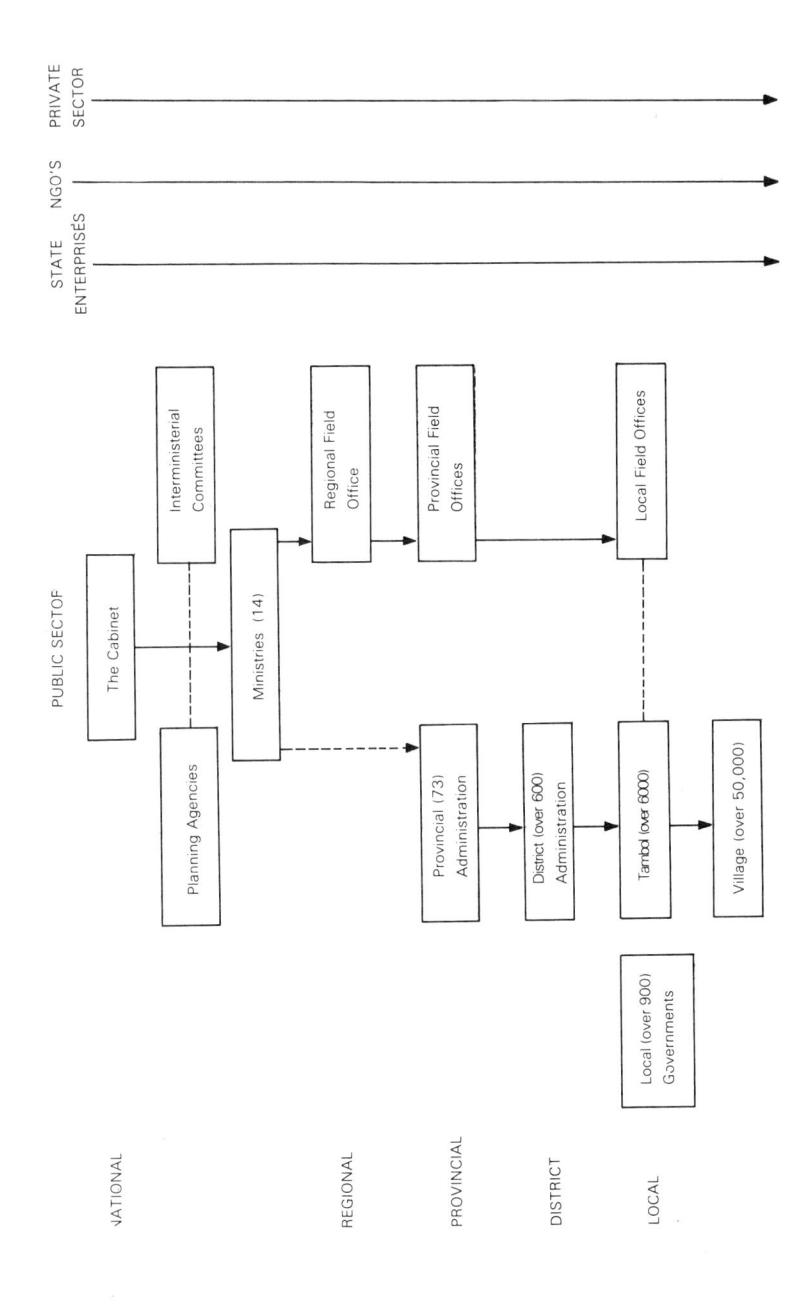

**Figure 3**   Framework of Institutional Arrangements at Different Levels

At the higher, policy-making level of the central administration, the ministers serve collectively in the Cabinet, which is a national policy-decision body under the leadership of the Prime Minister. Separately, each minister acts as a link between the Cabinet's overall policy decisions and the specific ministerial implementing mechanisms.

As the Cabinet is not a perfect agent of policy integration, the central administration must rely on many other mechanisms for integrating policies and services. Such mechanisms include the National Economic and Social Development Board, which is the central planning agency; the Budget Bureau; the Central Personnel Agency; the Council of Economic Ministers; and many more national-level committees.

It should be noted that the central administration is not confined exclusively to Bangkok. Central administration agencies are equipped with field offices at the regional, provincial, and local levels all over the country to oversee activities that are not entrusted to provincial administrations or local authorities.

*The Provincial Administration.* As of 1985, Thailand was divided on an administrative basis into 73 provinces, which were sub-divided into 723 districts, 6,325 sub-districts, and 56,404 villages.[16] Functionally, the provincial administration is designed to serve as the operating arm of the central "brain." As many agents of the central departments are stationed and function at the provincial level, the overall structure of the provincial administration is designed to integrate and coordinate provincial services through the governorship or district leadership. The governors are, however, not very successful in the integration mission because most department-based projects are highly structured by the central agencies, without much room for adjustment or reformulation. The more systematic and programmatic the formulation of projects at the center, the less likely will there be effective coordination at local level with the projects of other line agencies.

*The Semi-Autonomous Local Authorities.* Basically, there are three forms of local government organized on the basis of the socio-economic and demographic characteristics of local communities. As of 1983, there were 124 municipalities (or urban centers), 738 semi-urban communities (or sanitary districts), and 72 rural administrative organizations (*Changwad* Administrative Organizations).[17] There are, moreover, specially formed local authorities for areas with unique characteristics and problems, namely Pattaya City and the Bangkok Metropolitan Administration. However, since revenue sources and prescribed functions for most local authorities are so limited and barely touch economic activities in general or agricultural activities in particular, the roles of local authorities will not be discussed in this study.[18]

*Organizations Related to Agriculture.* The Ministry of Agriculture and Cooperatives, as indicated by its name, appears to many people as the agency exclusively responsible for everything concerning agriculture. A breakdown of the ministry by departments shows those activities or sub-sectors of major concern: Forestry, Fisheries, Livestock, Irrigation, Cooperatives, Crops, and Land Development. Moreover, there are eight state enterprises attached to the ministry to provide additional facilities and services. (See Figure 4.)

If agriculture is viewed in terms of processes, it is found that the functional responsibilities of most departments of the Ministry of Agriculture and Cooperatives are mostly focussed on production and related activities. Attempts have been made to supplement the ministry's production-oriented concerns through the establishment of several state enterprises to provide marketing, manufacturing, and storage facilities. These state enterprises have a number of regional offices or field units in provincial areas.

A comprehensive study by the UNDP has shown that 13 out of 14 ministries are in one way or another involved in agriculture or agricultural processes (the sole exception being the Ministry of Justice).[19] Another study has detailed the range of agricultural development services, and the names of organizations in Thailand's public sector which provide such services. The agriculture-related services are patterned along the lines of the Kulp model mentioned earlier. The list includes technology, marketing, supply, transport, incentives, extension, credit, group action, irrigation and land development, manpower planning, and budgeting. Some organizations providing services include the Department of Agriculture, the Marketing Organization for Farmers, the Department of Agricultural Extension, the Department of Fisheries, the Department of Community Development, etc. Details of these organizations are listed in Table 2, which also indicates which public institutions are involved in the service delivery system of the Thai agricultural sector.

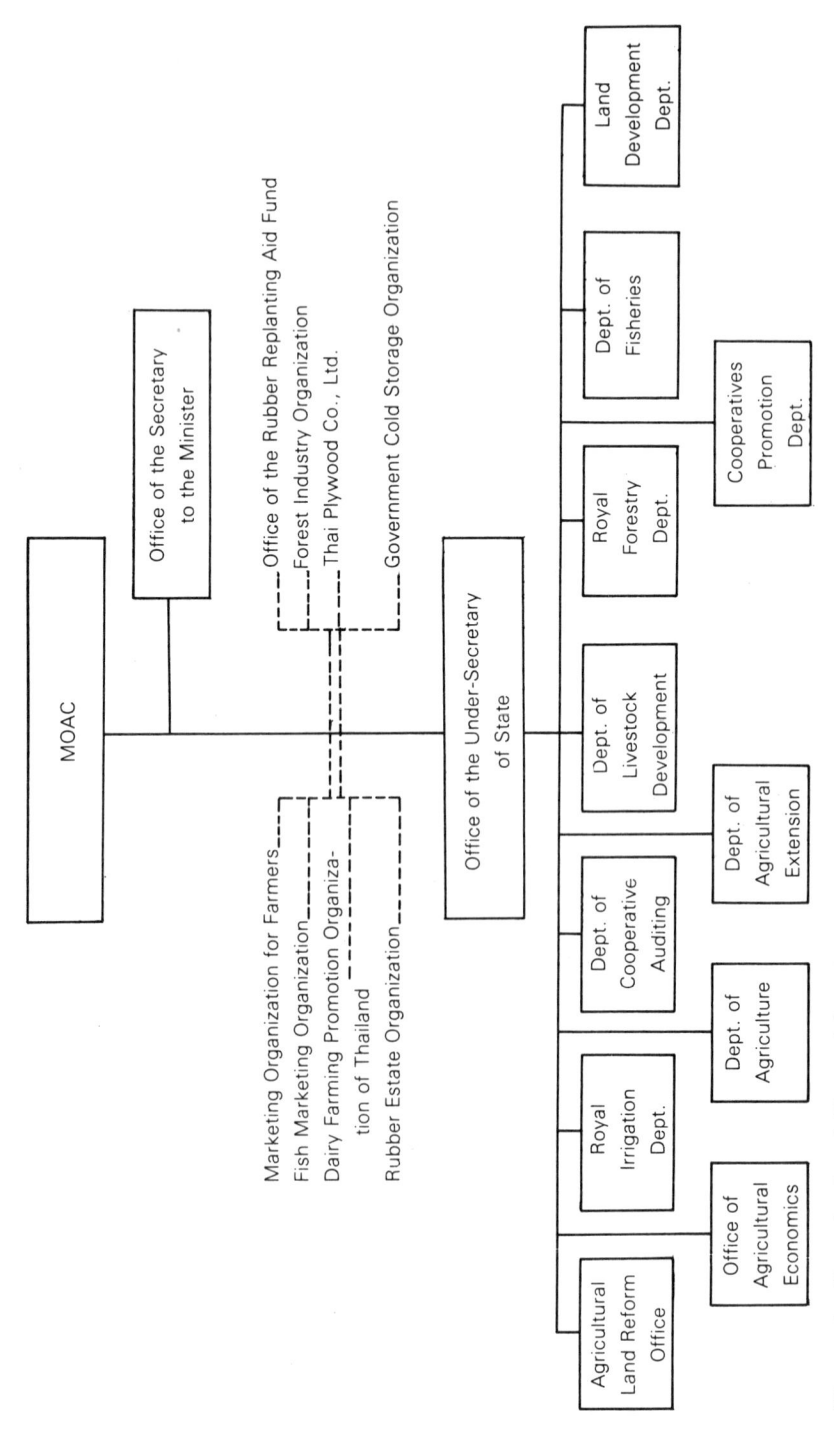

34  Delivery of Public Services in Asian Countries

**Figure 4** Organizational Chart of the Ministry of Agriculture and Cooperatives (MOAC)

**Table 2  Agricultural Development Services and Related Public Institutions in Thailand.**

| Services | Public Institutions |
|---|---|
| Technology | Department of Agriculture; research, experimentation, demonstration units in all other MOAC departments, universities and other academic institutions |
| Marketing | Marketing Organization for Farmers (MOF); Fish Marketing Organization; Cold Storage Organization; Dairy Farming Promotion Organization of Thailand |
| Supply | MOF; Dept. of Agricultural Extension (DAE) (seeds, insecticides); Depts. of Fisheries, Livestock, Forestry |
| Transport | Min. of Communications; ARD; Min. of Defense; public transport organizations; local governments |
| Incentives | Min. of Commerce; various Depts. in MOAC; provincial and local authorities administering the price support programs |
| Extension | Depts. of Agricultural Extension, Livestock, Fisheries, Forestry, Community Development |
| Credit | BAAC; Bank of Thailand (agri. bills discounting) |
| Group Action | Dept. of Cooperative Promotion, Dept. of Agricultural Extension (Farmers' Groups), Fish Marketing Organization (Fishermen) |
| Irrigation and Land Development | Dept. of Irrigation; Office of Land Reform; Depts. of Land Development, Forestry, Local Administration, Public Welfare (land settlements); Min. of Defence, King's projects, interagency committees |
| Planning | NESDB; Civil Service Commission, |
| Manpower and Budgeting | Budget Bureau; MOAC; provincial authorities; interagency committees |

Source :  National Institute of Development Administration (NIDA), *A Study of the Role and Functions of Regional Agricultural Offices in Thailand* (Bangkok: NIDA, 1980).

## Service Delivery and Institutional Performance

In order to clearly visualize how a system operates or to understand why the system acts or behaves the way it does, a study can be conducted at both the macro and the micro levels. As regards the agricultural sector, the focus can be on either an individual service or on overall sectoral performance.

*Service-Based Considerations of Service Delivery.* As earlier observed, the organizational set-up of the Thai central administration rests on a functional base. It is also the case that the extremely powerful central departments are not content to limit their role to planning, integration, and providing technical backing for the active provincial implementors. On the contrary, they have played very active roles in service delivery processes for a long time, right from policy planning down to the level of field operations and management.

A service-oriented or functional review of the operations of the Ministry of Agriculture and Cooperatives supports the above contention. Thus, although some departments do delegate a certain degree of service delivery responsibilities to the provincial administration, a considerable portion of duties and responsibilities still rests with the central administration. In Table 3, five major service areas in the ministry are selected for scrutiny: irrigation, livestock, agriculture (technical research development), forestry, and extension. Of these services, only agricultural extension and livestock allow a relatively large portion of administrative and implementation responsibilities to be performed by the provincial administration (with strict technical guidance from central departments). As for forestry, the majority of management and operation responsibilities in the forest areas are totally undertaken by the department. Only a small portion of licensing, law enforcement, and judicial processes are delegated to the provincial administration. In contrast, the delivery system of irrigation and agricultural technology services has not been patterned in terms of a partnership between the central and provincial administrations. They are, rather, administered exclusively by the central administration. Even though there are a large number of such field units as local irrigation project sites and local agricultural laboratories functioning in almost every province all over the kingdom, they do not constitute a part of the provincial administration hierarchy.

The attitudes of parties involved in such service delivery networks are mixed. To the official directly in charge of service delivery, the centralized delivery model and approach are acceptable, particularly on professional and technical grounds. If the delivery system of any service is discrete, semi-autono-

**Table 3** Organizational Back Up of Selected Services in the Central Administration (MOAC)

| National Departments | Irrigation | Livestock | Agriculture | Forestry | Extension |
|---|---|---|---|---|---|
| Regional agencies | 12 | 9 |  | 23 | 4 |
| Provincial & local agencies | 144 | 120 | 97 | 172 | 26 |

Source : Adapted from NIDA, *A Study of the Role and Functions of Regional Agricultural Offices in Thailand* (Bangkok: NIDA, 1980).

mous, and equipped with sufficient and effective channels and local outlets, it is quite natural for the service to be properly and easily planned, managed, processed, and controlled. In sum, a service-based or functionally-organized line of service tends to be effective and desirable from the standpoint of either the technocrats or bureaucrats directly responsible for providing it. However, the approach may not be as favorable if viewed in the broader perspective of the entire development context.

*Sectoral Considerations of Service Delivery.* A sectoral view of service delivery is virtually a macro-level or systems approach, in contrast to the micro-level or partial view obtained by the service-based approach examined above. For a number of reasons, the managers of a service strongly prefer a single-service type of organization as the most efficient and effective means for service delivery.

However, it is very important to point out that just to have a service reach its clients is not an end in itself. Most services defined on a functional basis are partial and complementary to each other. Together they play an instrumental role in achieving the ultimate goal of overall development.

The picture is clear from the standpoint of the farmer who receives the service. Conceptually, each farmer is engaged in a basic process in the agricultural sector ranging from growing and harvesting to marketing. It is evident that a single service or a combination of a few fragmented services (be they irrigation, credit, fertilizer, insecticides or pesticides, transportation, post-harvesting services, etc.) delivered to the farmers will not be sufficient for them to achieve developmental goals. What farmers really require is the whole package or an integrated combination of a few crucial services responsive to their needs.

Moreover, the goals must also distinguish between the subsistence and the progressive areas of the sector. For a subsistence economy, it may be sufficient simply to state that the goal is to increase productivity. However, for a progressive sector whose surplus production is transported to outside markets, the goal must be stated differently. Increasing productivity alone is inadequate and sometimes even harmful for the progressive sector. This is the case when investment in any agricultural product exceeds the capacity of the market to absorb it. Thus, the progressive sector must also establish goals of sensitivity, elasticity, or adaptability to market demands apart from that of increased productivity.

*Central and Provincial Interface in the Ministry of Agriculture and Cooperatives : Service Delivery Channels.* The overall feature of Ministry of Agriculture and Cooperatives service delivery is to channel services (which are mostly initiated by central departments) through existing organizational mechanisms to the receiving parties at the other end of the delivery pipeline in over 50,000 villages. The emphasis of ministry services is on the agricultural production stage and related activities (with additional manufacturing, storage, and marketing elements from a few state enterprises).

The basic organizational and managerial set-up focuses on the interrelationship between the central administration, which formulates and coordinates policies, plans, and projects as well as provides technical assistance, and the provincial administrative organs which implement or operate the service delivery system. In actual practice, however, the operation of the entire system differs somewhat from the aforementioned structural-functional set-up, as follows:

First, the extremely strong central departments play a predominant, if not determining, role in many instances. The scope or working boundary of most projects and the operational plans of regular tasks are formulated by the departments. Since the departments are structured and organized into divisions primarily on a functional basis, the scope and substance of activities of each task, project, or service initiated by a department tends to be confined to the limited functional responsibility of that department or, in many cases, a single division within a department. The activities of the numerous departments, or at a lower level, divisions, are not harmoniously integrated together within the framework of a single program, or comparable project-type operation. The ministry itself is not adequately equipped, organized, or authorized to seriously integrate or synthesize the projects proposed by the departments under its jurisdiction. It functions simply to loosely coordinate projects which are independently implemented by different departments and divisions.

Secondly, the central departments are not content with serving as the interface between the central and provincial administrations. As a number of activities are nominally delegated to the provincial administration by the central administration, this has led to a large number of agencies being set up in the countryside under direct control of the central departments themselves. These agencies perform a wide variety of functions including research and development, technical advisory, supervisory, coordinating, monitoring, evaluating, and in many instances, operations management. This point is evident from the fact that the Ministry of Agriculture and Cooperatives, a functional ministry with only 13 agencies of departmental status located in Bangkok, together with regular line units in all 73 provinces, 723 districts, and several thousand sub-districts, still manages to own and operate up to 988 offices located in the provinces but under the direct jurisdiction of the central departments. A detailed list of these agencies is given in the Appendix.

In sum, the service delivery systems of the Ministry of Agriculture and Cooperatives are highly centralized. Within the central structural framework itself, the influence of departments is overwhelming and far-reaching. The departments are so powerful that projects submitted by them are almost never rejected, modified, or reformulated by the ministry. In consequence, the provincial governors who head the provincial administrations play only a very limited role in coordinating a large number of centrally-assigned projects at the management and implementation level. Besides, the operations of the provincial administration are often closely supervised by central agents stationed in either regional or local offices. Furthermore, the provincial administration has to be aware of and accommodate a number of public services directly run by the central administration in each locality.

## Alternatives and Structural Adjustments

The above review and examination points to some weaknesses in the structural, organizational, managerial, as well as procedural aspects of the service delivery system in the agricultural sector in Thailand. In the following paragraphs, however, the structural elements which are regarded as a fundamental and overriding factor for the viability of the delivery system will be examined.

Initially, any alternatives or structural adjustment schemes designed to alleviate the existing difficulties and drawbacks have to have clear objectives.

With regard to the subsistence sub-sector of agriculture, the objectives are relatively clear: to create infrastructure, promote institution-building, identify the basic minimum needs of the sector, and provide the necessary means, facilities, and skills to farmers in keeping with the principle of self-reliance. In this regard, the body of concepts, methodologies, integrated policy packages, as well as the implementing mechanisms have recently been overhauled and restructured in what is known as the National Rural Development System.[20] There are as yet no major evaluative reports on the efficacy of this system. Consequently, the performance of the delivery system in this sub-sector cannot as yet be gauged. What should be noted, however, is that the agricultural sector can no longer rely on the expansion of areas under cultivation. Development strategies have to be intensive rather than extensive ones. Viewed in this light, it is likely that the desirable objective of future growth should be the maximum utilization of existing resources.

In the general context, there is nothing wrong with the goal of utility maximization, but extra care should be exercised if the idea is applied to the agricultural sector. Ironically, high productivity, which is generally acceptable, may not always be desirable as far as agricultural development is concerned. Over-production and high-yielding crops in the context of a limited market may become a penalty rather than a blessing for farmers. Thus, a proper perspective should be taken in formulating the appropriate strategies for sectoral development. It should also be kept in mind that agricultural system boundaries transcend local, regional, and national borders, to encompass international markets. In short, agriculture as a system cannot be regarded in terms of a single, oversimplified structure since it is extremely large, fragmented, and complex. The system embraces a vast network of activities required in the production and processing of various agricultural commodities. The flow process of each commodity cuts across the territorial boundaries of provincial administrations as well as the organizational boundaries of central functional departments or divisions. It is also important to note the unique nature and problems of each commodity when organizing service delivery systems.

In the current Thai context, the organizational structure of agencies responsible for agriculture-related systems is characterized mainly by functional departmentalization. Activities involving agricultural production, processing, and marketing are separately segmented and assigned to different agencies. The Ministry of Agriculture and Cooperatives is responsible primarily for production, the Ministry of Industry for processing, and the Ministry of Commerce for marketing, as shown in Figure 5. This type of organizational set-up has resulted in serious problems of cooperation, coordination, and integration of activities and services, even of the same commodity or product.

**Conclusions**

The role of the Thai agricultural sector, despite competition from the rapidly expanding industrial sector, is still of primary importance in the economy. Although its major products have recently become diversified, moving away from the traditional reliance on a few products, the overall sectoral structure is distinguished by a duality characterized by coexistent progressive and subsistence sectors in the economy.

The institutional framework for the activities of the agricultural sector embraces several ministries and departments in the central administration as well as the provincial administration and local government system. The Ministry of Agriculture and Cooperatives ordinarily plays a central role in delivering important services, especially with regard to the promotion of production.

It is generally found that most agriculture-related services delivered by public institutions are usually highly centralized due to a very powerful central authority and the status of the central departments vis-a-vis the provincial administration. A number of functionally-organized service lines directly administered by the central departments, combined with a traditional weakness of the provincial administration, together contribute to the fragmented nature of numerous public services in the sector. Attempts at coordination or integration on the part of the provincial administration have long been difficult and ineffective. Moreover, the very different nature and problems of agricultural commodities tend to call for specific governmental measures, rather than an over-arching general plan.

Since the focus of the study has been on structural aspects, the recommendations will be along the same lines. In general, the future structure of the agricultural sector must be far more receptive, adaptive, and responsive to changing market forces than in the past. Thus, the restructuring of the system is proposed in such a way as to curb organizational barriers, to provide a sensor of market signals, and provide an effective channel of communication among parties engaged in the same agricultural products, ranging from exporters to public organizations and, especially, the farmers.

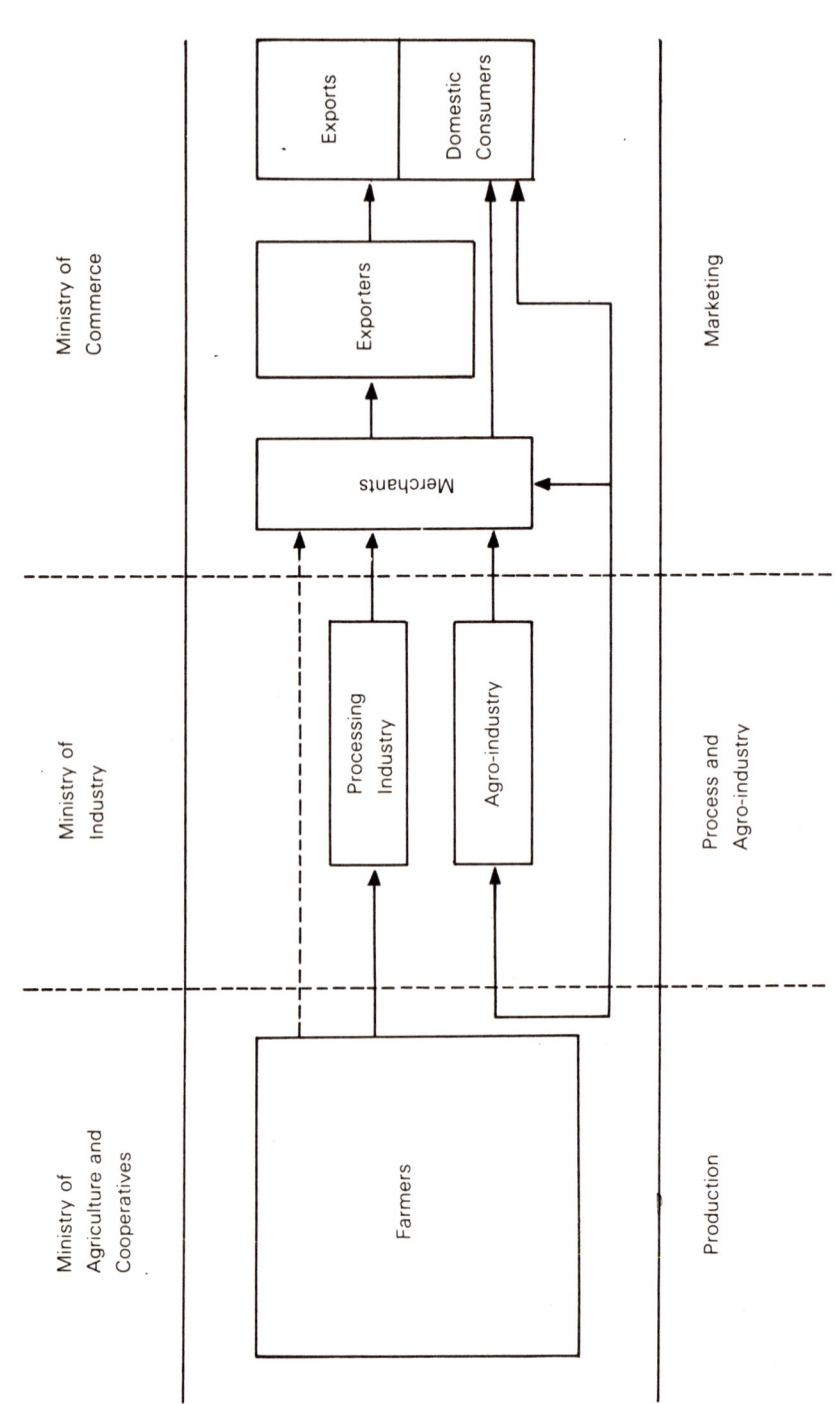

**Figure 5** Relationships Among Government Ministries and Private/Business Groups Related to Agricultural Activities

On the basis of the above discussion, the following suggestions are proposed:

Agencies of the central administration, which has been organized along specialist or functional lines, should confine their activities to their traditional mission, which is technical assistance. Thus, service delivery responsibilities should be confined to technical rather than administrative matters. Their roles in project or program formulation should be made in conjunction with other departments with the aim of creating multi-functional rather than specialized uni-functional projects, as has traditionally been the case. Their direct managerial or service deliveries in the field should be drastically curtailed and delegated to the provincial administration.

The provincial administration should be restructured to be able to play a more aggressive role in direct service deliveries. Each service should be designed according to the needs of the people rather than being dependent on the convenience or constraints of the rendering organizations. The organization of provincial and local services should be area-based rather than being based on functional or organizational factors. A very important point is that as the provincial administrations are charged with additional responsibilities, they should also be provided with sufficient authority and resources to carry them out.

The development tasks of certain specific areas in the provinces may deserve special treatment from the government in the form of an area-based integrated development project. For instance, in some irrigated areas where the government has allocated a large budget, the development potential for export-oriented investment is very high.

At the policy formulation and integration level, it is generally recognized that the entire agricultural sector is too large and complicated to serve as a single target unit for any meaningful policies or plans. It is here suggested that the organization of activities and services should be based on the processes or cycles of each commodity. In concrete terms, it is suggested that farmers' organizations should be set up according to the commodities they produce. At national level, a commodity board consisting of the representatives of farmers' organizations (of each commodity), government representatives from related organizations in the Ministry of Agriculture and Cooperatives, the Ministry of Industry, the Ministry of Commerce, bankers, exporters, etc., should be established. They should be provided with a strong secretariat organization in order to design and run an effective information system as well as to implement the decisions of the board. The board will consequently be assigned an active role in formulating policies and plans concerning each commodity. Also, the board secretariat should be equipped and financed to be well-informed about market trends and other factors affecting commodities, and keep all parties concerned, especially the farmers, well informed as well. The National Economic and Social Development Board is at present studying the feasibility of establishing such a body.

**Appendix** Number of Provincial Agricultural Agencies Belonging to the MOAC Central Administration

| Agencies | Number | Total |
|---|---|---|
| *Office of the Permanent Secretary* | | 15 |
| Regional Agricultural Offices | 4 | |
| Changwad Land Consolidation Offices | 9 | |
| Petburi Farm Demonstration Project | 1 | |
| Huey Sithon Demonstration Farm | 1 | |
| *Royal Irrigation Department* | | 156 |
| Irrigation Regional Offices | 12 | |
| Changwad Irrigation Projects | 24 | |
| Water Distribution and Maintenance Projects | 120 | |
| *Department of Fisheries* | | 30 |
| Changwad Brackish-Water Fisheries Stations | 8 | |
| Changwad Marine Fisheries Stations | 2 | |
| Changwad Inland Fisheries Stations | 17 | |
| Phuket Marine Biological Center | 1 | |
| Fisheries Development Unit in Ubol-Ratana Reservoir | 1 | |
| Fisheries Extension Unit at Huey Sithon | 1 | |
| *Department of Livestock Development* | | 221 |
| Zonal Livestock Offices | 9 | |
| Artificial Insemination Stations and Substations | 37 | |
| Veterinary Service Stations | 25 | |
| Livestock Development Centers | 28 | |
| Local Livestock Development Units | 9 | |
| Disease Inspection and Quarantine Units | 42 | |
| Livestock Breeding Stations | 13 | |
| Livestock Promotion Units | 9 | |
| Livestock Breeding Extension Centers | 10 | |
| Animal Nutrition Forage Crop Stations | 19 | |
| Forage Improvement Units | 5 | |
| Animal Husbandry Research Units | 1 | |
| Animal Disease Research Units | 1 | |
| Animal Disease Diagnosis Units | 3 | |
| Trichinosis Units | 8 | |
| Forage Experimentation Station | 1 | |
| Swine Improvement Research Center | 1 | |

Appendix (continued)

| Agencies | Number | Total |
|---|---|---|
| **Royal Forestry Department** | | 247 |
| Zonal Forestry Offices | 23 | |
| Khao Nang Ram Forest Research Station | 1 | |
| Bang Phra Nursery Station | 1 | |
| Zonal Wild Life Conservation Offices | 40 | |
| Wild Life Inspection Units | 5 | |
| Natural and Wild Life Study Centers | 6 | |
| Wild Life Parks | 4 | |
| Forest Reserves Improvement Centers | 13 | |
| Lac Research and Experimentation Centers | 8 | |
| National Parks | 24 | |
| Botanical Garden | 1 | |
| Foliage Gardens | 23 | |
| Forest Nurseries | 31 | |
| Watershed Conservation Research Station | 9 | |
| Basin Development Centers | 6 | |
| King's Watershed Development Projects | 4 | |
| King's Watershed Development Units | 38 | |
| Watershed Management Experiment Projects | 2 | |
| Northern Watershed Management Experiment Units for Rural Development | 8 | |
| **Land Development Department** | | 47 |
| Land Development Centers | 26 | |
| Land Development Units, Watershed Conservation Projects in the East | 13 | |
| Land Development and Consolidation Projects | 5 | |
| Marl Production and Servicing Station | 1 | |
| Acid Sulfate Soil Improvement Station | 1 | |
| Soil Conservation Station | 1 | |
| **Department of Agriculture** | | 111 |
| Tree Crop Experimentation Stations | 11 | |
| Rice Experimentation Stations | 22 | |
| Upland Crop Experimentation Stations | 18 | |
| Sericulture Research and Training Centers | 1 | |
| Sericulture Experimentation Stations | 14 | |
| Rubber Research Centers | 1 | |
| Rubber Experimentation Stations | 18 | |
| Crop Inspection Units | 26 | |

Appendix (continued)

| Agencies | Number | Total |
|---|---|---|
| **Department of Agricultural Extension** | | 32 |
| Regional Agricultural Extension Offices | 4 | |
| Pest Protection and Eradication Units | 24 | |
| Seed Multiplication Centers | 3 | |
| Grasshopper Protection and Eradication Center | 1 | |
| **Department of Cooperative Promotion** | | 95 |
| Cooperative Promotion Offices | 9 | |
| Cooperative Promotion in Irrigated Area Units | 10 | |
| Project Cooperative Demonstration Units | 10 | |
| Land Settlement Cooperative Units | 66 | |
| **Office of Agricultural Economics** | | 38 |
| Agricultural Economic Zone Offices | 19 | |
| Agricultural Economic Statistics Centers | 19 | |
| Total | | 992 |

Source : National Institute of Development Administration, *A Study of the Role and Functions of Regional Agricultural Offices in Thailand* (Bangkok : NIDA, 1980).

## Notes

1. Murray Weidenbaum, *The Modern Public Sector : New Ways of Doing the Government's Business* (New York : Basic Books, Inc., 1969), pp. 3-31 and Gary Fromm and Paul Taubman, *Public Economic Theory and Policy* (New York : The Macmillan Company, 1973), pp. 4-10.
2. Gerald E. Caiden, *Public Administration* (Pacific Palisades : Palisades Publishers, 1982), p. 128.
3. *Ibid.*, pp. 129-31.
4. Earl M. Kulp, *Designing and Managing Basic Agricultural Programs* (Bloomington, Ind. : International Development Institute, 1977), p. xxi.
5. John C. Bollens and Henry J. Schmandt, *The Metropolis : Its People, Politics and Economic Life* (New York : Harper and Row, Publisher, 1982), p. 266.
6. Kulp, *op. cit.*, pp. 16-17. See, also, Arthur Mosher, *Getting Agriculture Moving* (New York : Praeger, 1966).
7. *Ibid.*, p. 16.
8. George F. Gant, *Development Administration : Concepts, Goals, and Methods* (Madison : The University of Wisconsin Press, 1979), p. 37.
9. Regional Research and Development Center (RRDC), AIT, *Policy Study on Agricultural Development and Related Activities,* Vol. 2 (November 1983), pp. 10-11.
10. National Economic and Social Development Board (NESDB), *The Fifth National Economic and Social Development Plan (1982-1986)* (Bangkok : United Production Press, 1981), p. 43.
11. Center for National Rural Development Coordination (CNRDC), NESDB, *Handbook for the Rural Development System* (Bangkok : United Production Press, 1982).
12. RRDC, AIT, *op. cit.*, Vol. 1, p. 7.
13. See, for example, *The Nation,* July 1, 1985, p. 21; *The Nation,* July 23, 1985, p. 19; *The Nation,* October 10, 1985, pp. 1, 17; and *The Nation,* October 13, 1985, p. 19.
14. In 1969, there were just 102 civil departments and 856 divisions. See Voradej Chandarasorn, *Patterns of Organizational Expansion in the Thai Public Bureaucracy : A Study of Agencies' Functional Responsibilities, 1969-1982* (Ph.D. Dissertation, New York University, 1985), p. 152.
15. For general review of the role of central government organization in agricultural development in Thailand, see RRDC, AIT, *op.cit.*, Vol. 6, pp. 43-59.

16. Patom Manirojana, "Thai Public Administrative System," *Politics and Administration at the Subdistrict and Village Levels* (Bangkok : Asia Press, 1983), pp. 87-96. (in Thai)

17. *Ibid.,* pp. 97-136.

18. See World Bank, *Thailand : Toward a Development Strategy of Full Participation,* Report No. 2059 TH. September 1, 1978, pp. 124-25.

19. UNDP, *An Organizational Analysis of Agricultural Development in Thailand* (August, 1980).

20. Center for National Rural Development Coordination, NESDB, *Poverty Stricken Rural Development Plan, 1983* (Bangkok : Agricultural Cooperative Press, 1983).

# 3

# The Agricultural Delivery Service System in India*

## B.M. Verma**

In developing countries the 'theory of distributive justice' poses a problem of inequalities in the public distribution system in rural areas. Our changing society faces many challenges in resolving the need for means, methods, and materials required for the promotion and development of rural society. The institutional mechanism prescribed for public policy is very much determined by Harold Lasswell's[1] phrase, "who gets what, where, how." The eminent economist J.K. Galbraith[2] in the *Theory of Social Balance* concluded that our affluent society has largely solved the problem of production and wealth creation, but has failed singularly in its allocation of final output as between the supply of privately produced goods and services, and those of the state. The studies of Benson and Lund[3] and Jacob Harbert[4] show that there is an absence of clear links between the delivery of services and attitudes which are supportive of the regions. Economists have long been concerned with the production of services by local government, but have generally ignored the political and social aspects of distribution.

The term 'delivery system' is viewed as a static phenomenon under the existing policy framework, which, however, functions in terms of a dynamic inter-relationship between means and ends to achieve a tangible result. As a unidimensional concept, it may be regarded as serving to overcome poverty. In fact, it is nothing less than an efficient and effective implementation of the plans and programs of agricultural production. The agricultural delivery service system is designed to achieve developmental goals. The very nature of the delivery system is such that the delivery process, which is a dynamic one, seems to be an invisible concept. Operationally, when the community

---

\* This paper was prepared under the supervision of Dr. P.R. Dubhashi, Director of the Indian Institute of Public Administration, New Delhi, India. Dr. Dubhashi provided invaluable insights into aspects of rural development and agricultural administration, as well as comments and suggestions for improving the paper.

\*\*The Indian Institute of Public Administration, New Delhi, India.

structure - both tangible and intangible - and target group structure interact, the delivery system proves to be effective and successful. Thus, a better delivery system is a matter of organization in which the material inputs and services are made available for successful operation of the program.

The basic objective of the delivery system is to percolate from top to bottom the needs and requirements of agricultural programs, in both the production and service sectors. A number of inputs are required for agricultural production programs. Some of them are gifts of nature, such as sunlight, moonlight, rainfall, and other climatic factors. Other inputs include human factors and institutional arrangements for irrigation, seeds, manure and chemical fertilizers, labor, technology, electricity, and other resources such as credit, loans, and subsidies. "It is universally accepted that more equitable access to land, water and other agriculture resources is a prerequisite of agrarian reform and rural development strategy."[5]

As the public delivery system is directly connected with the productive capacity of farmers, the basic structure of the delivery system associated with the agricultural credit system will therefore be studied. Its administrative structure, organizational approach, design, methods, and procedures will also be screened in light of existing social and economic realities. The purpose of this chapter is to examine existing problems of the delivery of public services with regard to the administrative structure and to trace the development of the delivery system for carrying out the inputs, supply, and delivery of agricultural credit to rural areas. An attempt has been made to evaluate the cooperative credit structure - i.e., the role of various agencies such as cooperative and commercial banks - responsible for credit. In the framework of the general administrative policy of different plans and programs of agricultural production, this chapter evaluates different approaches to planned development and suggests some alternative solutions and structural adjustments in administrative capacity for improving the agricultural delivery service system in impoverished rural areas.

## Delineation of the Problem

With the increasing growth of population, modernization of agriculture, and achieving the goal of growth with social justice, India is making a great effort in rural areas by providing for basic needs and stimulating the various services required for agricultural production. According to Singh,[6] "unsatisfactory administrative and organizational arrangement was, by far, the most important single factor responsible for inadequate process in the sphere of agricultural production." Therefore, in order to sustain agricultural policy, a strong administration is required to support the smooth implementation of development programs. In the planned process of development, efforts have been made to formulate sound public policies concerning delivery systems for impoverished areas. Lessons learned over a period of more than three decades show that due to shifting foci in the approach towards strategy and planning, failures and limitations of human service programs and schemes geared for social action at grass-roots level, the efforts to accomplish desired goals have been defeated. Instead, public administrators are constantly involved in promoting new programs, techniques, tactics, and ideas. In order to reduce poverty and promote economic prosperity, the Government of India launched a number of rural development schemes, viz., the Community Development Program (1952), the National Extension Service (1953), the Small and Marginal Farmers Development Program (1970), the Drought-Prone Area Development Program (1972), the Rural Credit and Marketing Program, the Differential Rate of Interest Scheme, Antyodaya, the Minimum Needs Program, the Integrated Rural Development Program, and the National Rural Employment Program. It should be noted, however, that the fruits of these schemes for economic prosperity have not reached the rural poor, who are still unable to share in the growth process due to inadequacies of the delivery system. By and large, agricultural programs are not yet intensive enough and the organization of supplies and services has to become much more efficient. In order to increase agricultural production, it is necessary to examine the problems of the agricultural delivery system and to intensify efforts to supply agricultural credit. As the essential infrastructure, both material and psychological, is provided by different agencies and departments connected with agricultural administration, it is therefore essential to look into the general administrative structure in relation to the improvement of the delivery system at local levels.

No real progress can be made in agricultural production without the use of High Yielding Variety (HYV) improved seeds, an increase in fertilizer consumption, the use of pesticides and insecticides, and the use of modern implements. All these inputs entail a high level of capital investment. Agricultural indebtedness, however, has been a chronic feature of the rural economy in India. It is said that the Indian farmer is born in debt, lives in debt, and dies in debt. Given scarce resources and acute poverty, there is minimal utilization of agricultural inputs. The operations of an Indian farm must, rather, be looked at as a way of life rather than as a business enterprise. Analyzing the causes of rural poverty, the National Commission on Agriculture[7] in 1976 stated that low productivity of land and labor is one of the principal factors. Low productivity is characterized by low inputs and low outputs. Thus, the problem of low agricultural productivity in India is a very complex one and cannot be attributed to any single factor. On the other hand, a number of factors help to produce a 'vicious circle of poverty.' This circle comprises low productivity, low market surplus, low incomes, low savings, and low investments, which in turn lead to low agricultural product. The crucial deficiencies in Indian agriculture are related to land, capital, management, and organization. But what is more alarming is the die-hard traditional outlook of agriculturalists and the poor delivery of inputs for agricultural production. The basic characteristic of Indian agriculture is its variegated pattern in terms of natural endowments, social and economic overheads, institutional set-up, and cropping patterns. There is wide variation in per-acre productivity. Different regions have different patterns of, and problems relating to, agricultural planning and production. No generalization can, therefore, be made which would be applicable to all the areas without important qualifications.

An awareness of variations from one sector to another is accordingly as important as knowledge about the common elements. Only detailed and specific knowledge about conditions in each area can provide a firm basis for agricultural development. When viewing rural development in India in the wake of modernization processes and technological advancement, it can be said that physical and human resources have not been fully channeled. Guy Hunter[8] in *Modernizing Peasant Societies* puts forward the thesis that organizations need to be far more closely adapted to varying local conditions, and particularly to the stage of development which the farming community has reached. In this connection he further states that unless the choice of organization is right (for supplies, credit, marketing, storage, transport, and prices), the effort and cost of research will be wasted. Delivering the goods would be, according to Hunter, the agricultural problem of the 1970s. It is essential, therefore, that an adequate and functional delivery system be evolved and goods and services provided suited to the actual needs of the rural poor. In this context, it should be noted that a knowledge of the farming community and an awareness of agricultural programs, levels of leadership, habits, customs, and extent of apathy in local administration and extension agencies are intimately connected with the success of agricultural programs. It is the prime task of the agricultural administrator to motivate the individual farmers to adopt improved practices and to help organize agricultural production through education, aid, assistance, assurance, inducement, and institutional reforms - if necessary through large-scale public investment.

**Structural Analysis**

The notion of the delivery system, as it applies to agricultural production, can be traced historically as follows. In the pre-Independence era the British Government passed the Agricultural Loans Act and Taccavi Loan Act in 1882 to provide for some lending by the government to farmers. The Bengal Famine Commission[9] emphasized the need for distribution of fertilizers and other agricultural inputs. The Cooperative Societies Act of 1904 was enacted to enable the establishment of Riffeisen-type cooperative societies in Indian villages. In 1928, the Royal Commission on Agriculture[10] made certain recommendations with respect to providing support services and facilities to farmers, and accordingly cooperative credit societies were established in different parts of the country. Soon after the Grow More Food Campaign (1942), loans and grants were given by the central government to the states for distribution of essentials for generating food production. The Second Foodgrain Policy Commission[11] issued a statement on agriculture and food policy in India, with the objective of increasing the prosperity of cultivators and providing them with adequate resources for increasing production and diminishing dependence on the vagaries of nature.

In the post-Independence (1947) period, agricultural indebtedness and agricultural finance have received the attention of policy makers and planners. In the initial plan period of development, the Government of India took many decisions to modernize Indian agriculture, as evinced by the Community Development Program (October 1952). In accordance with national policy, agriculture, including irrigation and power, was given the highest priority in the First Five-Year Plan. In 1953 the Agriculture Extension Service as established with the objective of extending agricultural inputs and credit, and improving the package of services to farmers.

The subject of the agricultural credit system was examined by the All India Rural Credit Survey Committee,[12] established by the Reserve Bank of India. It was found that not more than 3% of total agricultural credit was handled by the cooperatives; farmers were dependent for the most part on money-lenders. The Committee therefore recommended a network of large-sized cooperative societies for a group of villages affiliated to the district cooperative center banks, which were ultimately affiliated to the Apex State Cooperative Banks. Both short-term and medium-term finances were prescribed not only for the small and marginal farmers, but also for tenant-cultivators. The National Development Council, in its meeting held in November 1958, suggested that suitable arrangements for more adequate agricultural credit through cooperative agencies should be worked out in consultation with the Reserve Bank of India. The Working Group on Cooperative Policy appointed by the Government of India in November 1955 stated in its report that the problem of providing adequate credit was important. The matter required careful and immediate consideration, and it was suggested that it should be speedily examined by the Government of India, the Reserve Bank of India, and other agencies concerned. The report of the Agriculture and Administrative Committee[13] reviewed the position regarding the distribution of nitrogenous fertilizers, improved seeds, improved agricultural implements, and pesticides. At the same time it was decided that delivery of agricultural inputs should be separated from the control of technical functions of the agricultural department and transferred to cooperative organizations in the various states.

In 1959, soon after the report of the Ford Foundation team on "India's Food Crisis and How to Meet It,"[14] a major change took place which consisted of a shift from the community approach to an entrepreneurial approach. The report suggested a package of services and practices for farmers. In 1960, the Intensive Agriculture District Program (IADP) was started and the notion of a selected area approach was discussed in the Development Commissioners' Conference, as well as in the Agricultural Administrative Committee and Manpower Report. In consequence, the delivery of inputs for agricultural production became of paramount importance.

During the Fourth Plan (1969-74), several central and centrally-sponsored schemes were launched in the fields of production, minor irrigation, land improvement, seeds and manure, etc. There was a perceptible increase in resource allocations, while procedures associated with the sanctioning and disbursement of assistance were also changed. In the Fourth Plan, a new orientation was imparted to agricultural policy to help the weaker and more vulnerable sections of society, as well as socio-economically backward areas. At the same time, the Rural Credit Review Committee[15] under the chairmanship of Dr. B. Venkatappiah recommended the creation of small farmer, marginal farmer, and agricultural labor development agencies to provide access to credit and supplies for potentially viable farmers. In July 1969, fourteen commercial banks were nationalized with the object of diverting the flow of credit to the priority sector of the economy. Farmers' service societies and Large-Sized Adivasi Multi-Purpose Societies (LAMPS) were created.

With the introduction of new technology during the Fifth Plan (1976-79), the supply of rural credit increased significantly. The National Commission on Agriculture[16] emphasized the need for integrated agricultural credit services and envisaged the greater involvement of commercial banks in financing agricultural development. The commission suggested that greater emphasis be placed on the needs of small and marginal farmers, and the provision of credit to them on preferential terms in respect of both interest charges and advances to enable them to upgrade and modernize agriculture. Suggestions were also made for improving farmers' service societies. Discussing other incentives, the commission recommended that selective subsidies should be allowed those classes, sectors, and key progams that needed support in the interests of balanced and rapid development, while bearing in mind the objectives of growth and social justice.

A more comprehensive integrated rural credit approach and accelerated rural development was emphasized in the Sixth Plan (1980-85), in order to create additional demand for credit. Under the 20-point economic program and the Integrated Rural Development Program as a means for eradicating poverty, greater coordination was required between the developmental agencies of state governments and the central government. During the Sixth Plan, District Rural Development Agencies were created in all the districts of the country for the implementation of the integrated Rural Development Program. These agencies identified farming families which could most benefit from the programs through loans extended by cooperatives and credit institutions such as primary agricultural credit societies, commercial banks, and regional banks. Depending upon the nature of the program, project, or scheme, 33 to 50 per cent of the financial input in the form of subsidies would be provided by the District Rural Development Agencies, and a substantial amount was to have been supplied by the banks. Advances to the weaker sections of society should have reached at least 25 per cent of designated priority sectors by March 1985. The banks were required to increase the share of advances for minor irrigation projects. Total agricultural finance reached a level of 17 per cent of total credit as of December 1981, against a target of 16 per cent. Direct finance constituted 13.2 per cent of total credit. Special programs were drawn up by state agencies to help designated castes and tribes. Policy action was taken to reorient the institutional structure in favor of the rural poor. The Reserve Bank of India stipulated in 1976 that at least 20 per cent of the funds of district cooperative banks should be advanced to societies for small and economically weak farmers. The Committee to Review Arrangements for Institutional Credit for Agriculture and Rural Development reported that in the case of cooperative credit, small and marginal farmers enjoyed a relatively better share which was 30 per cent for the whole country, compared to their share in total operated areas only, which amounted to 23.5 per cent. In the case of medium and long term credit, it is one of the objectives of the Agricultural Refinance Development Corporation,[17] established in 1963, to provide more credit to small and marginal farmers and other weaker sections' of society. The Agricultural Refinance Development Corporation is also committed to ensuring at least 50 per cent refinancing to its member banks under various schemes as against loans given to small farmers and other weaker sections. The share of small farmers in total disbursements of the Committee to Review Arrangements for Institutional Credit for Agriculture and Rural Development rose from 40 per cent at the end of March 1976 to 49 per cent as of March 31, 1979. In the case of commercial banks, the policy is to provide liberal credit to the priority sector, and within that special provision has been made for the allocation of credit to small and marginal farmers. In this context the national goals set out for commercial banks are as follows:

| Item | Target | To be achieved |
|---|---|---|
| Private sector advances to total advances | 40% | 1985 |
| Agricultural advances to total advances | 16% | 1985 |
| Agricultural advances to total priority sector advances | 40% | 1985 |
| Weaker sector in agriculture to total direct agricultural advances | 50% | 1983 |
| Differential Rate of Interest (DRI) advances to total advances | 1% | ongoing basis |

| Item | Target | To be achieved |
|---|---|---|
| DRI advances to Scheduled Castes/Tribes to total DRI advances | 66.7% | ongoing basis |
| Credit Deposit (CD) Ratio in rural areas | 60% | ongoing basis |
| CD Ratio in semi-urban areas | 60% | ongoing basis |

With regard to agricultural credit, it should be noted that insofar as Inda has followed a policy of active support for the development of agriculture, efforts have been directed at providing institutional credit for agricultural producers. At the national level the Reserve Bank of India formulates and regulaes credit policies. The Reserve Bank of India, nationalized commerdal banks, state governments, and the cooperative credit system have taken steps to liberalize credit policies and ensure a smooth flow of loan funds for agricultural development. In 1975 regional rural banks were established in selected areas to provide banking facilities to the credit cooperatives at grass-roots level. The land development banks in all the states are increasing their lending to cultivators. The Agriculture Refinance Development Corporation[18] and National Cooperative Development Council[19] were established in 1963 to prcvide a source of capital to cooperative and commercial banks for increasing project-oriented schemes for agricultural development such as minor irrigation, land reclamation, and plantations. The National Bank of Agriculture and Rural Development was established in 1982. As of June 30, 1982, there were 39,000 branches of commercial banks, of which 24,000 were located in rural areas and another 8,800 in semi-urban areas. Currently there are about 44,000 branches of commercial banks and about 6,500 branches of regional rural banks covering 227 districts.

The records of institutional credit in rural areas show that in 1951 only about seven per cent of total loans were obtained from the organized sector, while by 1961 this had increased to nearly 20 per cent. Institutional credit to agricultural producers was increasingly supplied through the cooperative credit systems. By 1965 they accounted for almost one-third of the estimated total, mostly in the form of short and medium term loans. The cooperative credit system numbered about 180,000 societies. Long term credit was made available for land development, irrigation, wells and pumpsets, and tractors. Additional credit was provided for development projects by the Agricultural Refinance Development Corporation. After the nationalization of banks from 1969 to 1978, the priority sector advances of public sector banks increased tenfold. from Rs.441 to 4,798 million. The percentage share of these advances in terms of total advances increased from 14.6 to 31.3 per cent in the same period. The total outstanding of all institutional loans directly advanced to farmers increased to Rs. 16,589 million on June 30, 1981 (see Table 1).

Of the total agricultural credit outstanding at the end of June 1981, cooperatives accounted for 55.7 per cent, commercial banks for 40.5 per cent, and regional rural banks for 3.8 per cent. The investment credit, which amounted to Rs. 10,117 million or 61.0 per cent of the total outstanding on June 30, 1971, increased to Rs. 42,080 million or 55.7 per cent by June 30,1981.

The National Commission on Agriculture[20] indicated that the share of agricultural advances to total advances by the commercial banks should rise from 8.8 per cent in 1974 to 15 per cent in 1985. It was estimated that credit requirements for full program coverage by 1985 amounted to Rs. 165,490 million, of which Rs. 78,840 million (47.6%) were estimated as short-term loan requirements. The Committee to Review Arrangements for Institutional Credit for Agriculture and Rural Development also projected a trend in the supply of credit during 1975-80. It was found that between 1974-75 and 1980-81, short-term loans issued by cooperatives and commercial banks increased at an average annual rate of Rs. 10,008 million and Rs. 773 million, respectively. In respect of investment credit, the average annual rate of growth of advances over the period 1975-80 amounted to Rs. 447 million in the case of cooperatives, and Rs. 1,162 million in the case of commercial banks. The total availability of institutional credit projected by the Committee to Review Arrangements for Institutional Credit for Agriculture and Rural Development for 1989-90 is given in Table 2. The inflow of credit from rural credit institutions is expected to reach Rs. 35,000 million in short-term loans and Rs. 26,800 million in investment loans.

The growth of total institutional credit during 1950-51 to 1980-81 on a per hectare basis has been set out in Table 3. The table represents short-term credit advanced per hectare of gross area sown, which amounted to only Rs. 3.67 during 1950-51. It increased, however, to Rs. 14.32 during 1960-61 and to Rs. 35.80 during 1970-71. Thereafter, further increases resulted in short-term credit advances amounting to Rs. 68.83 per hectare during 1975-76, and

**Table 1  Direct Institutional Loans for Agriculture, 1950 to 1981**

(Amount in Rs.million)

| Credit Institution | 1951 | 1952 | 1971 | 1975 | 1976 | 1977 | 1978 | 1979 | 1980 | 1981 |
|---|---|---|---|---|---|---|---|---|---|---|
| Cooperatives[a] of which | 351 | 2550 | 14225 | 21600 | 23571 (267) | 27957 (456) | 30741 (574) | 33831 (699) | 38303 (1010) | 42140 (1330) |
| (i) short-term | 291 | 1942 | 6472 | 9040 | 10121 | 12158 | 13476 | 15400 | 16973 | 18560 |
| (ii) term loans[b] | 60 (60) | 608 (370) | 7753 (6280) | 12560 | 13459 (10579) | 15799 (11934) | 17265 (12760) | 181431 (13337) | 21330 (15357) | 23580 (16710) |
| Government[c] (short-term) | NA | NA | NA | NA | NA | NA | NA | NA | NA | NA |
| Scheduled Commercial Banks of which | 140[e] | 160[e] | 2364 | 5630 | 9903 | 10310 | 13397 | 18246 | 23409 | 30600 |
| (i) short-term | NA | NA | NA | 2460 | 3638 | 4510 | 5466 | 7593 | 9469 | 12100 |
| (ii) term loans | 140 | 166 | 2364 | 3170 | 4265 | 5800 | 7931 | 10653 | 13940 | 18500 |
| Regional Rural Banks[d] | — | — | — | — | NA | NA | NA | NA | 1684 | 2864 |
| Total of which | 491 | 2666 | 16589 | 27230 | 31474 | 38267 | 44138 | 52077 | 63396 | 75604 |
| (i) short-term | 291 | 1942 | 6472 | 11500 | 13759 | 16668 | 18942 | 22993 | 28126 | 33524 |
| (ii) term loans | 200 | 774 | 10117 | 15730 | 17715 | 21599 | 25196 | 29084 | 35270 | 42080 |

a. Figures in brackets indicate the position of short-and medium-term loans financed by commercial banks and RRBs and routed through PACS.
b. Figures in brackets relate to long-term loans by LDBs.
c. Taken as short-term loans only, relate to April-March (financial year) and are based on State budgets. Small proportion may be long-term loans.
d. Taken as short-term loans only, even though some portion of it may be long-term loans.
e. Estimated indirectly as double of advances given in Table-1.

Sources: (1) Reports on Currency and Finance, various issues.
(2) **RBI**, "Chart Book on Financial and Economic Indicators", Nov. 1978.
(3) Statistical Statements Relating to Cooperative Movement in India-Part-1.

**Table 2** Estimate of Agricultural Credit Supply in 1989-1990

(Rs.million)

| Credit Institution | Short-term loans | Investment loans | Total |
|---|---|---|---|
| Cooperatives | 21000 | 9600 | 30600 |
| Commercial banks | 10500 | 13700 | 24200 |
| RRBs | 3500 | 3500 | 7000 |
| Total | 35000 | 26800 | 61800 |
| Per hectare (Rs.)* | 200 | 185 | 385 |

* Estimated on the basis of 175 million hectare of gross area sown for short-term loans and 145 million of net area sown for investment loans.

Source: Reserve Bank of India, Committee to Review Arrangements for Institutional Credit for Agriculture and Rural Development, January 1981, p. 41.

**Table 3** Trend in Institutional Credit per Hectare, India, 1950-51 to 1980-81

| Year | Short-term credit$^a$ (RS.) | Investment credit$^b$ (Rs.) |
|---|---|---|
| 1950-51 | 3.67 | 1.68 (0.68)$^c$ |
| 1960-61 | 14.32 | 5.81 (3.03) |
| 1970-71 | 35.80 | 71.86 (24.66) |
| 1975-76 | 68.83 | 124.56 (35.00) |
| 1980-81 | 124.33 | 294.68 (96.78) |
| 1989-90 (Projected) | 200.00 | –   (185.00) |

a. Advances during the year per hectare of gross area sown.
b. Outstandings at end June per hectare of net area sown.
c. Figures in brackets are advances per hectare of net area sown during the year.

Rs. 124.33 per hectare during 1980-81. From this, it can be seen that credit became important only after 1970. From a level of just Rs. 5.81 per hectare of net area sown as of June 30, 1961, it jumped to Rs. 71.86 per hectare by June 30, 1971; to Rs. 124.56 per hectare by June 30, 1976; and to Rs. 294,68 per hectare by June 30, 1981. The increase during 1980-81 was Rs. 96.78 per hectare of net area sown.

With regard to the crop loan system, the credit needs of cultivators are determined on the basis of production requirements with respect to different crops. Credit limits for individual cultivators are fixed according to repaying capacity. Credit is to be provided partly in cash and partly in kind on three components: firstly, a cash component to take care of the outlay on cultivation according to traditional methods; secondly, a kind component consisting of inputs such as fertilizers, pesticides, seeds, implements, etc. for improved cultivation; and thirdly, a cash component to accompany the use of inputs provided for in the second component. This last component is conditional on the extent of use made of the second component.

The operation of the crop loan scheme has been continuously improved. More than 50 per cent of farmers have become members of the primary cooperative societies, and the amount of short-term and medium-term credit disbursed every year has increased from 20 million rupees to Rs. 1,200 million during the last 30 years. Besides this, land development banks have been able to disburse investment finance of more than Rs. 200 million every year. While describing the achievement in the field of agricultural credit, the Working Party on Public Service Delivery Systems for the Rural Poor organized by the Government of India and ESCAP on November 8-12, 1979 at New Delhi, India, stated in its report :

> Institutional credit in the rural sector has, in fact, shown a sizable growth in the last 25 years and now accounts for more than half of the total supply of rural credit. More important, there has also been a qualitative change in the sense that a major portion of rural credit is now used for purchase of agricultural inputs and capital assets instead of consumption purposes, as was the case in the 1950s. Available figures show that short-term loans advanced by cooperatives will increase from Rs.6,910 million in 1973-74 to more than Rs. 14,000 million in 1978-79. Medium-term loans of approximately Rs. 1,130 million are estimated to have been extended during 1978-79 as against Rs. 710 million during 1973-74 while about Rs.3,070 million of long-term loans would have been disbursed for the same period compared with Rs. 1,470 million during 1973-74. The targets for the sixth five-year plan are Rs. 25,000 million for short-term loans in 1982-83 and Rs. 12,000 million and Rs. 25,000 million cumulatively during the plan period for the medium and long terms, respectively.[21]

**Contextual Factors**

In a developing country like India, both institutional as well as non-institutional credit systems play a vital role in accelerating the planned process of agricultural development. In the specific field of institutional agricultural credit, an ambitious plan of action has been imposed upon farmers. The willingness of farmers to adopt new modes of cultivation is greatly influenced by the exposure to modernization processes. In fact, credit requirements for refinancing and production purposes depend upon how farmers deploy their own resources and organization of production activity. Different types of inputs for use in agriculture have been provided by different types of loans. For example, irrigation projects may be financed by a medium-term loan, while the purchase and installation of pumping equipment may be financed by short-term loans. The evaluation reports of the success and failure of delivery processes indicates that the institutional mechanism of the cooperative credit structure plays a vital role; and a dynamic agricultural system requires a dynamic program of agricultural credit. Special attention is therefore paid towards credit for small and marginal farmers. Besides this, the significance of the concept of integrated development of agriculture has been realized in which credit has to be effectively linked with the supply of inputs, and with the marketing and processing of agricultural produce. The central banking institutions have extended support to the operations and activities of agricultural credit institutions. The majority focus of their policies has been to replace the exploitative traditional agencies (characterized by landlords, moneylenders, and traders) by institutional agencies. A multi-institutional approach to agricultural credit has been evolved to ensure that credit is not security-oriented but purpose-oriented, mainly to benefit a large majority of small farmers in the agricultural economy. As such, factors responsible for the resistance to change, lack of cooperation, laziness, and apathy on the part of the rural masses in response to the delivery system must be replaced by a revolutionary socio-economic transformation in life-styles of the rural poor.

The Indian cooperative movement evolved in terms of an integrated cooperative structure for supporting the modernization processes of Indian agriculture. It has at the same time become more and more oriented towards the advancement of small and marginal farmers. P.R. Dubhashi[22] has identified a number of deficiencies which have to be overcome:

> First of all, the structure itself has to be strengthened. There are weaknesses at the level of primary societies and even at the level of State District Cooperative Banks and State Apex banks. Secondly, proper cadres of the secretaries of the primary societies are yet to be established. The managerial personnel of the primary society and the District and Apex Banks need to be properly trained. Thirdly, District Banks are yet dominated

by the powerful sections of the rural society. Fourthly, proper traditions have to be established so as to allow the professional managers to play their managerial role without let or hindrance while the members of the Board of Directors lay down general policies and guidelines. Fifthly, utilization of credit has to be more effectively linked with agricultural extension and rural development. Links between credit marketing and processing have to be strengthened. Above all, the entire body of cooperative membership needs to be continuously educated about membership rights as well as responsibilities.

The weakest aspect of the agricultural sector is the defective or inefficient system of providing credit to farmers. Though the main responsibility for providing agricultural credit falls on cooperative institutions, it should be noted that after the period of bank nationalization commercial banks also entered the field of agricultural credit. Unfortunately, however, commercial banks have generally failed to attract farmers, particularly the small ones, for the simple reason that the procedures laid down for advancing loans are too cumbersome and time-consuming. Since farmers fail to obtain loans from banks expeditiously or easily, most of them are still dependent on village moneylenders who continue to charge exorbitant rates of interest. The entire machinery for providing agricultural credit therefore needs to be overhauled. Red tape and bottlenecks should be removed so that procedures for obtaining loans are simplified. It would be helpful if a clear schedule was prepared indicating the normal length of time taken at each stage of the process, right from submission of application to the granting of a loan. Facilities should be provided for the granting of loans to cultivators against their outstanding crops. The existing cooperative institutions should also be restructured so as to eliminate the operations of those with vested interests.

**Evaluation**

The public delivery system may be considered one of the most important strategies for combating rural poverty. The planned process of development has brought forth a network of public delivery systems in the fields of banking, cooperatives, and extension services to cater to the needs of the rural poor. It should be noted, however, that over the past three decades a unified approach has not emerged to solve the problem of the rural delivery system taken as a whole. The community mobilization project approach of the 1950s was replaced by the technocratic and entrepreneurial approach of the 1960s. During this period, the ideological background of cooperative development was weakened and operating agencies came to be looked upon as nothing more than institutional agencies. At the same time, policy decisions were taken for the introduction of commercial banks and regional rural banks in the field of agricultural credit, the establishment of agro-industrial corporations and commercial agencies for the supply of agricultural inputs, etc.

Another phase in the evolution of agricultural inputs began in the 1970s, as some of the distortions of the "Green Revolution" started to become apparent. It was felt that the Green Revolution measures of the 1960s had benefited only the well-to-do farmers, while the small and marginal farmers, agricultural laborers and the landless were left out. Thus, the new orientation of the 1970s characterized by the 'trickle down effect' did not work, and direct benefits had to be given to the poor in the Fifth Plan, by means of the multiple approach, i.e., the resource-based and problem-based approach, target group approach, intensive approach, and comprehensive area development approach. The 20-point Program introduced in The Emergency (June 1, 1975) by the late Prime Minister Smt. Indira Gandhi also asserted the importance for the revitalization of the rural economy and increased production. Policies such as the liquidation of rural debts and the rehabilitation of bonded labor were aimed at benefiting the underprivileged in rural areas. During 1978-79, the Sixth Plan was drawn up to provide direct benefits to the poor through the integrated rural development approach. Shri R. Venkataraman, the then Union Finance Minister, in a letter dated September 28, 1981, stated that the "Government of India is committed to development programme aimed at the upliftment of the weaker sections of society especially in rural area."[23] Thus, the strategy of development has shifted from macro-level to micro-level concerns, focussed on area-based and clientele improvement.

No systematic study at the micro level has yet been undertaken concerning problems of administration, agricultural production, and the delivery system. However, some attempts were made by K. Seshadhari,[24] T.N. Chaturvedi, R.K. Tiwari, and B.M. Verma,[25] T.N. Chaturvedi, M.L. Sudan, and M. Lasmiswaramma,[26] Kuldeep Mathur,[27] and J.A. Mollett,[28] to study the different facets of agriculture administration with respect to the rural poor and small farmers. They suggested changes in the administrative arrangement at district and block levels for effective integrated planning, management, and development in rural areas, since productive and social service programs relating to agriculture show signs of inadequacy in the delivery system at different levels. Problems in the delivery process appear due to defects in the framework of policy formulation, weaknesses in organizational and institutional structures, procedural ineffectiveness, communication gaps, and stresses associated with social transformation processes. The stages of the delivery process, highlighted by the Working Party on Public Service Delivery System for Rural Poor,[29] organized by the Government of India and ESCAP, are as follows:-

Stage 1: recommending and fixing norms for identification of beneficiaries and benefits;

Stage 2: actual identification of beneficiaries in the field;

Stage 3: selection of actual benefits for the individual beneficiaries or the community after matching the existing schemes and the needs of the community;

Stage 4: securing/selecting/constructing/approving the benefits to be given, including the question of timeliness or rationale of the benefits;

Stage 5: imparting knowledge necessary to the beneficiaries to be able to make optimum use of the benefits given;

Stage 6: follow-up actions to ensure that the beneficiaries do not transfer (either willfully or under duress) the benefits to another person (either within or outside the target group);

Stage 7: follow-up actions to ensure that the support services required for proper utilization of the benefits are made available.

**Alternative Solutions**

India's changing society is facing the challenge of how to alleviate poverty. In order to fulfill the basic needs of the rural masses and to achieve the objective of distributive justice, policy-makers, planners, and administrators have to modify the basic structure of the delivery service system and to look into its administrative organization, design, methods, and procedures. In fact, problems of the public delivery system are a function of economic factors or the productive aspects of development. Very little attention is paid to the social aspects of development. In order to establish a link between the productive and supportive services of the public distribution system, due attention should be paid to ideological aspirations, prescribed norms of the socio-political system within the prevailing socio-economic environment, cultural ethos, value orientations, and local conditions of the rural masses. Given the existing social and political realities of the country, a sound framework of administrative policies for agricultural development is required. In every action program, a new delivery system should be evolved through involvement of more voluntary organizations, associations, small groups, and farmers' service societies, in which lower level functionaries (officials and non-officials) should work with missionary zeal and play their roles effectively in nation-building and development.

Improvements in the capacity to administer the delivery system are closely related to institutional arrangements, processes, linkages, inter-departmental coordination, delegation, reporting, procedures of credit administration, recruitment of field staff and their training. Given the background of social stratification, diversity in socio-economic living standards, cultural patterns, value orientations, and ethos of the rural masses, efforts should be made to redefine the concrete objectives of the delivery system. The major focus of the agricultural service delivery system should be on how far resources, technological support and inputs, and supplies are properly utilized. The dependency syndrome on the part of the rural poor has generated a need for re-orientation at the level of the formulation of supportive services of the public delivery system. The delivery system dealing with the target group should be operated through a single agency. In order to create a framework for a new delivery system, it is therefore essential to redesign delivery policy, and organize and manage public service in the productive sector in favor of the rural poor. The decentralized administration should take care of the basic problems of coordination, communication, feedback, and follow-up action at field level. Some new methodologies and approaches need to be evolved for actual involvement and participation of small and marginal farmers in terms of a new perspective. Participation of farmers and their involvement in the delivery system is based on the strength of the linkage in the delivery circle. In spite of the network of the public delivery system in the field of banking, cooperative marketing and extension services for the rural poor to increase agricultural production, the latter have not benefited equitably from the public service delivery agencies. Half of all farming families are still outside the fold of cooperatives; specifically, the small and marginal farmers and Scheduled Caste farmers do not get their due share. Nearly 30 per cent of the total short-term credit is provided by the cooperative system. With the modernization of agriculture the need for agricultural credit has increased enormously and a credit gap has resulted. The management committees of cooperatives are dominated by vested interests. There is a need to reorganize and strengthen the cooperative structure and other supporting services for meeting the needs of poor farmers. The new cooperative ventures should facilitate the transfer of technology as well as arrange the supply of inputs, credit, and marketing. In order to solve these problems, P.R. Dubhashi[30] has suggested the following measures. Firstly, there should be a systematic drive for the enrolment of small and marginal farmers. Secondly, there should be representation of small and marginal farmers and the Scheduled Castes in the managing committees of cooperatives. Thirdly, there should be participation of the small and marginal farmers in reaping the benefits of the cooperative credit institutions. Finally, credit supplied by cooperatives should be supplemented by credit from the nationalized banks, commercial banks, and rural banks.

In order to achieve the multi-functional role of rural credit agencies, it is therefore essential that more finance should be given for production-input and asset distribution. This will promote forward and backward linkages to sustain growth at farm level and compete with the informal leaders who perform a multi-functional role by providing credit, labor, and community markets. The credit policy for determining loans to be advanced to farmers should in future be based on the previous year's advance. For this purpose credit and non-credit cooperative societies should come forward for mobilizing banks for providing credit and other services at mutually agreed terms and conditions. Training should be made an integral part for bank staff. Project formulation and implementation for lending purposes is highly desirable on the part of bankers. Regarding performance evaluation on the part of bank staff, it is desirable that a higher weight be attached to the task performed by the staff in assessing a farmer's potential to earn a higher and timely incremental income and enough cash to repay the loan, and that support linkages be organized to realize this potential.

**Conclusion and Recommendations**

The public delivery system is an important strategy that can be employed for eradicating rural poverty. The major task for developing countries, therefore, is to analyze the adequacy of the delivery system; to redesign conceptual and methodological approaches; to identify bottlenecks in planning, organization and management of delivery systems; and to explore the possibilities of new directives and methods of participation in the control of delivery systems.

In order to fulfill the task and to cater to the needs of the rural poor, a public delivery system network is necessary in the field of banking cooperatives and extensions. The contextual factors of the adoptive delivery strategies for agricultural production call for a change in the institutional arrangements of inputs. In the planned process of development for the proper utilization of resources (credit, loans, and subsidies) and generating a climate of work, every effort has been made and innovative practices introduced from time to time for the achievement of development goals. Nonetheless, the magnitude of the problems of the delivery system has not been simplified, due to the growth of population and the failure to adopt modernization processes and technological innovations.

A strong administrative structure is necessary to support the public delivery system for various agricultural development programs. Administrative strategy is a vital link in the implementation process. Different committees and commissions set up from time to time call for changes in the administrative structure and suggest an integrated approach to planning, implementation and supervision of agricultural development programs. Although the new agricultural strategy has succeeded in increasing production, it has generated intra-regional and inter-regional disparities. It has been found that merely adopting a project approach or a sectoral approach seems to be insufficient for leading to an overall development of large areas and a distribution of benefits to local populations. In spite of a massive investment in rural areas, the economic disparity among different sections of the rural population has increased. The less advantaged cultivating population has still to be brought into the network of information, services, and supplies in order to enable it to break away from the system of low-yield agriculture and to place it at a higher level of technology and output per unit of land.

Based on the study of Plan documents, the reports of different committees and commissions, and field surveys for macro- and micro-level researches in the field of rural and agricultural development, a realistic picture of those factors affecting the efficiency of the delivery system in the implementation process of agricultural development programs can be presented, as follows:

*Policy Framework.* An important factor affecting the efficiency of the delivery system is the lack of a comprehensive policy framework to provide productive and social assets for the rural poor. Different types of organization for the rural poor to provide the required inputs and supplies will have to be devised according to local conditions. It is, therefore, suggested that for improving the climate for implementation of plans and programs to benefit the rural poor, some better linkages and structural changes in policy direction are required to re-orient the district administration in light of changing circumstances.

*Organizational Structure.* For the implementation of agricultural production programs and management of the delivery system, efforts have not been made to strengthen block-level planning. The block organization has neither the competence nor the capacity to implement programs because it lacks decision-making authority. Due to the multiplicity of programs and a single-line authority, the processes of planning and coordination are not commensurate in the absence of administrative control. The workload of District Rural Development Agencies has increased without an increase in staff. There is no elaborate administrative and implementation machinery at the operating level of such agencies. The development staff are totally dependent upon state government assistance and other official and non-official agencies. There is therefore a need to strengthen the core staff of these agencies.

*The Institutional Support System.* In view of structural deficiencies, the bureaucratic system should be organized on functional lines so as to facilitate proper command and coordination. However, since rural and agricultural development cannot be broken up into functional components, a concerted effort and integrated action by a number of functionaries is required. This may give rise to problems of coordination, especially at the lower levels.

Another problem in the existing situation is that a number of lower- and middle-level functionaries have to operate under the dual control of the administrative hierarchy. A major structural defect existing at present is that scope for people's participation has not been provided at all in the administrative structure, or wherever provided it has not been institutionally possible to ensure that true representatives of the rural poor are selected as people's representatives in the organizations.

*Procedural Deficiencies.* Regarding procedural deficiencies, one major defect noted was that the procedure for monitoring and measuring progress is based on looking at either the expenditure figures or at the numerical figures of physical targets achieved. This very often means that the real purpose or objective of the delivery system or the programs gets overlooked. Over the years, a tendency has also developed in the delivery system to arrange for continued special campaigns for purposes of program execution and special schemes. The result has been that work now normally gets done only through such special campaigns and very little is achieved through regular routine work. Frequent transfers of staff and complicated procedures are inherited problems in the delivery system.

*Communication Gaps.* The problem of a lack of awareness involves shortcomings on both sides. Beneficiaries are often not aware of schemes and types of assistance so that they cannot secure benefits even though agencies may be available to provide them. They may also be unaware of the implications and background of various schemes. Thus, they may be apathetic towards the goods and services being delivered. Similarly, the officials at the lower level may not be aware of the true significance of the schemes. As such, they may give priority to the easy-to-perform tasks rather than to the vital or primary tasks, and thus fail to gain the confidence of beneficiaries. The role of the administration should be based on participatory management practices and the optimum use of human resources in support of the requirements of the rural poor.

*Social Transformation.* The traditional social structure in rural areas is weakening under the new socio-political environment and modernization processes, thus creating new problems for improving the delivery system for the rural poor. The delivery system shows signs of inequality against the landless. There is a great need for reorientation of the work system and attitudes of public service officials at different levels to make sure that the delivery system truly responds to the major concerns of the impoverished masses.

For evolving a new delivery system, there is a need to have an appropriate farm policy relating to products, inputs, prices, credit, insurance, mechanization, and marketing. A new delivery system should be evolved through involvement of more voluntary organizations, associations, and groups along with government agencies to replace the purely bureaucratic support system. The aim of decentralization efforts has been to reach the rural poor by building up a cadre of locally responsible leaders entrusted with the task of implementing development plans and programs. Linkage with village, block and district level panchayat and voluntary organizations should be strengthened. In order to modernize the agricultural sector, agro-service centers and mobile workshops should be set up for small and marginal farmers. They should be supported by advisory services and the timely supply of agricultural credit, improved seeds and fertilizers, plant protection services, and irrigational facilities on a priority basis. Crop insurance schemes should be implemented. Thus, the agricultural administration should be geared towards technological advancement, infrastructure, institutional support, and services. For establishing an effective delivery system, the extension, coordination, and integration of operations have to be ensured so that goods and services reach the rural poor. A lack of motivation due to socio-economic patterns of interrelationships caused by differences in position and/or status has resulted in cultural gaps which have ultimately become responsible for administrative failures, in both the productive as well as social service sectors of agriculture. It is, therefore, necessary to provide adequate motivational stimuli to the poor so that they can help themselves by forming their own organizations and associations which will be self-reliant. As far as the new development cadre are concerned, training should be imparted to executive functionaries to develop professional skills and to provide a sound delivery mechanism for the rural poor.

**Notes**

1. Harold D. Lasswell, *Politics: Who Gets, What, When, How* (New York: Peter Smith, 1950).

2. John Kenneth Galbraith, *The Affluent Society* (Boston: Houghton and Mifflin, 1958).

3. C.S. Benson and P. Lund, *Neighborhood Distribution of Local Public Services* (Berkeley : University of California, Institute of Government Studies, 1969), p. 190.

4. Jacob Harbert, "Contact with Government Agencies: A Preliminary Analysis of the Distribution of Government Services," *Mid-West Journal of Political Sciences,* Vol. XVI, No.1 (February 1972), p. 123.

5. F.A.O., *Review of Agrarian Reform and Rural Development in the Developing Countries since the mid-1960s,* Rome FAO, June 1979.

6. S.P. Singh, *Centre-State Relations in Agricultural Development* (New Delhi : Vikas Publishing House Pvt. Ltd., 1973), p. 4.

7. National Commission on Agriculture, *Ministry of Agriculture and Irrigation : Department of Agriculture* (New Delhi : Controller of Publication, 1977).

8. Guy Hunter, *Modernising Peasant Society : A Comparative Study of Asia and Africa* (London: Oxford University Press, 1969).

9. *Report of Famine in Bengal and Orissa,* 1875-76.

10. U.K. *Royal Commission on Agriculture in India,* Report London H.M. 50, 1928.

11. *The Second Foodgrain Policy Committee,* Report, Chairman, Parushottamadas, Thankurdas, Delhi Manger of Publication *(sic),* 1948.

12. *All India Rural Survey Report of Committee Direction,* Reserve Bank of India, 1954.

13. *India, Agricultural Administrative Committee,* Report, Chairman Raja Surendra Singh, Nalagarh, 1958. This Report known as Raja Nalagarh Committee Report has observed that the "problem for increasing agricultural production in India is more an administrative problem than technical one." The report stressed that "a streamlined agricultural administration is the urgent necessity and the food situation of the country can be appreciably increased if positive steps are taken to achieve the objectives. Administrative lapses have universally contributed towards shortfalls in implementation of agricultural schemes and thereby directly causes shortfalls in agricultural production." (p.4).

14. Ford Foundation, *Agricultural Production, Team Report on India's Food Crisis and Steps to Meet It,* 1959.

15. *All India Rural Credit Review Committe,* Report, Chairman B. Venkatappiah, Reserve Bank of India, 14 August 1969.

16. National Commission on Agriculture, *op. cit.*

17. *Agricultural Refinance Development Corporation,* 1963.

"ARDC was set up with an authorized capital of Rs. 25 million for providing long term loans to central land mortgage banks and other approved credit in situations to finance specific agricultural development schemes. The ARDC was to subscribe 90 per cent of these special debentures, leaving the balance to be contributed either by the public or the concerned state government. ARDCs disbursement totalled Rs. 135 million in 1975-76 (April-March) and Rs. 101 million in 1974-75 of which disbursement under IDA assisted schemes accounted for Rs. 103 million (60 per cent of the total in 1974-75)."

18. National Commission on Agriculture, *op. cit.*

19. *National Cooperative Development Council* (NCDC), 1963.

"NCDC indicates that as of 30 June 1982 there were about 3,000 primary marketing societies of different types. The number of primary agricultural credit societies affiliated to marketing societies was thus only 42 per cent of the total number. Moreover, of these, effective affiliation could be said to be in respect of 14,747 agricultural credit societies only, since it was only in respect of those societies that 257 marketing societies attempted linking of credit with marketing and recovered a total amount of Rs. 489 million from the members of primary agricultural credit societies." *Annual Report,* pp. 10-13.

20. National Commission on Agriculture, *op. cit.*

21. Economic and Social Commission for Asia and the Pacific (United Nations), *Public Service Delivery System for the Rural Poor,* Prepared in cooperation with the Government of India, Thailand, 1980, p. 6.

22. P.R. Dubhashi, "Credit, Cooperatives and other Financial Institutions for Small Farmers," Paper submitted in the working party on *Public Service Delivery Systems for Rural Poor,* organized by GOI and ESCAP, New Delhi, 8-12 November, 1979.

23. Economic Intelligence Service, *Secret Documents concerning India's Application for IMF Loan,* Center for Monitoring Indian Economy, Bombay, October 1981.

24. K. Seshadhari, *"Agricultural Administration in Andhra Pradesh,"* A Study of the Process of Implementation of Intensive Agricultural Development Program, Bombay, 1974.

25. T.N. Chaturvedi, R.K. Tiwari, and B.M. Verma, "A Case Study - Rehabilitation Scheme for Bonded Labor," *Kurukshetra,* Vol. XXVIII, No. 14 (April 16, 1980), pp. 4-11.

26. T.N. Chaturvedi, M.L. Sudan, and M. Laxmiswaramma, *Delivery System in Support of Small Farmers in the Context of Rural Development,* Center on Integrated Rural Development for Asia and the Pacific, Comilla, Study Series No. 18, May 1982.

27. Mathur Kuldeep, *Bureaucracy and the New Agricultural Strategy* (New Delhi: Concept Publishing Company, 1982).

The author depicts, "The picture that emerged of the operational machinery is that there is a multiplicity of organization working at the district. Separate organizations have been formed to perform individual functions. By and large, each input is provided on its own organizational basis while the Department of Agriculture performs the task of extension. With this functional diversity being embedded in separate organization, issues under the broad rubric of coordination emerge as a major problem area of implementation. This is compounded by parallel administrative systems running in district. In this administrative proliferation, Panchayati Raj scheme of local level participation has been imposed. The result is that there is a blurring of lines of responsibility, and areas of tension tend to rise," p. 57.

28. J.A. Mollett, *Planning for Agricultural Development* (New York: St. Martin Press, 1984).

The author viewed that capacity for improved agricultural performance is crucially a matter of management and of realistic planning properly implemented at the grassroot level. According to him, "Another reason for the serious gap between plan and performance is the lack of suitable administrative procedures and institutional organization, at all levels of government, to manage agricultural projects in developing countries tends to lag far behind official commitment of loans and grants, leading inevitably to failed targets and frustration," pp. 1-2.

29. ESCAP (United Nations), *op. cit.,* pp. 63-64.

30. P.R. Dubhashi, "Arrangement for the Provision of Credit, Delivery of Input and Marketing Farm Output in the Public Sector and Public Support to Arrangements in the Private Sector," Paper presented in the Round Table on Adoption of Administration to Rural Development: Decentralized Management and People's Participation in Poverty Focussed Program (16-18 August 1978) organized by GOI and ESCAP at New Delhi (India).

# 4  Structures for Health Service Delivery in the Philippines: The Case of the Primary Health Care Approach

*Victoria A. Bautista and Josie H. de Leon\**

### The Primary Health Care Approach

*Background.* The Philippine government has recently embarked on a new approach in the delivery of health services—the Primary Health Care (PHC) Approach. After piloting PHC in selected provinces in all regions of the country in 1980, it was formally launched throughout the country on September 11, 1981. The chief characteristic of PHC is the recognition of the need for citizen participation in planning and implementing health care activities which are at the same time integrated into socio-economic development of the local communities. This mandate may be aptly captured in the following policy statement issued by the Ministry of Health:[1]

> Primary Health Care is an approach that recognizes the interrelationship between health and overall socio-economic development by effectively providing essential health services that are community-based, accessible and sustainable at a cost which the community and the government can afford through community participation and active involvement towards the development of a self-reliant people, capable of achieving an acceptable level of health and well-being.[2]

---

\*College of Public Administration, University of the Philippines, Manila, the Philippines.

Letter of Instruction No. 949 issued on October 19, 1979 provides the legal basis for the official adoption of PHC. It gave the Ministry of Health (MOH) the mandate to design, develop and implement programs which focus on health development at the community level, particularly in rural areas.[3] This directive responds to the emphasis given to participatory decision-making in the planning and implementation of health services by the member states of the World Health Organization who joined the Alma Ata Conference in 1978. This directive in effect replaces the "top-down" approach of the Ministry of Health in defining and providing the kinds of services to be delivered to the people. PHC signifies the partnership of the government, non-governmental agencies and the people in identifying their health needs and in implementing the activities that could respond to these needs. PHC has been conceptualized from the awareness that citizens' capabilities have to be developed to respond to their own health needs in view of the limited resources and the rising population which the government may not singly face.[4] Furthermore, PHC as a concept stemmed from the realization of MOH "that developing countries uncritically adopted health care systems from developed countries with socio-cultural values, demographic characteristics, patterns of diseases and levels of economic development that are widely different from that of less developed countries."[5] As a result, "inequalities in health care coverage, costly urban-based curative and hospital-oriented, doctor-centered services" have been prevalent.[6] Furthermore, experts in public administration have considered citizen participation as a significant determinant of the effectiveness of service delivery.[7] This is because the kinds of activities pursued and implemented by the people are those intimately linked with their demands. Hence, satisfaction is witnessed in the kinds of services that they receive which they themselves help identify and undertake.

*Structural Arrangements.* To put into effect participatory involvement in the provision of health services, the organizational structure has necessarily been streamlined. This need has been suggested in Letter of Instruction 949 dated October 19, 1979 and Executive Order No. 851 issued on December 2, 1982.

Based on these two directives, Primary Health Care Committees have been directed to be constituted in the different levels of the hierarchy beginning with lowest political subdivision of the barangay, to the municipality, province, the region and then the national level. The Barangay Primary Health Care Committee (BPHCC) is envisioned to identify the health needs, mobilize local resources, manage and monitor health and health-related action programs of the community. The higher level committees are to oversee, monitor, and provide policy framework for PHC planning and implementation. These different committees serve as the "principal venues for close and binding inter-agency relationships" as they are to be composed of representatives from government and the private sector.[8]

It is of interest to note that the composition of the different PHC committees at the regional, provincial and municipal levels are expected to be the existing coordinating committees under the regional, provincial and municipal development councils.[9] The development councils are the existing planning bodies at the sub-national levels and are to be composed of representatives of the offices of operating agencies undertaking sectoral functions and respective elective officials of local government. The council is chaired by an elective official of the local government units. At the regional level, the chairman is appointed by the President. At the provincial level, the Provincial Development Council (PDC) is chaired by the governor; at the city/municipal level, by the mayor.

The health and nutrition subcommittee of each development council is to be tapped to serve as PHC committee in the region, province, and municipality. The MOH heads of offices in the different levels shall serve as PHC Coordinators and Chairman or member of the PHC Committees. They are: the Minister of Health (national office), Regional Health Director (region), Provincial Health Officer (province) and Municipal Development Officer (municipality). At the national and regional levels, the MOH Minister and the Regional Health Officer, respectively, shall be the automatic chairman of their respective PHC Committees. The chairman at the provincial and municipal levels is to be elected from representatives from the government and other citizen groups.

Since barangays do not have development councils like the higher local government units, the PHC committee shall be established by the local legislative body (the barangay council) with membership to be drawn from existing governmental and non-governmental organizations.

The programs are to be implemented in the barangay by volunteer workers called the BHWs (barangay health workers) who are the indigenous manpower to be trained in managing community-based health and health-related projects. These may include management of the Botica sa Barangay (drug store of the barangay), propagation and utilization of herbal medicinal plants, income-generating projects and other community-initiated projects, e,g., backyard gardening, toilet and drainage construction.

The BHWs complement or supplement the health promotion and disease preventive activities of the Barangay Health Station (BHS), as an old network of the MOH. The BHS is a satellite station under a Rural Health Unit (RHU). It is established at a strategic place to serve an average population of 5,000 covering three or more barangays. The BHS is manned by a midwife and has been set up to respond to primary care cases. Primary care is a medical service which requires minimum facility and equipment. This is often extended on an "out-patient" basis.

The Rural Health Unit (RHU) in turn is located at the center of the municipality and is staffed by a rural health physician, rural sanitary inspector, and rural health midwife.[10] Like the BHS, the RHUs can only respond to primary care cases because these have minimal facilities and equipment. Therefore, health care is extended on an "out-patient" basis. Other health related services are implemented by the RHUs and the BHS like nutrition, family planning, maternal and child care, environmental sanitation and disease control.

Secondary and tertiary cases are taken care of by the usual public health facilities under the MOH. Secondary cases are those requiring a physician with basic specialized training to attend to less complicated cases, but require basic hospital facilities and multidisciplinary support of other doctors and services.

Tertiary care is rendered by a specialist for complicated cases requiring specialized diagnostic and treatment facilities and multidisciplinary support service usually done on an "in-patient" basis. It also renders consultation and treatment in complicated cases on an "out-patient" basis.

As of 1984, there was only one hospital under MOH to serve 144,920 persons with medical problems. Primary health care can only be responded to by a total of 9,982 RHUs and BHSs altogether, or a ratio of one BHS/RHU to every 5,328 persons.

A significant feature of the reorganization plan as embodied in Executive Order No. 851 is the integration of health and medical units at the field operations level. First of all, this has led to recognition of the District Hospital as the integrating unit of all health and medical services in the catchment area. Formerly, the promotion of health and the campaign to prevent diseases had been supervised by the RHUs at the municipal level. Primary care cases were also attended to by the RHUs. In turn, the medical services were provided by the District Hospital and those below it, like the health center. By virtue of E.O. 851, this merging has led to the integration of the budget of the RHU and the District Hospital and the consolidation of administration of health and medical service at the municipal level.

Secondly, the reorganization scheme also provided for merging of the Provincial Hospital and the Provincial Health Office (PHO) to constitute an Integrated Provincial Health Office (IPHO). The IPHO is to be responsible for the complete integration of the preventive, promotive, curative and rehabilitative components of health care delivery system within the province. This merging also means integration of the budget for the Provincial Hospital and the PHO at the provincial level.

A third feature is the performance of higher management level activities by the Regional Health Office, leaving routine financial and administrative functions to the IPHO. Formerly, the Regional Health Office performed budgetary functions as well as overseeing health activities in the area (see Chart 1 for a comparison of the organizational network of PHC before and after the issuance of E.O. 851).

An additional feature of the organizational structure is the provision for a monitoring and evaluation system to determine the progress and performance of PHC. The regional, provincial and municipal offices of the MOH monitor the implementation of the respective plans of action at their level, to determine strengths and weaknesses of PHC implementation and the support needs of the field staff.[11] The national office in turn consolidates their reports to have a comprehensive understanding of the performance of PHC around the country. It must be pointed out at this juncture that cities are local government units in the Philippines but they had been deliberately excluded in the structures for PHC as the primary emphasis of PHC are the rural communities.

*Other Activities for PHC Implementation.* As the pivotal agency in designing, developing and implementing PHC, MOH had undertaken several activities towards its fulfillment. These activities may be classified into four categories, namely, social preparation, intersectoral collaboration, health services and the provision of implementation support.[12]

*1. Social Preparation.* This consists of activities to orient the government, the private agencies and the citizens concerning PHC at the regional, provincial, municipal and barangay levels. First of all, training is to be undertaken among the MOH staff and personnel to make them receptive to PHC. Based on the Progress Report of the implementation of PHC undertaken by PCF for MOH,[13] barangay midwives had been trained on community organization and community development; and had received skills training on maternal and child health, family planning, nutrition, and the control of diarrheal diseases,

Health Service Delivery in the Philippines 81

**Chart 1** A Comparison of the Organizational Network of PHC Before and After the Issuance of Executive Order 851.

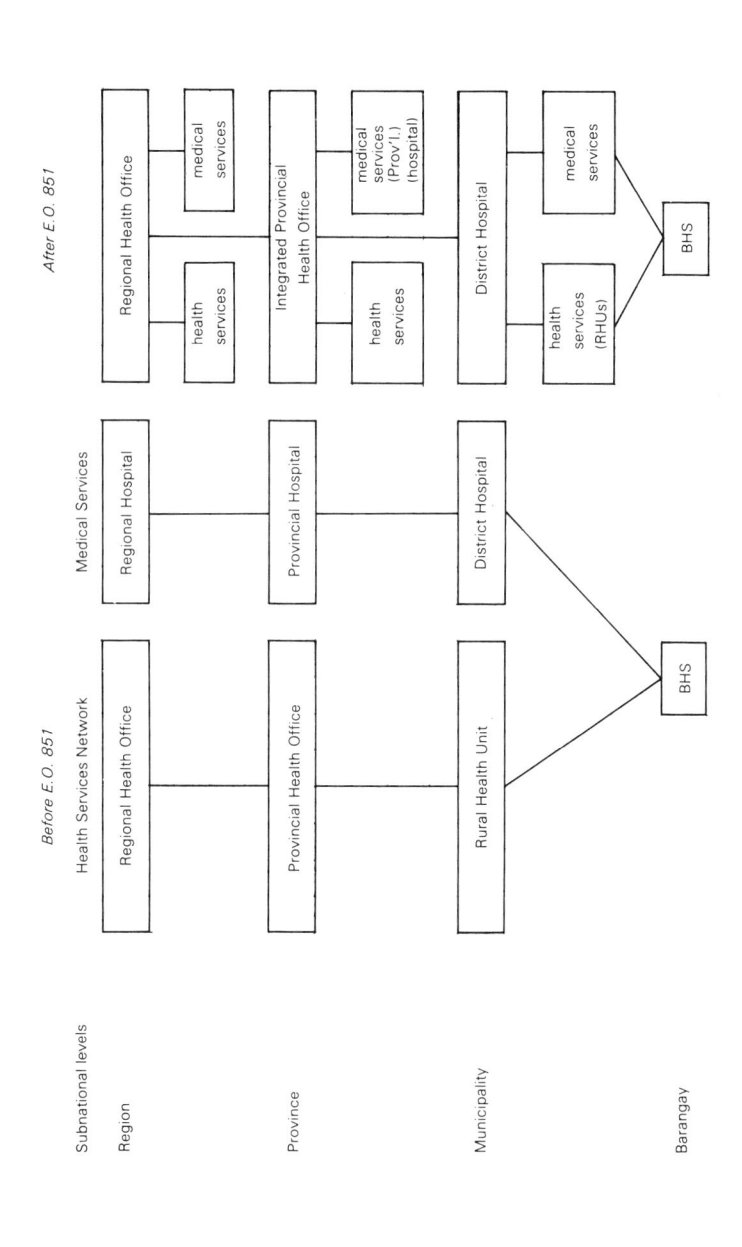

malaria and other endemic diseases. Public health nurses, health officers and chiefs of hospitals were also trained in the promotion of managerial competence in health development.

The clientele groups were also oriented to the concept and strategy of PHC by the conduct of dialogues with them. Indigenous health workers called the Barangay Health Workers (BHWs) were also tapped and trained to support PHC and to assist in the delivery of health services to the people. A total of 147,511 were reportedly trained as of 1983, yielding a ratio of five BHWs to every barangay initiated to PHC. By December 1984, MOH-PHC Unit statistics reveal a further increase in the total number of trained BHWs. A total of 262,553 had been trained, yielding a ratio of 6.96 BHWs to every barangay initiated to PHC.* Considering the MOH target of training one BHW for every 20 households, the data show a marked improvement in this ratio from 1:43 in 1983[14] to 1:26 in 1984.

*2. Intersectoral Collaboration.* The implementation guidelines require MOH to initiate coordinative efforts with the various agencies.[15] These agencies include the Ministry of Education, Culture and Sports for community and school health education programs; Ministry of Human Settlements in the promotion of home techniques; Ministry of Agriculture for backyard gardening and herbal medicines; Ministry of Local Government for community based infrastructure; Ministry of Social Services and Development for nutrition, self-employment assistance and disaster control programs; and Population Commission for population activities. Non-government organizations are also expected to be tapped such as women's organizations like the Catholic Women's League and Young Women's Christian Association; other religious groups; and socio-civic clubs.

*3. Health Services.* The activities undertaken under this category aim to provide the eight essential elements of PHC, namely: promotion of proper nutrition and an adequate supply of safe water; basic sanitation; maternal and child care, including family planning; immunization against the major infectious diseases; prevention and control of locally endemic diseases; education concerning prevailing health problems and the methods of preventing and controlling them; appropriate treatment for common diseases; and the provision of essential drugs.[16] These are often carried out by the rural health personnel,

---

*The total number of barangays initiated to PHC is 37,705 based on MOH data as of December 1984.

although encouragement is made through PHC committees for other agencies to cooperate where they can.

*4. Support Mechanisms.* The MOH continuously provides for technical support to assure the furtherance of PHC. These activities are realized through human resource development in the form of continuing education and manpower development for MOH field staff and the BHWs. In addition, MOH assures the provision of logistic support like essential drugs, information/education/communication (IEC) materials, and medical equipment and supplies. Also, research activities are encouraged to develop appropriate technology for PHC.

**A Case Study of Structural Arrangements for PHC**

*Area Profile.* Region IV, or the Southern Tagalog region, was chosen as the area of study primarily because it is the site of one of the more successful PHC programs in the country. The Population Commission of Region IV is an active participant in PHC, particularly in its family planning component. It provides contraceptive pills, IUDs, incentives for tubal ligation and premarriage counselling of couples on the methods of family planning. The Ministry of Agriculture, especially the Bureau of Fisheries and Aquatic Resources, is particularly tapped regarding food production.

Although several agencies participate in PHC, implementation is nevertheless still primarily under the initiative and supervision of the MOH. In line with this, the MOH of the region has formed PHC action groups at all levels, except the barangay level. The action groups are composed of purely MOH personnel. These action groups were tasked with organizing and implementing PHC under the guidelines set by Letter of Instruction No. 949 and Executive Order No. 851. They are virtually the executive arm of the PHC committee.

At the regional level, the Regional PHC Action Group (REPHCAG), was organized. This is composed of the different provincial health officers and selected MOH staff of the region. It is headed by the Deputy Director of the Regional MOH. As the lead agency for PHC, the MOH initially conducted information/education/communication (IEC) campaigns among its personnel to introduce the PHC approach. Conferences and dialogues were also undertaken with different sectors to familiarize them with the content and mechanics of PHC. Also, brochures on PHC were sent out to other agencies such as the

Ministry of Agriculture, Ministry of Local Government and the Ministry of Social Services and Development.[17]

*Provincial Level.* An inter-agency organization known as the Rural Information Council (RIC) acts as the Provincial Development Council for the province of Laguna. It is composed of the different line agencies at the provincial level, the provincial government and some private civic organizations based in Laguna. It is chaired by the provincial governor. However, there is a separate provincial PHC committee under the honorary chairmanship of the provincial governor. The composition of both the RIC and the provincial PHC are the same except that the chairman of the Provincial PHC committee is the provincial development communication officer. Aside from the chairman, the PHC committee also has a president in the person of the wife of the provincial governor, who is the representative of the Samahang Kababaihan ng Laguna (Women's Association of Laguna) in the RIC. The PHC committee was activated in July 1984.

Twenty-three member agencies from the national line ministries and local government constitute the Provincial PHC Committee.[18] Inter-agency collaboration is supported by memoranda of agreement with specific agencies, including non-governmental organizations. The Provincial PHC Committee, through the Provincial Health Office, has drawn up memoranda of agreement with the provincial MECS, the Samahang Kababaihan ng Laguna/National Federation of Women's Club (NFWC), the Center for Rural Technology Development, the UP-CCHP, the Masons, and the World Vision Philippines. Areas of collaboration vary according to the nature and purpose of the agency concerned. For the NFWC, cooperation in the area is nutrition and family planning. MECS is tapped for mass education of the prevailing health problems, the methods of solving them, the promotion of adequate food supply, proper nutrition, prevention and control of drug abuse, immunization, and the like. World Vision is tapped to provide medical and dental services, nutrition and family planning, tuberculosis control, environmental sanitation, training, etc.

The Provincial PHC Committee meets regularly, every last Wednesday of the month. The Provincial PHC Committee is provided technical support by the MOH through its provincial PHC action group (or PROPHCAG). In keeping with the reorganization scheme of MOH, the Chairman of PROPHCAG for Laguna is the Officer-in-Charge of the Provincial Health Office who is at the same time chief of hospital of the Laguna Provincial Hospital (LPH). The secretary of the PROPHCAG is the medical social worker of LPH and the treasurer is the senior pharmacist of Laguna. In addition, there are six district coordinators, all of whom are medical personnel of the IPHO (e.g., supervising PHN, Provincial Health Educator, Provincial Nutritionist, etc.). Other members include the five district hospital chiefs and a representative of UP-CCHP.

In order to comply with the requirement to submit monitoring forms (e.g., training accomplishment report forms, provincial/hospital monthly report forms, checklist for assessing performance, etc.) required by the Ministry and other agencies, the PROPHCAG created the position of collator with the specific duty of making sure that these forms are completed and that they are accurate and updated.

*District Level.* The district level is not a general political and administrative subdivision in the entire governmental system. Nevertheless, with the implementation of E.O. 851 integrating the health and medical services at the field operations level, a District PHC Action Group (DISPHCAG) was organized to "plan, supervise, manage and coordinate PHC activities" especially referral cases at this level. (See Chart 2 for clarification on referral system.) For Nagcarlan District, the chairman of the DISPHCAG is the District Hospital Chief. The District PHC Coordinator is a staff nurse of the district hospital. Other PHC personnel from the district hospital are the district PHC Collator who is also a staff nurse, and the PHC Secretary who is a clerk. The DISPHCAG regularly meets every month. They confer with other municipal health officers and other agency representatives in the area, as for instance, in the scheduling of "intervisitation" activities, or visits to different municipalities/barangays within the district, when necessary.[19]

*Municipal Level.* The structure for PHC implementation seems more organized at the municipal level in comparison with the other levels of the hierarchy earlier considered. This is indicated by well delineated roles in the structure for PHC at the local level. Furthermore, the different agencies are reportedly very cooperative in terms of fulfilling their respective roles and duties.

In Liliw, there is a Municipal Primary Health Care Task Force composed of the following members and equally drawn from the local legislature, the administrative bodies of the national and local governments, and the private sector: six representatives of the Sangguniang Bayan; two representatives from the municipal governement; two representatives from the Kapulungan ng mga Barangay (Association of Barangay Captains); one representative each from line agencies; six representatives from the religious groups and one represen-

86  *Delivery of Public Services in Asian Countries*

**Chart 2**  Flow Chart for Two-Way Referral of Patients

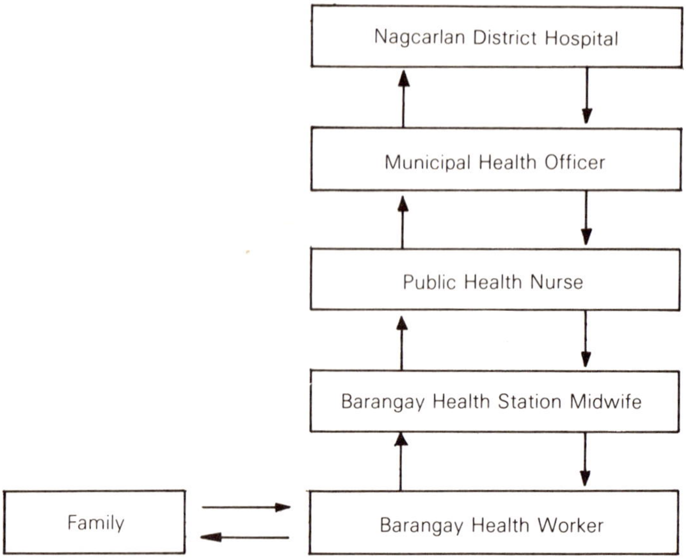

```
                    ┌─────────────────────────────┐
                    │  Nagcarlan District Hospital │
                    └─────────────────────────────┘
                              ↑      ↓
                    ┌─────────────────────────────┐
                    │   Municipal Health Officer  │
                    └─────────────────────────────┘
                              ↑      ↓
                    ┌─────────────────────────────┐
                    │     Public Health Nurse     │
                    └─────────────────────────────┘
                              ↑      ↓
                    ┌─────────────────────────────┐
                    │ Barangay Health Station Midwife │
                    └─────────────────────────────┘
                              ↑      ↓
     ┌──────────┐  →  ┌─────────────────────────────┐
     │  Family  │  ←  │    Barangay Health Worker   │
     └──────────┘     └─────────────────────────────┘
```

Source: Nagcarlan District Hospital, 1985.


tative from a civic group. The representatives from the Sangguniang Bayan are the mayor, the municipal secretary, the assistant municipal secretary and three councilors. The two representatives from the municipal government are the municipal assessor and the senior clerk of the Treasurer's Office. The representatives from the Kapulungan ng mga Barangay are the President and the Secretary of the association. The representatives from the line agencies are the Municipal Development Office from the Ministry of Local Government, an officer from the Ministry of Agriculture, a classroom teacher from the MECS who is also the guidance counsellor, an officer from the Ministry of Human Settlements, and a social worker from the MSSD. In addition, there is also a representative from the Malaria Eradication Office of the MOH because Liliw is classified as an endemic area for malaria. Representing the private agencies in the Task Force are five members of a religious group, the Knights of Columbus, and a representative from the Liliw Women's Club.

From the broad membership of the Municipal PHC Task Force, a smaller group called the municipal PHC Committee was formed which acts as the secretariat. There are seven members of the committee representing the following organizations: Ministry of Human Settlements, the municipal government, Sangguniang Bayan, Women's Club, Malaria Eradication Office and Knights of Columbus. The PHC Committee holds regular quarterly meetings.

Aside from these two organizations, a PHC action group is also organized at the municipal level. This is composed of the municipal health officer as the chairman with members coming from the rural health unit (i.e., PHC, dentist, RHM). This group takes care of the implementing and monitoring activities of PHC in the municipality.

*Barangay Level.* It is in the barangay level where the PHC effort is concentrated. In fact, PHC committees were first formed at this level. The Committee is headed by a chairman chosen by the MOH health team in consultation with the barangay. The basis for selection is one's credibility and acceptance in the community. Usually, the barangay captain is picked as the chairman since it was envisioned that the barangay council should serve as the "broad based political support of the PHC approach in policy planning and program implementation." (Provincial Health Office of Laguna, n.d.) However, this may not be so if the chairman is not receptive to the PHC.

The core of the PHC program is the barangay health worker who is expected to have capability in delivering primary health care services in the community. Hence, one of the support activities undertaken by MOH is the conduct of training for BHWs to prepare them for their role. Some of the criteria for the selection of BHWs are their acceptability to the community and their previous training in health care. Also preferred are the housewives, since it was observed that they are the ones who stay at home and have free time for community activities.

The barangay in focus for this study is Barangay Bongcol. The PHC at barangay Bongcol, Liliw, Laguna was organized immediately after the training of two BHWs on PHC on September 30, 1981. There are now eleven BHWs for the whole barangay, or an average of five families per BHW. This is higher than the MOH target of one BHW per 20 households for 1984.

Inter-agency linkages have been established with the Ministry of Agrarian Reform, especially with regard to land reform problems in the area; the Ministry of Agriculture and Food regarding swine raising technology; the religious sector, regarding the nutrition program; the Ministry of Human Settlements and the municipal government, for the provision of loans for income generating activities; and the Ministry of Local Government for the construction of the barangay health station and the activation of barangay brigades. The barangay health station, which was formerly a building for palay storage, was renovated with the help of domestic contributions and labor provided by the residents themselves. The PHC committee also negotiated for a *Samahang Kabuhayan* (Cooperative Livelihood Project) beneficiary loan from MLG for 5,276.58 Pesos for swine raising. To obtain this loan, the committee gave assistance in formulating a project feasibility study. The committee was also able to register the Samahang Kabuhayan with the Securities and Exchange Commission, as a requirement in receiving this amount.

To sustain the operation of PHC, each member family gives one peso per month. This serves as the emergency fund of the barangay.

The barangay has a very active barangay captain. His commitment to the community was recognized by receiving both the Outstanding Barangay Captain and Outstanding Farmer Awards. Chart 3 Provides a summary of the structural arrangements for PHC in Region IV and the other subnational levels.

**Chart 3** Structural Arrangement for PHC in Region IV

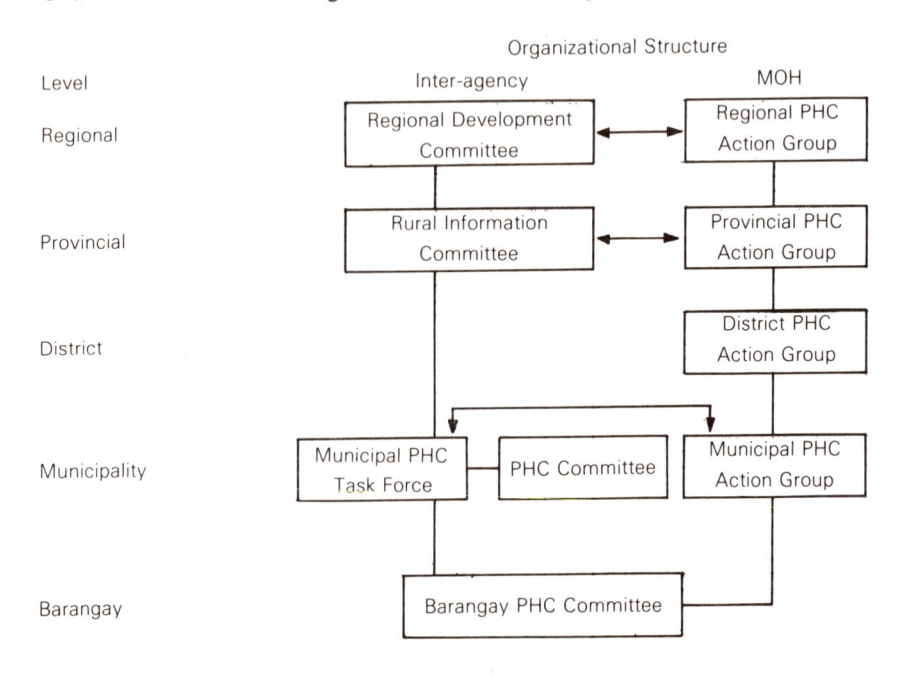

| Level | Inter-agency | MOH |
|---|---|---|
| Regional | Regional Development Committee | Regional PHC Action Group |
| Provincial | Rural Information Committee | Provincial PHC Action Group |
| District |  | District PHC Action Group |
| Municipality | Municipal PHC Task Force — PHC Committee | Municipal PHC Action Group |
| Barangay | Barangay PHC Committee |  |

## Status of Implementation

The extent of PHC implementation has expanded over time. Upon examining the 1983 data based on the PCF study,[20] 77 per cent of the barangays have been initiated to PHC. By the end of December 1984,[21] this has increased to 98 per cent. Only 1,345 barangays out of a total of 38,364 had not adopted PHC at the end of 1984. The regions that had the biggest percentage of barangays not yet initiated to PHC are the following, ranked from biggest to smallest:

| Region | Percentage |
|---|---|
| Region XII | 38.4% |
| Region VII | 24.6% |
| Region IV | 21.2% |
| Region VIII | 12.1% |
| Region VI | 3.5% |
| Region I | 2% |
| Total | 100% (total number of barangays not yet initiated to PHC) |

It may be noted that Region 12, which is a Muslim area, might have had poor performance in 1984 because of the earlier problems cited in PCF report.[22] It was mentioned that the peace and order problem was a primary impediment to its implementation. It was reported by the PCF team that 18% of the total barangays in the region had this problem. It was further pointed out that intersectoral collaboration was not effective because the coordinators responsible for initiating intersectoral effort were not doing their work as efficiently as they should. Furthermore, some agencies did not seem to be deeply involved in or committed to PHC as evidenced by poor attendance in meetings or the common practice of sending representatives who are not in a position to commit their respective agencies.[23] Other problems cited concern the inadequate skills of midwives in organizing the community for action and the lack of logistic support, i.e., doctors, market outlets for income-generating activities, etc.[24]

An analysis of the levels of PHC development in the different barangays initiated to the approach can be made based on the indicators formulated by the MOH-PHC Unit. There are four levels of health development namely:

1st Level - *(Social Preparation of Awareness)* where community leaders and the citizens are aware of the basic strategy of intersectoral partnership; community leaders have been trained for PHC.

2nd Level-*(Leadership Organizational Design-LOD)* where appropriate organizational structures for planning, implementation and evaluation had been identified; goal statements are expressly defined related to the needs of the community.

3rd Level-*(Program Planning and Management)* where community-based projects become operational including mobilization of local resources both human and material.

4th Level - *(Institutionalization of PHC)* where barangay councils serve as the broad-based political support of the PHC in policy-making, program formulation and management, supportive to PHC total development; policies and guide-lines in developing annual planning and management of PHC by community-level leadership are established and operational.

The MOH data as of December 1984 reveal that only very few (15%) of the barangays initiated to PHC have achieved the fourth level of development. The rest are below this level. More specifically, 46% are in the third level, 31% are in the second level, while 8% are in the first level.

The case of Region IV shows that of the total number of barangays initiated to PHC, 9% are in the fourth level of development. Those in the third level constitute 48% of the total; 39% are in the second; and 4% are in the first level.

**Problems/Issues Concerning Structural Arrangements**

Let us now consider some basic problems/issues concerning the structural arrangement for the PHC delivery system. As mentioned earlier, the peculiar requirement for inter-sectoral collaboration in the planning and implementation of PHC has necessitated the formulation of coordinative bodies in the different levels of the hierarchy. Coordination is a basic feature in the formulation of PHC Committees which are the structures responsible for overseeing and monitoring the planning and implementation of the PHC approach.

The evaluative study of PHC in the pilot provinces[25] reveals a basic problem that PHC committees are not formed according to the implementation guidelines. In addition to the utilization of existing development councils, some coordinative activities for PHC had been forged through the formulation of special coordinating bodies such as the case in Pangasinan where a PHC committee is not the Health and Nutrition Sub-Committee of the Provincial Development Council. The Provincial PHC is chaired by the Governor with the Vice-Governor as Chief Executive for Committee policies.[26] In certain areas where no coordinative bodies were available or where coordinative bodies were available but did not perform their jobs, the MOH staff assumed most of the responsibilities such as the case in Carmen, Agusan del Norte. In this area, the initiation of PHC was performed by the Public Health Nurse.[27] Hence, MOH personnel had their hands full with health activities but were not able to respond to non-health activities.

The difficulty in harnessing inter-agency collaboration, which has been noted in programs relying on coordinative bodies,[28] has also been observed in the PHC Committees. This difficulty has been manifested in a number of ways. First is the non-attendance of any activity of PHC Committees by certain agencies. Another is the dwindling attendance of regular representatives during committee meetings. Non-cooperation is further manifested through the attendance of proxies to committees, instead of regular representatives, thus preventing continuity in pursuing PHC concerns.

This difficulty may perhaps be attributed to the very nature of coordinative bodies that draws support from representatives of various agencies and whose loyalties and commitments belong to the primary agency of their affiliation. In certain instances, agency representatives may indeed extend their commitment to PHC but their respective agency programs and priorities may demand more of their attention.[29] For example, in Region V, the presence of the Bicol River Basin Development Project (BRBDP) which pursues an integrated area development approach and encourages citizen participation had also left PHC coordinators responsible for PHC. However, the participating agencies "were pre-occupied with their own responsibilities and problems" and were "paddling their own canoe" by performing the usual activities.[30]

Another possible issue that could be raised regarding structural arrangements is the potential conflict that may arise between community-based concerns and the regular MOH programs and projects that are expected to be carried out in the different communities (i.e., nutrition, family planning, maternal and child health, etc.). This may possibly occur as the PHC committees are constituted preferably from the members of the sub-committee on health and nutrition of the different development councils in the region, province and municipality. Formerly, the sub-committee on health and nutrition forges the programs and projects of the MOH. A potential conflict may arise in representing the community's interests and the concerns of the national office if the community-based needs and demands run at cross-purposes with the requirements of the national program. As borne out by the data on the communities studied by PCF,[31] income-generating activities take precedence over health and health-related activities. Another study analyzing integrated vis-a-vis sectoral mechanisms in health service delivery also shows that the people prefer to embark on income-generating activities.[32]

Another observation about the structural arrangement is the assignment of responsibility of monitoring and evaluating only to the MOH network of personnel in the different levels of the hierarchy. Hence, the national leadership of the other cooperating agencies are not able to keep track of the number of field personnel who participate or refuse participation in community-based activities. This lack may suggest to the field personnel that they are not obliged in the furtherance of community-based concerns.

**Other Contextual Variables**

Certain contextual variables in which the structural machinery of PHC is embedded may militate against or facilitate the full implementation of this strategy. These factors include organizational and extraorganizational factors. Organizational factors are those pertaining to components of the organization other than structure, which are necessary for the fulfillment of the activities under PHC. Extraorganizational factors include those pertaining to the sociopolitical milieu within which the structure is embedded.

*Organizational Factors.* Some of the organizational factors that surfaced in the case study of Region IV concern the significant role played by the local leadership in forging PHC, financial resources and the schemes adopted for monitoring the progress of the PHC approach.

*Commitment of Local Leadership.* Earlier studies on health delivery have identified the critical role that project leaders play in the success or failure of projects in the area.[33] In the case of the region under study, the local officials have been very cooperative in providing the technical support for PHC activities. The rural health midwife was able to tap the resources of the municipality to initiate the negotiations for a loan, together with the barangay's PH Committee, to finance income-generating projects for the area. Furthermore, Bongcol did not experience any problem gaining the support of the mayor of the municipality. She was even instrumental in the approval of the said loan by the Sangguniang Bayan (Municipal Council). The barangay captain has also been very active and has in fact received awards for being an outstanding captain and an outstanding farmer in the province. The actions of the leaders of the community show a commitment to pursue programs and projects which they think would rebound to the benefit of the people in the area. Their support facilitated implementation of PHC in Bongcol.

*Financial Support for PHC.* Another reason for the relative success of PHC in Barangay Bongcol is that it was able to receive funding from several agencies, including international organizations like the World Health Organization. It must, however, be borne in mind that not all areas have the same resources and opportunities that Bongcol had in the establishment of PHC.

Logistics have always been a problem of organizations and even the regional office has complained of the limited logistic support given to them for PHC. PHC personnel have also decried that no incentives are given even for coordination, despite the fact that it is an additional workload for them. They are not even entitled to a travel expense allowance, for instance, when they go to the region on PHC matters.

The self-reliance ethic is indeed one of the means of coping with the limited resources of Third World countries, but one is left with the nagging question of whether the prioritization in budget allocations has been based in favor of certain activities, e.g., defense, rather than health.

*Monitoring Forms Voluminous and Under-Utilized.* Field personnel from the study sites also complained that monitoring forms are too many and too complicated. It also takes too much of their time which should have been spent in more productive endeavors. Monitoring seems to be concentrated more in producing data which are not immediately useful to the field units. At the level of the district, for instance, the staff nurse has to allot at least two days of ward duty just to complete the forms which were more than a foot high on her table. What is tragic is that many of these forms end up piled, or at least filed, on the desks of higher level units. Lower units (i.e., provincial) have also complained of difficulty in retrieving data from the regional office because of its disorganized filing system.

*Extra-Organizational Factors.* The extraorganizational context in which the structural machinery of PHC is formulated may militate against or facilitate the full implementation of this approach. These variables include the following: the tendency towards centralization since martial law was declared in 1972; economic status in the area; varying types of natural resources and other physical factors in the different regions of the country; the occurrence of natural calamity; and, the peace and order situation.

*Centralization Tendencies.* One basic ecological factor that could militate against the workability of the structures for PHC is the tendency of the national government to withdraw local government autonomy since martial law was declared in 1972. In spite of the fact that the 1973 Constitution has expressed concern for the state "to guarantee and promote autonomy" of local government units "to ensure their fullest development as self-reliant communities" contradictory policies and practices have worked against its fruition. According to local government experts like Romeo Ocampo and Elena Panganiban, "local governments were progressively stripped of important functions and powers during the last decade."[34] For example, the traditional functions of administering police services, local finance and local utilities were referred back to the national ministries. The local governments only perform minor administrative roles in public markets, garbage collection and street maintenance. While they assume local taxing powers, the revenues from this activity are for the most part, transferred to the national coffers, and further utilization of local resources is restricted by policies regarding budgetary formulation and expenditures. Hence, in spite of the huge earnings of some of these units, they have to depend on the allotments and aid from the national government.

In rhetoric, the RDCs seem to offer a lot in terms of formulating plans responsive to the needs of the people in the area. In practice, however, we have earlier pointed to the fact that the national offices pursuing sectoral programs primarily determine the priorities of their respective field offices. Hence, development councils have only operated as "talking forums" rather than as bodies that formulate substantive programs responsive to local demands. Furthermore, central control is further enhanced by presidential appointment of the Chairman from the core of elective officials in the region. Previously, this position is obtained after one is elected by the other members of the RDC. It may not be surprising, therefore, why PHC Committees find difficulty in furthering community-based interests. The limited resources extended to local governments and the prescriptions regarding local priorities by line agencies of the national government may restrict concerned representatives of government agencies to propagate the interest of the local communities.

Politically speaking, local government units had for a long time been denied the opportunity to undertake local elections to determine its local leaders. Some have remained in power since martial law was declared in 1972. Others emerged through political appointment. It was only in 1980 that elections to the provincial, municipal and city governments were restored. Barangay elections were also held only in 1982. To aggravate this delay in local elections, other factors have also weakened the political system. These are as follows:[35]

1. "Sectoral" representation was introduced into the local councils; thus, the traditional representative system based on general citizenship was curtailed.
2. Local bodies were linked up to the national power structure by a system of "nested" federations at different levels.
3. In Metropolitan Manila, save for the mayorship, the constituent municipal and city governments were abolished, and the Metropolitan Governor (who is concurrently the Human Settlements Minister) has dominated political and administrative processes in the area.

Thus, political participation of the citizenry is at a low level and could be a militating factor against community organization and participatory decision-making. Nevertheless, credit should go to private agencies that have funded, initiated and have applied the community-based approach in the delivery of services. These organizations have certainly contributed in paving the way for the politicization of the citizenry and for making them self-reliant communities.

The experiments undertaken for greater local autonomy in Regions IX and XII or the so-called Regional Autonomous Governments, at first blush seem to provide promise in devolving rather than deconcentrating local powers and responsibilities. A Regional Executive Council (or *Lupong Tagapagpaganap ng Pook*) is constituted to perform the responsibility of overseeing, planning and implementing development projects in each region. As area manager, the body, through its chairman, has been granted greater powers than the other regions, by assuming regulatory and supervisory powers over the local governments and the regional offices of the line ministries.[36] The Council, however, does not perform activities that are within the jurisdiction and competence of the national government such as national defense and security, foreign exchange, etc. The Ministries of Health, Education, Public Works and Highways, Agriculture, Social Services and Development, and Human Settlements are the ones under the jurisdiction of the Regional Executive Council. The Council has the power to recommend the transfer of the regional director outside the autonomous regions. The threat towards the Council's autonomy is the power of the President to appoint the members and the chairman upon the recommendation of the local legislative body (Sangguniang Pampook). Furthermore, Presidential Decree 1618 stipulates that the President may remove the chairman or members upon the recommendation of three-fourths of all the members of the local legislative body.

P.D. 1618 has also restricted the Council's prerogative to supervise the national line ministries' field offices as it stipulates that implementation be "done in accordance with duly approved plans, prescribed schedules and procedures, and specifically allocated resources." Hence, the internal operations of the regional field offices remain the responsibility of the regional directors. This is because the funds for undertaking sectoral projects are released directly to the field offices rather than the Council. Full supervision can only be undertaken for projects funded by the autonomous government. In effect, this decree has stripped the Council's powers to supervise and implement projects of line ministries. Thus, the Council has once again been reduced to perform "coordinating" functions like the other regional development councils.

The very adoption of PHC as an approach to health care was effected through a Letter of Instruction, without the program going through the usual pilot-demonstration-full implementation phase. Specifically, the centralization tendency could be discerned in the formulation of targets which each region had to accomplish within a given period, e.g., number and level of barangays initiated to PHC, number of new BSB sites, etc. In the province under study, some MOH personnel complained that they are pressed to accomplish targets which are difficult if not impossible to meet because they were based on performance levels as perceived by the central office, and not on the performance levels as perceived by the central office, and not on the local capability as perceived by the residents themselves. Some complained that the time frame set to meet targets has not been arrived at realistically. There were also reports of lower levels being pressured to alter statistical data, such as those regarding PHC level of development, to paint a favorable picture of PHC status in the area. In Laguna, intervisitations conducted monthly revealed the existence of barangays still in levels 1 (social preparation or awareness level) and 2 (leadership organizational design level) although official figures showed the majority of these barangays already classified in level 3 (program planning and management level).

*Economic Factors.* Economic factors have definitely influenced the degree of PHC implementation in Laguna. In Bongcol, for example, unemployment is one of the problems that have been noted with 14.25% of the household heads not having gainful employment according to our survey. In fact, the major reason given by respondents for non-participation in PHC activities was lack of time, which in turn was brought about by their preoccupation with earning a living *(paghahanap-buhay)*. Even the BHWs have found it difficult to find sponsors who would be willing to shoulder their travelling and other expenses. Sometimes, the local councils provide assistance but these are more often not enough. If they are attending training in the municipality for a number of days, their personnel resources are usually drained to the limit.

The operation of the *botica sa barangays* (BSBAs) has also been affected by economic factors. One of the reasons BSBAs find it difficult to sustain the operations of boticas is the practice of many residents to borrow medicine but to conveniently forget (or are unable) to pay for it later.

Another effect of this is the fast turnover of BHWs. Many trained BHWs, especially males, transfer to other areas to seek higher paying jobs.

*Geographic and Other Physical Factors.* The geographic location of the area is also another variable which has affected PHC implementation in Barangay Bongcol. Barangay Bongcol is only about two to three kilometers away from the town proper of Liliw. Its accessibility to Liliw and to Manila has definitely accounted for easier coordination and monitoring, particularly for the MOH regional office, which has selected Bongcol as its pilot area for PHC. However, there are far-flung mountain areas in Laguna which can be reached only by foot, and it is here where coordination has proved to be much more difficult.

The size of the area can also be considered as a factor affecting PHC implementation. Bongcol is really only a small barangay with only a total of 66 households. This seems to be a pivotal factor in the success of PHC in the community. However, in larger areas, management could indeed be a problem.

Other ecological variables may also affect the full realization of PHC in various degrees. For example, the uneven distribution of natural resources in the different regions of the country may determine the kinds of socio-economic activities PHC-initiated communities are likely to undertake. The areas with rich resources have greater potentials to reap benefits, provided of course that the citizens have the sufficient capabilities to tap these resources. An example is Central Visayas (Region VII) which is richly endowed with 61% of Philippine gold reserves, with mines producing one-third of the country's total mining output, with abundant fishing areas and with agricultural products for export.[37] On the other hand, local capabilities do not seem to be at par with these vast potentials as the masses still suffer from low income and unemployment. The poorest in the region earn a monthly income of 83.33 Pesos. This is not even sufficient to cover two days basic cost of living.[38]

Another environmental condition is the varying topography of the Philippine geography. The Philippines is made up of lowlands, mountains, hills and slopes spanning 7,100 islands. Hence, communication is very difficult and access to distant places is aggravated by the need to travel hilly portions.

*Natural Calamity.* Natural calamities also constitute another factor that may militate against total development efforts in the country. The Philippines is often beset by typhoons, earthquakes and volcanic eruptions which cause destruction to property, injury to some and death to many, and, susceptibility to calamity--related and caused diseases. In 1984, when typhoon "Undang" struck the Visayas Region, the province of Capiz' fishpond industry was severely hit. Capiz supplies 80 percent of the milkfish and shrimps sold at one of the biggest markets in Manila. It also produces over half of the national production for prawns.[39] In September 1984, the Mayon Volcano spewed out lava in Albay, Bicol. Twenty-one barangays in seven towns of the province were buried deep in mud. The situation was aggravated by heavy rains caused by typhoons which washed tons of volcanic debris down the slopes of the volcano. A total of 60,500 families were affected by this calamity.

*Peace and Order Situation.* The peace and order situation is another important contextual variable. Laguna has been fairly peaceful in recent years, although militarization of the area seems to be evident as witnessed by the presence of many checkpoints when passing through from one municipality to the other within the district. Recently, the Liliw police station, which is right next to the town hall, and the Nagcarlan police station have been the scene of an arms snatching *(agaw armas)* operation allegedly led by the New People's Army. Despite these isolated incidents, however, Liliw and Nagcarlan seem to be generally peaceful. This is probably one of the reasons Bongcol has been chosen to be a pilot area for many government projects. For instance, even in agriculture, Bongcol is a successful pilot area.

Unfortunately, the same cannot be said for other areas. Recent news accounts point to the growing strength of insurgent groups especially in the rural areas. In one area in Laguna, the UP Comprehensive Community Health Program was forced to withdraw because of the worsening peace and order situation.

**Recommendations**

Considering the fact that non-health related activities take precedence over health concerns in the community, a rethinking may be made in terms of the entry point within which community-based activities are pursued. In lieu of PHC, the Community-Based Approach (CBA) may instead be undertaken. With this approach, the substantive components of the strategy shall be spelled on the basis of the needs and demands of the community and should not only be emphasized for health. At the lowest level, this could be the barangay, as PHC has envisioned to address. The Community-Based Approach shall include the basic characteristics of PHC which is participatory and requires intersectoral collaboration among the governmental agencies, the private sector and the community. It shall necessarily be *integrated* in the kinds of services it delivers because the problems that beset a community are often complex and interrelated. The existing *development councils* in the Philippines may once again be tapped as the coordinative body to oversee community-based activities, which MOH has considered primarily for PHC through its subcommittee on health and nutrition.

At present, the Philippines' development council is indicative of the coordination effort among the elective officials of the local government, heads of national government agencies and other leaders of organizations who play a significant effort in the development efforts in the area.[40] A critical bottleneck in its operation, such as the ones experienced by the PHC Committees as a subcommittee of the development council, is the difficulty in effectively integrating decisions and directing the action projects on a unified basis because of the coequal status among the field officials in the development councils. The chairman of the council does not have any supervisory power or administrative control over the development council's members.[41] Furthermore, being financially dependent on the national government, regional decisions on program priorities and budgetary requirements are subordinate to central office decisions.[42] Despite the meticulous development-oriented activities for the identification of programs and projects to meet the development needs and objectives of the regions, it is regrettable that a majority, if not all, of the projects that get funded are centrally-initiated and/or identified.[43]

Hence, to strengthen the capability of the development council to be a more responsive structure for a community-based approach to service delivery, the chairman should be granted administrative powers over its members, composed of national representatives in the field, similar to the ones being tried in Regions IX and XII (but with more vigor). Furthermore, priorities should not be dictated by the national leaders but should be determined by the local governments. Also, greater autonomy could be provided by allowing the chairman of the council to be elected by the members rather than appointed by the President from the core of local elective officials. However, certain functions can still be retained by the national government, such as those expressed in the establishment of the Regional Autonomous Governments.

Instead of a BHW at the lowest level, a Barangay Development Worker (BDW) may be trained to undertake community organizing activities. Projects shall be pursued based on problems identified by the community through a Barangay Development Council which will plan and oversee the implementation of the activities they themselves identify. The Barangay Development Council can be composed of intersectoral representatives from the community, whose participation may be determined by election.

To effectuate this new approach, social preparation activities must be undertaken to enable the different sectors--government, the private agencies, and the community--to understand and facilitate the implementation of the community based approach (CBA). Support systems must also be provided once CBA is underway such as technical support and provision of facilities for human resource development, both carried out through intersectoral collaboration. Monitoring and evaluation must be undertaken to determine progress and performance, preferably involving or undertaken by citizens themselves.

A critical issue that may be raised regarding the fulfillment of CBA is how prepared the national leaders are in granting local autonomy? How willing are the heads of the line ministries to extend substantial powers to local government units?

**Conclusions**

The effort to nationalize an innovative strategy for service delivery is indeed commendable. For the first time, the Philippines has adopted a national policy to implement health care and related services through the Primary Health Care Approach. This is characterized by citizen participation in planning and implementing health service delivery, and, intersectoral collaboration of the government, private sector and the community.

The lesson we have learned from PHC's implementation is that the coordinative bodies designed and implemented by MOH, primarily constituted from representatives from the government sector, have not prepared themselves to respond to the community-based concerns of barangays initiated to PHC. These bodies are commonly plagued by non-cooperation among the different agencies in fulfilling the major tasks of overseeing, monitoring, and providing able technical support to the barangays. This difficulty may perhaps be attributed to the major structural defect of relying on the existing subcommittee on health and nutrition whose concerns for respective national programs each member represents may compete with the areal concerns of the barangay. Furthermore, the PHC Committees as subcommittees of the development councils may suffer as well from the limited powers extended to the development councils. Hence, the very structures formulated for the furtherance of PHC may themselves find very little contribution in assisting community-based activities.

Furthermore, PHC as an approach has only generated prime concern for the initiation and propagation of socio-economic activities among the barangays. Health is almost always not a priority.

In seeking measures to correct the basic structural defect of PHC Committees, one cannot but help re-examine the macro structure in which it is embedded--the development council at the regional, provincial and municipal levels. It has been suggested that these councils be granted more autonomy so that *areal* concerns take precedence over *sectoral* concerns represented by the field officials of the line ministries.

Furthermore, it has also been suggested that instead of assuming a PHC approach, a community-based approach be emphasized as the latter would provide more leeway in forging more particular interests of the barangays.

These recommendations would therefore have implications for national-level relationships and would require major revisions in the national-local political and administrative structures.

## Notes

1. Ministry of Health (MOH), "What Is Primary Health Care," in *Health for All Filipinos Through Primary Care* (Manila : MOH, 1984), p. 19.
2. *Ibid.*
3. Amparo Banzon, "Primary Health Care in the Philippines," Paper presented to the 8th SEAMIC Workshop in the Philippines, February 3-9, 1981, p. 6.
4. *Ibid.*, p. i.
5. MOH, *op. cit.*, p. 20.
6. *Ibid.*
7. Lediviña Cariño and Associates, *Integration, Participation and Effectiveness : An Analysis of the Operations and Effects of Five Rural Health*

*Delivery Mechanisms* (Manila: Philippine Institute for Development Studies, 1982), p. 6.

8. University of the Philippines, College of Public Administration Research Team (U.P. - CPA), "A Study of the Implementation of the Primary Health Care Program in Twelve Regions," A Study Commissioned by the MOH, Vol. 1, 1982, p. 32.

9. Population Center Foundation (PCF), "A Progress Report on the Status of the Implementation of Primary Health Care Approach in the Philippines," Prepared for MOH by PCF, December 1983, pp. 106-108.

10. Ma. Concepcion Alfiler, "Primary Health Care in the Philippines: A Closer Look at a Policy and a Program," Paper prepared for the Commission on Audit's Policy Audit Seminar, State Auditing and Accounting Center, Quezon City, September 3-14, 1984, p.5 (mimeo.).

11. PCF, *op. cit.,* p. 14.

12. *Ibid.,* p. 13.

13. MOH, *op. cit.,* p. 98.

14. PCF, *op. cit.,* p. 19.

15. MOH, *op. cit.,* p. 22.

16. PCF, *op. cit.,* pp. 23-24.

17. Interview with the Regional Director of the Ministry of Health, Region IV, June 14, 1985.

18. These agencies are: (1) Ministry of Local Government; (2) Ministry of Agrarian Reform; (3) Bureau of Animal Industry; (4) Bureau of Agricultural Economics; (5) Provincial Assessor's Office; (6) Ministry of Social Services and Development; (7) Provincial Engineer's Office; (8) Bureau of Fisheries and Aquatic Resources; (9) Ministry of Justice; (10) National Food Authority; (11) Bureau of Land Transportation; (12) Ministry of Education, Culture, and Sports; (13) Office of Development Communication, University of the Philippines at Los Baños; (14) National Cottage Industry Development Administration; (15) Bureau of Plant Industry; (16) UP Comprehensive Community Health Program; (17) Laguna Red Cross; (18) Laguna Provincial Library; (19) National Media Production Center; (20) Provincial Treasurer's Office; (21) Office of the Governor; (22) Integrated Provincial Health Office; and (23) Bureau of Agricultural Extension.

19. Interview with District PHC Coordinator, Nagcarlan District, June 18, 1985.

20. PCF, *op. cit.*

21. Based on MOH-PHC Unit Statistics as of May 27, 1985.
22. PCF, *op. cit.,* p. 89.
23. *Ibid.,* p. 92.
24. *Ibid.*
25. U.P.-CPA, *op.cit.,* pp. 66-67.
26. *Ibid.,* p. 37.
27. *Ibid.,* p. 38.
28. PCF, *op. cit.,* and U.P.-CPA, *op. cit.*
29. PCF, *op. cit.,* p. 37.
30. U.P.-CPA, *op. cit.,* p. 67.
31. PCF, *op. cit.,* p. 64.
32. Ledivina Cariño and Associates, *op. cit.*
33. For more detail see, Ma. Concepcion Alfiler,"Comparative Case Studies of Community Based Projects in Health and Family Planning : An Integrated Report," U.P. College of Public Administration, 1981.
34. Romeo B. Ocampo and Elena M. Panganiban, "Local Autonomy and Centralism in the Philippines," Paper presented at the International Studies Association Convention, Atlanta, Georgia, March 27-31, 1984, p. 4.
35. *Ibid.*
36. Victoria Bautista, *Structure of the Philippine Administrative System* (Manila: U.P. College of Public Administration (mimeo.), 1984), p. 10.
37. Ibon Facts and Figures, "Central Visayas," *84* (February 15, 1982), p. 1.
38. *Ibid.,* p. 3.
39. Ibon Fact and Figures, "A Stormy Year: Regional Profiles," *153* (December 1984), p. 2.
40. Raul P. de Guzman, "Towards a More Effective Coordination of Planning and Implementation of Development Programs/Projects: The Integrated Area Development Approach (IAD)," Paper prepared for the National Conference of Local Government Executives, 31 January - 5 February 1979, Philippine Plaza and the 24th World Congress of the International Union of Local Authorities, 5-9 February, Philippine International Convention Center, 1979, p. 4.
41. *Ibid.*
42. Narcisa Santos, "Towards the Reduction of Regional Imbalances," *Philippine Budget Management,* Vol.7, No. 1 (March 1983), p. 18.
43. *Ibid.,* p. 78.

# 5    Delivery System of Public Health Services in Rural Areas: The Korean Case

*In-Joung Whang* *

The purpose of this chapter is to make a descriptive analysis of the delivery system of public health services for rural development in Korea. Rural development involves a complex process of changes in both the nature and interaction of rural sub-systems leading to improvements in rural income, employment opportunities, income distribution, rural welfare, and other aspects of rural life. These changes, although interrelated, range from improvements in agricultural productivity, innovation in farm technology and green revolution, and rural industrialization and non-farm job opportunities, to increases in educational opportunities, welfare facilities, health services, and the physical infrastructure.

The critical importance of any of these factors and the priority for government intervention for the initial take-off of rural development depends on the stage of development. In particular, the health status of rural residents may be viewed either as a critical factor for further improving agricultural productivity and income, or as a target commodity for improving the quality of life and welfare, or as both. In Korea, rural development in general has been promoted through the rigorous implementation of the Saemaul Undong (the New Village Movement) for the last fifteen years.[1] However, health services for rural residents are insufficient to meet the need in view of both accessibility as well as affordability. Once rural income and the physical infrastructure in Korean rural communities have been raised significantly through the nationwide rural development movement, it is natural that demands for health services and for better standards of rural living by the rural population tend to increase. Hence, this study will focus on health service delivery in the rural areas.

What is meant by a "delivery system"? Generally, it signifies the physical movement of a subject from one to another point of location in order to make it readily available. Hence, delivery is defined by four major variables:

---

* Korea Development Institute, Seoul, Korea.

(a) *services* for which government intervention is critical in order to enhance the availability,[2] (b) *sources* which produce or provide services to improve availability to end-users, (c) *channels* through which services flow from source to end-user, and (d) *client groups,* or end-users who badly need the services.[3] Therefore, a delivery system is defined in this paper as a system which secures the smooth flow of services through proper channels from qualified sources to the right target group at the right time. Getting health services available to rural client groups requires proper channels, including the private market channel, NGO channel, government channel, or community channel. Sources of health services may consist of private clinics, hospitals, NGO-operating hospitals, pharmacies, herb clinics, public health centers, and so on. Sources of services tend to have their own channels depending on their influence and their respective objectives. From the clients' point of view, however, government intervention is necessary for the optimum combinations of channels to secure the efficient delivery of services.

This chapter attempts to provide a descriptive analysis of the current delivery system of public health care services[4] in remote rural areas in order to identify overriding problems and to clarify the contextual variables related to improving the delivery systems. The following questions are therefore relevant:

(a) To what extent are health care services readily available to residents in remote rural areas?
(b) What are structural characteristics of the public health delivery system for rural areas and how does it work in the present context of remote rural communities?
(c) What are contextual variables which determine the performance level of the public health delivery system?
(d) What are alternative solutions in terms of structural adjustment for improving the public health delivery system?

In this chapter, the health service is defined in broader terms, inclusive of curative medical services, than its usual connotations. The analysis of the public health delivery system for this study is based on data collected through a survey conducted by the Korea Institute of Public Health (KIPH) and a literature survey.

### Extent of the Accessibility to Health Services in Rural Areas

*Overview of Health Delivery System.* Health services in Korea are provided by both the public and private health system, although the Korean health system as a whole is heavily dependent upon the private sector. As of May 1984, approximately 38% of the total hospital beds and less than 20% of the total number of physicians, for example, were administered through the public health system.[5]

To meet the increasing demand for health services due to the increase in income and in the health consciousness of the population, various measures and channels are provided for improving the accessibility of health services. These measures include a medical insurance scheme and the public medical assistance program. As of the end of 1984, approximately 41% of the total population were covered by a medical insurance scheme, which was established for workers in organized sectors such as government employees, military personnel, industry workers, and associations of self-employed in various categories. Approximately 8% of the total population are covered by medical care services (medicaid) under the public assistance program, which has been in operation for those under the poverty line or disabled persons identified according to the Livelihood Protection Law of 1961.[6] In other words, approximately 0.6 million indigents and 2.6 million low-income citizens benefit from the medicaid service with out-patient care provided free of charge. Fifty percent of inpatient costs for the low income group are subsidized, while indigents receive care free of charge. On the other hand, more than half of Korea's total population are without access to health care assistance, which they therefore must cover with their own resources. However, it is noted that the current fifth five-year plan is targeting the improvement of the population coverage from 38% in 1981, up to 66% in 1986. The present level is achieved by vigorous government programs as envisaged in the plan.[7]

Nevertheless, the regional distribution of health resources should be considered as a significant factor in examining the accessibility to health services. Although only 54% of the total population live in 52 cities in Korea, 88% of the doctors are urban dwellers and 89% of hospital beds are located in cities. These statistics imply that access to health care for the rural population remains very low.[8] The imbalance in the distribution of health resources is due to the free-market system of private health care. The private sector tends to invest more health resources in urban cities where the effective demand for health care is greater than in rural areas.

A question thus arises: To what extent are health services accessible to rural residents particularly in remote rural and island areas? The accessibility to health care services can be defined in terms of the availability of health resources, the pattern and level of health care services, and the level of satisfaction with the services. Due to the lack of data on the current status, this study is based on a recent sample survey which was conducted by the Korea Institute of Population and Health (KIPH) during November 1981,[9] before the introduction of various measures for improving the health delivery system since 1982 onward. Hence, the data in this section do not necessarily reflect the current status of health service delivery in rural areas. The survey covered 38 Myons (townships) which were selected through stratified sampling and systematic sampling methods. A Myon is the lowest level of local administration serving the rural people. Approximately 375,000 persons live in these 38 Myons. From this sample area, 4,185 households were interviewed with regard to accessibility to health care services.

*Availability of Health Care Services.* Available health resources in these remote rural areas include physicians, dentists, nurses, nurse-aids, pharmacies and herb clinics. According to the sample survey conducted in 1981, approximately 125,000 persons lived in 14 Myons without any medical personnel, 148,000 persons lived in 15 Myons, each with a clinic doctor, and the remaining 102,000 persons lived in 9 Myons with one or two doctors. The availability of physicians therefore was severely limited, with an average of only one doctor per 12,930 persons. The ratio of population per nurse was also extremely high, with as many as 93,745 persons per nurse. These ratios from the sample rural area were ten times higher than those in urban cities, indicating that health manpower was an extremely scarce resource in remote rural areas (Table 1).

In addition, physical accessibility to health care facilities was examined in terms of distance. Of those closest to a pharmacy, 84% replied that the pharmacy was located either in their own Myon (68%) or more conveniently in their village (16%). Only 37% of those closest to a hospital or clinic had these services in their own Myon or village (Table 2). Physical accessibility can be analysed further in terms of mode of transportation most frequently utilized. Table 3 indicates that buses were most commonly used in visiting hospitals or clinics, while the residents who were close enough to visit pharmacies on foot did so.

**Table 1** Number of Population per Health Resource, 1981

(No. of persons)

| Sample Myons<br>Classified by availability of clinic | Health Manpower Resource |  |  | Health Facilities |  |
|---|---|---|---|---|---|
| | per physician* | per nurse | per nurse-aid | per pharmacy | per herb clinic |
| Doctor-less Myon | — | 124,700 | 3,563 | 3,118 | 13,856 |
| One-doctor Myon | 9,859 | 147,881 | 4,108 | 5,281 | 7,783 |
| One or more doctor Myon | 7,314 | 51,199 | 3,531 | 2,926 | 9,309 |
| Average | 12,930 | 93,745 | 3,750 | 3,641 | 9,615 |
| Cities average | 1,409 | 1,308 | - | 1,397 | 10,480 |

Sources: Based on Song, et al., *Baseline Survey on Health Status in Remote Rural Areas* (KIPH, 1983), p. 41 for the sample rural areas. The statistics on cities were provided by Ministry of Home Affairs, *Municipal Yearbook of Korea, 1982* (Seoul, 1983), pp. 366-369.

**Table 2** Location of Health Care Facilities

| Location | Hospital or Clinic (%) | Pharmacy (%) |
|---|---|---|
| His/her village | 0.6 ⎫ 37.4 | 16.0 ⎫ 83.5 |
| His/her Myon | 36.6 ⎭ | 67.5 ⎭ |
| Other Myon | 51.9 | 14.0 |
| Other County | 2.2 | 0.7 |
| Urban city | 8.3 | 1.8 |
| Unknown | 0.4 | - |
| Total | 100.0 | 100.0 |

Source: Song, et al., *op. cit.*, p. 43.

**Table 3** Available Transportation to Visit the Closest Health Service Facility

(%)

| Health Service Facility | Bus | Train or Vessel | Others | by Foot | Total |
|---|---|---|---|---|---|
| Health Sub-center | 41.9 | 5.7 | 3.6 | 48.8 | 100 |
| Hospital/Clinic | 75.2 | 6.6 | 3.1 | 15.1 | 100 |
| Pharmacy | 33.3 | 5.5 | 3.4 | 57.8 | 100 |

Source: Song, et al., *op. cit.*, p. 43.

The percentage of those who could reach the closest public health sub-center and the closest hospital or clinic within 30 minutes' time were only 20% and 8% respectively (Table 4). On the average, rural residents spent 48 minutes and 65 minutes, respectively, travelling to public health sub-centers or to private hospitals and clinics.

**Table 4** Time Required to Visit Treatment Sources

% (minutes)

| Treatment Sources | 0-29 minutes | 30-59 minutes | 60-89 minutes | 1½ hour or more | Total | Weighted average |
|---|---|---|---|---|---|---|
| Public Health Sub-Center | 20.3 | 40.8 | 27.9 | 10.9 | 100 | (48.4) |
| Hospital/Clinic | 8.3 | 32.2 | 35.5 | 24.0 | 100 | (65.3) |
| Pharmacy | 26.0 | 39.5 | 23.3 | 11.2 | 100 | (46.3) |

Source: Song, et al., *op.cit.*, p. 44.

Due to the lack of availability of health services and the physical difficulties involved in reaching the presently available health resources, the most preferred health facility among rural residents for their initial consultation and service were pharmacies (68%), followed by private hospitals and clinics (24%). Least popular were the public health sub-centers; only 6% of rural residents prefer them for initial consultations and services.

*Pattern of Health Service Utilization.* To what level and in what way did rural residents actually utilize the health services? Out of those who needed health care services for the last 15 days before being interviewed, 59% (or 2,312 households in the sample area) had contacted a health treatment source. This figure, similar to that of those living in Myons, was lower than that of the urban population which registered 78% (Table 5 ).

**Table 5** Contact Ratio for Last 15 Days

(% of population)

|  | Sample Area | Cities | Myons |
|---|---|---|---|
| Those who were sick for last 15 days (a) | 21.1 | 34.5 | 30.4 |
| Those contacted with Health Service (b) | 12.4 | 26.8 | 18.0 |
| Those not treated | 8.7 | 7.7 | 12.4 |
| Contact Ratio (b)/(a) | 58.7 | 77.8 | 59.2 |

Source: Song, et al., *op.cit.*, p. 76, for the sample area; and KIPH, *Household Survey for Organization of National Health Network 1981* for Cities and Myons.

The health service utilization in the sample area depends heavily on pharmacies. While 72% of those contacting a health treatment source relied on pharmacies, the utilization of hospitals or clinics was relatively low (14%). Only 5% used the public health sub-centers. This health service use pattern was consistent with the order of preference of health service facilities.

The degree of health services utilization by rural residents in the study area was extremely low; only 15% of those who approached health service facilities in a year visited a hospital or clinic. The average frequency of visits to any kind of health treatment source in a year was 4.3 times per capita. Specifically, pharmacy visits averaged 3.2 per person and hospital visits 0.6 per person.

The relatively limited contact with health treatment sources, the high dependence on pharmacies rather than hospitals, and the low frequency of hospital visits in this rural area were primarily due to the lower level of education and income of the area residents and to the restricted availability of health resources in the area.

*Satisfaction with Health Care Services.* The extent to which rural people are satisfied with the health care services can be measured by: (a) the convenience in utilizing a particular health care service, (b) perceptions of the effectiveness of treatment, and (c) costs paid by rural residents. Convenience means physical ease of access to health care services, and includes variables such as location, availability of transportation, and the required time involved. Out of 2,312 sample households which needed health care services, 43% contacted health service facilities within their Myon (Table 6).

On these occasions, the most frequently utilized means of transportation was the bus (49%), followed by walking (28%). On the average, the time spent to visit any health treatment source in the sample area was 55 minutes. Those who used hospital or clinic services spent 76 minutes on the average, while those visiting pharmacies spent 51 minutes on the average to obtain services.

Approximately 77% of 1,714 persons who utilized pharmacy services were satisfied with the results, as opposed to 71% of 307 visitors of hospitals/clinics. As for the credibility of service, which is closely related to the level of satisfaction, hospitals/clinics seemed to be the most trusted by rural residents. It should also be noted that public health centers or sub-centers were regarded as less credible than pharmacies (Table 7).

**Table 6** Location of Health Care Service Facilities Actually Visited Within Last 15 Days

% (household)

| Location | Hospital/Clinic In-patient | Hospital/Clinic Out-patient | Public Health Centers | Pharmacy | Herb Clinic | Others | Total |
|---|---|---|---|---|---|---|---|
| Within his/her Myon | 4.3 | 16.1 | 58.3 | 49.4 | 17.5 | 28.4 | 42.8 |
| Other Myons | 39.1 | 38.1 | 20.4 | 27.2 | 28.7 | 3.0 | 27.7 |
| Cities | 56.5 | 39.1 | 6.8 | 13.9 | 40.8 | 7.5 | 18.5 |
| Home Treatment | - | 6.7 | 14.6 | 9.4 | 15.0 | 61.2 | 11.0 |
| Total | 100.0 | 100.0 | 100.0 | 100.0 | 100.0 | 100.0 | 100.0 |
| (N) | (23) | (299) | (103) | (1702) | (102) | (67) | (2,312) |

N means the number of those who visited a health service facility in last 15 days.

Source: Song, et al., *op.cit.*, p. 112.

112 Delivery of Public Services in Asian Countries

**Table 7** Credibility and Satisfaction with the Service

(%)

|  | Hospitals/ Clinics (N = 307) | Public Health Centers (N = 109) | Pharmacies (N = 1714) | Herb Clinics (N = 151) |
|---|---|---|---|---|
| Satisfaction: |  |  |  |  |
| satisfied | 71.0 | 60.6 | 77.0 | 54.3 |
| dissatisfied | 9.8 | 15.6 | 7.9 | 21.2 |
| unknown | 19.2 | 23.8 | 15.1 | 24.5 |
| Total | 100.0 | 100.0 | 100.0 | 100.0 |
| Credibility: |  |  |  |  |
| credible | 83.7 | 67.9 | 74.5 | 62.4 |
| not credible | 13.4 | 23.8 | 20.2 | 29.6 |
| unknown | 3.9 | 8.3 | 5.3 | 10.0 |
| Total | 100.0 | 100.0 | 100.0 | 100.0 |

Source: Song, et al., *op.cit.*, p. 116.

The cost of health services seemed to be a little higher in view of their perceived level of service quality, although the total average health care expense during 1981 was W99,264 per household in the survey area.[10]

**Rural Health Delivery System**

*Private vs. Public Services in Rural Areas.* The rural health delivery system (RHDS) consists of two broad systems: (a) private commercial channels and (b) the public health network. The private sector includes private clinics, hospitals, pharmacies, and herb clinics. The public health network again consists of (i) a cluster of public health centers and sub-centers operating in rural areas and recently, (ii) community health practitioners working for those who could not reach any health clinics within 30 minutes time.[11]

As of March 1983, there were 1,450 physicians working in the 139 counties representing the whole rural sector of Korea. Approximately 40% of these physicians were at private hospitals and clinics while the remaining 60% were working in public health centers and sub-centers and were mostly obliged to serve for only a limited period of time by law (Table 8).

**Table 8** Physicians in Service Areas of 139 Health Centers

|  | No. of Physicians | (%) |
| --- | --- | --- |
| Public Health Centers | 111 | (7.6) |
| Public Health Sub-Centers | 761 | (52.5) |
| Private Hospitals/Clinics | 578 | (39.9) |
| Total | 1,450 | (100.0) |

Source: Song Keun Yong, Nam Jae-bong, et al., *Organization and Functions of Health Centers in Rural Areas* (KIPH, 1983), p. 71 (in Korean).

Health services at the local level come under the administrative control of the Ministry of Home Affairs (MOHA), although technical guidance and support with regard to substantive matters are provided by the Ministry of Health and Social Affairs (Health Ministry for short). This Health Ministry is responsible for policy planning, coordination, and supervision of the overall national network of public health services. The Health Ministry licenses all health practitioners, supervises production and distribution of drugs, and controls the rights and obligations of hospitals and clinics to serve the public. MOHA, on the other hand, is responsible for the financing and actual management of authorities and health centers through the provincial and local governments, which are under MOHA's control (Chart 1).

Health services are available only when the necessary health resources such as health manpower, medical facilities and instruments, drugs, and other materials are duly mobilized to meet the health care needs of clients. Since private commercial channels are reluctant to provide health services in rural areas, the rural population tends to depend primarily on the public health network. The public health delivery system consists of public health centers at the county level and health sub-centers at the Myon level. In order to supplement the public health network, community health care stations were recently introduced on a selective basis at the village level. Therefore, the primary health care services in rural areas are available through three sources: (a) the private clinics or hospitals; (b) the public health network; and (c) the community health care system. This chapter focuses on analysing the public health network with emphasis on public health centers and the community health system, both of which are of primary concern for government policy innovation.

The performance level of RHDS depends on its structural characteristics in terms of organization and functional prerequisites. The middle range variables mobilized for the organizational analysis of RHDS include (a) the

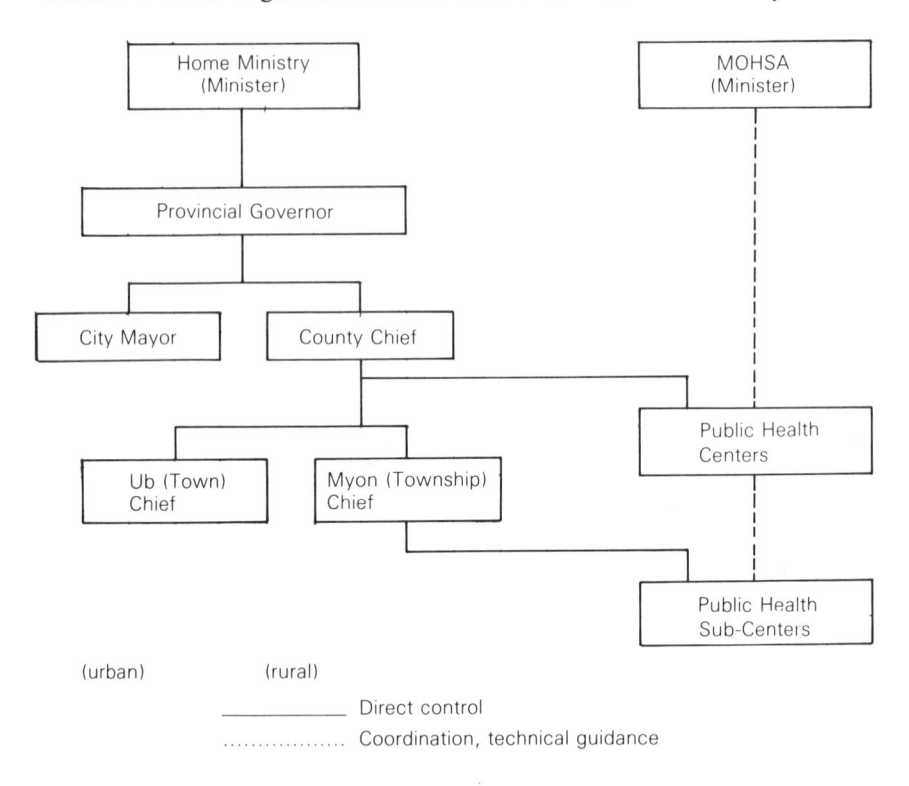

**Chart 1** Formal Organizations for Public Health Service Delivery

```
   Home Ministry                          MOHSA
    (Minister)                           (Minister)
        |                                    |
        |                                    |
  Provincial Governor                        |
        |                                    |
   ┌────┴────┐                               |
City Mayor  County Chief                     |
              |                              |
              |                     ┌────────┴────────┐
              |                     │ Public Health   │
              |                     │ Centers         │
              |                     └────────┬────────┘
      ┌───────┴────────┐                     |
  Ub (Town)       Myon (Township)            |
    Chief              Chief                 |
                        |                    |
                        └──────────┬─────────┘
                                   |
                          ┌────────┴────────┐
                          │ Public Health   │
                          │ Sub-Centers     │
                          └─────────────────┘

  (urban)           (rural)
              ─────────── Direct control
              ··········· Coordination, technical guidance
```

major doctrine or goals of RHDS, (b) leadership, (c) internal structure, (d) programs and activities, (e) resources, and (f) environmental linkages.[12]

*The Public Health Network.* As of April 1985, there were 139 public health centers to cover all counties and 1,303 public health sub-centers to cover all Myons in Korea. Of the 139 health centers, 27 are located in cities, even though they are designated to serve rural residents in their respective counties. Thirty centers are in towns within their service counties which are close to cities, while some 82 health centers are located in towns within their designated counties but are apart from cities. These 82 centers deserve special attention from the government in order to improve the performance of the rural health service network.[13]

The network of public health centers has been evolving at the county level since 1961 and has expanded through the addition of sub-centers at Myon level throughout the 1970s. From one perspective, an individual's health and medical care might be regarded as a private concern. Particularly in rural areas, however, government intervention in the form of public health centers and sub-centers became inevitable in Korea from a humanitarian as well as developmental point of view.

As far as professional and technical matters are concerned, public health centers are managed by physicians. However, they are under the direct control of the county chief, who holds authority over budgeting and financing, personnel (including nurses and technical staff), and major decision-making. In other words, administrative leadership for public health services is exercised by the county chief, while professional leadership is held by physicians. Therefore, the successful performance of individual health centers often depends on the relationship between the county chief and the health center head (physician) and, in particular, on the individual personality of the county chief. The leadership crisis and the lack of autonomy in public health centers are obstacles to the efficient delivery of public health services to rural persons. Public health sub-centers can be viewed as branch offices of the health center operating at the Myon level. Their utility maintenance and management expenses are borne by the health center. However, a working relationship between the health centers and sub-centers has yet to be formally established. There is no direct line relationship between the two; formal communications between the two flow through the county chief and the township chief (Chart 1). In this sense, one can say that there is no structural consistency.

Health centers provide both preventive and curative health care services to the public. Preventive services include laboratory tests, vaccinations, communicable disease prevention, parasite control, family planning, maternal and child health (MCH), and nutrition. Curative services include diagnosis of out-patients, prescriptions, and medication. Depending on the population of its service area, the structural device of the health center may or may not include a medical service function (Chart 2).

In addition, 71 health centers have a Maternal and Child Health (MCH) center directly under the health center head. However, in order to provide equal opportunities for primary health care services throughout the countryside, some existing public health center services should be strengthened. These services include emergency services, dental care services, X-ray tests, health statistics, health education, and nutrition. Furthermore, psychotherapy, adult diseases, and rehabilitation programs should be provided as additional services.

Physicians are still a critical element of health resources. Since qualified physicians seem reluctant to work in rural areas for economic and socio-cultural

**Chart 2** Internal Structure of Public Health Centers

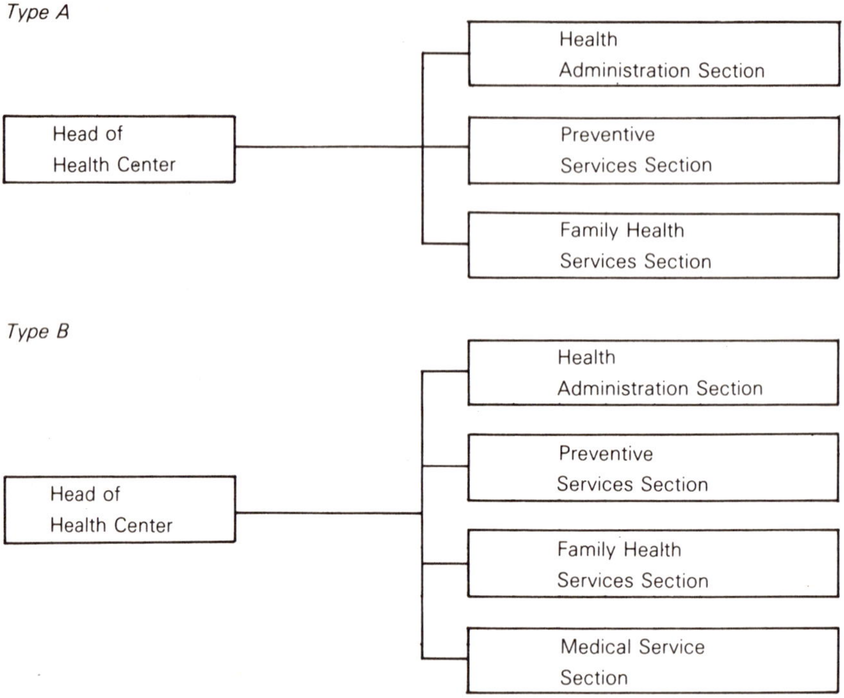

*Type A*

```
                          ┌── Health Administration Section
Head of Health Center ────┼── Preventive Services Section
                          └── Family Health Services Section
```

*Type B*

```
                          ┌── Health Administration Section
                          ├── Preventive Services Section
Head of Health Center ────┤
                          ├── Family Health Services Section
                          └── Medical Service Section
```

reasons, physicians are scarce resources for RHDS. Therefore, most of the physicians currently serving in the countryside have been forced by a special law to work there. As of December 1984, 1,232 physicians were working in 1,303 health sub-centers. The majority (67%) are "public health doctors" who are mobilized by law to serve people in remote rural and island areas where health care services are severely limited (Table 9). Their obligation to serve in the rural area for three years is a substitute, if they wish, for their military service obligation. This option became possible through the Special Law for National Health Service of 1978, which was introduced to cope with mounting pressure on the government to provide basic needs, including health and education, during the last two decades. The law indeed provided an incentive scheme for newly qualified doctors to serve as "public health doctors" at public health centers or sub-centers in remote mountainous and island areas. This policy measure enabled the government to effectively cope with the problem of the shortage of physicians in rural areas. However, there still remains the problem of their relatively poor motivation and quality of services.

**Table 9** Physicians in 1,303 Public Health Sub-Centers

|  | Number | (%) | Obligation Period |
|---|---|---|---|
| Total Number of Doctors | 1,232 | 100 | — |
| Public Health Doctors | 830 | 67 | 3 yrs |
| Limited Area Doctors | 272 | 22 | 3 yrs |
| Contracted Doctors | 124 | 10 | 1-2 yrs |
| Doctors on Scholarship | 4 | — | 2-5 yrs |
| Others | 2 | — | 2 yrs |

Source: Ministry of Health and Social Affairs, *Status of Public Health Services, 1985* (as of December 1984).

In spite of its strong functional capabilities as well as the linkages provided with government authorities like MOHA and Health Ministry, the public health system suffers from poor diffusion linkages which are essential for effective and efficient service to rural residents. This deficiency arises primarily because contextual variables such as socio-economic and physical characteristics of rural communities are unfavorable and are beyond the control of the public health system, at least in the short run. It is also noted that linkages between the health centers and the community seem to be lacking, due primarily to the bureaucratic mode of operation and the authoritarian behavior of the public health center workers.

*The Community Health Care Service* (CHCS). In order to play a complementary as well as a supplementary role, the government enacted a drastic measure to introduce the community health care system. Specifically, the Special Law for Rural Health Care Service was an official response by the Korean government to the ideological dominance of "Health for All by the Year 2000" adopted by the Alma-Ata Declaration.[14] The 1981 law is designed to improve the accessibility of rural residents to health care service. By incorporating the 1978 Act, this law also enabled the Korean government to introduce community health care stations into remote rural areas where residents had no access to a clinic or doctor within a 30 minute radius. The program was formally introduced after a three-year experiment monitored by the Korea Health Development Institute (KHDI, presently KIPH).[15] This program gives the residents in remote rural areas more easy access to simple health care services. Each community health care station covers 3-5 villages and serves approximately 500 to 700 persons.

The government has expanded the program annually since 1982. As of the end of 1984, the total number of community health care service stations amounted to 1,404 units, serving 6,349 villages and 2.9 million people. It is expected that 1,629 community health care service stations will be in operation by the end of 1985.[16]

The critical manpower resource for this program are the community health practitioners (CHP), who are selected from among local nurses. The CHPs are assigned to a community after a 6-months training program. By the end of 1984, 1,477 CHPs had been trained at several training institutions.[17] Their salaries are fully subsidized by the local governments serving their assigned communities, and their obliged period of service is a minimum of two years. The government also provides buildings and instruments, while materials and drugs are provided by the communities themselves through their Community Health Program Management Board. This Board is identical with the community development committee, because it consists of the same members who in most cases include the village chief and Saemaul community leaders. Thus, the community health practitioners program was introduced as an integral part of an already on-going, successful program for integrated rural development, namely, the Saemaul Undong. It should be noted that the new program became relatively successful as it could take advantage of the already established community development program.[18]

The Management Board decides rates to charge for services. In other words, the managerial leadership of the community health care service stations stems from the community organization itself. As the public health system is limited without a positive response from the community, this innovative program tries to invite considerable community involvement. In view of its establishment and government subsidies as well as technical assistance, this program can be viewed as an extended version of the public health delivery system, in spite of the growing concern over community involvement.

Due to the limited number of available health resources, especially CHP nurses, community health care service stations for the most part provide preventive services such as environmental sanitation, family planning, and health education. However, in spite of their legally limited duties, the 1981 Special Law enables CHPs to provide certain medical care services such as vaccinations, urgent but simple treatment, simple tests, assistance in the evacuation of patients, and other simple medical tasks.

This community health care program is based partly on community involvement and participation, while also establishing enabling linkages with local government and functional linkages with the public health centers and sub-centers. It is noted that the mode of operation at the public health centers is the top-down delivery of services and is bureaucratic in nature.

*Managerial Issues in the Rural Health Delivery System.*[19] In concept, the public health network, private commercial channels and the community health care system should work together to provide equal access to health services for rural people. This client satisfaction and the insufficient performance of the public health delivery system indeed form a vicious circle disrupting the entire management process. Within the public sector health delivery system, the optimal allocation of both financial and manpower resources, efficient organization, and increased productivity and incentive of health manpower are targets for management improvement.

## Contextuality of the Rural Health Delivery System

The process of health service delivery is affected by contextual variables. Contextual variables include political, administrative, organizational, socio-economic, ecological, managerial and other environmental factors. The political context in rural areas in Korea is characterized by the relatively weak voice of rural residents and lack of aggressiveness as far as health issues are concerned; their ability to aggregate and articulate their concerns over health problems seems to be very limited. This problem arises because their primary interest in aggregation and articulation stems from concern over rural income and, in particular, the pricing of agricultural products.[20]

In terms of the administrative context, the traditional tendency towards the centralization of decision-making power and public resources tends to prohibit creative adaptation of RHDS to local situations and needs. In addition, the bureaucratic setting of the public health network encourages authoritarian and unkind behavior of doctors and nurses working within the public health network.

The socio-economic context is represented by levels of income, education, age and perceptual patterns of population. The data for analysis of these variables were drawn primarily from the survey which was utilized for discussion in Section II. The implications of these variables in terms of the contextuality of the rural health delivery system may be examined through comparison with those in other areas. Additional information was obtained from other survey data or government sources.

The major reasons for treatment not being sought in spite of health care needs are degree of sickness, economic limitations, and geographical distance.[21] According to the previous survey, the lower the age or the higher the income level, the higher the contact ratio in remote rural areas. The contact ratio is also higher if health care service is urgently needed, or there are a greater number of seriously ill people. Finally, if the source of treatment is close enough in terms of time-distance, then the contact ratio is high.[22]

It is interesting to note that the population structure by age is characterized by a higher ratio of aged people in remote rural areas as compared with those in cities and towns (Table 10). The greater percentage of elderly in the rural population that is primarily due to the urban-ward migration of working population in the rapid industrialization process[23] requires special attention in the delivery of health services to this group. In particular, the age distribution of married women who may need certain preventive services such as MCH and family planning is also characterized by a greater portion of older women in the rural areas. Table 11 shows that the majority of women in rural areas are between 35-44, while in large cities most women are between ages 25-34.

**Table 10** Population Structure by Age

(%)

| Age Group | Cities | Towns | Sample Area |
|---|---|---|---|
| 0-14 | 36.6 | 36.7 | 37.0 |
| 15-59 | 58.5 | 55.8 | 51.7 |
| 60 and more | 4.9 | 7.5 | 11.3 |
| Total | 100.0 | 100.0 | 100.0 |

Source: Song, et al., *op. cit.*, p. 49 for the sample area; and KIPH, *op. cit.*

The educational level of the rural population particularly in the sample area is much lower than that of the urban population despite the fact that the educational level of the country as a whole has been tremendously improved as demonstrated by the 1980 Census.[24] Approximately 23% of rural residents in the sample area have had no schooling, compared to only 6% of urban residents. Another 23% of rural residents have studied at the primary school level (Table 12). The share of non-educated females is greater (30%) than of males (15%);

## Table 11  Age Distribution of Married Women

(%)

| Age | Sample Area | Rural Area Cities | Small-medium Cities* | Large Cities |
|---|---|---|---|---|
| Below 24 | 12.4 | 14.2 | 13.4 | 12.1 |
| 25-29 | 18.0 | 22.1 | 27.4 | 29.4 |
| 30-34 | 20.2 | 20.4 | 24.2 | 24.3 |
| 35-39 | 20.0 | 19.3 | 17.9 | 17.9 |
| 40-44 | 29.4 | 24.0 | 17.1 | 16.2 |
| Total | 100.0 | 100.0 | 100.0 | 100.0 |
| (N) | (1,893) | (1,561) | (974) | (1,816) |

N = Sample size

Source: Song, et al., *op.cit.*, p. 134, for sample area and for other areas (1982 data).

## Table 12  Educational Level of Population

(%)

| Educational Level | Cities | Towns | Myons | Sample Area |
|---|---|---|---|---|
| Pre-school children | 16.0 | 18.8 | 12.7 | 12.6 |
| Students enrolled in: | | | | |
|   primary school | 15.5 | 16.6 | 17.7 | 18.1 |
|   middle-high school | 11.2 | 12.9 | 13.0 | 11.0 |
|   college | 2.5 | 0.9 | 0.4 | 0.2 |
| Other categories: | | | | |
|   no schooling | 6.0 | 10.2 | 18.2 | 22.6 |
|   primary school | 12.1 | 20.6 | 24.1 | 22.9 |
|   middle-high school | 28.0 | 22.5 | 13.8 | 12.1 |
|   college | 8.7 | 2.5 | 0.8 | 0.5 |
| Total | 100.0 | 100.0 | 100.0 | 100.0 |
| (N) | (11,441) | (5,958) | (21,264) | (18,846) |

Source: Song, et al., *op. cit.*, p.50.

in particular, of 1,893 married women between the ages of 15-44, approximately 22.4% are uneducated and 61.6% are only primary school-educated. Further, 40% of the women from the age group 40-44 are non-educated. The low level of education among the rural population deserves due contemplation when considering approaches to rural health education and delivery of health services.

There is no quantitative information regarding the level of household income in the sample area. No doubt the income level is much lower than that in cities and towns, in view of lower ratios of those owning television sets, refrigerators, electric cookers, and telephones.[25] In addition to income, another device enabling rural residents to gain access to health care services is medical protection through institutional measures, which include the medical insurance schemes and the medicaid program. In this sample area, only 16% of the rural residents benefit from medical protection and insurance, compared to 43% in cities and 31% in towns (Table 13).

**Table 13** Population under Medical Protection

(%)

|  | Cities | Towns | Myons | Sample Area |
|---|---|---|---|---|
| Not protected | 57.4 | 68.5 | 82.7 | 84.2 |
| Protected | 42.6 | 31.5 | 16.3 | 15.8 |
| Total | 100.0 | 100.0 | 100.0 | 100.0 |
| N (Sample size) | (11,441) | (5,958) | (21,264) | (18,846) |

Source: Song, et al., *Baseline Study*, p. 56, for the sample area; and KIPH, *op.cit.*, for other categories.

In addition to the relatively lower income, the lower percentage of coverage by the medical insurance and medicaid program tends to result in lower affordability for rural residents and poor accessibility to health care services when compared to cities and towns. Because the needs for health care service are closely related to the self-assessed health status of people, the improvement of RHDS is intimately concerned with the perception of health conditions by rural residents. Sixteen percent of rural residents in the sample area reported that they were not well. In particular, 34% of those aged 45 and over thought that they were sick (Table 14).

Mass communication media such as TV, radio, and newspapers seem to be relatively well spread throughout the countryside. However, the coverage of health education through mass media is limited unless the rural population is interested in health information and education. In view of lower levels of education, the rural population tends to be less concerned with health problems compared to the urban population.

**Table 14** Self-Assessed Health Status

(%)

| Age Group | Healthy | More or Less Healthy | Unhealthy | Total | (N) |
|---|---|---|---|---|---|
| 0-14 | 84.6 | 11.3 | 4.1 | 100.0 | (7,003) |
| 15-44 | 70.0 | 16.1 | 13.9 | 100.0 | (3,963) |
| 45-64 | 43.2 | 22.4 | 34.4 | 100.0 | (3,963) |
| 65+ | 46.4 | 19.8 | 33.8 | 100.0 | (1,393) |
| Total | 68.0 | 15.9 | 16.1 | 100.0 | (18,825) |

Source: Song, et al., *op.cit.*, p. 70.

The above analysis of socio-economic factors implies that the latent demand for health and medical services in the rural sector should be higher in view of the relatively low income, lower education and old aged, although the manifested demand for health and medical services seems to be lower than in urban areas. Rural citizens tend to be reluctant to contact health service sources until they become seriously ill or face urgent needs for such services. This socio-economic context is not conducive to a more active role of private medical channels in rural areas. In addition, due to the traditionally male-dominated Korean culture, the all-female CHP nurses cannot make an impact on community health education and public information services, although the attitude of rural people toward CHP recently has become favorable.

It is already confirmed that relatively poor investment in rural transportation, in terms of the number of available buses and trains, conditions of existing roads, village-connecting roads, and time-distance to health services, create a reluctance on the part of the rural population to contact health service suppliers. However, the Saemaul Undong in rural villages has made an enormous impact on community structures as well as productive effect particularly in improving the rural physical infrastructure.[26]

Nevertheless, community organizations in the majority of rural villages are little concerned with community health issues because the Korean culture perceives health problems as a personal matter which should be treated as an individual responsibility. Thus, the community response to the government-offered community health care program is relatively low in most cases. Furthermore, the Management Board, consisting of the village chief, Saemaul leaders and other influential community members, seems little concerned and relatively unsupportive of the CHP in most cases. In other words, their program orientation to public health is limited because the community organization is primarily oriented towards village infrastructure and income boosting projects. Indeed, the limited acceptance of the CHP by communities has been illustrated by its infrequent utilization by the client population and also by its heavy dependence on government subsidies for the maintenance of community health care stations and CHP salaries.[27] This problem is acute in villages where the sense of community is poor. The success of community health care programs primarily depends on the active participation and response of the community rather than on the quality of the CHPs themselves.

**Toward Structural Adjustment: Conclusions**

What are the policy implications which could be drawn from this study? With regard to the basic approach, there are two distinct strategies of government for rural development: maximum and minimum intervention through the use of government funds and state authority. In the Korean context, however, rural development and, in particular, health development cannot be achieved simply by the maximum influx of public resources into rural areas without a proper response or a broadly-based community initiative. Therefore, Korea's approach to rural development in general was to adopt a minimum intervention strategy in which the government tries to induce desired changes in rural areas by using the population's own initiative indirectly through supportive policies and incentive schemes and through public information and social education activities.[28] The public health services delivery system in the rural sector follows this minimum intervention strategy.

Two sets of criteria are applicable to the evaluation of PHDS, namely, the performance level of RHDS as well as intermediate indicators. The performance of RHDS is defined in terms of its immediate objectives, which are to increase (a) the contact ratio or service ratio (the percentage of those who contacted treatment sources to those who needed health care services); and (b) the level of satisfaction with the treatment or the quality of health care services. Another set of criteria for evaluating the overall capacity of the RHDS could be stated in terms of intermediate indicators, which include availability, accessibility, affordability and acceptability of health care services to the rural population. These indicators monitor whether or not RHDS assures timely availability and sufficient supply of quality services by reliable sources of treatment to the population at reasonable cost.

In pursuit of the national health policy objective, namely "Health for All by the Year 2000," the Korean government recently attempted to provide more opportunities for the rural population to gain access to health care services through improving the public health care system toward a "comprehensive delivery system."[29] This rigorous intervention by government includes (a) the expansion of public health centers at the county level as well as sub-centers at the Myon level by assigning newly qualified physicians to serve as "public health doctors" in lieu of their military obligations, and (b) the introduction of community health practitioners (CHPs), although only in limited areas as of 1985, by subsidizing their salaries and facilities. It is also noted that the integration of CHP into the on-going Saemaul Undong (integrated rural development program) was a wise approach for its successful adoption.

These two innovations are the skeleton of the Korean approach to government intervention into primary health care system for the rural sector, in particular, and for private commercial channels. It is a dual structure in which the regular service channel (including both local private clinics and the public health centers and sub-centers) provides primary health care services to the rural population, while CHPs provide the rural population with simple health care services where services from regular qualified sources are scarcely available. In view of the gradual recognition of "para-official" role of CHPs among the rural population[30] as well as the increasing need for health care services due to the improvements both in the income and education of rural residents, it seems desirable to increase the number of CHPs in order to cover more of the target population. The extensive health education of client groups through CHPs will contribute to the absorptive capacity of rural people to eventually improve the delivery system of public health services in the future. However, the introduction of CHPs should be a temporary measure only, until regular services, either public or private, become extensive enough to meet the health service needs of the rural population.

In order to let all partners work more closely and in a complementary manner, coordination is essential in the service area of the public health center. In spite of some physical access difficulties, the county or the service area of a public health center should be a primary unit, within which close coordination between public health center, sub-centers, and private clinics could be encouraged. Authority and power for coordinating health care services -- presently in the hands of the county chief -- have not been properly exercised so far; therefore, as far as health administration is concerned, authority to initiate necessary action for coordination should be delegated to the head of the public health center. Easy communication among working partners is another element of better coordination. The improvement of RHDS through better coordination calls for institutional reforms by the public authority to coordinate health manpower in the jurisdictional boundary of rural local areas, and to improve the formal and informal communication network between working partners in the health field.[31]

Furthermore, some existing functions of public health centers and sub-centers should be strengthened and specialized, while additional functions should be properly developed. These actions will improve the quality of health care services and thus enhance the credibility of the public health delivery system in rural areas.

It may be necessary to set up a special orientation program before their assignment to the field which will enable public health doctors, who are semi-voluntarily mobilized by the government enforcement scheme, to become further motivated, to make a stronger commitment, and to be ready to devote themselves to the improvement of rural health. Additionally the working environment including medical facilities and tools should be improved through a more generous allocation of the government budget. Because physicians are the most critical health resource and are also the managers of public health centers or sub-centers, a strong commitment from them induces attitudinal changes among health workers, including nurses and nurse-aides. Indeed, the major reasons why the rural population is reluctant to approach the public health network are the low credibility of the health service and the "bureaucratic" attitude of public health workers.[32]

Efforts to improve the RHDS require due consideration of the demand side of health care services. Although a longer time-span is needed, the improvement of the general education level as well as the income level of the rural population should be emphasized. In addition, public investment in rural transportation should be stressed, and a rigorous program for public information, education, and communication activities on rural health should be organized either through the public health network or local administration channels.

In view of functional / structural prerequisites as well as contextual variables impinging upon the public network of the health service delivery system, the limitations of its performance seem to be unavoidable. Hence, government policy may have to focus on fostering the role of NGOs, and encouraging them to work more closely with government agencies in a complementary fashion, and again on helping private commercial channels to become more amenable and accessible, both physically and financially, to the rural people.

Lastly but most importantly, consideration should be accorded to innovation in community organization by encouraging participation by rural citizens in their own community health care service program through the elevation of the self-help spirit of the rural population and also through reorientation of community development activities toward health care.

**Notes**

1. Whang In-Joung, *Management of Rural Change in Korea* (Seoul: Seoul National University Press, 1981), pp. 238-243.

2. They include not only governmental services but also non-governmental services in the nature of "public" by which government intervention seems to be essential for effectively and efficiently meeting the needs of the populace.

3. Those four middle-range variables are derived from E. Rogers, *Communication Strategies for Family Planning* (New York: Free Press, 1973), pp. 47-53.

4. Throughout this paper, health care service and health and medical care services will be used interchangeably due to their mutually inclusive concept.

5. Sung-woo Lee, "Introduction of Korean Health Plan: Organization and Financing," *World Hospitals,* 20 (August 1984), p. 27.

6. This law was enacted in 1961 but became effective only after 1969.

7. For statistical data, see Ministry of Health and Social Affairs, "Status of Public Health Services, 1985" mimeo. (in Korean); and for information regarding targets of population coverage by health services, see Ministry of Health and Social Affairs, *The Fifth Five Year Economic and Social Development Plan, 1982-86, Health Planning* (March 1983) (in Korean).

8. Sung-woo Lee, *op, cit.,* p. 29.

9. Song Keun-yong, et al., *Baseline Survey on Health Status in Remote Rural Areas* (Seoul: Korea Institute of Population and Health, 1983) (in Korean).

10. *Ibid,* pp. 117-126.

11. See note 6 above.

12. These are selected from variables of an institution-building model because RHDS could be viewed as an institution building process which infuses "health" values into the rural population. For concepts of these variables, see Milton J. Esman and H. Blaise, "Institution Building Research--Guiding Concepts," Pittsburgh, University of Pittsburgh, GSPIA, 1966 (mimeo); and also Martin Landau, "Linkage, Coding, and Intermediacy: A Strategy for Institution Building," in Joseph Eaton (ed.), *Institution Building and Development* (Beverly Hills, California: Sage, 1972), pp. 91-109.

13. See note 6.

14. International Conference on Primary Health Care, Alma-Ata, USSR, Sept. 6-12, 1978.

15. KHDI, *Primary Health Care Demonstration Projects in Korea; 1976-1980: Planning, Achievement and Evaluation* (Seoul, 1982).

16. See note 6.

17. Kim Jin-soon, "Summary Report on Training in Community Health Practititioners," KTPH, 1984, mimeo, pp. 7-8 (in Korean).

18. For the conceptual framework and its actual performance, see Whang In-Joung, *op.cit.,* pp. 9-36.

19. Primarily derived from interviews with officials of the Ministry of Health and Social Affairs, and officials of the county office as well as of public health centers at the local level.

20. Kim Dong Hee, "The Present Status and Prospects of the Korean Agriculture," in Korea Rural Economics Institute, *Korean Agriculture in Transitional Stage* (Seoul, 1979), pp. 17-47 (in Korean).

21. Song, et al., *op.cit.,* p. 82.

22. *Ibid,* pp. 48-80.

23. See Young-sik Kim and Dong-hee Kim, "Transfer of Resources Between Sectors and Adjustment of Agricultural Structure," in Dong-Hee Kim (ed.), *Korean Agriculture in Transition* (Seoul: KREI, 1980), pp. 64-97 (in Korean).

24. For simple indicators, see Economic Planning Board, *Social Indicators in Korea, 1984* (Seoul: EPB, 1985), pp.150-151.

25. Nevertheless, it should be noted that the level of farmers' household income has been greatly improved to be almost equivalent to the level of urban workers' household income. See Suh Sang-Mok, "Economic Growth

and Change in Income Distribution,"presented at KDT Forum on Trade Promotion and Industrial Adjustment," Seoul, Korea, Sep. 6-15, 1983.

26. Whang In-Joung, *op.cit.,* pp. 178-206.

27. Yeon Ha-Cheong, *Primary Health Care in Korea* (Seoul: Korea Development Institute, 1981), p. 40.

28. Whang In-Joung, *op.cit.,* pp. 5-6.

29. Yeon Ha-Cheong, "Rural Community Health Care in Korea," presented at International Social Security Association, Round Table Under Extension of Social Protection to Marginal Groups in Rural Zones, Mexico City, 13-16 November, 1984, pp. 205-208.

30. For role of "para-bureaucracy" in rural reform, see John Montgomery, "Allocation of Authority in Land Reform Programs: A Comparative Study and Administrative Procedures and Outputs," *Administrative Science Quarterly (1972), p. 66.*

31. Factors such as authority, structures and communications are regarded as most critical to improving coordination among administrative units. See James Price, *Organizational Effectiveness* (Homewood, Ill.: Richard Irwin, 1968), pp. 163-167; and also Whang In-Joung, "Integration and Coordination of Population Policies in Korea," *Asian Survey,* Vol. XIV, No. 11 (1974), pp. 985-999.

32. Song Keun Yong, et al., *op. cit.,* p. 95.

# 6

# Urban Low Cost Housing in the ASEAN: A Comparative View*

*Jürgen Rüland**

Most Third World countries are presently confronted with an urbanization process unprecedented in human history. Their urban population is growing twice as fast as the national population, which in most cases is increasing at rates way beyond the two percent margin. Between 1950 and 1980 the urban population of developing countries increased by more than 700 million, while in the industrialized countries it grew by only somewhat more than 300 million. According to the latest U.N. projections, the urban population in the Third World will grow by another 1.1 billion until the end of the century. By the year 2000, 43 percent of the expected total population in the developing world will be city dwellers (1950 = 17 percent). The roots and the effects of this rapid growth are well documented in a vast body of literature. For our purposes it is sufficient to bear in mind that - unlike in the developed countries, where urbanization went hand in hand with a secular economic upswing (urbanization and industrialization stimulating each other), a marked increase in employment opportunities and a decline in the rural population - in the developing countries it is primarily a process resulting from both inherited (colonialism) and self-made socioeconomic

---

*The author is indebted to several institutions and individuals who contributed to this study in various ways. I am particularly grateful to the Foundation Volkswagenwerk, Hannover, West Germany, for its funding of the author's current research project on "Rapid Urbanization and Local Government in Southeast Asia." Without this support many of the data presented here could not have been collected. The author is also grateful to the Arnold-Bergstraesser-Institut, and its Director, Prof. Dr. Dieter Oberndörfer, for his encouragement and continuous support for the author's urban research. The institutional and logistical support which has been rendered to the author by the Social Research Institute, Chiang Mai University, and its Director, Dr. Bhansoan Ladavalya, in recent months, are gratefully acknowledged. Last, but not least, I would also like to thank my wife, Dr. Dorothea Rüland, for her encouragement and willingness to discuss issues related to this paper.

**Arnold - Bergstraesser -Institut, Freiburg, West Germany.

structural deficiencies (unbalanced capital-intensive, urban-oriented industrialization strategy).

Here, in the majority of cases, urbanization is accompanied by an increasing concentration of poverty, unemployment and - as the most visible indicators of rapid urban growth - sprawling slums and squatter settlements. The tremendous housing shortage, which primarily affects the lower income groups, is made evident by the fact that today more than one-third of the urban population in Third World countries lives in slums and squatter settlements.

Unfortunately, in many countries authorities began to respond relatively late and hesitantly to the increasing housing shortage and a plethora of other complex social problems brought about by rapid and at times haphazard urban growth. It was the international organizations (the U.N. and subsequently the World Bank) as well as concerned academicians from various disciplines (in particular urban planners, architects, sociologists and anthropologists), from developed as well as developing countries, who gave the initial impulses for an in-depth study of the problems and the search for viable solutions. In the meantime, a lot of ingenuity has been devoted to achieving a better understanding of the multiple social and economic forces influencing the housing conditions of the poor. Experiments with various approaches have been made in order to bring affordable housing and security of tenure into the reach of low-income families.

This chapter assesses the impact of major low-cost housing strategies on the living conditions of the poor. It centers on the question why, despite tremendous efforts on the part of governments and academic research institutions alike, the delivery of urban low-cost housing services is still far from satisfactory. The sequence in which these strategies appear marks the changing attitudes toward the provision of low-cost housing services and a process of continued learning. At the same time, it illustrates the government housing agencies' enormous difficulties in entering into a clearcut, consistent, long-range, low-cost housing policy. In addition, this chapter derives some conclusions from the discussion of the different strategies and identifies major factors contributing to a more effective delivery of low-cost housing services.

This chapter primarily concentrates on the delivery of low-cost housing services in three ASEAN countries--i.e., the Philippines, Thailand and Malaysia-- where the author has been able to collect data during several field research stays of varied length. As far as the Indonesian and Singaporean housing policies are concerned, reference is made to the relevant literature, but very little is known about the provision of housing services in Brunei, which became the sixth member-state of ASEAN in 1984.

**Slums and Squatter Settlements: A Case of Diversity**

Literature on the physical and socioeconomic structure of low-income settlements is legion. But there is a widespread tendency to regard poor urban communities as settlements which share more or less the same characteristics: a high rate of unemployment, low and irregular household incomes, substandard and overcrowded housing conditions, inadequate infrastructure (such as water and electricity supply, access roads, drainage) and lack of other basic services such as waste disposal, health care and educational facilities. Such a generalizing view, however, overlooks the diversity of sub-standard urban settlements which has far-reaching implications for the practicability and adequacy of approaches to remedy the problem.

First of all a distinction has to be made between slums and squatter settlements. Slums are long - established, overcrowded, inner-city living quarters of dilapidating housing stock. Their inhabitants usually have entered some form of a contractual relationship with the landlord (mostly on a temporary basis), which legalized their residential choice.

Squatter settlements usually emerge on invaded public or private land. In many cases these settlements are located on marginal land with relatively little economic value such as swamps, along railway tracks or at dump sites. They can be located right in the heart of the city, but more often they are found at the urban periphery. Because squatters are settling on invaded land, their legal status is highly precarious. Squatter settlements are generally more recent in age than slums; they tend to be less densely populated, more makeshift, more temporary, in the majority of cases - especially if located at the urban fringe; and their inhabitants, owing to their recent arrival in the city, are less established in the urban economy. In other words, they have smaller and less stable incomes than the average slum dweller.

The incidence of slum dwellers and squatters is different in urban Southeast Asia. It varies according to the level of national socioeconomic development, the pace of urbanization and city size (see Tables 1 and 2). While in Thailand, and in particular in Bangkok, slums are more prevalent, squatting is the predominant housing arrangement for the poor in Philippine and Malaysian cities. Substandard housing is more serious in Indonesia and the Philippines, and

## Table 1  Metropolitan Areas in ASEAN Countries

| Country | Per Capita Income (in US$) | National Urbanization Level (percent) | Population of Metropolitan Area (in Millions) | Percentage of Slum and Squatter Population in Capital |
|---|---|---|---|---|
| Indonesia | 510 | 20 | 6.5 | n.d. |
| Malaysia | 1,961 | 29 | 1.1 | 25 |
| Philippines | 656 | 37 | 5.9 | 45 |
| Thailand | 794 | 17.5 | 5.5 | 30 |

## Table 2  Incidence of Slum Dwellers and Squatters in Regional Centers

| City | Percentage of Slum Dwellers and Squatters |
|---|---|
| *Philippines* | |
| Davao City | 40 |
| Marawi | 44.5 |
| Butuan City | 43.5 |
| Baguio | 27 |
| Cebu City | 18 |
| *Malaysia* | |
| Johore Bahru | 25 |
| Ipoh | 20 |
| *Thailand* | |
| Chiang Mai | 15 |
| Songkhla | 25 |
| Nakhon Sawan | 10 |
| Khon Kaen | 2 |

is less severe in Thailand and Malaysia (although with a trend to increase). Only Singapore has been able to overcome its housing shortage and offer adequate housing to the lower strata of society. In absolute numbers the housing problem is more pressing in metropolitan areas than in secondary centers, although in some rapidly growing Philippine regional cities (such as Davao City, Cagayan de Oro and Butuan City) the percentage of slum dwellers and squatters is approximating or even exceeding that of the metropolitan area.

While living in depressed areas in all cases means hardship, inadequate access to most basic services, and insecurity, there are marked differences among ASEAN countries in the socioeconomic status of the urban poor. For example, the urban poor in Thailand and Malaysia seem to be somewhat better-off (at least in monetary terms) than their counterparts in the Philippines and Indonesia. In addition, the structure of low-income residential quarters varies from country to country. While in the Philippines, especially in Metro-Manila and Davao City, there are several large slums and squatter settlements, poor communities are on the average much smaller and more scattered over the whole urban area in Thai and Malaysian cities. This diversity of low-income residential areas has to be kept in mind, when solutions for the different countries as well as individual cities or the settlements themselves are discussed.

**Eviction and Resettlement**

For a long time slums and squatter settlements were not recognized by the authorities as a social problem. To the better-off sectors of society and the governments they were hardly more than eyesores, breeding grounds of crime, health hazards, in short an obstacle to modernization and a threat to property, law and order. Squatting was primarily viewed as a legal problem. To tolerate the illegal occupation of invaded land was seen as an encouragement to further "unlawful" land invasions. As a consequence municipal as well as national authorities categorically ruled out the integration of these settlements into the urban system and their provision with basic public services.

Nevertheless actual policies toward slums and squatter settlements were inconsistent. They ranged from tacit toleration and occasional promises of electioneering politicians to work for improvement of the poor's living conditions to periodic outbursts of outright oppression, allegedly to cure the problem once and for all. Usually not even resettlement or alternative housing was offered, except that in cases, when the evicted families had some form of a contractual agreement over the occupation of the land with the landowner, (as in the case of slum dwellers in Bangkok) a small amount of compensation was paid. At other times, such as in the Philippines, the evicted squatters were returned to their home provinces (through a program called "balik pro-binsya") or relocated to remote areas beyond the urban periphery. Not surprisingly, this initial phase of dealing with low-income residential quarters was called a "period of hostility."

In the Philippines, relocation as a policy of slum clearance started very early. Already in the fifties and early sixties the authorities relocated some 7,274 squatter families to sites outside Manila.[2] As these programs had practically no impact on the capital's fast growing squatter population, the authorities finally resorted to drastic measures. While formerly evictions took place on a piecemeal basis, affecting relatively small numbers of people, in 1963 the government began mass-scale evictions. Between December 1963 and March 1964 almost 15,000 squatter families of the capital lost their homes; 4,500 of them were relocated to Sapang Palay, a hilly, infertile resettlement site in the Province of Bulacan, some 40 kilometers north of Manila. Virtually no preparations had been made to absorb the sudden influx of such a huge number of people, so that the relocated squatters found themselves without employment, shelter or public services. In 1968 and 1974 additional resettlement sites were opened in San Pedro (Laguna), Carmona and Dasmariñas (Cavite) with living conditions similar to those in Sapang Palay. By the end of 1981, at least 46,186 families were relocated to these four resettlement centers.[3]

It is obvious that the eviction-cum-resettlement approach cannot alleviate the housing problems of the poor. On the contrary, these measures produced economically and socially undesirable effects. The demolition of shanty towns is a waste of existing - though admittedly sub-standard - housing stock and property. Numerous studies have shown that poor settlers over time make considerable investments in their houses.[4] Moreover, as demolitions do not spare the complex informal sector economy that has emerged in these low-income residential quarters, existing employment opportunities within the cleared areas are destroyed as well. Eviction and relocation have serious repercussions on the living conditions of the people. Relocation requires them to start anew. It brings about a multiplication of costs in all sectors of life. The inadequacy of the relocation approach becomes apparent in the following objections raised in a considerable number of case studies:

1. Relocation means economic uprooting. While employed family members frequently lose their jobs in the process of relocation, alternative employment is not available in the resettlement sites. Industrial estates inaugurated several years after the opening of the relocation center may at a later stage have a positive effect on employment prospects, but the initial generation of relocatees will hardly benefit from them.

2. Job opportunities are concentrated in the capital or the urban center. The family budget of relocatees is thus additionally burdened through a second accommodation for the household head near his place of work or high transportation costs by commuting.

3. Due to additional transportation costs and a longer chain of middlemen, relocation inflates household expenses for food and other commodities, which have to be "imported" from the urban center.

4. Infrastructure development and site preparation are either inadequate or not completed when large numbers of relocatees arrive in the resettlement areas.

5. Relocation causes socio-psychological disorientation among the settlers. Social networks which sometimes have developed over decades in slums and squatter settlements are all of a sudden torn apart by relocation. As a consequence severe problems of integration into a new environment arise and amorphous social structures emerge.

6. Due to a lack of planning and coordination among government agencies, relocation often took place as an ad hoc exercise. Frequently more people were evicted than there were lots available in the resettlement sites. In Manila, for instance, the overspill population had to be accommodated in Emergency Relocation Centers before being moved to a permanent relocation site.

As a result of disadvantageous living conditions, many relocatees simply abandoned the relocation sites. As of 1981, in the resettlement sites adjacent to Manila, more than 36 percent of the relocated families returned to the capital, settling again in one of its 415 depressed areas.[5] Relocation brings about only a spatial shift of the squatter problem: to areas outside the city, or due to the high re-migration rate, merely to other squatter settlements within the inner or intermediate parts of the cities, where the vicious circle of eviction, relocation and re-migration starts again, creating a stratum of "urban refugees."[6] But also from the viewpoint of regional planning, relocation is more counterproductive than it is helpful in the alleviation of urban growth problems. Relocation of slum dwellers and squatters to rural areas does not contribute to a dispersal of urban growth. On the contrary, these sub-standard urban satellites reinforce the trend of conurbation and metropolitanization. While this rather negative approach to the housing problem persisted to a varying degree (more in the Philippines, less in Thailand and Malaysia) throughout the sixties, governments adopted more sophisticated strategies in the following decade. First the Philippines and Indonesia and subsequently Thailand responded to the on-going international debate on low-cost housing and seemed to rank it higher among their development priorities. Surprisingly, however, punitive actions against slum dwellers and squatters did not terminate. In the Philippines, through P.D. No. 296, and, more explicitly P.D. No.772, an antisquatting law was introduced. While until 1973 squatting was only treated as a public nuisance, under the new decrees it was declared a criminal offense, punishable by imprisonment or fine.[7] Periodical anti-squatting campaigns were mounted. Thousands of squatters were ejected and relocated prior to the Miss Universe pageant (1974), the visit of U.S. President Ford (1975) and the IMF-World Bank Conference (1976.) Again large anti-squatting drives were initiated in June/July 1982 and 1984 which forced the authorities to open a new relocation site in Tala Estate, Novaliches (north of Manila). But the way in which relocation was carried out did not differ markedly from the earlier relocations.

The introduction of sites-and-services and slum-upgrading programs notwithstanding, evictions were also on the rise in Bangkok. According to the Thai National Housing Authority's (NHA) Bangkok Slum Eviction Survey, about 200,000 persons (or 38 percent of the total slum population) were evicted from 129 out of 410 depressed areas between 1978-1980 or were threatened by eviction.[8] Amazingly, while in other Southeast Asian cities the threat of eviction usually looms higher for people settling on private land the opposite is true for Bangkok. Although about 60 percent of the slum dwellers and squatters settled on private land, more than two thirds of those evicted or threatened with eviction settled on public land.[9] The attractiveness that the relocation approach still enjoys is also made evident by the results of a survey conducted by the author in cooperation with the Social Research Institute, Chiang Mai University, among local politicians and municipal administrators in Chiang Mai. Fifty percent of the respondents felt that resettlement (to prepared lots at the urban fringe) is the best way to cope with the slum and squatter problem in Chiang Mai.

Only in Malaysia does there seem to be a decline in evictions and resettlements, possibly influenced by the dramatic change in the ethnic composition of slum dwellers and squatters. Whereas in 1966 nearly 68 percent of the squatters in the Federal Territory were Chinese, and only 21 percent Malays, the remaining 11 percent being Indians, by 1980 the proportion of Malays had sharply risen to 47 percent, while that of the Chinese had declined to 38 percent, with the proportion of Indians slightly increasing to 15 percent.[10]

The observation that evictions and *ad hoc* relocation continue to play an important role in the attempts of the authorities to cope with rapid urban growth[11] requires some explanation. One reason for this attitude is that authorities are caught in a dilemma which is caused by various conflicting factors. The new low-cost housing strategies (such as high-rise housing, sites-and-services and slum upgrading) rarely produced quickly visible results (and thus legitimacy), and this encouraged powerful vested interests, especially when slums and squatter settlements stood in the way of plans to change land use into more profitable uses, to exert political pressure on the housing authorities. As there is a widespread tendency among bureaucracies (especially the less prestigious agencies) to avoid protracted conflicts, they usually adhere to the demands of the more powerful protagonist. Squeezed into such an unpleasant position, housing authorities periodically tend to overreact when the pressure becomes unbearable; they resort to large-scale evictions and resettlements in the hope of eradicating a social problem by making it invisible. Apart from that, in a society like Thailand, where state interventions into the economy are rare by tradition, evictions are the effects of more or less unchecked market forces on a shrinking land market. Interestingly, in numerous cases government agencies behave very much in the same way as private landlords, seeking to sell their land for commercial development at market value. Not surprisingly, centrally located slums and squatter settlements are under the greatest threat of eviction. The percentage of evictions is declining with increased distance from the center. The higher the land value, the greater the potential for eviction.[12] As shown by Somsook Boonyabancha[13] road construction, commercial developments (shopping complexes, shophouses), the construction of public buildings and residential development (townhouses, row houses, flats) are the major types of alternative uses that have created those pressures for eviction.

Another important reason why authorities continue to resort to evictions and relocations is that the state tends to regard the urban poor as a political threat. The fact that the urban poor played a major role in both the Nicaraguan as well as Iranian revolution seems to support this view. However, with the partial exception of the Philippines, this fear is largely unjustified for Southeast Asian countries. The poor quite often have different perceptions of what is considered to be social injustice than foreign observers, domestic intellectuals or governments. For many of them the city is a haven of vast chances for upward social mobility - and even the depressing life in slums or squatter settlements is regarded as progress compared to their former existence as dependent, landless agricultural laborers with very little prospects for change in their living circumstances. This also explains why urban low-income settlements occasionally have been termed "slums of hope."[14] Only when this "hope" has been doomed time and again by repeated experiences of eviction, police harrassment and other punitive acts by state authorities, and only if the move to the city has not led to at least some modest socioeconomic status improvement, can the accumulated frustration provide some basis for collective anti-government actions. But even then the barriers working against horizontal mobilization and solidarism are high. In general, slum dwellers and squatters are a highly heterogeneous group which are rather conservative in their social values and political outlook and, apart from that, often compete for the same scarce resources. As the urban poor are also divided along ethnic lines, according to social status, place of origin, income and location of their settlements (with the exception of the Philippines, low-income settlements tend to be small poverty pockets which are dispersed all over the urban area), there is little room left for horizontal bonds of solidarity and the emergence of class-based politics. In many instances, political organization of the urban poor follows the traditional vertical patron-client relationships which link them to the state.[15] In virtually every Malay squatter settlement, for instance, the United Malay National Organization (UMNO), the dominant party of the country, is represented with a party branch.[16] While in Thailand there is very little political organization of the urban poor, in the big slums and squatter settlements of Philippine cities the state is facing organized opposition.[17] Ironically it is exactly the threat of eviction and relocation which finally amalgamates the urban poor into political organizations. But even in the Philippines, despite the attempts of radical political forces to cash in on the social discontent of the urban poor for revolutionary purposes, the overwhelming majority of the urban poor have other priorities which fall short of radical social changes: their demands primarily focus on employment, security of tenure, better public services - in other words a more stable and secure environment to live.

## Conventional Social Housing

The first positive steps to counter the growing housing shortage and poverty in Southeast Asian cities were the conventional social housing programs of the fifties and sixties. Although the demolition of slums and squatter settlements was still the main response, occasionally the evicted population was offered rehousing in cheap flats in high-rise buildings. By this strategy the authorities, which regarded slums and squatter settlements primarily as remnants of backward-oriented social and cultural norms, hoped to achieve a more rapid adaptation of the poor to "modern" urban lifestyles. Moreover, aesthetic norms imported from the West served as a further justification for such a housing strategy. It is evident that this first phase of public housing policies was mainly guided by the ideas of prevailing modernization theories. While in Thailand and the Philippines the efforts to deliver low-cost housing units in walk-up apartment blocks remained sporadic, Malaysia and in particular Singapore embarked on vigorous high-rise housing programs.

With the exception of Singapore, however, the majority of conventional social housing projects did not achieve their goals. In this regard, there is little difference to the public housing programs of a great many industrialized countries, which are also plagued by a number of problems. The major reasons for the rather limited success of these high-rise housing projects can be summarized as follows:[18]

1. High-rise housing is capital - intensive and, as a result of considerable inputs of imported machinery and building materials, has relatively high foreign exchange requirements. In addition, there are high costs for infrastructure development as well as progressively rising administrative costs after completion.[19]
2. Although rentals or amortization payments (in case of purchase) were considerably lower than in the open market, they were beyond the means of the poor, because they were based on cost rather than family incomes.[20]
3. Due to financial constraints, management problems, and corruption, the programs had no quantitative impact on the housing shortage. In the Philippines, for instance, between 1948 and 1973 only 13,500 dwelling units were constructed in 19 projects—most of them located in Metro-Manila,[21] while in Thailand the combined output of all government housing agencies amounted to only 11,268 units between 1942 and 1973.[22] Even the ambitious Urban BLISS project which, inaugurated in 1979, was originally announced as a housing project for low-income families, had virtually no impact on the housing shortage in Manila. As of mid-1983, only 2,471 Urban BLISS units had been completed in Metro-Manila.[23]
4. As a result, low-income families were strongly underrepresented in these projects. The beneficiaries of public housing were primarily middle and upper class households. A good case in point is the Urban BLISS project. In 1982 the construction costs had spiraled to 75,000-90,000 pesos per unit - costs which are affordable only by the upper middle class and above.[24]
5. Rising costs of construction forced the use of building materials of minor quality, thus accelerating the process of early dilapidation of the units.

6. Frequently the dwellings were not adapted to the needs of the occupants who in many cases responded by altering or extending their dwellings by "illegal" constructions.

So far high-rise social housing programs have been successful only in the city states of Hong Kong and Singapore. Between 1960 and 1983 the Singaporean government was able to construct 451,414 flats, thus providing 1.95 million or 77 percent of Singaporeans with public housing.[25] With monthly rents not exceeding a margin of 11 - 13 percent of the family income, Singapore's housing program was even able to reach large sections of the poor - except for the bottom ten percent of households.

But it is not exclusively Singapore's status as a city state which favorably contributed to its housing success story. While immigration admittedly can be relatively easily controlled in an insular city state, there are other factors which were at least as important for its effective delivery of housing services:[26] a rapidly expanding and relatively stable economy with broad and marked spread effects and long-term real income increases; an active family planning program to curb the natural population increase; and a sophisticated financing system.

## Sites-and-Services and Slum Upgrading

By the end of the sixties the stereotypes which had beset the image of slum dwellers and squatters were successfully refuted in the pioneering works of Abrams, Laquian, Mangin, Turner and others.[27] The major conclusions drawn from their writings can be summarized as follows:

1. Slums and squatter settlements are a rational and functionally adequate response of the poor to their status of socioeconomic deprivation and the shortage of cheap and centrally located housing.
2. As slums and squatter settlements offer housing which can be easily produced through self-building or the application of simple, yet appropriate building techniques, they satisfy an important basic need.
3. Without security of tenure, some infrastructure development and the provision of basic public services, there is no prospect for improvement of the living conditions of the urban poor. According to Turner, housing has to be seen as a "process," meaning that over time the poor are willing to invest significant proportions of their savings in the improvement of their houses, as long as they are secure from evictions.

This re-assessment of the slum and squatter theme eventually led to far-reaching changes in the official housing policies of developing countries (and within the ASEAN as well). It became gradually accepted that:

1. The costs per housing unit had to be reduced drastically in order to make housing affordable to low-income households.
2. This target could be best realized through Turner's concept of "housing as a process."
3. Sophisticated building techniques do not serve the needs of the poor.
4. Building and design standards derived from industrialized nations should be avoided.
5. Evictions and relocations have to be confined to a minimum, thereby conserving existing housing stock. Substandard housing is still better than no housing.
6. Housing services have to be provided with the participation of the target group in order to ensure that they are actually "user-oriented."
7. The self-help potential of the poor must be mobilized.

Alarmed by the unabated rapid urban growth and concomitant poverty as well as the failures of their former growth-oriented development strategies, international organizations like the World Bank and the U.N. joined the reform debate on slum improvement and urban development. It was at that time (1972) that the World Bank established its urban division. As a facet of their new basic needs development strategy, the World Bank and other development aid organizations propagated low-cost housing projects which were designed to rely on self-help of the beneficiaries, thereby adopting, if only rhetorically, Turner's concept of "housing as a process." Known as "sites-and-services" and "slum upgrading" these new types of low-cost housing programs were soon adopted by many governments in developing countries. Within ASEAN, the Philippines and Indonesia were the first countries to experiment with these strategies, later on followed by Thailand - and more hesitantly Malaysia, which still places priority on the construction of walk-up apartment blocks.

Slum upgrading is the introduction of basic infrastructure, e.g., water, electricity, drainage, footpaths, access roads, toilet facilities, sewerage, etc., into depressed areas. The improvement of the dwellings, however, is left to self-help activities of the residents, their time and financial capacities. Very often upgrading necessitates measures to decongest the area for infrastructure development. This is done by "reblocking," meaning that the typically irregular structure of the settlements is re-arranged through moving the dwellings along a rectangular layout. Reblocking, however, entails the relocation of an overspill affected by the decongestion measures.

Sites-and-services projects usually serve a twofold function: to accommodate the overspill population of upgrading projects and to increase the housing stock at low cost. In sites-and-services projects some basic infrastructure is provided together with a shell house (including sanitary core) that the settlers must complete themselves according to their resources.

In the past the recovery of costs for infrastructure development and core house construction from the beneficiaries was an integral part of sites-and-services and slum-upgrading projects. The rationale behind cost recovery is that the scarce resources of the public sector do not allow for government subsidies and that recovered funds can be used for the repetition of these projects.

In the Philippines, Thailand and Indonesia the on-going upgrading and sites-and-services projects are without doubt by far the most comprehensive effort of the public sector to mitigate the housing problem. Sites-and-services and upgrading have brought cheap housing in a shorter time into the reach of more low-income households than ever before. But compared with the total demand for low-cost housing they are still far from offering a final solution.

This problem is compounded by the fact that the public housing agencies tend to grossly overstate their actual capacities in the delivery of housing services. The National Housing Authority of the Philippines, for instance, came out with a target of constructing 171,000 new units (especially sites-and-services) and renovating 175,000 units in Metro-Manila alone between 1978 and 1985.[28] If, in the meantime, these targets have been achieved by only 50 percent, it could already be considered as a tremendous (quantitative) success. In a similar vein, Thailand's low-cost housing program proved far too ambitious as well. While the Thai NHA had targeted the construction of some 120,000 low-cost housing units under the Fourth Five Year Plan (1977-81), as of the beginning of 1980 only 17,800 units had actually been completed and 14,200 were under construction.[29] As a consequence the NHA had to revise its program, scaling it down considerably. For 1978 - 1982 the construction program was reduced to 32,600 units in sites-and-services, 5,600 low-income rental units and 3,500 units in projects intended to generate profits. Apart from that, another 17,500 units were scheduled for upgrading.[30]

While experience so far suggests that the "as is where is" approach of upgrading is somewhat cheaper and more adjusted to the needs of the poor than is sites-and-services, there is much evidence that both - upgrading as well as sites-and-services - are still too expensive for many low-income families. In his study of the upgrading and sites-and-services projects in Tondo and Dagat-Dagatan, Manila, Oberndörfer found that only 30 - 40 percent of the beneficiaries could afford to pay the rents regularly.[31] According to preliminary observations in Philippine regional cities, the affordability rate seems to be somewhat higher. The relatively low affordability of these project types must be attributed to four main factors:

First, infrastructure development is frequently far beyond what low-income households can afford. This is due to technically sophisticated public works (for instance land reclamation) or unduly high design standards (as is the case with roads, foot paths and drainage systems). However, it must be noted that the standards for physical improvements in such projects are much more modest in Thailand and Indonesia than in the Philippines.

Second, feasibility studies are generally based on the assumption that poor households can afford to spend 15 - 20 percent of their monthly income on housing (in Kuala Lumpur even 30 percent).. This *a priori* excluded a large proportion of the target population from the project's benefits, for most surveys on the spending behavior of low-income households indicate that expenses for housing rarely exceed 10 percent of the monthly income. Furthermore, cost recovery is at times based on rather unrealistic expectations of income increments. As cost recovery has to be stretched over a long period (usually 25 - 30 years), income projections are based on average increases, thereby ignoring the adverse impact of recessions and economic slumps on the budgets of the poor, which among all social groups are affected most owing to an overproportionately high percentage of consumption expenses. Thus a temporary economic crisis not only jeopardizes the ability of poor households to continue with their rent or amortization payments, but also threatens their status as project beneficiaries, especially if there are provisions like in Philippine low-cost housing projects which endow the government with the right to expel beneficiaries who have failed to fulfill their obligations for three consecutive months.

Third, while cost recovery inappropriately burdens the household budgets of the poor, most projects do not generate additional employment that would provide the beneficiaries with secure jobs and regular incomes. Cost recovery overlooks the fact that about two-thirds of the households have highly irregular sources of income. Unfortunately, integrated projects which included an employment component have had only modest success. In Manila, for instance, an industrial estate adjacent to the Tondo and Dagat-Dagatan project sites, expected to create 20,000 jobs, has not yet got off the ground, while projects to promote small-scale industries could not significantly boost the income of the project beneficiaries. Thus, although planned as integrated projects, the physical components predominated, while social and economic conditions could be changed only marginally.

Fourth, planning, the hiring of foreign consultants, and project management cause considerable administrative overhead costs. Burgess estimates that 20 percent of the final cost per housing unit is due to administrative costs.[32]

Other objections could be added: coordination problems among implementing agencies triggering long delays, problems with the collection of rents and the paternalistic or even authoritarian style of planning and implementation. Moreover, an aspect of major concern for most project beneficiaries is the persistent insecurity over land tenure. In the Philippines and Thailand, authorities are reluctant to grant land titles to the beneficiaries. Basically it is their policy to grant land titles only to those who opted for purchase of their lot and house and only after full amortization of the development and construction costs. The "certificates of award" which were distributed to the beneficiaries in the meantime, were, however, only of limited legal value.[33]

These problems have received too little attention from the project implementing agencies. Confronted with the gigantic task of providing shelter for an increasing number of low-income households, and often put under severe pressure by domestic and foreign critics, they tend to gauge the success of their projects primarily on the basis of quantitative and formal criteria. Thus, a project has been implemented "successfully" when the respective facilities have been established and the costs recovered. Economic considerations thus gain priority over social aspects.[34]

Some other long-term social and economic effects of upgrading and sites-and-services projects require further research. There are indications that the above-mentioned deficiencies favor processes of social segregation within the project areas: increasing land prices (due to the improvements), lack of employment and the greater financial obligations in the wake of cost recovery have caused an exodus of the lowest income groups among the target population. Increasingly they will be replaced by middle income groups. Silas, for instance, has found that in Surabaya, in improved areas the rents rose between 50 and 200 percent, thus driving out the renters (who usually are the economically weakest group in low-income residential areas). In addition, in upgrading projects there are serious problems in maintaining the improved facilities. If slum upgrading is restricted to a one-time action without regular follow-ups there is much danger that the improvements will be subjected to a process of gradual degradation over the years.[35]

**Self-Help: Panacea or Deadlock?**

While the limitations of the sites-and-services and upgrading approaches as discussed above are increasingly recognized by scholars and practitioners, the search for further improvements in the provision of low-cost housing services continues. New proposals primarily dwell on the considerable potential for self-help inherent in sites-and-services and upgrading. Accordingly, it has been suggested that the state should encourage self-help initiatives to the utmost extent. But in light of the tremendous housing backlog, the question arises as to whether the potential of the poor for self-help activities is not grossly overestimated.

The proponents of self-help primarily argue the concept's economic advantages: of all approaches self-help building requires the least capital inputs and thus ensures a highly efficient utilization of scarce public resources. Apart from this, the democratizing potentials of self-help are emphasized: not only does self-help have decentralizing effects insofar as to a great extent it ensures the utilization of local know-how and skills, it also recognizes the individual needs of the users and facilitates the organization of the poor as a major precondition for the effective articulation of their demands.

Criticism against the self-help approach was first aired by Marxist scholars. Self-help has been characterized as "myth,"[36] "palliative," and "ideological bluff."[37] Burgess sees in it a strategy for the preservation of the present societal status quo in developing countries which forestalls necessary structural reforms.[38] For Steinberg,[39] self-help is unduly prolonging the working day of the poor or, as Skinner[40] has termed it, it is a form of "overexploitation." In this view self-help indirectly leads to a long-term decline in real wages, because it reduces the pressures for wage increases as long as workers construct their homes themselves, thus keeping costs for the reproduction of their labor at a low level.[41] Doubts have also been raised as to whether self-help can solve the housing problem in quantitative terms. Burgess, for instance, suspects that self-help projects rarely go beyond an experimental or pilot stage.[42] In the long run, these authors maintain, the housing problem can only be solved if it is recognized as a structural problem of peripheral capitalism. Unfortunately, however, most of them fall short of offering an alternative. Burgess and Steinberg, for instance, both of whom are rather skeptical about the chances for significant changes in housing policies, merely present a shadowy vision of a socialist society.[43]

But objections have been raised even from non-Marxist authors against a self-help concept that is misleadingly taken as a panacea for the housing problem. The concept suggests harmony, where in reality social conflicts are simmering.[44] Oberndörfer warns about self-help romanticism. Slums and squatter settlements are not "egalitarian communities of the poor," but are characterized by considerable income disparities and internal relationships of mutual expropriation.[45] And, according to Sarin, without a certain minimum income and savings even the most modest concepts of self-building turn out to be illusionary for the poor.[46] In the meantime, even the World Bank has arrived at a more cautious assessment of the potentials of self-help approaches, after experiences with Bank projects suggesting that the labor surplus in poor households is much smaller than anticipated.[47]

## Toward a Solution of the Low - Cost Housing Problem?

From the foregoing discussion several major conclusions can be drawn:

1. Even taking into account the commitment of the housing agencies and their officials to find viable solutions, it has to be conceded that slums and squatter settlements will be concomitants of socioeconomic change for a long time to come. This holds true even if the population growth slows down considerably - which so far has been the case only in Thailand. City-ward migration will persist in the face of transformations in the agricultural sector, the exhaustion of cultivatable land resources, unrest and insecurity in rural areas.
2. There is no panacea and no universally applicable model for the efficient delivery of low-cost housing services.
3. Low-cost housing is an extremely complex problem. As the urban poor are a highly heterogeneous group, their living conditions and socioeconomic circumstances vary considerably from country

to country, city to city, and according to location inside the respective urban area.
4. From this it follows that effective delivery of low-cost housing services must rely on a whole range of complementary strategies.
5. Improvements in low-cost housing services will be incremental, unless the economy undergoes a major crisis. Such a crisis has twofold effects: it accelerates the influx of impoverished rural migrants into the urban areas, while public resources for coping with the problem are decreasing or at best stagnating.
6. Housing policies must be consistent. There should be no frequent alternations between negative responses, such as eviction and large-scale resettlements and positive measures, such as the various low-cost housing schemes.
7. There is a delicate balance between the need to steer urban growth in an orderly fashion, i.e., urban planning, and social priorities caused by the poverty of at least 30-40 percent of the urban population.

Furthermore, the low - cost housing problem is neither merely technical nor financial in nature. The phenomenon of slums and squatter settlements is influenced by a variety of variables such as the state of the national economy, the national development strategy, employment opportunities, income distribution and the structure of the political system. A housing policy which disregards these variables cannot do more than cure the symptoms.

There are two preconditions which to a large extent will influence the outcome of future housing policies. First, there must not only be sustained economic growth, but this economic growth must be redistributed in a much more effcient manner than in the past. Economic growth must be associated with broad spread effects which benefit the poor in the form of more employment and higher real incomes, so that better housing will be made affordable for these groups. Such a priority, however, should not be mistaken as a call for a "growth first, redistribution later" policy which implies serious dangers of increasing existing socioeconomic disparities. Instead, in order to actively reduce such disparities, economic gains must expeditiously translate into social policies with tangible effects on large sections of society, such as, for instance, affordable low-cost housing. Second, there must be the political will to rectify structural deficiencies in the distributive system which so far has primarily worked to the advantage of the urban middle and upper classes.

Although low - cost housing is a theme too complex to permit the presentation of a comprehensive scheme for alleviating the problem in the context of this chapter, it is nevertheless attempted in the following sections to sketch some major components which such a scheme should encompass. We will distinguish between components which primarily aim at the national level and those which have to be considered at the local (i.e. urban) level.

## National Level Strategies

The capitalist state, which as claimed by Burgess primarily represents the interests of the landed elite, the corporate interests of the construction and real estate industry, and the finance capital,[48] is not an impediment *per se* to effective low-cost housing services. Even under the auspices of capitalism there is enough room to maneuver for interventionist and redistributive (social) policies which would spread the benefits of economic growth to the lower income groups. Welfare policies are no luxury for developing countries (and particularly not for newly industrializing countries). On the contrary, well designed social policies may lead to an increase of purchasing power among low income households, which in turn may become a supporting force for sustained economic growth and diversification.

With regard to low-cost housing, redistributive policies must primarily focus on the land issue. Low-cost housing programs can only then curb the housing backlog if the public sector has enough land resources to implement large - scale projects expeditiously. In ASEAN countries (with the sole exception of Singapore) a major reason for the non-achievement of planning targets are the complicated legal procedures involved in the acquisition of land by the public sector. In Thailand, for instance, this process can take three to four years. A good case in point is the land acquisition program of the Thai NHA. For completion of its projects under the Fifth Five Year Plan (1982 - 86), the NHA had to acquire 3,780 *rai* of land, but when the planning period started in January 1982, no sites had been purchased for the 1982 projects. Although the NHA has been endowed with eminent domain power since 1979 this prerogative has still to be applied.[49] The Philippine housing agencies are also very reluctant to enforce expropriations (against compensation). Lim[50] is certainly correct when he attributes this failure to the fact that the right of land ownership in free - market (or better: "laisser faire") economies is often treated as a highly sensitive, ideological and emotional issue. Without positive intervention, "land for housing the poor" will become increasingly scarce.[51] The high degree of (a continously increasing) urban land concentration is well documented in work of Goh Ban Lee. In the six Malaysian towns he studied, a mere one percent of the landowners own about 17 percent of private land in Kota Bharu, 24 percent in Bukit Mertajam, 28 percent in Kulim, 32 percent in Georgetown, 36 percent in Alor Star and 40 percent in Butterworth.[52]

In a similar vein, Noranitipadungkarn and Hagensick[53] report about Chiang-Mai that within the municipal area (at that time 17.5 km$^2$), "three owners hold about 7 km$^2$" (= 40 percent). Hence, in order to control spiralling land prices and rampant speculation there must be "appropriate and tough legislation to allow the authorities to acquire land speedily and at reasonable cost for public purposes."[54] In Singapore, for instance, the Land Acquisition Act (1966) and the Land Acquisition (Amendment) Act (1973) gave broad powers to the government for compulsory land acquisition. But the legal side has to be matched by law enforcement, which is a weak point especially in the Thai and Philippine administrative systems.

To keep housing costs at a low level it is therefore imperative for the public sector to establish land banks. Land banking is the reservation of land for future urban use. Land banking may preclude other land uses which otherwise would compete with, and in the end outbid, land use for low-cost housing. Land banking may also result in considerable savings. According to an analysis of the Thai NHA, estimated savings due to advance land purchases ranged from 25 - 67 percent in Bangkok and Chiang Mai housing projects.[55]

As the housing problem cannot be separated from the urbanization process as a whole, a major precondition for its alleviation are measures to steer urban growth through a national urbanization policy. Such a policy must attempt to divert urban (population and economic) growth from metropolitan areas to regional or smaller centers in the hinterland. Moreover, in order to avoid that such a regionalization strategy degenerate into a mere "growth pole" approach, it must at the same time establish linkages between these lower-order urban centers and the rural hinterland. This necessitates changes in the present industrialization policies which so far have concentrated on the primate cities in Southeast Asia. Complementary measures consist in the promotion of agro-based industries (i.e., the creation of nonagricultural jobs in rural areas), better marketing and storage facilities for agricultural products, infrastructure improvements, etc.   In the Philippines and Thailand, such regionalization programs (Regional Cities Development Project) are currently underway.

They are a reflection of the increasing scholarly attention devoted to small[56] and secondary cities.[57]

Without a marked decline of the natural population growth rate, strains on the housing market will not ease significantly. Apart from Singapore, a noticeable deceleration of the population growth rate has occurred only in Thailand, where the growth rate slowed down from 3.0 percent (1960 - 1970) to 2.0 percent in 1985 (the target for 1986 being 1.5 percent).

The provision of low-cost housing services is a late-comer in development policy. This is reflected in the rather weak position of the national housing agencies (especially in Thailand and the Philippines) within the government set-up. There is considerable need for a strengthening of these authorities in terms of financing and staffing. Without a significant improvement of management capacities of these bodies, low-cost housing projects will continue to suffer from delays and coordination problems. The staffing pattern should also be modified in such a way that a greater number of social scientists (preferably sociologists, psychologists and anthropologists) will be hired so that more competence is available as far as the social impacts of housing projects are concerned. Apart from the fact that many architects, planners and engineers are young graduates, thus lacking much needed experience, there is a high turnover rate of these professionals. In the Philippines, for instance, they leave government service after two or three years in order to join the private sector or to work in the Middle East.

**Urban Level Strategies**

Due to the heterogeneous social, economic, ethnic and spatial structure of low-income settlements, housing policies must be highly flexible and adaptable to varying local conditions. Instead of imposing a certain low-cost housing strategy on the whole spectrum of low - income households, future schemes should take into account the fragmented social structure of the urban poor. Thus, existing strategies should be applied in a selective and flexible way to different target groups. We recommend that, first, as virtually all low-cost housing strategies have excluded the bottom 20-40 percent of the low-income group, slum upgrading at very modest design standards (like the Kampung Improvement Projects in Indonesia) or outright subsidization seem to be the only viable options for this group. The upgrading approach should be a cornerstone in the housing policy of less affluent countries which - like Indonesia or the Philippines - have a numerically substantial urban population living below the poverty threshold, while subsidization of the poorest of the poor is only recommendable for countries with greater resources and a higher GNP.

Second, relatively better-off sections of the low-income population which can bear the additional financial burden of suburban life could be targeted for sites-and-services schemes. But care must be taken that only those families are chosen who have employment within a certain radius around the project site. Otherwise many of the problems discussed in connection with the relocation schemes emerge. In addition, as the trend of constructing low-cost housing in suburban areas will continue, cheap and fast mass transit systems to the inner city (where most income generating opportunities exist) must be developed.

Third, slums and squatter settlements in inner city locations should not be demolished. The land-sharing approach as outlined by Angel and Chirathamkijkul[58] may provide an alternative, if the intricacies involved in cross-subsidization can be managed.

Fourth, despite its various disadvantages high-rise housing should not be dismissed outright as a component of a more efficient delivery of low-cost housing. It might be affordable for NICs such as Malaysia, Taiwan or Korea. For reasons given above, countries with fewer, public resources, however, should not embark on walk-up apartments as the predominant strategy in the delivery of low-cost housing. But even here one target group might be an exception: the upper stratum living in low income settlements which has been well established in urban life, who can afford the rents and does not reject apartment housing for sociocultural reasons.

Low-cost housing is an important component of social policies and thus by nature conflicts with the economic rationale of cost recovery. Not surprisingly, cost recovery has been successful only when lower middle or middle class families were the target group of housing programs. In most upgrading and sites-and-services schemes the authorities have been reluctant to enforce cost recovery for fear of social unrest and political conflicts. That cost recovery is not the exclusive key to the reduplication of low-cost housing projects has been proven by the Indonesian Kampung Improvement Projects where no cost recovery was involved.[59] Also in the slum improvement component of the Thai Regional Cities Development Project cost recovery has been dismissed as not feasible.

Eviction and relocation should be limited to an absolute minimum. Even in the West, urban renewal which involved the relocation of a large segment of the population has always been a source of intense conflict in urban politics. If relocation cannot be avoided, disruptive effects on the living conditions of the affected families must be cushioned to the utmost extent. Thus relocation should take place only after careful timing, site preparation and provisions that the relocatees do not lose their employment.

Public housing projects should provide mechanisms for the participation of the target group. The formation of authoritative representation and pressure groups of the poor should be encouraged by the state instead of being suppressed.[60] The acceptance of the poor as legitimate participants in planning and decision-making may have long-term stabilizing effects on the political system insofar as it forestalls developments in which the poor become the "available mass" of radical organizations, be they groups with leftist leanings, Islamic fundamentalists or communalist extremists.

Despite the objections raised against it, self-help will continue to play an important role in low-cost housing policies for a transitional period of yet undetermined length. The duration of this transitional period will very much depend on overall economic growth and diversification and will only come to an end when broad sections of the population benefit from economic growth through rising real incomes. Housing policies must thus provide a workable framework for "freedom-to-build" so that self-help initiatives of the poor can crop up where the state cannot immediately provide adequate shelter. In such areas authorities should therefore refrain from imposing rigid building and design standards, and implementing building code regulations copied from western countries.

Low-cost housing should be considered as an integrated approach which has to be linked to employment generation and go hand in hand with rising, regular and secure household incomes. Especially in the less affluent countries like the Philippines, Indonesia and Thailand due attention must be paid to the informal sector economy. As the informal sector serves as a niche of survival for the poor, stiff anti-hawking drives by urban authorities have an adverse impact on the income of the poor. Instead, productive informal sector activities should be actively promoted, with the perspective of establishing closer linkages between the modern and the informal sector economies.

New financing models have to be developed, which take into account the reluctance of low-income families to enter into long-term financial commitments. Due to the highly insecure and precarious financial situation of the poor, credit facilities (e.g., low-interest rates and avoiding long-term repayment schedules) must be developed which are tailored to the specific needs of this target group.

**Notes**

1. W. Doebele, "The Provision of Land for the Urban Poor : Concepts, Instruments and Prospects," in S. Angel, et al. (eds.), *Land for Housing the Poor* (Singapore : n.p.,1983), p. 358.
2. J. Rüland, *Squatter Relocation in the Philippines: The Case of Metro Manila* (Bayreuth : University of Bayreuth, 1982), p. 19.
3. *Ibid.*, p. 25.
4. A. Laquian, "Slums and Squatters in South and Southeast Asia," in L. Jakobson and V. Prakesh (eds.), *Urbanization and National Development* (Beverly Hills : n.p., 1971), p. 188; E. Jimenez, "The Value of Squatter Dwellings in Developing Countries," in *Economic Development and Cultural Change*, Vol. 30, No. 4 (1982), pp. 739-752.
5. Rüland, *op. cit.*, p. 83.
6. S. Boonyabancha, *"The Causes and Effects of Slum Eviction in Bangkok."* in Angel, et al. (eds.) *op. cit.*, p. 254.
7. P. Makil, "Squatting in Metro Manila," Paper read at the Breakfast Dialogue of the Bishops-Businessmen's Conference (BBC), Makati, 1982, p. 8.
8. Boonyabancha, *op. cit.*, p. 255.
9. *Ibid.*, p. 258.
10. J. Diamond, et al., "Urban Poverty Group Study in Kuala Lumpur," *Occasional Papers of the INTAN*, No. 2 (1980), p. 23.
11. ESCAP, "Policies Towards Urban Slums and Squatter Settlements in the ESCAP-Region," *Case Studies of Seven Cities* (Bangkok : n.p. 1980), p. 91.
12. Boonyabancha, *op. cit.*, p. 266.
13. *Ibid.*, p. 267.
14. P. Lloyd, *Slums of Hope? Shanty Towns of Third World* (Harmondsworth: n.p., 1979).
15. R. Hampel and J. Rüland, "Verstädterung in der Dritten Welt : Wachstum ohne Entwicklung?" in *Der Burger in Staat* (Stuttgart : forthcoming, 1985)
16. P. Chan, "The Political Economy of Urban Squatting in Metropolitan Kuala Lumpur," in *Contemporary Southeast Asia* (1983), p. 496.
17. J. Rüland, "Political Change, Urban Services and Social Movements in Metro Manila," in *Public Administration and Development*, Vol. 4, No. 4, (1984), p. 327 ff.

18. R. Ocampo, "Development of Philippine Housing Policy and Administration (1945-1959)," in *Philippine Journal of Public Administration*, Vol. XXII, No.1 (1978), pp. 1-9; A. Ancog, "Bagong Barangay Housing Project: An Experiment in Social Housing," in *Philippine Journal of Public Administration*, Vol. XXII, No.1 (1978), pp. 79-99.

19. P. Herrle, P. Lübbe and J. Rösel, *Slums und Squattersiedlungen* (Thesen zur Stadtplanung in der Dritten Welt, Stuttgart, 1981), p. 156.

20. O.F. Grimes, *Housing for Low-Income Urban Families* (Washington: n.p.,1976), p. 9.

21. ILO, *Sharing in Development : A Programme of Employment, Equity and Growth for the Philippines* (Geneva : n.p., 1974), p. 213.

22. ESCAP, *op. cit.*, pp. 78-92.

23. M. Reforma and L.M. Briones, "Housing Services in Metro Manila," mimeographed paper, Freiburg/Manila, 1983, p. 52.

24. *Ibid.*

25. Information Division, Ministry of Culture, Singapore, *Facts and Pictures 1984* (Singapore : n.p., 1984), pp. 137-141.

26. D. Oberndörfer and J. Rüland, "Slum und Squatter-Sanierung in der Dritten Welt," in M. Von Hauff and B. Pfister-Gaspary (eds.), *Entwicklungspolitik : Probleme, Projektanalysen und Konzeptionen* (Saarbrücken/Fort Lauderdale, n.p., 1984), p. 222.

27. C. Abrams, *Housing in the Modern World : Man's Struggle for Shelter in an Urbanising World* (London : n.p., 1966); A. Laquian, *Slums are for the People: The Barrio Magsaysay Pilot Project in Philippine Urban Community Development* (Honolulu : n.p., 1969); W. Mangin, "Latin American Squatter Settlements : A Problem and a Solution," in *Latin American Research Review* (1967), pp. 65-98; J. Turner and R. Fichter (eds.), *Freedom to Build* New York: n.p., 1982).

28. Metro Manila Commission, *Metro Manila : The First Three Years, November 1975 to December 1978,* (n.p., 1979), p. 11.

29. World Bank, *Thailand, National Sites-and-Services-Project* (Washington: n.p., 1980), p. 3.

30. *Ibid.,* p. 4.

31. D. Oberndörfer, *Strukturdaten zum Squattergebiet Tondo/Manila, Beschreibung und Analyse der amtlichen Förderungsmassnahmen in dieser Region* (Freiburg : n.p., 1979), p. 81.

32. R. Burgess, "The Limits of State and Self-Help Housing Programs," in E. Bruno, et al. (eds.), *Development of Urban Low-Income Neighborhoods*

*in the Third World* (Darmstadt : n.p., 1984), p. 36.

33. W.J.Keyes, *Freedom-to-Build-Philippines: Experience with the Freedom-to-Build Project at Dasmarinas, 1976-1982* (Bangkok : Human Settlements Division, Asian Institute of Technology, 1983), p.13.

34. J. Rüland, *Politik und Verwaltung in Metro Manila. Aspekte der Herrschaftsstabilisierung in einem autoritaren politischen System* (München : n.p., 1982), p. 173.

35. J. Silas, "*Spatial Structure, Housing Delivery, Land Tenure and the Urban Poor in Surabaya, Indonesia,*" *in* Angel, et al. (eds.), *op.cit.*, p. 222; P. Baross, "Kampong Improvement or Development? Appraisal of the Low-Income Settlement Upgrading Policy in Indonesia," in Bruno, et al. (eds.) *op.cit.*, p. 330.

36. F. Steinberg, *Die Städtische Wohnungsfrage in Sri Lanka, Perspektiven der Wohnungspolitik für die Armen* (Saarbrücken : n.p., 1982), p. 308.

37. R. Burgess, "Self-Help Housing Advocacy : A Curious Form of Radicalism. A Critique of the Work of John F.C. Turner," in P.M.Ward (ed.), *Self-Help Housing: A Critique* (London : n.p., 1982), pp. 86, 91.

38. *Ibid.*, p. 86.

39. Steinberg, *op.cit.*, p. 318.

40. R. Skinner, "Self-Help Community Organisation and Politics : Villa El Salvador, Lima," in Ward (ed.), *op. cit.*, p. 226.

41. Steinberg, *op. cit.*

42. Burgess, *op. cit.*, p. 91.

43. In his latest article Burgess (in Bruno, et al., 1984) modifies his critique of the self-help approach by distinguishing between state-sponsored self-help projects and autonomous self-help. While he maintains his earlier critique against self-help approaches as far as state-sponsored projects are concerned, he describes autonomous self-help as a possible alternative for mitigating the low-cost housing problem.

44. Herrle, et al., *op. cit.*, p. 174.

45. Oberndörfer, *op. cit.*, p. 37.

46. M. Sarin, *Urban Planning in the Third World: The Chandigarh Experience* (London : n.p., 1982), p. 164.

47 World Bank, *Shelter* (Washington : n.p.. 1980), p. 20.

48. Burgess, *op. cit.*, pp. 20-24.

49. R.S. De Voy and C. Rodrongruang, "Basic Land Banking Concepts and Their Application to Low-Cost Housing in Thailand," in Angel, et al. (eds.), *op. cit.,* p. 423.

50. W.S.W. Lim, "Land Acquisition for Housing with Singapore as a Case Study," in *ibid.,* p. 409.

51. *Ibid.,* p. 408.

52. Ban Lee Goh, "Patterns of Landownership : Case Studies in Urban Inequalities," in Kee Check Cheong, et al. (eds.), *Malaysia: Some Contemporary Issues in Socio-Economic Development* (Kuala Lumpur : n.p., 1979), p. 69.

53. C. Noranitipadungkarn and C.A. Hagensiek, *Modernizing Chiengmai : A Study of Community Elites in Urban Development* (Bangkok : n.p., 1973), p. 15.

54. Lim, *op. cit.,* p. 404.

55. De Voy and Rodrongruang, *op. cit.,* p. 421.

56. O.P. Mathur (ed.), *Small Cities and National Development* (Nagoya : n.p., 1983); D. Kammeier and P. Swan (eds.), *Equity with Growth? Planning Perspectives for Small Towns in Developing Countries* (Bangkok : n.p., 1984).

57. D.A. Rondinelli, *Secondary Cities in Developing Countries : Policies for Diffusing Urbanization* (Delhi : n.p., 1983).

58. S. Angel and T. Charithamkijkul, "Slum Reconstruction : Land Sharing as an Alternative to Eviction in Bangkok," in Angel, et al. (eds.), *op. cit.,* pp. 430-460.

59. Baross, *op. cit.,* p. 322.

60. S.R. Cheema, "The Role of Voluntary Organisations," in S.R. Cheema and D.A. Rondinelli (eds.), *Decentralization and Development : Policy Implementation in Developing Countries* (Beverly Hills : n.p., 1983), pp. 203-228.

# 7

# Delivery of Public Services in Urban Korea with Special Reference to Shelter Problems

*Chung - Hyun Ro\**

There is probably not a single major city in the world without some form of housing problem. This is more true in primate cities in the Third World. Therefore, housing is a serious public issue and urban Korea is no exception.

Housing is often called "shelter." In some societies this is literally all that housing provides.[1] People in arctic wind and tropical downpour need protection from the elements. Shelter itself, especially for the millions of urban poor, is certainly a part of what is meant by "housing." It is this shelter which, with clothes and food, we Asians in our long history regarded as a key necessity of life. Today, shelter is an important indication of the welfare of the people and this is one of the important public services that national and local governments should be able to deliver.

In the last two decades Korea has made remarkable progress in economic growth. In 1962, for instance, the per capita income was only US$87, but in 1984 the per capita income of the Korean people increased to US$1, 998. That means the Korean income grew 23 times in the last 22 years.

However, the housing supply rate was not able to increase along with the economic growth. In 1960 the housing supply ratio of Korea was 84.2% but in 1980 the housing supply ratio decreased to 70.2%.

Therefore, the national government, in its 5th five-year economic plan (1982 - 1986), planned for the public sector to supply 618,000 housing units and for the private sector to supply 1,437,000 housing units. However, the housing construction business has not made as much progress as was planned. Thus, the housing supply rate dropped sharply to 66.6% as of now.[2] And the housing situation in the urban sector became even more serious.

---

\*Yonsei University, Seoul, Korea.

For these reasons, this chapter will examine:
1) the current housing situation,
2) the causal factors for the increase in the housing shortage,
3) structural aspects of housing administration,
4) housing policies, including finance, and
5) finally, this study will discuss the fundamental problems of housing in Korea and provide some policy alternatives and recommendations.

## The Current Housing Situation

The housing situation in Korea poses a growing problem because of the relatively slow increase of supply against the rapidly rising demand for new houses.[3] Ever since 1970, the housing demand has kept rising sharply, mainly due to the natural growth of population, the increasing number of households (owing to a trend toward the nuclear family system and especially the rural-urban migration) as well as natural loss by decay and demolition for urban renewal projects.

As of 1981 there were 8,150,000 households and there were 5,580,000 housing units. This means that we have a shortage of 2,570,000 housing units. Those who do not own their own house naturally have to live in rental space. Some households rent an entire house but many other households live in one or two rented rooms. More than 50% of all the households in large cities have to live in small rented rooms, rather than an entire rented house.[4] Furthermore, a great number of urban poor have to live in squatter settlements. In the Special City of Seoul alone, there are at least 150,000 squatter units.[5]

The fact that more than 50% of the people live either in rented rooms or squatter settlements is not only a quantitative problem but a problem of the quality of life as well. According to the survey conducted by the Korea Research Institute for Human Settlements (KRIHS), the average number of people who live in a rented room is 2.3 persons and the average household rents 1.8 rooms. Thus, the density of lower income housing is very high in urban Korea.

Density is not the only problem; infrastructure and other facilities are also problems. Water supply, bathrooms, and modern toilets are also still seriously lacking in the low income housing community.

## Causal Factors in the Housing Shortage

One can cite many cases illustrating the causal factors in the housing shortage. Among many factors, the Korean War and the rapid population movement from rural areas to large cities are the major causes of the housing shortage in Korea. During the Korean War, 514,955 houses were destroyed. This created a very serious housing problem. War-torn Korea and the government could not do much about this but provided for some temporary shelter for the homeless population. Korea took almost one decade for the reconstruction of housing and other public buildings from the ashes in the 1950s. Once this reconstruction period was over, industrialization and urbanization took place during the last 20 years. The huge waves of the rural-urban migrants to the large cities began. Between the years 1969 and 1970, for example, the city of Seoul alone had a 750,000 population increase. This sudden increase of population was primarily due to the social movement that is rural-urban migration. Such an enormous number of migrants created shelter problems in the urban sector, and they either had to live in one or two rented rooms or create a squatter settlement.

Another factor is that the housing supply has not been able to cope with the increasing housing demand. As one can see in Table 1, the increase of households nationally in 1970-75 was 19.2% and in 1975-80 it was 19.9%.

**Table 1**  Population, Household Trend and Housing Shortage, 1970-80

| Classification | 1970 | 1975 | 1980 |
|---|---|---|---|
| Population (1000 persons) | 30,882 | 34,707 | 37,436 |
| No. of households (1000 units) | 5,576 | 6,648 | 7,969 |
| Housing stock (1000 units) | 4,359 | 4,734 | 5,310 |
| Rate of housing shortage (%) | 21.8 | 28.8 | 33.3 |

| Classification | 1970 - 75 | 1975 - 80 |
|---|---|---|
| Rate of increase in households (%) | 19.2 | 19.9 |
| Rate of increase in housing stock (%) | 8.6 | 12.4 |

Source: Economic Planning Board, Korea.

The housing supply rate in these respective periods was 8.6% and 12.4%. Especially in the case of urbanized areas, the household increase in these respective years was 40.1% and 40.2%. Thus, the gap between demand and supply for housing is widening.

Another reason for the housing shortage in urban Korea is the demolition of existing shelter. In 1981, for instance, 30,000 existing housing units were demolished. Some were demolished by natural disasters such as flood and fire, but the vast majority of the existing shelter was demolished by government policy under the urban renewal project. This makes shelter problems even more severe, and the low income families living in such shelter as squatter units have to suffer even more. When the government demolishes one unit of squatter housing, two or three households living under the same roof lose their living base. If the policy for demolition of existing shelter continues, there will inevitably be uneasiness and even fear among the squatter dwellers. The consequence of this will create social tension and will have a great impact on social stability. It is therefore imperative to preserve existing shelter by means of self-improvement, rather than impose urban renewal projects which mean the demolition of existing shelter.

The government of Korea has so far been concentrating all its effort in developing key industries, and consequently has given low priority to the housing sector. This was evident by the fact that the average rate of investment in housing construction to the GNP during the last decade was 3.7%, as compared with the 6 - 8% recommended by the United Nations for the ESCAP region.[6]

In general, housing investment in Korea is broadly classified into that of the public and private sectors. The amount of housing investment in the public sector has been too small, as compared with private investment. This means that the private sector has been playing a leading role in the field of housing construction.

Table 2 shows the amount and sources of housing funds in the public and private sectors in 1975, and Figure 1 illustrates the schematic diagram of the housing fund flow.

Obtaining funds from the public sector does not seem to be improving. In 1980, for instance, 210,000 housing units were constructed, for which 2,613,000,-000,000 Won was invested. Only 18% of this total amount was from public funds; 82% of the funds came from private sources. This is a clear indication of how small a proportion of finance for housing was provided by the public sector until the early 1980s.

## Table 2  Amount and Sources of Housing Funds (1975)

| Sector | Amount of Funds Invested (Won) | Source of Funds | Conditions Terms (yrs.) | Interest Rate (%) |
|---|---|---|---|---|
| Public | 74 billion (22.7%) | National Budget Appropriation<br>National Housing Bond<br>Housing Lottery<br>Bank Funds<br>  Debentures<br>  Installment of Deposits<br>Housing Special Accounts in Local Governments<br>Foreign Loans<br>  AID<br>  IBRD | <br>5<br>20<br><br>15<br>20<br><br><br>20 - 25<br>20 | <br>6<br>4<br><br>8<br>14<br><br><br>8 - 10<br>8 |
| Private | 352 billion (77.3%) | "Non-Systemized" Funds<br>Key Fund, Savings<br>Real Estate Disposal<br>Retirement Fund<br>"Kye" Fund*<br>"Systemized" Funds (Borrowings)<br>Private Loans<br>Company Loans<br>Bank Loans<br>Other Financial Agencies | | |

Note: *"Kye" is a private installment deposit system consisting of 10 - 20 members of relatives or friends.

Source: Study on raising funds and housing financing system (summary) by KID, 1976.

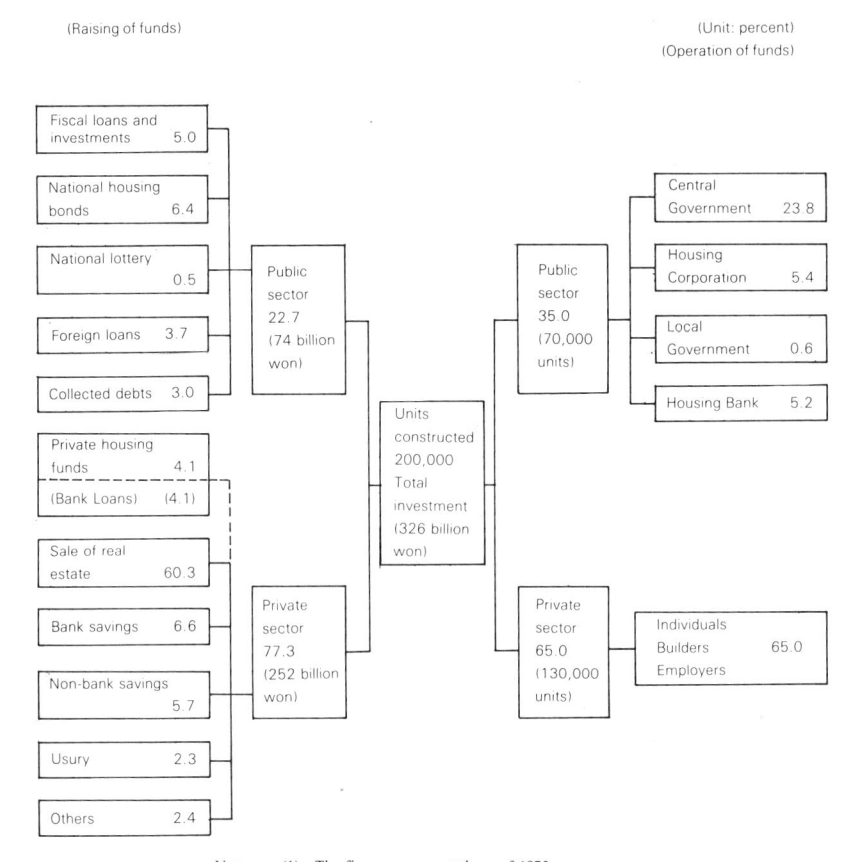

*Shelter Problems in Urban Korea  163*

(Raising of funds) (Unit: percent)
(Operation of funds)

| Raising of funds | % |
|---|---|
| Fiscal loans and investments | 5.0 |
| National housing bonds | 6.4 |
| National lottery | 0.5 |
| Foreign loans | 3.7 |
| Collected debts | 3.0 |
| Private housing funds | 4.1 |
| (Bank Loans) | (4.1) |
| Sale of real estate | 60.3 |
| Bank savings | 6.6 |
| Non-bank savings | 5.7 |
| Usury | 2.3 |
| Others | 2.4 |

Public sector 22.7 (74 billion won)
Private sector 77.3 (252 billion won)

Units constructed 200,000
Total investment (326 billion won)

Public sector 35.0 (70,000 units)
Private sector 65.0 (130,000 units)

| Operation of funds | % |
|---|---|
| Central Government | 23.8 |
| Housing Corporation | 5.4 |
| Local Government | 0.6 |
| Housing Bank | 5.2 |
| Individuals Builders Employers | 65.0 |

Notes: (1) The figures represent those of 1975
(2) The figures for the private sector are based on KID survey
(3) Source: Study on raising funds and housing financing system (summary) by KID, 1976

**Figure 1** Flow chart of housing funds

## Structural Aspects of Housing Administration

*Central Housing Administration Organization.* As the central housing administration organization, the Ministry of Construction (MOC) carries out the direct housing administrative functions with reference to the national housing policy formulation, and the Economic Planning Board (EPB), the Ministry of Finance (MOF), and the Ministry of Home Affairs (MOH) execute indirect housing administrative functions in cooperation with the MOC. In addition, the Annuity Bureau of the Ministry of Government Administration carries out special administrative functions in respect of housing.

MOC carries out the administrative functions pertinent to housing survey, long-term housing demand estimation, the establishment of the housing construction plan, and supervision and control over various housing projects. EPB has the administrative function of establishing a housing investment plan, in addition to the establishment and execution of an economic development plan, budgeting, resource mobilization and investment fund allocation, technical development, international economic cooperation, etc.. MOF controls and supervises the Korea Housing Bank (KHB) in addition to its main role of management of currency and financial affairs, the taxation system, foreign exchange and public properties. MOH has the function of supervising and controlling the housing projects being carried out by the local authorities. In addition, the Annuity Bureau of the Ministry of Government Administration deals with housing projects for homeless civil servants, and the Office of Veterans deals with the provision of housing for soldiers, both active and retired.

In this framework of a horizontally decentralized administrative system, MOC establishes and executes housing construction plans in cooperation with other central administrative agencies. For instance, the establishment of a comprehensive housing plan, the conduct of housing surveys and the keeping of statistical data, the functions of supervision and control, and design and technical development of housing are the principal functions vested in the MOC. The function of design and technical development includes: (1) approval of housing project design; (2) preparation and diffusion of standard designs; (3) supervision and control over technicalities in housing construction operation. Miscellaneous functions are: (1) urban development and redevelopment plan, construction and remodelling; (2) inspection and technical examination of housing complex plans; (3) approval of housing complex development projects; (4) designation of housing complexes.

As for the housing administrative functions on the local government level, these are carried out by the Housing Bureau of the Seoul City government, by Construction Bureaus of each provincial government and the Pusan City government, and by the Construction Section of each city and county office. The local housing administrative functions differ according to area and the level of local government, because of the different housing situations and size of budgets.

*Korea National Housing Corporation (KNHC)*. The Korea National Housing Corporation was established in July 1962 for the purpose of ensuring housing stability for the people and stepping up public welfare in conformity with the government's welfare policy. Since then the Korea National Housing Corporation has been playing a leading role in alleviating the housing shortage.

The KNHC has contributed substantially in effecting changes, particularly in the field of housing construction. From its establishment in 1962 until 1983 the KNHC has completed a total of 293,037 housing units, intended for homeless people. These include apartment houses as flats, and row houses. Many of these were smaller type dwelling units, supplied to the urban low-income class. The size differences were as follows: 50% were smaller than 43 square meters; 48% were 43 - 83 square meters; and 2% were larger than 83 square meters.

These completed housing units were located across the nation at 76 locations, including 47 cities. This reflects the KNHC's intention to ensure a balanced development and growth among the smaller towns and cities. However, due to the rapid population increase in the large cities (which was prompted by the nation-wide industrialization process), more than 46% of the housing construction had to be concentrated in four major cities, namely Seoul, Incheon, Pusan and Taegu. The number of housing units completed in Seoul was just over 29% of the total.

Although the KNHC is basically in charge of the housing construction for the low income class, it has also built houses for other special purposes, such as for workers working on industrial estates; for the evacuees from the urban redevelopment areas; for the families of the dead or wounded veterans of the Korean and Vietnam wars; and for the victims of various natural disasters who are in need of subsidies from the state. Another function of the KNHC is the building and managing of rental houses for foreign diplomats, members of the UNC personnel and other special groups.

Of the housing units completed by the KNHC, 71% are ownership houses for sale, 25% are rental houses, and the remaining 4% are houses built under contract. The large proportion of ownership houses in the total housing scene reflects the Korean people's long held, traditional preference for house ownership. This strong feeling, that one must live in one's own house, is practically unchanged.

To help the low income class acquire houses smaller than 83 square meters, the Government is providing long-term and low-interest loans.

**Table 3** Housing Construction by KNHC (1962 - 1983)

| Total Number Completed | Leased | Sold | Built Under Contract |
| --- | --- | --- | --- |
| 293,037 | 73,237 | 207,251 | 12,549 |
| ('61 - '82) | (25%) | (71%) | (4%) |

Source: Korea National Housing Corporation, 1985.

On average, the KNHC built 1,100 houses a year during the period from 1962 to 1970, but this figure increased to 10,000 units by the mid-1970s, then to more than 30,000 units in 1979 and to 40,000 units in the 1980s. This escalation in the KNHC's housing construction may be partly attributable to the population increase. However, a series of earlier economic development plans brought about growth in the national economy, which increased investment in public housing construction. Thus priority was given to housing construction, resulting in the development of this field.

Due to the social disintegration caused by the division of the nation into the south and the north, following Liberation in 1945, and by the ensuing Korean War in the early 1950s, it has taken a relatively long time before the investment in housing construction and housing policies could regain its proper and stable functioning. In 1962, the Korean Government launched its first five year economic development plan, incorporating the housing construction programs and establishing the Korea National Housing Corporation as an agency of the Government, to execute the programs. However, in the following 10 years, until the time when the second five-year economic development plan had terminated, top priority was given to the development of industries. Thus, inevitably the KNHC's housing construction activities remained at a very low level.

In 1977, with the beginning of the fourth five-year economic development plan, the situation changed. The Government chose as one of its three major policy goals the social development programs designed to promote the welfare of the public. This meant a new turning point in the growth in the supply of public housing and a boost for the housing construction of the KNHC.[7]

**Chart 1**   Public Housing Construction in 1984

Unit: 1000

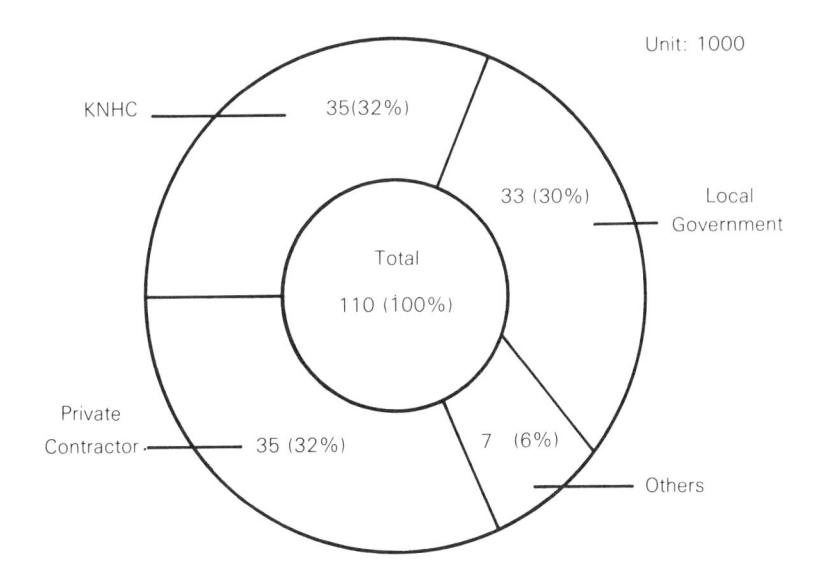

- KNHC: 35 (32%)
- Local Government: 33 (30%)
- Others: 7 (6%)
- Private Contractor: 35 (32%)
- Total: 110 (100%)

Source: Korea Housing Corporation, 1985.

The Korean National Housing Corporation has established two subsidiary companies to supply a large number of housing construction components, precast panels, and building bricks. The Hansung Prefab. Company was established in 1971 to supply such prefabricated components as PC panels and other components exclusively to the KNHC. The annual production capacity of the PC panels is equivalent to 5,200 housing units of 13 pyung (42.9m$^2$) type apartment. The Korea Silicate Bricks Company was established in 1975 with capital of 2,500 million Won, invested wholly by the KNHC, and a loan of 11 million D.M. in kind from the Dorstener Company, West Germany. The Company has an annual capacity of approximately 154 million bricks composed of N.F. (Normal Format) and D.F. (Dunn Format) sizes, in order to construct 10,000 housing units of 15 pyung (49.5m$^2$) type.

*Korea Housing Bank.* The Korea Housing Bank was established as a special corporation in 1967, in accordance with the enactment of the KBH Law aimed at supporting and promoting housing construction for low and lower-middle income people. Its main functions are to loan funds and deal with the related matters of management of funds for housing construction, housing transactions and site development.

The major sources of funds are its capital assets, contract savings, issuance of housing bonds, borrowings from government, foreign loans and the issuance of housing lottery tickets. The funds secured from these sources are directly loaned to the low and middle income groups or indirectly to the KNHC, local authorities, public agencies and private commercial builders. National housing funds, which are usually secured from the issuance of housing bonds and the introduction of foreign loans, are sub-loaned at an annual interest rate of 8%, with a repayment period of 15 years. Private welfare housing funds, which are secured from the operation of KHB funds, are loaned to those who have the means of loan repayment and are capable of bearing partial financial burdens in the construction and purchasing of houses. However, the conditions of the loan often have the effect of isolating the potential customers, owing to the size of the amount involved and the repayment terms, thus resulting in a heavy financial burden to the low income group. In addition, undue limitations in the operation of KHB funds hamper the positive and broader performance of its function, which is to further housing construction.[8]

*Other Agencies.* There are provincial and city governments that have administrative units for housing. They are primarily concerned with the construction of low cost housing for low income people.

Thus, one can see a good number of housing administrative units at the central level as well as at provincial and local levels. The problem, however, is lack of administrative coordination. When the city of Seoul, for instance, is to plan housing construction, there is very little means of coordination with the Housing Bureau of the Ministry of Construction. Nor does the city of Seoul consult with the Korea National Housing Corporation, which is established primarily for the construction of housing for middle and low income people.

Because of this lack of coordination in the construction of housing, there seems to be some duplication and confusion in housing administration.

**Fundamental Problems and Some Policy Alternatives**

As mentioned earlier, there are two aspects to the fundamental problem. The first problem is the rapid increase of housing demand and the slow supply. According to the Ministry of Construction, the ratio of the household increase between 1971 and 1984 was 3.5 and the ratio of housing supply was only 0.9. Because of this gap, the price of houses went up 39 times and the price of the housing site went up 108 times. During the same period average household earnings increased 28 times. Therefore, one can easily see that the price of housing and especially of the housing site greatly exceeded the income of households.

The government has just begun to realize the importance of supplying houses in the public sector, and it was planned that the public sector will construct 200,000 units of housing next year, against this year's 150,000 units.[9] Again these houses will be built in large cities such as Seoul, Pusan and Taejon.

Another problem is that, while urban Korea has an increasing shortage of housing, the size of newly constructed houses is getting larger and more luxurious. According to a survey made by the Economic Planning Board (EPB), the average size of a house in 1970 was 22 pyung;[10] by 1980, the average size had increased to 43.29 pyung. This shows that the space of the average house doubled in the last ten years. Houses larger than 40 pyung increased in the same period to 378%, or nearly 4 times. It is understood that the average size of a house in Japan is 24.3 pyung. Korea, which has about 1/5 of the per capita income of Japan, has houses twice as large as the average Japanese house. This creates the price hike in housing and also creates the problem of social disparity. If this trend continues, low income people will have to face ever increasing difficulty in purchasing their own house. Furthermore, a greater degree of social tension is inevitable between the class which owns larger houses and the low income masses who see a slim chance of ever having their own house, and who have to live in one or two small rented rooms or sometimes in a squatter settlement.

*Some Alternatives.* In order to overcome these housing shortage problems in Korea, there is a strong need to develop a house building industry, particularly by the private sector. Most of these house builders in Korea do not have enough capital and the government needs to support the house building industry, especially the medium size builders at provincial levels.

Because of the capital shortage and limited amount of low interest loans from the Korea Housing Bank, the housing construction firms have to get the loan from private financial sources, with high interest. This is the reason why the price of a house has increased so much. If a private housing construction firm is to build 300 apartment units for low income families, the company needs to have 11.6 billion Won, in which case the public sector, such as the Housing Bank of Korea, supplies 21% of the total cost and the company has to invest the remaining 79%.

If the house builders cannot sell the houses and are not able to collect the money, they will have to suffer because of high interest rates, and sometimes they may even face bankruptcy. Therefore, it is imperative that the public sector put higher priority on supporting the housing construction industry, through financial means and other incentive systems. However, it has to be very clear that these housing industries are not for the construction of large and luxurious houses but for smaller, inexpensive houses for low income families.

Building material is another important aspect of the housing industry. The cost of materials in house building in Korea accounts for an average of 70% of the total cost, with some variations, depending on the type and quality of housing. Therefore, the housing administration authorities should be able to encourage the house building industry to standardize to produce greater quantities of building materials, and to create distribution channels for the materials in such a way that the end user can purchase directly without exploitation by the middle man.

Housing site supply is also an important aspect of the housing problem. As rapid urbanization is taking place, the price of land has gone up even higher, and there has also been the problem of land speculation. The major source of housing sites has been the government's land readjustment plan, and also the site development projects undertaken by the KNHC. This system has played an important role of being the basic site supply channel for new town development projects, aimed at preventing the over-concentration of population and the influx of industrial facilities into large cities.

Another channel of housing site supply is the housing site development activities carried out by private real estate dealers. Of course, the size of these as compared with the public source is rather small. However, this sometimes creates the problem of speculation. Therefore, the newly established Korea

Land Development Corporation should be able to develop a massive housing site, particularly for low income families.

The housing distribution channel must be improved. Most of the housing transactions are conducted through brokers who are called *Pok Duk Bang*. Often these brokers are older people, ill-qualified and inexperienced, mostly not fit for any other productive job. Therefore, there is a strong need for real estate brokers to be licensed by the government, according to their qualifications. As massive apartment complexes have been erected by big export-oriented companies, a group of younger brokers has also emerged. They sometimes play the intermediary roles between the apartment builders and the speculators. Sometimes they themselves speculate, and this has created an enormous social problem. Therefore, there is a strong need to establish the legal code, not only to regulate the qualification of brokers but to control their anti-social activities.

Finally, it must be understood that the role of the public service is not to look after all the problems of society, but to create favorable conditions so that the people can easily solve their own problems. Housing is a good example. Government has to increase loans so that people can construct their own houses with these loans. For this reason this chapter seeks to illustrate how such a policy can be implemented through legalization and self-help projects for their own shelters.

## An Experimental Study on the Improvement of Squatter Settlements

*The Case of Nankok-Dong, Seoul, Korea.* The writer and his Institute of Urban Studies and Development have done a research experiment for the improvement of a squatter settlement in Nankok-Dong. The reason for doing the study in this particular area is that there is highly concentrated squatter housing and to try to see if there is any possibility of legalizing the squatters and improving the squatter settlement through self-help projects.

*General Background of Residents.* Through surveys, it was found that 92% of the householders are male, and that householders aged from 30 - 50 are 89.2% of the total. This age spectrum shows that most of the householders are persons having active economic ability.

In regard to the householders' occupations, 38.7% of them are laborers and this percentage forms the largest portion of the occupational group. Most of the squatter residents in this area (76.7%) are migrants from provincial areas; in particular, 60.8% are from agricultural and fishery areas. This shows that the rural population moving into the Seoul metropolitan area is concentrated heavily in this kind of squatter area. The average number of family members in each household is 5 to 6 (51.4%) and 22.8% have more than 7 family members. The remainder consists of households with 4 or less family members. This indicates that the urban poor have a greater number of children than ordinary households in Korea.

*Physical Conditions and Residential Environment.* The survey found that the plot size and floor space of each is very small, in that 62.7% of the houses are less than 8 pyung in plot size. This size of living space is far short of 2.4 pyung per person, which corresponds to the minimum required residential space. Houses with less than two bedrooms are 76.9% of the total, and thus in most of the families children use one bedroom, without separating male and female children. The residents in this community mostly feel dissatisfaction with the existing residential conditions and they are especially dissatisfied with their children's life environment.

*Legalization of the Squatter Houses.* The survey result of the Nankok-Dong area shows clearly that the residents of the squatter houses hope that the city government will legally stabilize the existing settlement condition. The reasons that the residents hope for a policy of legalization are as follows: 1) the lack of economic capacity (18.6%); 2) the belief that the living environment can be improved over the present situation (12.8%); 3) the hope of having their own houses (12.3%).

In regard to home improvement, 73.6% of the respondents answered that they will improve their existing squatter house in the area if their situation can be legalized and methods for on the spot improvements are suggested, such as: rebuilding or repairing the current house (55.3%), and new construction after pulling down the existing squatter house (23.5%).

As to the building site, 79.6% of the respondents answered that they will pay for the land, which is currently owned by the public sector, on a long term basis.

*Some Proposed Policies.* Some alternatives for a desirable solution of the problems of squatter areas are suggested as follows. The first step is to legalize the existing squatter houses. The second step would be to improve the housing on the spot. The third step would be to construct some community employment facility, in order to improve the residents' earnings, by making use of the unemployed labor force of the area. The fourth step is to remake the area into a new residential compound, in which reasonable, small size housing or low storey apartment buildings can be erected. Some effective housing financial systems should be established so that residents can get a good portion of low interest loans from the National Housing Bank on a long term basis. The city government, of course, has to build an infrastructure for this community, and the mass production of building materials of a certain standard should be encouraged, so that low income people can purchase building materials at a reasonable price.

If all these conditions are met, it will be much easier for urban poor such as these people to own their own house. In fact these houses can be built by the residents themselves because they are in many cases, the carpenters plasterers, and other skilled laborers who have made a great contribution to the development of this great city of Seoul today. This is a concrete example of how the housing situation can be improved through legalization and self-help projects on the spot.

**Concluding Remarks**

In conclusion, the writer would like to stress the following points:

1. Higher priority should be given to national housing policies, particularly for low income families.
2. The public sector should be encouraged, by giving low interest loans and even subsidies to house builders for the supply of rental housing. This is important because newly married couples and nuclear families are not able to purchase a house immediately, and they can in the meantime live in a rental house until they save enough money to purchase their own house. Furthermore, there should be a conceptual change from the idea of owning a house to the concept of residing in a house, even a rented one.
3. The Housing Policy Council has already been established in recent years under the chairmanship of the Minister of the Economic Planning Board, to screen the housing policies proposed by various agencies concerned with housing. However, there should be a better means of administrative coordination between housing administrative agencies such as Housing Bureau of MOC, Housing Unit of City of Seoul, Korea Housing Bank, Korea Housing Corporation, Korea Land Development Corporation, and other housing administrative units of local governments.
4. Finally, the delivery of public service should be performed at the grass-roots level, with clientele-oriented policy, not bureaucrat-centered policy. It must also be understood that delivery of service can be made possible by the people themselves. The self-help housing project is a good example.

Korea has reached a critical point in housing. Merely building many apartments or housing units is not enough; the people who need housing have to be able to afford it financially. For example, 6,642 apartment units constructed by the Korea National Housing Corporation and 4,447 units built by the private sector are still vacant. This is 20% of the total number of apartment units constructed by the two sectors. The greatest problem is not the actual construction of housing units, but the ability of people to pay for them.

As Francis Bacon once said, "Houses are built to live in and not to look on; therefore, let use be preferred before uniformity, except where both may be had."

**Notes**

1. Wallace F. Smith, *Housing: The Social and Economic Elements* (Berkeley: University of California Press, 1970).

2. *Dong A Ilbo,* June 15, 1985.

3. Sung Do Jang and Hang Koo Cho, "Low Cost Housing in Korea," in L.J. Goodman, et al. (eds.), *Low Cost Housing Technology* (Honolulu, Hawaii: East - West Center), p. 136.

4. Myung Chan Whang, *Jutaek Chung Chaek Ron (Housing Policy)* (Seoul: Kyung Wha Won, 1985), p. 58.

5. For detailed information see Chung - Hyun Ro, *An Empirical Research for Improvement of Squatter Settlement: Case of Nankok-Dong* (Seoul: Institute of Urban Studies and Development, Yonsei University, 1983), pp. 323 - 326.

6. *Ibid.*

7. Korea Housing Corporation, *KNHC: Annual Report, 1985.*

8. Sung Do Jang and Hang Koo Cho, *op. cit.,* pp. 145 - 147.

9. *The Korea Times,* September 28, 1985, p. 5.

10. One pyung is equal to 6 × 6 feet.

11. For details see Chung - Hyun Ro, *op. cit.*

# 8

# Strategies Management in the Delivery of an Effective Transportation System in Singapore

*Chee Meow Seah**

The transportation system of any polity can be evaluated from the perspectives of the users, the suppliers and the coordinators. Even then, each of these groups is also involved in different levels and patterns of transport requirements. In a sense, transportation is not as simple as seeking the means of connecting human and non-human resources from the sources of supply to situations of need. Had it been a simple logistics exercise, perhaps much of the perplexities, bewilderments and agonies which have confronted policy makers might not have occurred. There are just too many intervening and contextual variables which policy makers must recognize and user and supplier groups must at least grudgingly acknowledge.

One basic formula in discussing transportation stems from the so-called "distance/time" ratio. According to this premise there are certain built-in economic, social, personal or related costs which affect the propensity on the part of people to travel. This factor is also responsible for the size of towns or settlements. Distance/time ratio, however, can be improved by technological developments in the realm of locomotion. The use of animal powered transportation, for example, has enabled men in the past to travel a much longer distance than had that been done by unassisted commuting. Similarly, the development of mechanized transport modes has enabled even longer distances to be covered within the same period of time, and consequently, even settlements or urbanized areas could expand spatially while people could afford not to live too close to their place of employment or economic activities. The same could be said of traffic management and engineering skills which have enabled better efficiency to be obtained with prevailing transport modes.

Yet, technology and infrastructural improvements do not provide a logical extension to the distance/time ratio. The increased tempo of economic develop-

*National University of Singapore, Singapore.

ment could lead to a larger number of passenger trips, while towns might not have the capacity to absorb these people or even acquire the means of transport. Over-congestion would simply lead to inefficiency and greater societal costs while persistent aggravation of this problem could ultimately lead to the decline of the cities.

At the same time, there are also inherent contradictions even in the realm of technological and infrastructural developments. For example, improvements in audio-visual communication could reduce the need for interpersonal (or face-to-face) contacts and hence, a noticeable decline in the number of transport trips could be registered. However, to merely place one's hope on such expectations could be disappointing. Transport trips have been increasing rather than affirming the correctness of the inverse relationship between communication improvements and trip frequencies. There thus seems to be more variables which have prevented such a formula/relationship to be realized. For policy makers, their dilemma has not been ameliorated, for unless urgent solutions could be found, the very vitality of their polities could be seriously undermined.

What role could policy makers take? While the range of inter-modal and intra-modal improvements could increase the options available to them, the policy makers would have to decide on role-definition. Should they assume the role as suppliers of transport facilities? Should they abstain altogether and let the economic and market forces realize an appropriate equilibrium? Should they try to intervene in affecting supply/demand? Could the problem of efficient transport ever be solved, especially in the built-up urban areas? Or should not the policy makers think of even more drastic means such as the relocation of urban areas, thus preventing existing problem areas from aggravation?

There are unfortunately no tailor-made solutions. The importance of a viable transport policy has always been clouded by other more pressing considerations such as strategies of economic growth or types of political demands and goods. Even the nature of the political culture could affect the policy makers' judgement on transport solutions.

The difficulties in seeking an appropriate transportation policy does not mean that such a policy is not desired or necessary. Yet, it would seem that on the whole, the commuters could also absorb innumerable inconveniences while the government could at times, try not to seek any solution at all. These two factors do not mean that the prevailing situation could permit governmental ineptitude since manifested public frustration could lead to systemic instabilities of a widespread nature. Ultimately, therefore, policy makers have to work out some forms of solutions as the bare minimum for political survival; they too would have to depend on the bureaucrats for administrative, managerial and technical expertise in ensuring that their people would have access to an important social facility, namely, the right to get where, when, how and at the minimum cost.

For Singapore the importance of an efficient form of domestic transport would seem rather patent. As a city-state whose survival is based on its keen competitive edge and service facilities, the importance of an efficient domestic system of transportation would thus seem obvious. Yet, the logic of a comprehensive policy on transport seems to have eluded the government until about two decades ago when tentative moves were made toward what could eventually be termed as a comprehensive strategy in regulating the patterns of domestic transportation. Presumably the bulk of the trip patterns would be adequately catered for.

This chapter discusses the background of the transportation problem in Singapore. The first section shows that the problem certainly went back to a relatively early period and that *ad hoc* measures were mainly proposed as attempts to lighten the problem. The second section discusses the philosophy of the government on this issue and how the approach to the transportation problem is conditioned also by contextual variables which would make the resort to other forms of strategies management difficult. The third section discusses the policy measures which were subsequently taken to solve this issue. While the problem may have been largely resolved and the implementation of a comprehensive transportation policy seems to have been realized, it is argued in the final section that the style which was responsible for much of the policy making process in the 1970s might become less relevant. Attention is focused on what in perspective may seem to be an innocuous issue, namely the taxi (or paratransit) issue.

## The Problem Defined

The beginnings of the transportation network were established by Sir Stamford Raffles shortly after he founded this island for the British in 1819. Raffles proposed different zones for the main religious-racial-cultural communities, but at the same time, he suggested that the town of Singapore be based on the grid-pattern. This pattern would undoubtedly facilitate domestic transportation since accessibility and mobility would be a matter of knowing the "grid-point" references. The network implied relatively even terrain and indeed many of the small hillocks in the designated town area were thus levelled. This action also enabled most of the swampy grounds along the Singapore River to be filled up. Once the grid-pattern was established the construction of dwellings followed suit, with houses merely following the decided pattern. Even today, the implications of the grid-pattern on land-use could still be seen in the older parts of the city.

In those days, the main forms of locomotion were animal-assisted. Horses and oxen indeed provided much of the transport trips and as mechanized locomotion was not easily foreseen, even the grid network did not take into account the impact which could be made by such modes. In any case, it would appear unrealistic to expect Raffles or the colonial officers to plan extremely wide road infrastructure to cater for an unknown future. Their problem was mainly to ensure how many of those roads would not deteriorate. Deep ruts and potholes were far too common on laterite roads. These were caused by the frequent thunderstorms and the heavily-burdened carts drawn by oxen.

Yet, even in the 19th century, the issue of efficient transportation did surface. The search for a slightly more efficient mode and also to prevent congestion along the then "arterial" roads was pursued. There was even a suggestion that a canal be dug between Outram and the Singapore River so that goods could be moved by ferry boats using the canal's gradient as a main source of power. The idea, though mooted and discussed, was finally shelved mainly because news of mechanized locomotion such as the use of railways was creating a new source of interest. Indeed, the early railway lines transversed the heavily-built "Chinatown".[1]

The beginnings of the automobile certainly injected a new dimension into the issue of domestic transportation. Cars could be found alongside animal-assisted carriages and cyclists. As the number of cars increased, new forms of regulation had to be introduced. Signals at road intersections were essential, and in view of the grid-pattern, there were far too many signals which had to be installed. Traffic speed was thus reduced to a crawl. By the late 1930s, a commission chaired by G. Trimmer was appointed to examine problems of domestic transportation. The issues raised by the commission seem familiar to most transport planners even today: the problems of traffic-mix, the extent of government regulation, the issue of congestion costs, the indiscriminate use of roadspace for unplanned purposes, such as goods placed alongside roads, the issue of parking and roadside parking and how to deal with the "stop-go" situations inherent in a network full of road intersections. The commission suggested solutions equally familiar to road planners today: revise the ordinance on building controls so that tall buildings would have to incorporate parking facilities, the possibility of multi-storied car-parks in the Central Business Area (CBD), the segregation of traffic by the construction of separate cyclist lanes and rigid traffic enforcement to ensure that cyclists would not meander into the main transport network, the conversion of two-ways to one-ways, and a general statement to motorists and car owners not to expect "point-to-point" accessibility and to refrain from "garage" (or long-term) parking in the city areas.[2]

Despite the recommendations, there was administrative inertia. Indeed, the various matters pertaining to road planning or matters affecting existing and proposed roads were left to the Singapore Improvement Trust (SIT), itself set up on the recommendation of an earlier committee to look at the issue of urban housing congestion and public health. The issue of road transportation was thus shelved and was never to be reviewed subsequently.

Even at the end of the war, transport was seldom mentioned as a factor to be given attention. The concerns then, other than political agitations, were to ensure that the basic needs such as employment and housing could be catered for. The magnitude of the housing problem was largely responsible for the Master Plan. This Plan basically sought to review in a fundamental manner the premises of town planning itself dated to the days of Singapore's founding. The Master Plan was granted legislative authorization and subsequent development had to conform with the guidelines of the Master Plan. Briefly, the Plan hoped to freeze the existing size of the city and channel new growth in the forms of new or satellite towns. In a sense, the planners felt there was a certain "optimal" size for the city, perhaps; transportation requirements were also implicitly acknowledged.[3]

This blueprint was partially modified by the People's Action Party government which took over office in 1959. In its zeal to construct as many housing units as possible, the government, through the Housing and Development Board (HDB), had to build such units on whatever land that could be available. Land thus had to be "salvaged" from whatever sources (taking into consideration certain constraints such as limits on acquisition of private property). A familiar source of land were those areas made available as a result of massive fires which razed large squatter areas. If the provisions of the Master Plan were adhered to, then there would be further constraints on the HDB and issues such as density ratio and permissibility of land for housing purpose could drastically reduce the number of such units that could be constructed. Some of the provisions of the Master Plan were thus given less recognition.

The success of the government in public housing has been acknowledged - whether measured in terms of cost reduction, number of units built or improvements in quality of accommodation.[4] However, the presence of these early housing estates also resulted in a new series of problems. For example, relatively inadequate attention was given to the issue of road space or ancillary facilities such as car parks, since it was assumed (rightly, if the purpose of low cost housing were taken to mean housing for the poor) that the people would not be in a position to afford private vehicles. When an increasing number of them, however, did purchase such vehicles, the congestion problem became extremely serious. Secondly, as these early estates were constructed mainly for purpose of dwelling, unnecessary trips were generated simply because the residents had to commute elsewhere for work, schooling, and even for the payment of services such as public utilities. The residents, too, had to commute to social, shopping and cultural areas since such facilities were not found in the housing estates. As the main public transport were the buses, and as the bus companies had difficulties in providing adequate ridership capacities, long and unpredictable commuting time became a main source of complaint. This had the effect of encouraging many working members in the households to pool their resources for the purchase of private vehicles which could be used to supplement the poor level of service afforded by the bus companies. At the same time, the resort to other forms such as "pirate" taxis or the unauthorized use of vans and lorries for passenger trips became a serious issue for the law enforcement agencies.

Yet, despite these problems it would seem that most residents tend to have developed a certain stoicism by bearing up with these difficulties. The problem did not become a political issue and the ruling party continued to consolidate more support than ever before. Yet, the government realized the need to review the Master Plan and reexamine new possibilities of land-use for Singapore. A team, with United Nations Development Program (UNDP), came up with what could be termed as the Concept Plan. This team which first started work in 1967 could be said to have sufficient latitude in its conceptualizations, for by then, the government was sufficiently bold to decide that as the housing situation was no longer that critical, it was possible to embark on urban redevelopment or renewal. The Concept Plan served mainly as a guide, but it did not have legislative authorization. Thus, most government plans were guided by both the Concept and the Master Plan.

The planners should be complimented on the multi-variable approach adopted. Transport needs were noted as well. Among the highlights of the Concept Plan were the suggestions of corridors of intense development (which incidentally favored the development of expressways and mass rapid transit), and a pattern of new towns, expressways, and even a MRT to cater to Singapore's future.

In the meantime, the government continued to pursue a vigorous policy of urban redevelopment. New places such as Golden Mile, Shenton Way and the Golden Shoe projects were conceived and many of these areas saw intense development. More office space - and employment - was generated in the CBD. The logical consequence was the additional burden placed on the transportation facilities. To the government, the makings of a political bombshell were all there - serious regulatory problems caused by illegal public transport operators, inadequacy of parking and related facilities, the long waiting periods for most commuters, the unevenness in the quality of public transport, and conflict of interests among the bus companies and even their workers. Even private car owners had their grievances. Also, of even greater consequence for the government was the effect of a deterioration in domestic transportation service on the continuing vitality of Singapore's CBD. Policy measures had to be found to ensure that congestion costs would not outweigh whatever economic benefits were associated with the CBD.[6]

## Government Philosophy and Impact of Contextual Variables

A major dilemma facing the government was the type of role it should adopt. The government was noted to be "interventionist," but what was not clear was the extent of its involvement. For example, in public housing, public utilities and even in certain areas of economic development, the government would directly participate and even assume responsibility for the management of these facilities. Should it do the same for domestic transportation, an issue with immense significance and probably affecting the bulk of Singapore's population?

The government had chosen not to take over the role as the main supplier of transport needs. It would still stick to its regulatory role, except that it would be extremely active in initiating measures as deemed essential for the alleviation of the transport problem and, hopefully, contributing to the development of a comprehensive transportation policy. By not seeking to assume responsibility for the running of public transport, the government perhaps was aware of the dilemmas facing many national, state and even town or county governments desperately having to bail out commuter services under their control. Economic and financial viability were crucial factors to the government even though assuming total control of this key service could have immediate (though perhaps questionable long-term) political dividends.

A major contextual problem was the time variable. Transport trips in congestion situations were costly in terms of time, and the congestion problem was such that those affected would also want immediate, remedial measures. The Concept Plan did outline the main additions to the infrastructural network, but even the implementation of that would take time and would not necessarily guarantee success. If the issue could be contained within the shortest possible time, adverse political consequences could also be forestalled.

The second issue was the nature of land use planning in Singapore. While the HDB had in the meanwhile shifted to the concept of comprehensive planning for new towns, there was no doubt that the major generator of economic and employment opportunities would still be in the CBD. The decision to proceed with urban renewal would merely accentuate the congestion problem in the CBD as new jobs and office spaces would be created and more trips thus generated. Planners had thus to assume that a large part of the commuting to the city area would remain a permanent feature and what could be done would be to minimize unnecessary trips to the CBD wherever possible.

The third dimension of the problem was the differentiated nature of the clientele groups and the methods of commuting. The main group having to use public transport would be the relatively less affluent having to depend on the buses. Walking or cycling had never been popular, perhaps for practical reasons such as the difficulties of avoiding the high humidity and the frequent thunderstorms. Taxis performed a supplementary role to the public transport network, although their importance could be enhanced with more vehicles and effective management. On the other hand, private car users were not restricted to the group with wealth even though this group would be associated with multi-car ownership. A large number of "salary-men" would have saved enough to purchase cars and there would also be a percentage of those who could own such vehicles on the basis of pooled resources among family members. While it would be easy to label them as "marginal owners," their need and usage would not always be marginal. As the level of public transport further deteriorated, the number of such marginal car owners increased.

The fourth dimension to the problem was the inadequacy of the administrative structure to handle the problem. Matters on transportation were generally handled by a division in a ministry. It was only in 1967 that the Ministry of Communications was created specifically to be responsible for all modes of transport. Yet, this Ministry, while an important development in itself, would have to depend on the over-riding political goodwill and also the assistance of other agencies or ministries. Among those external agencies would be the Public Works Department, the Police Department and even the Ministry of Finance. Inter-ministerial coordination was thus essential, although in the Singapore context, the direction and extent of political clout was undoubtedly important.

Finally, one important dimension which has to be noted was the elitist nature of decision making. This decision making was also of a closed-door nature. As effective solutions to the transport problem would involve not merely improving logistics linkages but also behavioral patterns of commuters, the almost silent neglect of public participation in policy formulation could create situations of administrative "overkill" or gaps existing between policy implementation and feedback. Undoubtedly, the political leadership was of the opinion that it had access to its various institutionalized grassroots organizations for feedback while it could also ensure that the bureaucratic agencies would remain responsive.

Nonetheless, the government was in a fortunate situation insofar as the popular mood was one of anxiety, if not desperation, with respect to the need to improve the level of transportation effectiveness and efficiency. Under such circumstances the people were more than willing to bear with inconveniences if there were convincing promises of a more effective remedy in the forthcoming future. By capitalizing on this mood, it was possible to initiate a wide ranging series of measures while simultaneously silencing those groups with adverse reactions to specific or the general approach of the government's measures.

**Policy Measures and Effectiveness**

In the area of transport planning four groups of measures could be analyzed. The first would be the improvement of existing modes. The second would be traffic management schemes. The third would be infrastructural improvement schemes, such as increases in the length of existing road network, or traffic engineering schemes such as computerized signalling. There would also be the final package of solutions which examined new modes for possible incorporation. Yet, whatever the measures introduced, it would be a fallacy to try to solve the transport problem: at the most, the objective sought for would be the amelioration of the problem to a manageable dimension.

The more immediate approach for policy-makers would be to decide whether the solutions are of a short or long term character. Short term measures would undoubtedly be essential in view of the need to satisfy the public with some immediate results. Crisis management style would thus be more appealing although hopefully, these short term remedies could provide the basis for long term self-sustaining solutions as well. There are also measures which would take some time for realization such as changing the behavioral attitudes of the people and modifying land use patterns to shift the incidence of the problem to different locations.

Yet not all the short term measures necessarily alleviate the transport problem. Indeed, short term measures that increase road capacity at selected congestion nodes merely "transfer" the problem elswhere rather than solve the problem. At the same time, long term solutions should have well-defined objectives, especially if they are more than a continuation of short term measures. From what the government had then been advocating it would seem that its approach at strategies management in the area of transportation could be summarized thus:

(a) there was a clear recognition that effective transportation should be provided (even though not necessarily borne financially by the government) at minimal social and financial cost to individuals;

(b) that the amount of public investments in infrastructural investments would be limited not just by budgetary constraints but also by the spatial restrictions familiar to land-scarce Singapore;

(c) that a strategic mix in intra-modal and inter-modal transport should be present although the bulk of transport trips would be borne by forms of public conveyance;

(d) that public conveyance should stress high ridership capacity and thus those with smaller passenger capacity should play a subsidiary role;

(e) that drastic measures would have to be employed to curb the growth of private vehicle ownership and restraints had to be imposed on the patterns of such usage;

(f) non-transport factors such as health, safety, and the aesthetic qualities of life should not be compromised in the search for a transport policy and, wherever possible, should be incorporated in such a policy;

(g) the costs of pursuing whatever solutions should not result in excessive bureaucratization;

(h) the key to the success of the transport measures would be the willingness of the people to change their attitudes.

In a sense, the government's objective could be summarized thus: quality of life in an urban setting should not deteriorate if modifications and adjustments were made by all concerned. The government was not anti-motorists, but motorists should adjust their trip patterns to accommodate those of the non-motoring majority. Vehicle operation is thus not an individual right, and social obligations have to be respected. The other commuting groups too have to make adjustments, although not as drastic as the car-owning clientele group.

Perhaps, one feature which did facilitate administrative effectiveness was the high level of acceptance of public authority. The respect for governmental authority remained high and indeed the ruling party continued to monopolize all parliamentary seats in the 1970s - the period in which major transport measures were introduced.

The 1970 Government White Paper on the *Reorganization of the Motor Transport Service in Singapore* could be said to be the major starting point in the search for and implementation of a viable transportation program. Prior to that, there were frequent attempts to curb illegal para-transit, but the main problem - namely, to ensure efficiency in transportation - was not fully addressed. In the 1970 White Paper it was proposed that the twelve bus companies of varying size, operational capabilities and vehicle makes be reorganized. The main company, the Singapore Traction Company (STC), was allowed to remain as a distinct entity while the 11 other Chinese bus operations were reorganized into three companies. Considerable government pressure had to be applied to these bus operators to accede, notwithstanding innumerable problems of assessing the relative value of each of these companies. At the same time, an Australian public transport expert was invited to provide a new set of service routings.

This was necessary though it did not immediately realize its objectives. The routings were based on point-to-point accessibility, which meant excessive layover of transport equipment as some of the routes took almost two hours (in peak traffic conditions) to complete, as in the case of the service plying from one end of Singapore (Changi) to the other (Jurong). Also, the STC was no longer viable. Its financial collapse meant that a further reorganization of bus operations was necessary. Hence the decision to merge all bus operations into one major organization, the Singapore Bus Service (SBS). In making this decision, the government argued that economies of scale would result and wasteful competition could be reduced. It is worth noting that there was a relatively high outpouring of letters to the press - many of which were emotional rather than rational.

The government's more immediate solutions would come within the purview of (a) improvement of existing modes and (b) traffic management schemes. The reorganization of the bus operations was an example of the desire to improve existing modes and indeed would constitute the main underpinning in this category of reforms. In the 1970 White Paper the government advocated an active interventionist strategy by stating:

> No objective person can deny that reorganisation of the Public Transport service is long overdue in Singapore. That being the case, we must therefore make a determined effort *now* so as to put a stop to its laissez faire growth over the years.... It is no consolation to our people that traffic snarls and jams have to be accepted as being part and parcel of the price for our strong economic growth over the last decade and that other cities are experiencing similar problems more acutely. The dissatisfaction of our bus commuters, who, after all, form the vast majority of our two million population, must be boldly faced and met....[7]

Yet, the government did not want to nationalize or take over the bus operations. Instead, it resorted to an ingenious method of pressuring these operators to accede, often with the backing of public pressure, to the extent that the owners of bus operations felt uncomfortable for not agreeing to what was in the so-called public interest. Another point worth noting was the decision to upgrade bus operations. Politically, the National Trade Union Congress (NTUC) supported the Singapore Industrial Labour Organization (SILO) in bringing together bus workers under its wings. This was no mean achievement. At the management level, the government seconded government officers to head critical managerial and operational aspects of the bus company. In a sense, the government was managing the company even though the capital was from the private sector, giving perhaps another twist to the pragmatic democratic-socialist profile of the ruling party. By such means, bus operations did improve. Profits for the owners were kept to a low ceiling so that the excess could be plowed back into the company in the form of assets acquisition such as rolling stock. Passenger comfort and safety was also increased by shortening the permissible operational life-span of buses to 17 years instead of the previously acceptable 22 years.[8]

Other means of improving existing modes included mobilization of school buses to ply selected traffic corridors during morning and evening peaks, the use of lorries for transporting workers, and increasing the number of taxis (though these were given to the NTUC-cooperative, COMFORT). Shuttle-bus service was also provided. It was hoped that while existing bus commuters would find travel more bearable, a large number of private car users would also switch to public transport. It was in the realm of traffic management schemes that the government could be said to have made significant impact. In a sense, the traffic management schemes suggested and implemented were not unusual - they were textbook solutions. But what was critical was the determination of the government to pursue these measures (and defy unpopular feedback) and to introduce them with great rapidity. The list of traffic management measures that were introduced (though not necessarily in chronological order) were:

(a) toughen regulatory measures against motorists found to commit various infringements. These included higher fines and "point demerit system" in which a motorist could be barred from driving if he were to accumulate a stipulated number of "points" for such infringements;

(b) reduce the number of cars by periodic hefty increases in import taxes and by raising operational costs through increases in road tax and on fuel;

(c) reduce parking facilities in the CBD to deter motorists from driving to the city;

(d) prohibit large vehicles with three or more axles from entering the CBD during peak hours;

(e) encourage car-pooling and staggered working hours;

(f) introduce 14 km. of reserved bus lanes to be exclusively used by such vehicles during peak periods;

(g) discourage "garage" parking by upward revision of fees for cars/vehicles which park for slightly longer periods in the CBD's existing lots;

(h) introduce a road pricing scheme, namely the Area Licensing Scheme (ALS); the CBD was largely designated as a restricted zone; and,

(i) construct fringe area car parks to encourage motorists to adopt a "park-and-ride" attitude. Shuttle buses would frequent these car parks and bring such motorists to the CBD.

Three interesting observations about the bureaucracy should be noted. First, the bureaucracy did not have many precedents to rely on. *Ad hoc* measures had indeed been carried out in several cities, but there was no precedent in which a staggering series of measures would be introduced within a short span of a few years. Second, the political leaders gave every encouragement to the bureaucrats concerned with policy advising and implementation. Not all measures could be successful, and, indeed, there were notable failures such as the staggered working hours campaign and the costly fringe car parks which failed to draw motorists. The political leaders supported the bureaucrats by strongly identifying with these measures and even gave credit for trying out new ideas. Third, the government encouraged inter-agency coordination. The most important mechanism was the Road Transport Action Committee (RTAC), which comprised permanent secretaries of ministries with some interest in transport issues. These involved the Ministry of Finance (which dealt with taxes and other forms of revenue), the National Development Ministry (whose Public Works Department was responsible for the infrastructural and engineering/technological aspects of imposing traffic restraint measures), the Home Affairs Ministry (the Police Department of which was responsible for law enforcement), and the Ministry of Communications which oversaw all these measures. Setting up a high-powered committee was a reaffirmation of the government's (and bureaucracy's) commitment to this issue. It also revealed the desire to reduce inter-agency delays and differences of views, since all the related agencies would be collectively responsible.

Interest group agitations against traffic restraint measures were kept to a minimum. While this could be attributed to the type of political culture in Singapore and the relative desire to avoid open agitation, it would have been difficult for interest groups to go against measures aimed at the social good. However, dissatisfaction was voiced whenever discrepancy in treatment occurred. For example, a government circular allowing senior civil servants who worked in the CBD to have free access into the restricted zone during hours of enforcement was severely criticized. The circular was quickly withdrawn and the privilege thus rescinded.

As a longer term solution, the government proceeded with two groups of measures. The first was traffic engineering and infrastructural improvements. Traffic lights in the CBD were computerized and synchronized to allow uninterrupted flow of traffic whenever possible. Infrastructural improvements took the form of road widening and construction of expressways. All these projects were actually proposed in the Concept Plan. A major aim of the expressways was to promote direct access between the major towns and also to allow east-west traffic to by-pass the CBD. The expressway construction program was speeded up, but its effect in the 1970s was not very noticeable since expressways took a relatively longer period to complete, unlike the traffic management measures. By 1990, the network of expressways will have been completed.

The second long term solution was to examine whether a Mass Rapid Transit was necessary for Singapore. First mooted in the Concept Plan, the government appointed a team of consultants, Wilbur-Smith and Associates, to look into the proposal. This team suggested a rail-bus combination, and a second report showed that the proposal was economically viable. Without the heavy rail MRT to cater to a sizeable part of the peak hour trips, the whole of the CBD would, in the team's analysis, be swamped by buses and with all the usual inconveniences associated with such a situation. The government, too, had its own committees, including a team from the Ministry of Defense, to look into these issues. At the same time, a team comprising mainly Harvard dons, the Hansen team, was asked to examine Wilbur-Smith's recommendations. This team felt that the situation of congestion was well under control. It questioned the premises of Wilbur-Smith's reports and suggested that other measures such as, a change in land-use planning to include residence-cum-working opportunities in the CBD to reduce transport trips, more liberal treatment of buses (e.g., more reserved bus-lanes), and vehicle restraint measures be extended to include the expressways, so that these could be used by express and semi-express buses. The conclusion of the Hansen team was that an all-bus system was viable in Singapore and could even be more efficient than the rail-based MRT. However, should the need ever arise (if these measures and the provision of more CBDs did not work), then limited MRTs such as the "aero buses" should be recommended. They would be cheaper and would provide a more pleasant environmental ride for the commuters, as opposed to the rather monotonous subway journeys.

It was only at this juncture that the elitist concept in decision making was slightly modified to allow for popular participation. The reports (some of which were abbreviated) were made available to the public - a far cry from previous practice of treating them as secret documents. The people were encouraged to comment, and there was indeed a discussion on television featuring representatives of the two foreign consultancy groups, the PWD senior civil engineer, a senior member of the SBS and a don. Mainly directed at the relative merits of the two sets of reports, the discussion did not arouse too much enthusiasm. A provisional MRT Authority was set up, presumably to coordinate matters pertaining to the formulation of a long term transportation policy and to undertake further studies. Another study was made to examine the Hansen report and also to propose solutions.[10]

It should be noted that this departure from elitist monopolization of decision making could perhaps be due to the relatively ambivalent position held by some members of the Cabinet. A decision seemed forthcoming when the report, *Comprehensive Traffic Study - Phase A,* came out in favor of the MRT, urging that the inconveniences of an all-bus system might be beyond toleration limits. The government subsequently made a policy pronouncement on the decision to proceed with the MRT. Engineering and related studies were undertaken and the MRT Authority became a full-fledged statutory board.

To what extent was the decision motivated by long term transportation policy? This is probably difficult to answer as non-transportation arguments were raised to support MRT, the most important being strategic, namely, the stations could be modified as air-raid shelters. Had no MRT been constructed, the government presumably would have had to build such shelters. This defense-related justification put to rest arguments regarding the type of MRT systems, the aero-bus concept and the light rail concept, which did not feature as viable alternatives. Many previously-held concerns such as the fear of a non-viable system were also demolished with the announcement that the main development costs would be borne by the sale of reclaimed land at Marina Center. A certain degree of urgency was injected into the decision making process, with the announcement that a multi-phase approach would be adopted to have the system operational as soon as possible.

Although the construction and blueprint differed to some extent from Wilbur-Smith's, the MRT construction was finally underway. This was a massive S$5 billion project (the costs having escalated since the Concept Plan). By 1987, perhaps, the first phase will be operational.[11]

Presumably with the completion of MRT, it is possible to argue that a comprehensive approach to transport planning has finally been attained, which could well be the first since the rudimentary town and transport planning made by Stamford Raffles. In transportation policy, strategies management seems to be the main style of the government. MRT marks an attempt to have a pro-active approach rather than devising measures which are a reaction to specific problems. Nonetheless, questions are still raised: is the transport issue being finally resolved? Would not the old issues continue to plague present and future governments? Will there be a consistent pressure to ease existing traffic restraint measures now that the congestion problem has eased sufficiently? Will the premises of the 1970s (and for that matter, the political style) be as relevant today or in the future? Will bureaucrats be given a relatively free hand in designing modifications to the transportation system?

Already elements of contradiction appear. The logic in the single bus organization has been seriously eroded, and a new bus company, the Trans-Island Bus Service (TIBS), has been given operational status and routes. Some of these routes compete with those of SBS. The rationalization of the government (presumably with bureaucratic advice) has been that such competition will make SBS more competitive and less complacent. The bulk of the ridership would thus benefit from enhanced efficiency.

Yet, the Singapore experience does suggest some lessons. First, the administrative structure does not require too much expansion. What is more important is the congruence of interests among the political and bureaucratic elites in trying to solve the problem. Second, a certain degree of administrative flexibility is required; there have been instances in which regulatory agencies had to modify routine administrative processes to cater to the impact of proposed policies, such as the decision to revise road taxes immediately or to put into effect a policy that would make ownership of old vehicles more difficult or cost-prohibitive. The third factor is the need for coordination and to make all the related agencies collectively responsible. The RTAC effectively pooled the resources of at least four ministries while making them accountable for the state of the transportation problem. We caution against any resort to new administrative structure, since this would merely lead to a more cumbersome bureaucracy. The MRT authority was finally convened after it became apparent that a go-ahead decision could not be reversed. Finally, there are no miracles or shortcuts in transportation, insofar as each and every policy measure helps in some form to reduce the problem. Indeed, in the midst of the traffic restraint measures in 1975, the Minister of Communications commented that as long as each of these measures could marginally reduce the problem, the net effect of all the measures would be significant.[12] An incremental approach is thus the best method - to rely exclusively on the "big kill" such as MRT for salvation would probably end in utter disappointment.

**The Taxi Issue : Old Problems in a New Guise**

A basic contradiction in the realm of transport planning is the perennial presence of the taxi problem. Whatever measures that have been proposed could only ameliorate the situation, although the extent of continuing effectiveness would depend on the existing as well as future contextual variables. There is also a tendency to slide back to the same problems which have previously haunted the transport planners, who had expected that the various policy measures would have lasting positive effects. The same could be said of the situation in Singapore. The more recent taxi controversy - which has not been fully solved - illustrates in a vivid manner that old problems continue to appear in new guises.

Taxis are basically a form of para-transit with limited ridership capacities. Their role should be of a supplementary character, but they are noted for personal convenience which other forms of public transport do not provide. A key question to ask, therefore, is what role should be assigned to taxis. If too many, they could well defeat some of the goals of the government as regards traffic restraint measures. Ultimately, the hope of the government (and transport planners) is not just a reduction in car ownership, but also a change in behavioral and attitudinal norms of the people, to the extent that they would take to the main transport system as the modal form for commuting.

By the end of 1983, there were a total of 11,193 taxis or an increase of 565 over the preceding year. The number of taxi drivers or those with licenses to operate as taxi drivers in that year was 33,727. The number of taxis and taxi driving licenses were decided by a governmental taxi advisory committee, comprising bureaucrats from the Ministry of Communications, political leadership and the major public transport operators. The number of taxi drivers exceeded the number of taxis by a ratio of almost 3 to 1, implying that many of the taxis were operated on a shift-basis. The amount of compensation which the shift drivers would have to pay to the vehicle owner would depend on the informal "market" mechanism. There were also informal guidelines on such payments and the hours designated for changing of shifts.

Most of the vehicles were supposed to be in use for the larger part of the daily 24 hours, but there were no rigid rules on such usage. For vehicle owners, the need to "sub-let" vehicles to shift drivers would depend on assessment of several factors, such as the relatively short authorized life-span of the vehicle (currently seven years, although owners are encouraged to replace their vehicles after five years), the potential additional maintenance costs of possibly less-responsible shift drivers, income needs as well as the use of vehicles for personal reasons. Most of the taxi owners had their vehicles through the auspices of the taxi cooperative, COMFORT, a move initiated mainly by the government. Lately, certain organizations such as SBS have decided to enter the taxi business as part of the desire to seek new avenues of continuing employment for their retired or retrenched employees.

A perplexing question facing most commuters and the government as well was the relative difficulty in securing a taxi. Long queues were familiar and frustrating experiences. There was the usual list of accusations: taxi drivers were selective of the types of passengers they would ferry; they preferred their own operating schedule which did not take into consideration such factors as peak hour loads; taxi drivers were predisposed to gambling (pictures of unattended taxis at the race course would occasionally appear in the newspapers); taxi drivers preferred tourist-related activities.

The pressure on the government for more taxis to be put on the road kept increasing. Yet, fare meter readings such as trip journeys indicated that most taxis were underutilized. As the meters were compulsory, it could be asserted that the meter readings would convey an accurate picture of the extent of under-usage. It would have been preposterous, therefore, for the government to increase the number of taxis on the road, as this would adversely affect the government's vehicle-restraint policy and still be unable to account for the underutilization of the existing vehicle stock.

While this problem had yet to be tackled, the government too was rather wary over the increase in the number of private vehicles. For example, in 1983, 43.3 per cent of the registered 476,288 vehicles were private cars. In that year, the number of cars went up by 12 per cent over the preceding year. Compared with increases of 11.5 per cent for 1982, 6.6 per cent for 1981, and 6.8 per cent 1980, there were indeed worrisome signs for the political leadership. Higher motoring and petrol taxes were introduced in 1983, but this was one solution which could not be resorted to *ad infinitum*. Yet, unless some equilibrium could be attained in the demand-supply situation for taxis, the growth in private car ownerhip could exceed the expectation of the political leadership. Such a possibility was not unlikely in view of the feeling of euphoria of high wage increments associated with the early years of the 1980s.

Yet, if the demand for the taxis was to spiral what could be done? It was found that many of the taxi trips were used for rather "flippant" reasons such as commuting to office while avoiding the inconveniences associated with other forms of public transport. Some of these commuting trips were taken by those in relatively junior employment situations such as clerical workers and receptionists. The shortage of taxis was artificially induced in the sense that many of these passenger trips were of a questionable nature and could indeed distort the character which taxis as para-transit were supposed to implement.

It was under such conditions that in the 1985 Budget proposals the second generation leaders decided to implement a series of measures aimed at solving this and related problems of transport. On the issue of private vehicle ownership, the government had proposed a further increase in operational costs, namely, to increase the *ad valorem* tax on petrol from 50 to 60 per cent. In terms of pump prices the increase was tantamount to an additional 25 cents per liter over the previous price level.

On the issue of the taxis, the government decided to increase the diesel tax on taxis to $6,000 per year with effect from October 1985. In justifying this move, the Finance Minister pointed to the apparent discrepancy between the higher diesel tax which the privately-owned diesel car owners would have to pay as compared to the largely diesel-operated taxi fleet. The proposed tax would thus "harmonize" the tax structure on vehicles using diesel fuel. In the course of the Budget debate it was pointed out that the main purpose was to seek a solution to the taxi problem by restoring it to its "proper" role. Increasing the number of taxis would not help because, to quote the Communications Minister, a taxi was just a car by another name.[13] Since the government's policy was to restrain car ownership, the logic on taxi policy was thus apparent to the people.

To ensure that taxi drivers would not have their take-home income adversely affected by the hike, the government revised the tariffs which the taxis would have to charge. Citing statistics to show that fares charged by Singapore taxis were too low as compared to those in selected capital cities of Asia and the OECD countries, it was argued that these low fares indeed were the cause for the "abuse" in taxi usage.

Unlike the previous flag-down fare of $1.20 and a consistent rate for subsequent distance travelled, it was decided that the flag-down should be $2 for the first 2 km. and that the fare would go up by about 10 cents for every 300 meters up to the first 10 km. and 10 cents for every 250 meters thereafter. Other rates and surcharges included a waiting time rate of 10 cents for every 45 seconds; 50 cents surcharge for the third and fourth passengers; 50 per cent surcharge of the metered fare between midnight and 6 a.m. and $1 for any luggage placed in the boot. All these were in addition to other prevailing surcharges such as the $3 airport surcharge, $1 for trips to the CBD, $1 for radio calls and $2 for radio booking.

The response from the two affected groups was immediate and vocal - perhaps exceeding what the political leadership had anticipated. Car owners were undoubtedly disgruntled with the hefty increases. Quite a number of them had done their own calculations and found that a liter of premium grade petrol was S$0.665 cheaper in Johore Bahru, taking into account the pump price there of $1.06 per liter and the lower exchange rate of the Malaysian ringgit. Many motorists thus decided to purchase a full tank of petrol in Johore Bahru, obtaining a net saving of at least $20. In due course, petrol stations in Johore Bahru were working at full capacity. The loss of revenue to the Singapore government was considerable.

The main source of discontent was from the taxi drivers and commuters who used this form of transport. The increased cost was certainly prohibitive, and many commuters switched over to buses, though not without protest. (A major bus company reported a 10 per cent increase in the day's takings.) Taxi drivers could not find enough passenger trips to ensure economic viability, and the reverse scenario appeared, viz., too many taxis waiting for the occasional passenger to stroll to the taxi bays. Take-home income was rather pathetic for some of these drivers, who reported an income of only a few dollars after the usual deductions for operational and rental costs.

What was of interest was the rather agitational protest at the government's measures. This could be attributed to the fact that the younger ministers were not held in high esteem and respect. Hence, the people could feel grossly aggrieved by the new measures. Second, the approach adopted by the government reaffirmed the same exclusive form of elitist decision-making. There was hardly any significant discussion with the major taxi cooperatives or the important clientele groups. Neither COMFORT nor the Consumers Association of Singapore (CASE) was consulted, even though these two organizations ironically had governmental support and hence were regarded as rather sympathetic to governmental opinions or views. Indeed, the adviser of COMFORT was none other than a candidate (though defeated) of the ruling party in the last December election. Apparently, the old political style of the old guards could not be duplicated by the new guards and there was indeed a credibility gap. Never had the response of the affected public been so negative and whatever arguments were put forward by the Communications Minister seemed to fall on deaf ears.

But was the government turning a deaf ear to the public, if not to itself? The results of the last December general election were notable in producing two opposition members of parliament while there was a distinct swing of 13 per cent from the ruling party. These were certainly significant signals to the ruling party and indeed, one of the responses of the ruling party was that it would be more deliberative or consultative in nature. Yet, barely less than four months after the election, the new measures on transport did not have the benefit of prior consultation of either the public or the major affected groups such as COMFORT. While a senior minister did mention that this "oversight" was merely a transitional problem since the proposed policy had already been in the "pipe-line" for quite some time,[14] it would seem that even such an explanation was irrelevant given the attested hall-mark of the ruling leadership in its responsiveness to political sensitivities and realities. Alternatively, it could be argued that perhaps the bureaucrats involved in the policy-advising role had not developed sufficient maturity or acumen in handling "shifts" in the political climate and thus assumed that the same style of governance should prevail given the continuity of the existing ruling party.

COMFORT found itself in the invidious position of having to articulate the needs of taxi drivers. It thus had to agitate and was successful in getting rather quickly a modification of the existing tariff rate, namely, the permission of the government to allow its members to offer a 20 per cent "discount" on the new fares. Through this move, it was hoped that sufficient ridership could be generated, thereby enabling taxi-drivers to improve their income "yield."

The move, however, did result in considerable confusion. Not all members decided to heed COMFORT's advice and there were also other taxi drivers who chose to adhere to the approved fares. Also, as not all the meters were adjusted to the new fares, the drivers (and passengers) found themselves having to juggle with the fare conversion card (issued by the Registry of Vehicles) and the discount rate to arrive at the actual fares to be paid. Notwithstanding the discount, the number of passenger trips did not increase appreciably.

Yet, the impact of these two measures on easing transport problems could be seen in other sectors. Many small and medium-sized restaurants and hawkers complained that their patronage was adversely affected, as people were disinclined to eat out because of the higher costs of travelling. In view of the less than usual rate of economic growth, the effect on this service sector was thus compounded. The government had no intention of rescinding these two decisions, especially that pertaining to taxis even though assurances were given to the effect that the situation would be carefully monitored.

Representatives of the various taxi operators continued to mull over the issue, and in June 1985 a petition was submitted to the Minister for Communication and Information for a reduction of fares. Although the proposed fares represented the work of COMFORT, they also incorporated the views of the Singapore Taxi Drivers Association, Singapore Taxi Transport Association, Singapore Commuter, Singapore Airport Bus Services and SBS Taxis. This petition was approved after modifications. The flagdown fare would be $1.60 for the first 1⅛ km and staggered rates for subsequent distances. The main implication of the change was that short distance trips would cost slightly more than the 20 per cent "discounted" fare although the fares would be cheaper for longer distance travel. These measures took effect from 1 June and with it, there was the hope that the take-home income would be improved as more passengers would use taxis for short distance travel. It could be argued that the compromise was forced on the government even though the taxi drivers were equally guilty of making unfounded claims on the adverse effect of governmental measures on their income. The earnings have stabilized to some extent although many of those that changed their mode of transport have no intention of going back to the taxis.

Yet, there was a certain amount of administrative untidiness, perhaps not a good reflection of the government's standard for impeccable output. For example, a new conversion card (printed a different color for easier identification) was issued by the Registry of Vehicles, since the meters had not been completely readjusted again. In June, there were still taxi meters which had not even been adjusted to the post-April fare structures and there were thus taxis plying in Singapore displaying pre-April, the immediate post-April and the readjusted June fare schedules.

The taxi fare problem was certainly not a storm in the tea-cup. Of course, not everyone (including taxi drivers) was satisfied, and there were still hopes that the diesel fee might be modified or abandoned by the government prior to its implementation in October. Only the slightest pretext was required for further agitation. This came about from a much bigger issue, namely, the slow-down in economic performance of the country.

By August the government was announcing a negative outlook for the economy and it was feared that there would be zero growth for the second quarter. Several moves were introduced by the government to try to revive the economy, ranging from removing obstacles to business and industrial activities, injection of new capital sources in selected fields, a call to freeze existing wages and a desire to reduce some of the overheads facing the business-industrial sectors. The slow-down ensured that the government would have to review its policy measures on transport as well. By the end of August the government introduced two measures. The first was equivalent to rescinding its earlier measure on private cars by reaffirming that petrol taxes would revert back to the 50 per cent *ad valorem* duty. In proposing the change, a senior government minister argued that as "...the economy had slowed down more than expected, people are driving around less, and also buying fewer cars. For as long as this is the case, there is no need for the higher tax on petrol."[15] In regard to the taxi issue, the government decided that the diesel tax would be implemented, except that the quantum of $6,000 would be reduced to $1,100. This amount would be bearable to taxi drivers as it would represent approximately between two to three per cent of daily earnings. The important role of taxis was further reaffirmed (though by a different minister who was also secretary-general of the National Trade Union Congress) to the effect that "...taxi drivers provide a public transport service, (and) they are an essential part of our transport system. We want to help them to make a decent living."[16] This view seemed to be different from another minister who argued that the ultimate aim of the government was to impose the full diesel tax and that the reduced amount was acceded to "in view of the current recession" -- the full tax would be introduced "only when economic conditions permit."[17] For most taxi drivers, such fine distinctions seemed not to matter much since their aim of not having to incur "additional expenses" had been largely achieved. The taxi issue may still not be allowed to rest although the focus of public concern has since then switched over to graver issues such as ensuring continuing employment, existing income level, and pondering when the country could emerge from the recession. It should, however, be noted that notwithstanding the recession, the people are not in the same economic straits of the immediate post-Independence period.

The taxi issue shows that the government was merely dealing with another facet of the transportation issue and persuading Singaporeans. The contextual variables, however, have been modified between the period of the 1970s and those of the 1980s. There is a new generation of voters, many of whom had not experienced hard times and have been used to a better quality of life. This upward aspiration has to be satisfied and it would be extremely difficult to tell them to forego owning a car. The MRT could be a tantalizing alternative, but its effects are yet to be seen. The concept of privacy and pride in a vehicle of one's own is hard to repress and indeed, in many advanced countries including Japan, the trend has been increasing. (In Japan the so-called "My-car zoku" has certainly caught the imagination of the younger generation.) Secondly, the new generation of voters is slightly more educated than in the past, in terms of average literacy level, and it would be indeed difficult to prevent these voters from questioning the actions of the leaders or the bureaucracy. It may be essential for the leaders to seek an acceptable *modus operandi* in dealing with the voters.

Two aspects, perhaps essential in dealing with new problems, could emerge in the foreseeable future. The first is to seek new channels of communication with the people to ensure adequate representation of interests. The political culture of Singapore seems to have undergone shifts in orientation and a new sense of self-sufficiency could be detected among the people. There is also the belief in not only to be heard but also have their proposals acted upon. The "hand-me-down" approach so typical of the leadership style of the past will become increasingly less relevant, notwithstanding the bona fide intentions of the leaders making these pronouncements.

Second, perhaps there should also be greater interaction among the bureaucrats and even the interest groups prior to the formulation of proposed measures. Such joint deliberations were not given sufficient attention in the past, but if responsiveness is what the government has hoped to achieve, this form of consultations would have to be given greater elaboration. Joint consultations again would be of a more meaningful type rather than those used merely to endorse government decisions. Neither the political leaders nor the bureaucrats could pride themselves for being main repositories of expertise and there is an increasingly large number of qualified professionals even in the private sector who could match the skills of the bureaucracy or those of the political leaders.

These two comments are of course equally applicable to other areas as well and not only on matters pertaining to transportation issues. The public wants to be informed and to have a share in the decision-making process. In a sense, Singapore is approaching a more mature political system and the spirit (if not the codes) of democracy would indeed be taken rather seriously. The vote has become a symbol and a means of exercising public concern and interest.

## Conclusion

The above discussion on the transportation problem illustrates the importance of contextual variables in helping to shape the effectiveness of policy measures.

Yet, the same contextual variables could change or modify within a relatively short time-span. The Singapore situation in many ways enjoyed certain peculiarities which have made policy implementation a much easier task. Its spatial limitations have enabled prompt feedback and analysis of policy measures. Both the political and bureaucratic elites need not wait to measure the feedback - in several instances, the feedback could be almost instantaneous. Second, the fact that the survival theme has long been stressed and accepted has made it possible for greater public responsiveness whatever the constraints which the people or selected clientele groups would have to adjust to. There is no rural-urban migration to complicate the existing transportation problem in the urban areas while the effect of the modified land-use policy which facilitates the existence of intense corridors of development, population and employment has made transport planning a much easier exercise.

A comprehensive approach, involving the management of different strategies, has been designed to deal with the transport problem. Even though the effects of long term solutions are not yet known, there is no doubt that the improvements to the transport issue have been significant. Yet, complacency cannot be tolerated for as shown even in the case of the recent (and perhaps; on-going) taxi issue, the old problems could indeed re-surface. However, unlike the 1970s, the latitude afforded to the leaders - political and bureaucratic - would be restricted and not as unimpeded as in the past. Changes in the contextual factors would require a change in political style and while the political and bureaucratic elites could still play leading roles, their posture would have to be softened or adapted in a manner which the clientele groups would accept. In a word, while the new "structure" of the transport system has been affirmatively set out, tinkerings with the system in the present and future would demand as much acumen and maturity as those of the 1970s.

**Notes**

1. References to infrastructure in the 19th century can be found in some of the memoirs and social history written in those days. See for example, Walter Makepeace, *One Hundred Years of Singapore* (London: John Murray, 1923).

2. Elaboration on this issue could be found in Seah Chee Meow, "Some Key Issues in Singapore's Domestic Transportation," in Wu Teh Yao (ed.), *Political and Social Change in Singapore* (Singapore: Institute of Southeast Asian Studies, 1975), pp. 72-112.

3. The Master Plan is generally available. It is of course possible to propose amendments although the procedure is not that convenient.

4. See Jon S.T. Quah, *Administrative Reform and Development Administration in Singapore: A Comparative Study of the Singapore Improvement Trust and the Housing and Development Board,* unpub. Ph.D. dissertation, Florida State University, 1975, for a detailed discussion of the SIT.

5. Refer to H. Wardlaw, "Planning in Singapore," *Royal Australian Planning Institute Journal* (April 1971), p. 2 ff.

6. The main fear of most policy makers has to do with the deterioration of the city's "inner-core" and the concomitant social, economic and political problems. Many city authorities have in more recent times attempted to rehabilitate these inner cores.

7. *Reorganization of the Motor Transport Service of Singapore.* Cmd.21 of 1970 (Singapore, 1970), paras. 1.1 and 1.2.

8. See Seah Chee Meow, "Government Policy Choices and Public Transport Operations in Singapore," *Transport Policy and Decision Making,* Vol. 1 (1980), pp. 231-251, for an elaboration of measures taken to improve the bus system.

9. See Seah Chee Meow, "Mass Mobility and Accessibility: Transport Planning and Traffic Management in Singapore," *Transport Planning and Decision Making,* Vol. 1 (1980), pp. 55-71. Studies on some of the specific measures are available such as Peter Watson and Edward Holland, *Relieving Traffic Congestion: the Singapore Area Licensing Scheme* (Washington: World Bank, 1978).

10. A summary can be found in Seah Chee Meow, "The MRT Debate in Singapore : To Do or Not to Do?" *Southeast Asian Affairs* (Singapore : Institute of Southeast Asian Studies, 1981), pp. 290-306.

11. The general economic recession world-wide too has a determining influence on the MRT proposal. Presumably, the massive construction projects of the MRT could help to promote economic growth and confidence in Singapore during the current "lean" years.

12. In a discussion with the author on the issue. This minister has since retired from politics.

13. The Budget debate in 1985 was given wide television coverage and the Minister's remarks were also given ample air-time by the mass media. His remarks on the taxis could thus not be lightly dismissed.

14. From a recent discussion between the minister and the writer.

15. *Sunday Times,* 1 September 1985.

16. *Straits Times,* 2 September 1985.

17. *Sunday Times,* 1 September 1985.

# 9

# Toward Effective Delivery of Public Services at the Local Level: Restructuring of Local Government in Peninsular Malaysia

*Shamsuddin Kassim**

In 1976, the Malaysian Government with the agreement of the State Governments embarked on a program of restructuring the local government system in Peninsular Malaysia. The restructuring exercise was essentially aimed at improving the capacity of local authorities in providing services to people living within areas under their jurisdictions. Although it is now almost ten years since the restructuring exercise was first started, most of the restructured local authorities, particularly the District Councils, have not shown any remarkable improvement in their capacity to deliver services to their clientele. Indeed many of them continue to be beset by the same problems that were faced before they were restructured.

This chapter analyzes current problems faced by the restructured local authorities in Peninsular Malaysia, to identify the relevant critical issues and to suggest alternative solutions to overcome the problems.

*Local Government in Malaysia.* In Peninsular Malaysia the term local government refers to the government of urban areas, rural areas or a combination of urban and rural areas subordinate to the state government, but enjoying an independent legal existence from that government. It represents the third tier of the Federal structure, and therefore it is the level of government that is closest to the people. The existing system and pattern of local government were established according to the provisions of the Federal Constitution. Under the Constitution, local government, other than that for the Federal Territory, is a subject that falls within the purview of the State Governments in accordance with the Ninth Schedule of the Federal Constitution. Thus, State Governments have direct authority and responsibility for local government in their respective states.

---

*National Institute of Public Administration, Kuala Lumpur, Malaysia.

However, under Article 76 (4) of the Federal Constitution, Parliament may enact legislation to ensure that there is uniformity in the laws relating to local government for the nation as a whole. To ensure that local government laws passed by the Federal Parliament under Article 76 (4) of the Federal Constitution are accepted and applied by the State Governments, a National Council for Local Government was established in 1960 following an amendment to the Federal Constitution. The National Council for Local Government is chaired by the Minister responsible for local government with members representing each of the 11 states in Peninsular Malaysia and 10 members representing the Federal Government. Sabah and Sarawak send a representative each to the meetings of the Council as observers.

The National Council for Local Government was established to play a role in the formulation of national policy for the promotion, development and control of local government. It serves as a forum for consultation between the States and the Federal Government as well as provides advisory services on local government laws and policies to the various State Governments. All decisions of the National Council for Local Government are binding on the Federal Government and the States, the exception being Sabah and Sarawak. The present system of local government in Malaysia is shown in Appendix 1.

*The Need for Restructuring.* The history of local government in Malaysia can be traced back to the beginning of British colonial rule in the Malay Peninsula in the early 19th Century. The local authorities established during the colonial period were assigned the basic functions of protecting public health and safety and collecting taxes. The system of local government was also introduced as part of the effort to introduce democracy in stages to the people, and much later on as a measure to counteract the influence of subversive elements in the new villages which were created during the period of Emergency (1948 - 1960). The local government introduced by the British did not form a single integrated system. It consisted of a large number of mainly isolated local authorities, the majority being small units which were both understaffed and underfinanced. A few, such as Georgetown Penang, Ipoh and Melaka, were substantial and able to provide adequate urban services but they operated within narrowly defined boundaries. Legislation was inherited, outdated and inadequate while control was dispersed through the States and given little priority.[1]

When the Federation of Malaya became independent in 1957 it inherited over 300 local authorities of various sizes and established under a variety of federal and state legislations. By the early 1960s it was increasingly felt by the Federal and State Governments as well as by many of the local authorities themselves that change was needed to improve the situation. It was also becoming apparent that many of the local authorities were incapable of performing their functions because of poor financial resources. Matters were in such poor shape even in some of the bigger local authorities that State Governments had to step in to take direct control of their operations. In 1965 the Federal Government set up a Royal Commission under the chairmanship of the late Senator Datuk Athi Nahappan to look into the affairs of local authorities in Peninsular Malaysia. Although only parts of the recommendations of the Royal Commission were eventually incorporated into the Local Government Act of 1976, it nevertheless served as an impetus for subsequent deliberations on the future of local government in Malaysia.

**Contextual Factors**

*The Restructuring.* The restructuring of local authorities in Peninsular Malaysia was started at the end of 1976. This was preceded by the passing of The Local Government Act, 1976 (Act 171). The objectives of the restructuring exercise may be summarized as follows:[2]

1. To ensure that local authorities are able to become an effective third tier level of government to provide good and efficient service to the people.
2. To enable local authorities to plan and implement development in a systematic and integrated manner as well as to facilitate infrastructure and socioeconomic development in the towns and rural areas.
3. To recognize the administrative structure, the membership of the Council, service delivery and development activities in the local authorities so that they are in consonance with current social, economic and political demands as well as in line with the goals of the New Economic Policy.
4. To provide opportunities for the people to participate in the process and activities related to the formulation of policy and implementation of development at the local government level.

The Local Government Act of 1976 stipulates that after restructuring there would be only two types of local authorities, namely Municipal Councils and District Councils. The process of restructuring was rather slow because it depended on the initiative of individual State Governments. The exercise involved the organization of about 374 local authorities of various categories including City Councils, Municipal Councils, Town Councils, Rural District Councils, Town Boards and Local Councils. The restructuring of the local authorities in Peninsular Malaysia has now virtually been completed. Today, except for the local authorities of Maran, Rompin and Pekan, all in the State of Pahang, all the local authorities in the Peninsula have been restructured to form 75 District Councils and 16 Municipal Councils (including the City Council of Kuala Lumpur). The local government system in Sabah and Sarawak was not affected by the restructuring exercise.[3]

The restructuring under Section 3 of the 1976 Local Government Act was effected in a number of ways as follows:
    i. by declaring an existing local authority as a new local authority area under the Act;
    ii. by increasing the area under a local authority through incorporating within it adjacent smaller local authorities, new villages or surrounding areas;
    iii. by amalgamating two or more contiguous local authorities to form a new local authority;
    iv. by enlarging the size of a local authority through incorporation of areas that were not previously under any local authority;
    v. by declaring a new area that had not been previously administered under any authority as a new local authority;
    vi. amalgamation of existing small authorities or new and traditional villages to form a larger local authority.

A local authority is classified as a Municipal Council if it meets the following criteria: (i) if it is a major town such as the capital of a State, (ii) having a population of more than 100,000 living in dense urban setting, (iii) having an annual revenue of not less than Malaysian $5 million, (iv) with an existing administrative center situated in a central location, and (v) where the pressure on the administration is for better urban services rather than the provision of infrastructure. On the other hand, a local authority is classified as a District Council if it is (i) rural-based and located outside the major towns, (ii) having a population of less than 100,000 living in scattered manner, (iii) having an annual revenue of less than Malaysian $5 million, (iv) with limited ability to carry out all its functions because of inadequate communication facilities, and (v) where the need is to provide more basic infrastructural facilities rather than local services.

*Implications.* A major outcome of the restructuring exercise is that not only are the new authorities larger in terms of area and population than their predecessors, but also that smaller villages and sparsely populated rural areas have become part of a local authority for the first time. Before restructuring was undertaken as much as 90% of the land area and 40% of the population living in Peninsular Malaysia were outside the existing local government structure. With the completion of the restructuring exercise, almost all the Peninsula's land area and population fall within the new system of local government. This increase in size and population has far reaching implications for the local authorities particularly on their capacity to deliver services to their clientele. Thus, the new Municipal Councils and District Councils require additional funds, staff and equipment simply to extend the existing local services over a wider area and to a larger population.

With restructuring, local authorities have now wider functions and responsibilities. The scope and implications of the restructuring exercise on the functions and responsibilities of local authorities are reflected in the three major pieces legislation accompanying restructuring, namely, the 1976 Local Government Act, the 1976 Town and Country Planning Act, and the 1974 Streets, Drainage and Buildings Act, which govern the activities of the new local authorities.

The 1976 Local Government Act which became the basis for the establishment and restructuring of local authorities contains specific provisions outlining the role, responsibilities and functions of local authorities in local government. Briefly, local authorities are entrusted with the responsibility and given the authority to protect, control and promote the social welfare and economic interests of the local population. Thus, apart from the collection of taxes, the responsibility includes areas such as public cleanliness and health, safety of buildings, control of public places, environmental pollution, cemeteries, provision of basic amenities, enforcement of by-laws and others which are directly or indirectly related with the health and welfare of the public. An important aspect of the Act is the 'developmental' role that local authorities are expected to play. They are empowered to participate in economic and commercial activities as part of the effort to develop the local economy for the benefit of the local population as well as the local authority itself.

The 1974 Streets, Drainage and Buildings Act provides wide ranging responsibilities and powers to the local authority to control physical development, such as buildings, drainage, and streets, to ensure that the activities are carried out according to conditions and standards set under the Act. This involves the exercise of wide ranging control and enforcement functions on the part of the local authority to ensure the appropriateness and safety of buildings and other physical structures constructed within the local authority area.

The 1976 Town and Country Planning Act recognizes the local authority as the 'local planning authority' and provides it with wide powers and responsibilities to control planning and all activities related to physical development in the local authority area. Local authorities are required to ensure that all development planning by government agencies as well as the private sector conforms to the planning standards established under the Act. Local authorities are required to prepare structure and local plans to ensure orderly development within the area under their jurisdiction.

Considered together, the three major pieces of legislation discussed above reflect the wide and comprehensive role and responsibilities that the restructured local authorities have been called upon to shoulder.

*Administration and Personnel.* Although the restructuring exercise proceeded rather smoothly, albeit somewhat slowly, a number of problems have been identified that act as constraints to the local authorities in improving their capacity to perform even their traditional functions of providing services to the people.

The effects of the restructuring exercise in improving the administrative and operational capacity of the local authorities are at best minimal. This is particularly true of the District Councils. The larger and more established Municipal Councils tend to derive more benefits from the restructuring because they have a stronger foundation to build upon.

In respect of the appointment of Councillors of local authorities, the 1976 Local Government Act stipulates that a Councillor should be appointed on the basis of: (i) being a resident in the local authority area, (ii) having achieved prominence in a certain profession, trade or industry, (iii) has experience in the running of a local authority, and (iv) has the ability to represent the interests of his community. In practice, however, State Governments seldom adhere to these criteria in the appointment of Councillors. Almost all Councillors of local authorities are appointed from amongst politicians. This practice has often resulted in the appointment of persons who are unable to contribute meaningfully or who have little interest or dedication in the running of the local authority.

Local authorities, particularly District Councils, have not been able to match the increase in their area and scope of responsibility with a corresponding increase in personnel. In theory, local authorities are empowered to recruit their own staff. However, before they are able to do so approval has to be obtained from the State Government, and for the senior category of officers approval of the Federal Treasury and the central personnel agency has to be obtained because of the financial implications involved. A problem that is continuously faced by local authorities is their inability to fill existing vacancies because of the refusal of State Governments to grant permission to fill such vacancies. Likewise local authorities depend on State and the Federal Government for approval for the creation of new posts. Even when all the necessary approvals are granted, it is difficult to get candidates to apply for higher level posts because service with a local authority lacks the attractions that other services in the public and private sector can offer.

The general problem of filling vacancies in local authorities and their general inability to develop a core of personnel adequate in number and varied enough in expertise constitutes one of the major reasons why most local authorities, especially the District Councils, have not been able to improve their organizational and administrative effectiveness, particularly in light of their increasing responsibilities and functions brought about by restructuring.

*Finance.* Local authorities derive their income from property taxes, rents, licensing fees and profits earned from trade, services or enterprises, as well as payments received from time to time from the Federal or State Governments. For most local authorities, particularly District Councils, income from taxes is limited - the bulk of their income being derived from grants provided by the Federal or State Governments. Income from sources outside the local authority includes contributions-in-aid of rates, road maintenance grants, balancing grants and grants for small projects. Without these sources of income from outside, most local authorities would find themselves in dire financial straits.

The Federal Government provides local authorities with an annual grant and a launching grant as incentives for them to implement the restructuring policy of the Government. The grants also serve to ease the financial burden of local authorities which has increased considerably as a result of restructuring. The launching grants are designed specifically to assist local authorities to purchase equipment and vehicles for garbage collection, as well as to carry out other projects that have become necessary. Grants for implementing small projects are also given out by the Federal Government to assist local authorities in providing basic amenities such as public markets, public toilets, drains and roads.

The increase in the size of local authorities and their new 'development' role as a result of restructuring have very serious implications on the finances of local authorities. The increase in land area and population and, therefore, in responsibility has taken place without a corresponding increase in revenue, especially in the case of District Councils. In addition, they are now confronted with the need to carry out development projects out of their already meager resources, while at the same time having to provide basic services for an increased number of people.

At the same time local authorities continue to suffer the ills of the past. They are unable to undertake revaluation exercises of properties in their areas because of insufficient capacity to do so. Most local authorities are still using rating and valuation methods that are out of date, thereby further depressing their revenue source. They are unable to raise property taxes without approval of State Governments, and approval is rarely given for various reasons.

Shortage of qualified and experienced personnel also prevents many local authorities from enhancing their revenue. Their inability to enforce laws adequately leads to loss of revenue and backlog in the collection of property taxes.

Although with restructuring, local authorities are provided with direct financial assistance by the Federal Government, it appears that most of them, particularly the District Councils, are experiencing very serious financial problems. This situation is reflected in the poor performance of local authorities in carrying out their administrative and operational functions. It is apparent that the restructuring of local authorities requires major investment of funds to enable local authorities to properly carry out their increased responsibilities and functions. The objective of establishing an effective and viable system of local government would not be easily attained if the financial problems of local authorities are allowed to persist.

*Overlapping of Responsibilities and Functions.* Prior to restructuring, local authorities had existed side by side with the long established institution of District Office. The division of responsibilities and functions between the two was clear cut. While the District Office was responsible for the overall administration and development of the district, the local authority concentrated mainly on the provision of basic services such as disposal of garbage, street maintenance works, clearing of drains, providing street lighting, etc. Only the bigger and more affluent local authorities provided discretionary services such as public facilities, public housing, public transportation and so on. The District

Office has traditionally been the center of administration for the district. The District Officer, acting through various committees such as the District Action Committee and the District Development Committee, plans and coordinates development for the district as a whole.

Restructuring has introduced a new element into the picture. The newly restructured Municipal and District Councils may physically cover entire Districts or major sub-divisions of existing Districts. The fact that a local authority is also assigned a developmental role and given powers, by virtue of its being also the local planning authority, to coordinate and control development activities within its boundary, has given rise to the possibility of conflicts and duplication of responsibilities and functions. At present these are minimized by the mere fact that the local authority does not possess the capacity to perform all its assigned functions. In any case, District Officers are in many instances appointed as Presidents of District Councils and in this capacity are able to play their traditional role unhindered.[4] However, where the posts of District Officer and President of the local authority are occupied by different individuals, the potential for conflict is very real. Again, the practice of appointing a District Officer as President of the local authority is not without its disadvantages. As the chief administrator of a district his responsibilities and functions are very broad. Most of his time is taken up by meetings of numerous committees and attending to ceremonial functions. As a result he has very little time to devote to the affairs of the local authority. Invariably, the tasks of running the local authority fall upon the administrative officer or secretary of the council. A District Council caught in this situation is unable to take the initiative in planning, coordinating and controlling development activities undertaken by various government agencies within the area under its control. This situation is not conducive to the development of public confidence in the ability of local authorities to be the initiator and coordinator of development at the local level, which is so important at this initial stage.

Other government and semi-government bodies are also involved in the implementation of socioeconomic development projects in the area under the control of a local authority. Regional development authorities that had been established prior to restructuring and became incorporated into a local authority area had also been given powers and authority of a local government unit for the purpose of providing basic local services to residents in their area. In such a situation, a measure of confusion and overlapping of roles has arisen. For as long as the newly restructured local authority is incapable of extending services to areas under a regional development authority things will work fine, but once a local authority has developed the capacity to plan and extend its services complications are bound to arise.

The question of overlapping of responsibilities and functions did not appear to have been seriously considered. While at the initial stages this may not be a serious problem because of the limited capacity of the newly restructured local authority, it may be costly in the long term and may prove difficult to sort out.

## Solution Alternatives

The restructuring of the local government system in Peninsular Malaysia was undoubtedly a step in the right direction. Malaysia is too small a country to afford the luxury of so many local authorities that are incapable of delivering basic services in an efficient way, much less participate in the socioeconomic development of the nation. The reform introduced in 1976 established the structure of a new system of local government in Peninsular Malaysia. The 1976 Local Government Act, which became the basis of the restructuring and accompanying legislation, confers upon local authorities not only powers that could be utilized to improve the delivery of services, but also powers to undertake a very wide range of activities for the benefit of their communities. However, considered as a whole the progress achieved by 1985 only partially meets the expectations. The newly restructured local authorities still lack the capacity to take on their new role.

The lack of success in developing the capacity to undertake their new role on the part of local authorities is inextricably linked to the way power and resources are distributed in the Malaysian federal system. The restructuring exercise has not altered the power and authority relationship between local government, State Government and the Federal Government. Admittedly, the local authorities have been placed on a more solid footing by the reorganization of boundaries and given more powers through various legislations to undertake traditional and new responsibilities. However, the actual exercise of these powers still depends on the discretion of the State. The reform therefore has not altered but confirms the dominance and control of the State in all respects. Particularly important are the States' control over the appointment of Councillors, areas of local authorities, budgets and loans, appointment of senior staff, development plans and rating lists.

The States, in their dealings with their own local authorities, face several constraints. One major constraint is the constitutional imbalance between the responsibilities of the States and the fiscal resources available to them to carry out their responsibilities. The difference between the States' revenue and expenditure is met partly from statutory grants from the Federal Government under the constitution, partly by loan from the Federal Government and partly, in the case of the poorer States, by the Federal Treasury covering the deficits. This fiscal imbalance not only can contribute to poor relationships but also prevents the States from establishing strong and efficient administrations to carry out their functions and responsibilities effectively because they do not have resources to do so. Thus, faced with this constraint themselves, their lack of total commitment and less than generous attitude towards their own local authorities can be readily understood.

From the foregoing, it would appear on the surface that one way by which the capacity of the local authorities could be strengthened is to give them more powers over finance and personnel. These two are closely linked and constitute the life-blood of an authority. This would entail amendments to the Federal Constitution which would in effect mean a redistribution of powers between the Federal, States and local Governments. Given the realities of a federal system, however, such a suggestion is impractical and unrealistic. Under the circumstances it can be assumed that the Federal Constitution is unlikely to be changed to any significant extent in respect of the various levels of government. Given this assumption, it makes good sense to concentrate on the present framework and to search for ways by which the capacity of the new local authorities could be strengthened.

In view of the fact that financial and personnel resources constitute the sinews of any local authority, the search for solutions to the plight of the local authorities should begin in these two major areas.

Evidently, existing sources of revenue are no longer adequate to meet the needs of local authorities to deliver basic urban services to the people, not to mention the need to undertake development activities called for by the Local Government Act of 1976. Ways will have to be found to provide additional sources of income for the local authorities. In this respect there is a need for a study to be carried out to identify additional sources of revenue to enable them to be financially independent in the long term. As this task is beyond the capacity of any individual local authority, save the larger Municipal Councils, it should be undertaken by a higher level of government. Once these additional sources are identified a guideline should be prepared for use by local authorities.

As noted earlier the restructuring exercise was accompanied by various legislations conferring various powers on the local authority. These legislations are practically useless to most local authorities as they do not have the necessary by-laws to enforce them. As it is beyond the existing capacity of most local authorities to develop their own by-laws they should be assisted in doing this by the relevant authorities. Such by-laws would not only assist local authorities in law enforcement but also provide additional income through fees, fines and other penalties.

A high proportion of local authorities have not carried out revaluation exercises of properties within their area for a considerable length of time. Those that have carried out revaluation face the prospect of stiff resistance from several quarters. Assistance given to local authorities to carry out revaluation exercises has to be intensified, as most do not have the capacity to undertake this function on their own. At the same time State Governments should adopt a more pragmatic and bolder approach to the question of raising assessment rates to more realistic levels to reflect current economic conditions. Hard decisions will have to be made to make local authorities a going concern. In the long term resistance to increased rates may be mellowed when the increased tax burden is compensated by an improved level of services.

Financial assistance will have to continue to be provided to local authorities, particularly the poorer ones, to enable them to reach a stage where they are in a position to finance their own day-to-day operations and at the same time carry out basic socioeconomic activities in their area. From time to time assessments should be made on the financial position of such local authorities to ascertain whether further assistance would be justified.

There is also a need to review the formula presently being used by the Federal and State Governments in the granting of financial assistance to local authorities. Apart from area size and size of population other factors that should be taken into account include the stage of socioeconomic development as well as resource endowment of a local authority. Local authorities that are located in remote areas and which are less developed should be provided with greater financial assistance. The level of increase to be given could be made on a selective basis.

As the financial malady afflicting local authorities had been inherited and allowed to persist for such a long time, it may take some years to nurse them back to sound health. Continuous commitment on the part of higher levels of government is therefore a prerequisite for eventual recovery and take-off.

Closely interlocked with the question of finance is the question of personnel. As noted earlier, most local authorities, particularly the District Councils, face perpetual problems of filling vacancies and creating new posts, owing to financial constraints and the control exercised by the States and Federal Government. Admittedly, the constitutional division of powers and the financial position of the States themselves make the controls a necessary evil. However, the higher levels of government should be ever mindful of the fact that without the necessary manpower to work at the local level, no amount of legislation, powers conferred or responsibilities given to the local authorities would lead to improved performance in the provision of basic services or in carrying out development activities as expected.

The service of a local authority is small by its very nature. Thus, a local authority will continuously face the problem of attracting capable and qualified personnel. To overcome this problem in the short term a policy of seconding officers from other agencies of the government to the services of the local authorities should be vigorously pursued until such time as a local authority is able to develop a sufficient cadre to operate on its own. In the long term, the idea of setting up a common service for all local authorities should be seriously examined. Such a service would be able to provide avenues for promotion and career advancement, which the separate local authority services do not now possess, to attract capable and qualified candidates.

The creation of new local authorities with enlarged boundaries to include whole districts or parts of several districts has given rise to the possibility of duplication of functions and responsibilities with existing agencies and institutions, particularly the District Office. Serious duplication has so far been avoided because of the lack of capacity on the part of local authorities to carry out all their assigned responsibilities and functions as provided in the various legislations. It is the planning and developmental role of the local authority that places it in a position of competition with the District Office and other government agencies engaged in development activities within the area covered by the local authority. The problem of duplication of responsibilities and functions between the local authorities and other government institutions and agencies deserves close scrutiny by higher levels of government to avoid unnecessary expenditure of time and money. Pending a resolution to this problem, it would be beneficial for local authorities to concentrate their efforts in providing improved urban services to their communities, especially in view of the limited financial and manpower resources at their disposal.

As noted earlier, the present system of nominating councillors of local authorities does not appear to encourage public participation. In the first place, the members are limited in number to a maximum of twenty-four. Secondly, there is a tendency among State Governments to appoint political figures and to emphasize balance among the components of the ruling party. This practice has led to the appointment of persons who do not meet the rather specific requirements of the Local Government Act of 1976. Moreover, the brief tenure and transitory nature of the office make the role of councillors unattractive. In such a situation it is questionable whether the interests of the local population are adequately articulated in the council.

Development after all concerns the welfare of people, and people should have as direct a say as is feasible as to how improvements in their welfare are to be achieved. Since autonomy, in the sense of a strong local initiative, is impractical because it is not acceptable in the hierarchical structure of Malaysian Government, new strategies will have to be found to provide more opportunities to the public to say what and how services are to be provided to them. The State authorities need to review their practice of appointing local authority councillors to conform to the requirements of the Local Government Act of 1976 and to ensure that the genuinely concerned and the interested are not excluded from the councils of local government.

## Summary and Conclusions

It may be too early at this juncture to measure the performance of the restructured local authorities in Peninsular Malaysia. The restructuring exercise, at least in the physical sense, that was set in motion in 1976 is now almost complete.[5] Today, practically the whole of Peninsular Malaysia is covered by a local authority; Municipal Councils for the larger urban areas and District Councils for the predominantly rural districts. This in itself is no simple task considering the nature of Malaysian Federalism.

However, actions that have been taken thus far to provide the necessary resources for local authorities appear to be inadequate. Whatever is provided seems to be provided with hesitation. A solution to the perennial problem of local government financing is still a long way off. The issue of staffing for local authorities is still unresolved. The issue of the possibility of duplication of responsibilities and functions at the local government level seems to be conveniently set aside.

In terms of the delivery of basic urban services the restructuring appears to have raised some expectations. Launching grants provided by the Federal Government have enabled even the poor District Councils to purchase additional vehicles and equipment to improve garbage collection and other services. As to how long this situation can be maintained depends a great deal on the availability of continuous support.

The period that has elapsed since restructuring was started may not have been adequate to enable the local authorities to overcome the problems and weaknesses they have inherited and which have been rampant for such a long time. The next five years should prove critical not only for individual local authorities but also for the local government system as a whole. If measures currently undertaken fail to produce the desired results in the next five years, then serious thought should be given to answer the question as to whether the existing system of local government is viable in the context of the country's social, economic and political environment and whether the structure, concepts and principles that form the basis of the existing system should be reviewed. If after such soul searching it is decided that the system of local government is worth preserving, then the next question that has to be answered is whether there is readiness to modify the existing patterns of relationships between the three tiers of government, with the aim of providing the necessary powers as well as resources to local government units to enable them to carry out their responsibilities and functions effectively.

The existing model of local government has all the potential to succeed. But to do so, it needs the continuing support and commitment of the States and Federal Government. If these are forthcoming, there is no reason why the local government system could not be an effective partner in the socioeconomic and political development of the nation.

**Notes**

1. Malcom Norris, "Restructuring of Local Government," *Malaysian Management Review,* Vol. 15, No. 1 (1979).

2. Department of Local Government, Kuala Lumpur, "Strategi-Strategi Kementerian Perumahan dan Kerajaan Tempatan Dalam Konteks Rancangan Malaysia Ke 5." Paper presented at INTAN, Kuala Lumpur, at a Conference, 3 - 8 May, 1984.

3. There are 3 Municipal Councils and 19 District Councils in Sabah. The Municipal Council of Labuan has been changed in status to Federal Territory. Sarawak has 3 Municipal Councils and 21 District Councils.

4. The practice of appointing Presidents of Municipal and District Councils is not uniform throughout the States. Municipal Councils may have as their Presidents, the Chief Minister, a full time seconded officer or a politician. A District Council may have a District Officer or a politician as president.

5. Only three remain to be restructured - Maran, Rompin and Pekan, all in the State of Pahang.

218  *Delivery of Public Services in Asian Countries*

**Appendix I  Structure of Local Government in Peninsular Malaysia**

Level of Government

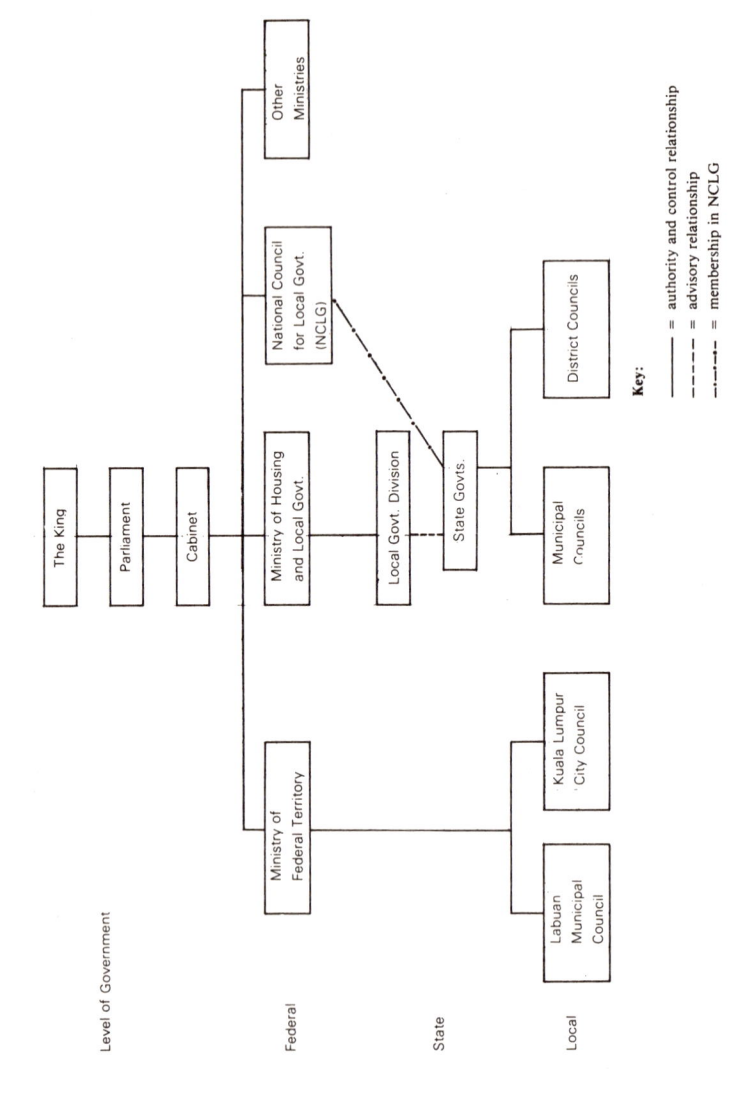

Federal: The King — Parliament — Cabinet — Ministry of Housing and Local Govt. — Local Govt. Division; Ministry of Federal Territory; National Council for Local Govt. (NCLG); Other Ministries

State: State Govts.

Local: Municipal Councils; District Councils; Kuala Lumpur City Council; Labuan Municipal Council

Key:
———  = authority and control relationship
- - - - -  = advisory relationship
—·—·—  = membership in NCLG

# 10

# The Delivery of Services at Sub-District Level: the Concept of Service Centers in Nepal

*Khagendra Nath Sharma\**

Nepal is one of the few countries in Asia which has never been colonized. This fact, in conjunction with the country's relative isolation, may explain why up until 1950 there were virtually no traces of socioeconomic or politico-administrative development. In 1951, however, the ruling aristrocratic family of the Ranas - who had up until then overshadowed both the monarchy and the people - were overthrown in a revolution headed by the king. This revolution heralded the beginnings of fundamental socioeconomic and administrative reforms in Nepal, one of which was the first organized development program, launched in 1952 under the name of the Tribhuban Village Development Program.[1]

Before 1951, the government performed only extractive and regulatory functions. For this purpose about 35 districts and a few sub-districts were created under the supreme unitary command of the prime minister. Under the village development program, development blocs were created within the districts and each bloc had a team of development experts headed by a bloc development officer. Under the command of the bloc development officer there were village development workers who worked under the direction of technical supervisors. These development workers served in an area encompassing a few villages and moved from village to village. There were advisory bodies at the bloc level and village level, but they were hardly functional.

After 1962, when the panchayat system of partyless democracy was established,[2] the village development program was replaced by a new panchayat development program. What were previously blocs were converted into districts. Villages were clustered into village panchayats, while at the district level, district panchayats were created as politico-developmental institutions. The chief executive of the district panchayat was a panchayat development officer, who

---

*The Central Panchayat Training Institute, Lalutpur, Nepal.

supervised the village panchayat secretaries that also worked as multi-purpose development workers. The so-called panchayat sector was responsible for local level (i.e., district and village) infrastructural development. Other development sectors created their own line agencies with separate offices at the district headquarters. They had some field workers who worked in the villages in mobile teams.

The village development program and the panchayat development program contained two different conceptions of local development. While the village development program had created a pool of technical experts under the direction of the bloc development officer, the panchayat development program functioned in a manner where all expertise was organized on a unilinear basis. During the period of village development programs, the people were only nominally involved, whereas during the period of the panchayat development program, panchayat institutions were created with political and legal support. Thus, the emphasis was on institutionalized development. The concept of guided development in the village development program became the concept of participatory development in the panchayat development program, where the major responsibility for local development rested with the panchayats. The panchayats in turn were elected institutions which called upon the people to participate in development programs.

**Delivery of Services at the Local Level**

Until 1951, the idea of serving the people was only a philanthropic concept and not a regular duty of the government. A semblance of justice was provided through courts manned not by jurists but by favorites of the ruling family. Some medical services were provided in a few district headquarters, which reached about 1 to 2 per cent of the population. For the other 98 - 99 per cent, however, shamans provided consolatory relief. In the field of education, some schools and a college in Kathmandu were opened, but the population in general remained illiterate.

During the decade after the overthrow of the Ranas, services were initiated in different sectors of development. The village development program provided the following services: agricultural inputs, credit through cooperatives, animal husbandry and veterinary services, school-level education, health services, cottage industries, etc.; but the delivery was done at bloc headquarters which were not very accessible to the majority of people because of the distance, physical difficulties, and high cost involved. Extension services were provided through mobile agricultural workers and the village development workers. The people obtained their first notions of organized development - but it was only the beginning of change.

The panchayat development program brought about structural changes in the organizational pattern of development. The bloc team separated into autonomous units engaged in sectoral development with support from the line departments and ministries at the center. The panchayat sector adopted an institutional pattern through the creation of panchayat institutions, where elected representatives of the people made decisions directing the course of local development. The quantum of service was increased over time, although the beneficiaries remained virtually the same. A number of banks were created including an agricultural development bank.

**Contextual/Structural Constraints**

The process of development in Nepal is fraught with constraints, some avoidable and some unavoidable. While the government is trying its best to alleviate problems concerning the delivery of basic services in rural areas, there are inherent limitations that tend to thwart attempted improvements. Some of these constraints are discussed below.

*Unavoidable Constraints.* The most obvious example of an unavoidable constraint is the problem of creating a surface transportation system in the hills and mountains. About 15 percent of the total land mass consists of uninhabitable mountains. About 50 percent of the population inhabit the lower mountains and hills. Experience has shown that even along the foothills, construction and maintenance of roads is problematic in terms of both cost and durability. In consequence, most villages in the hills are not connected to a good road system. Concomitantly, the difficult topography also inhibits the growth of services such as irrigation, drinking water, communications, and health care.

The lack of a properly developed transportation system has in turn inhibited the development of marketing networks. Consequently, although many areas have started growing apples and other fruits and vegetables, they cannot sell their produce in lower Nepal because of the prohibitively high transportation costs. The situation is such that the price of apples imported from Kashmir in India, thousands of miles away, is lower in Nepalganj than the price of apples brought from Jumla, which is only half-an-hour's flight from Nepalganj.

The cost of development in Nepal will remain a perennial problem. Because Nepal is landlocked with its inherent limitations, this will always result in higher expenditures on imports compared with countries with seaport facilities. Added to this is the internal cost of aerial transport or carriage by porters or animals. A bag of cement, for example, sells along Nepal's southern border with India for Rs. 100, while in a hill district about one hundred miles away, it costs over Rs. 500.

*Manageable or Avoidable Constraints.* In the socioeconomic context the caste system, compounded by unequal distribution measures, creates the problem of imbalance. The rich are usually literate also, and can manage to absorb the bulk of development inputs. The poor and the lower castes are the illiterate sector of society, and benefit very little or not at all from the 'trickle down effect' of socioeconomic development. Agrarian reform was initiated in 1964, but this has only been partially successful. Thus, more can be done in pursuit of balanced socioeconomic development.

The socio-political context is a reflection of socioeconomic factors. The managers of local institutions mostly come from the upper stratum of society, and they have easy access to the delivery system. In contrast, the lower strata have much fewer opportunities to access the delivery system, and have no way of influencing the decision-making process. In short, political benefits for the lower strata of society are minimal.

In the administrative structures created for delivery of services, the following problems are apparent: first, the district headquarters is the main center for service deliveries, but for many villages it is too remote. Second, apart from physical distance, there is the social distance between an educated officer in charge of delivery and the illiterate villager in need of services. This problem is compounded by superficial bureaucratic formalities that do not accommodate the needs of villagers. Third, qualified and trained personnel prefer to stay away from rural areas. There is, therefore, a dearth of technical services at the local level. Fourth, local institutions such as the *sajha* (cooperative) have failed to enlist the participation of the general population. Similarly, institutional credit from the Agricultural Development Bank has also failed to reach the more needy sections of society, who are then forced to turn to money lenders for loans. Fifth, except for the programs of the panchayat sector, other development sectors like agriculture, health, education, forestry, cottage industries, etc., have no formal link with local institutions. This has been a major factor inhibiting popular participation. Finally, the basic problem underlying the process of development, including delivery of services, is that of coordination. When the line ministries were separated, no formal structure was provided at district level for coordination of their programs.

## Attempted Improvements

Given the above circumstances the delivery of services has been only partially effective and only a small segment of society has benefited from it. Efforts are constantly being made to solve this problem, however, including the introduction of a periodic planning system in 1956.[3] Five five-year plans and one three-year plan have been completed up to now. The sixth five-year plan was initiated in the current fiscal year, beginning July 16, 1985. Nepal has been divided into 5 development regions, 14 administrative zones, and 75 districts. In addition to the development line agencies that work in these 75 districts, there are 75 district panchayats, 29 town panchayats, and 4023 village panchayats that work in local development. The village panchayats are further divided into 8 wards, each ward having a committee of five persons elected by the adult population of the area. The village panchayat is responsible to a larger body called the village assembly, which is the final legitimizer of development activities at village level.

At district level the following sectoral line service/development agencies have been created: district panchayat secretariats; agricultural development offices; agricultural development banks; agricultural input corporations; health extension hospitals; education institutions; cottage industries; forestry agencies; soil conservation agencies; postal services; cooperatives; public works (engineering); drinking water (in a few districts); irrigation agencies; and family planning offices.

The main objectives of development plans have been to create employment and provide basic services. Five development regions were recently created to offset regional imbalances in the development process, where the eastern and central regions overtook the west in almost all aspects. Now the west obtains an equitable share in resource allocations. The regional directorates supervise, monitor, and evaluate their respective sectors at the district level.

There was no formal intersector relationship at the district level until 1973. The above-mentioned development agencies and other regulatory and revenue agencies worked independently of each other. There was, however, the office of the chief district officer, who was regarded as the chief government agent. The government introduced an executive order in 1974 known as the District Administration Plan, which made the chief district officer responsible both for the maintenance of law and order and the coordination of local development. This provided a loose relationship among the district level development agencies under the leadership of the chief district officer. The District Administration Plan, however, was not an effective mechanism for development for two reasons: first, the chief district officer was generally preoccupied with law and order and thus provided only nominal leadership for development; second, the continued control from the central line agencies, combined with a refusal on the part of most development ministries and departments to delegate administrative power to the chief district officer, dealt a severe blow to the District Administration Plan. Thus, although the District Administration Plan has never been rescinded, neither has it been of any use in shaping the delivery systems of public services in Nepal.

In 1978-1979 the government implemented on a trial basis in four districts a new approach called the Integrated Panchayat Development Design, which empowered the district panchayat to coordinate and regulate all local development programs. Because of the political turmoil of 1979 and the subsequent referendum, however, the government virtually dropped this approach.[4] Instead, the government started the Integrated Rural Development Project with bilateral and multilateral assistance.[5] Although the Integrated Panchayat Development Design had introduced the concept of delivery services at sub-district levels, the program was abandoned before the concept could take hold. In contrast, the Integrated Rural Development Project became an effective instrument of rural development. There are at present 8 projects covering 23 districts, the details of which are set out in Table 1.

**The Concept and Practice of Service Centers in Integrated Rural Development Projects**

The Integrated Rural Development Project adopts a multi-sectoral approach that aims, *inter alia,* to increase production and income levels and generate employment opportunities. IRDP projects support the development of infrastructure to provide for an effective delivery system. As delivery facilities for government services have centered hitherto around the district headquarters, which have been inaccessible to most people, the growth that was originally intended

**Table 1** Integrated Rural Development Projects in Nepal

| Se:No. Project Name | Donor |
|---|---|
| 1. Koshi Hill Areas Dev Project (KHARDEP) (4 districts) | - U.K. Govt. |
| 2. Sagarmatha IRD (3 districts) | - Asian Development Bank (loan) |
| 3. Rasuwa Nuwakot IRD (2 districts) | - World Bank (loan) |
| 4. Integrated Hill Development Program (IHDP) (2 districts) | - Swiss Govt. |
| 5. Dhading IRD (1 district) | - Govt. of the Federal Republic of Germany |
| 6. Rapti Rural Areas Development Program (5 districts) | - U.S. Govt. |
| 7. Karnali-Bheri IRD K-BIRD (3 districts)* | - Canadian Govt. |
| 8. Mahakali Hill Areas IRD (3 districts) | - World Bank (loan) |
| Total coverage - 23 districts. | |

*K-BIRD may eventually cover the 10 districts of Karnali and Bheri Zones. But now it is implemented in two districts in Bheri and one in Karnali.

has not been achieved. Hence, more accessible points have been considered necessary. Bringing the entire district mechanism down below the district level has not been feasible because of cost and political considerations; but certain basic services can be increased by proliferating distribution points below the district level. Thus, appraisals concerning integrated rural development have included identification of locations most frequently used or which are usable by people in the surrounding areas, such centers being little towns where people shop for or sell their products. In the absence of such facilities, temples or schools can be convenient points for this purpose.

Service centers are intended to make the service delivery points accessible to the majority of people, and to promote the growth of local institutions. The service center is a pool of development inputs and technical services, and is expected to provide technical services in response to the needs of village panchayats. One of the main components of the panchayat development program is people's participation in the process of development. The service centers will be able to provide support for this movement by offering services to satisfy both individual needs (medical, veterinary, and agricultural), and collective needs (community projects). The main components of service centers are oriented toward civil engineering; agriculture; health; veterinary care; cottage industries; banking; forestry and soil conservation; and panchayat.

Districts have been divided into nine politico-electoral areas, each represented by one district panchayat member. The ultimate spatial distribution of service centers will be one service center in each of those nine areas; but in the initial stage a smaller number of centers have been opened in the integrated rural development districts. The following statistics are derived from the Ministry of Panchayat and Local Development regarding the present status of service centers in integrated rural development districts (see Table 2).

A thorough evaluation of the service centers has not been done, but initial results have been so satisfactory that the government has decided to gradually expand the service scheme in all 75 districts under the decentralized planning process. In the fiscal year which started on July 16, 1985, 14 districts were selected for intensive implementation of the scheme.

*Decentralization.* Planning in Nepal, as in most other developing countries, has been highly centralized. The National Planning Commission controlled and directed the allocation and use of resources except for a small proportion of local resources, with a misleadingly high percentage assumed to be contributed by the people. The local Panchayat Acts of 1962 (the District Panchayat Act, the Town Panchayat Act, and the Village Panchayat Act) resulted in a planning framework to be legitimized by local bodies, but central control of resources made the local institutions dependent on central allocations.

An attempt was made in the fifth five-year plan (1980-85) to reverse this process and start a process of planning from the bottom up. However, resource control still remained in the hands of the National Planning Commission, and there were no substantial changes in that period. The central government was, nonetheless, committed through pledges made during the 1980 referendum to initiate measures for effective decentralization of development functions. Consequently, a Decentralization Act was passed in 1982 which was implemented at the beginning of the 1986 fiscal year, which coincided with the beginning of the sixth five-year plan.[6] The planning aspects of the Decentralization Act are being implemented in all 75 districts, but the government has chosen cnly 14 districts - one in each zone - where all the provisions of the Act are to

**Table 2** Service Centers Operating Under Different Integrated Rural Development Projects

| Name of IRDP | District | No. of Service Centers |
|---|---|---|
| 1. KHARDEP | 1. Dhankuta | 3 |
|  | 2. Bhojpur | 3 |
|  | 3. Sankhuasabha | 3 |
|  | 4. Terhathum | 3 |
| 2. Sagarmatha IRD | 1. Siraha | 9 |
|  | 2. Udayapur | 9 |
|  | 3. Saptari | 9 |
| 3. Rasuwa-Nuwakot IRDP | 1. Rasuwa | 3 |
|  | 2. Nuwakot | 9 |
| 4. IHDP* | Dolkha | 2 |
| 5. Rapti RADP** | 1. Dang | 1 |
|  | 2. Salyan | 1 |
|  | 3. Rukum | 1 |
|  | 4. Pyuthan | 1 |
|  | 5. Rolpa | 1 |
| 6. K-BIRD Project | 1. Surkhet | 2 |
|  | 2. Dailekh | 2 |
|  | 3. Jumla | 1 |
| 7. Mahakali Hills | 1. Baitadi | 6 |
|  | 2. Dadeldhura | 5 |
|  | 3. Darchula | 3 |
| 8. Dhading project has not opened service centers yet. | | |
| | Total Service Centers | 77 |

* Sindhupalchowk district is only partly covered by the Integrated Rural Development Project.
** Rapti Rural Areas Development Program aims at running five service centers in each district, but has at present only one center in each district.

Source : Ministry of Panchayat and Local Development.

be implemented. The creation of service centers is one of the main provisions of the Act. The planning process is as follows:

The National Planning Commission provides advance information on the resource ceiling for both periodic and annual plans for all local development programs. Local agencies develop their plans and projects in the following manner. At ward level (nine wards in a village panchayat), the ward committee initiates the planning process indicating its demands, priorities, and strategies of implementation. At the village panchayat level, the village panchayat aggregates the ward level action plans into a composite village panchayat plan and places it before the village assembly, which consists of all the nine ward committees, the chairman and vice-chairman of the village panchayat, together with the chairman of class organization primary committees. The village assembly finalizes the village plan and sends it to the district panchayat.

At the district level, the district panchayat makes a composite plan which includes three types of activities: all the village plans; all programs undertaken by the district panchayat; and all district-level sectoral programs of development. There are five plan formulation committees to examine projects of respective sectors which include construction and maintenance, agriculture and irrigation, health and population, forestry, soil conservation and industry, and education. The formulation committees send their respective recommendations to the district panchayat which then aggregates all these activities into one coherent plan and places it before the district assembly, which consists of the district and all chairmen and vice-chairmen of village panchayats and town panchayats, together with one-third of the town panchayat members wherever there are town panchayats in a district. The district assembly is the final legitimizer of local plans. The central government is bound to accept the decision of the district assembly within the resource ceiling provided. The local panchayats can also access a variety of local resources. No sectoral plan will be funded unless it is approved by the district assembly.

*The Case for Service Centers.* As mentioned earlier, the creation and operation of service centers is one important aspect of the Decentralization Act. This major change in policy was taken after a review of the flaws in the existing delivery system and an examination of the operation of the service centers in the integrated rural development projects.

The following flaws in the existing delivery system have been identified:

1) Resources were allocated at the discretion of the center and not on effective demand of the local population.
2) There was a lack of coordination among the development/service agencies at district level.
3) In some areas services or programs were duplicated but major areas were left out.
4) The so-called multipurpose development worker who worked as the village panchayat secretary was not used by development sectors as their agent. The services of the other sectoral 'front line' workers were inadequate, as the numbers of such workers were too small to cover the large areas involved.
5) Qualified technical personnel were not available to work at the village level.
6) Out of the available services the only ones who benefited were the village elite. Thus, there was very little trickle-down effect, especially in remoter areas of districts.
7) Local electoral institutions were not directly involved in the delivery system. This precluded the participation of the people at desired levels.
8) The local cooperatives, called *sajha,* suffered at the hands of the bureaucrats and failed to emerge as real institutions of the people. Thus, although most of them were supposed to supply agricultural inputs, they failed to respond to the needs of the people.
9) The Agriculture Inputs Corporation had its offices at the district headquarters and used the local *sajha* for delivery, so its services were correspondingly not as effective as they could have been.
10) The Agriculture Development Bank also depended on the services of the local *sajha* for agri-credits, with similar results. In this context, it should be noted that the Agriculture Development Bank only provided direct credits on collateral, which precluded participation by the poor.

These features have made it desirable to create a more effective service delivery system at lower levels. The experiment with service centers at sub-district level under the integrated rural development projects has been found to be a more effective delivery system, with the following advantages:

1) Service delivery points have been made more accessible to the majority of people.
2) Concomitantly, the proximity of the service area will provide the following benefits: a more direct dialogue can be started with the recipients of services; direct feedback on the use of inputs or services can be gathered through personal supervision; it will encourage participation on the part of the needy; the actual needs of the people can be estimated and immediate services rendered; it will foster the growth of local institutions by involving them in the delivery system.
3) There will be more effective coordination among the service agencies because they can develop and implement action plans on the basis of mutual cooperation.
4) The district monitoring system will operate more effectively as it will operate under conditions of direct information and feedback.
5) It will reinforce the development of market mechanisms for basic supplies, as the service centers will gradually grow into commercial centers.
6) A pool of technical experts at this level will meet the need for village skills.
7) Training in different aspects of rural development can be provided to needy rural people.

*The Service Center Scheme Under Decentralization.* Article 17 of the Decentralization Act of 1982 provides for the creation and management of service centers in the following manner:

1) The government can open service centers, usually in the middle of the nine electoral areas of the district, with a view to providing physical and technical assistance in development activities of the neighboring village panchayats.
2) Such service centers will be the lowest administrative units involved in local development.
3) The functions of the service centers will be as follows: to provide necessary services to the village panchayat in formulating, implementing, and reviewing development plans and projects; to assist in the formation and work of users' committees in the village panchayat area; to provide technical assistance to village panchayats for development programs; to help the village panchayats by pro-

viding financial and material assistance; to periodically review the progress of village panchayat development efforts; to forward the problems and needs of the village panchayats to higher levels for inclusion in development plans; and to encourage a spirit of competition among the village panchayats, and to facilitate sharing of experiences by organizing meetings, conferences, seminars, etc. at the area level.
4) Other functions and responsibilities of the service centers will be as specified in the by-laws.

According to Rule 32 of the Decentralization By-laws passed in 1984, the rights, duties, and management provisions of service centers are as follows:

1) The government can establish service centers at the center of each of the district panchayat electoral areas on the recommendation of member village panchayats in the area.
2) The following general conditions will be considered in establishing service centers: the village must be geographically convenient and have potential for the growth of basic services and facilities for the people of the area; from the transportation point of view, it must lie in or nearly in the center of the area; it must be a place which has market facilities for the basic needs of the local people; the village must be a place where there are already all or some of the following public facilities, viz., post office, health post, school, police check post, warehouse, cooperative organization, etc.; it must be a place which has been chosen by the government as an investment priority for area development. If it is not feasible to establish service centers in all the nine areas of a district, the government may set up some service centers which will also provide services to neighboring areas until such centers are opened up in those areas as well.
3) After the service centers have been established, all development sectors shall open branch offices to provide services in the areas covered by them. If the opening of branch offices is not feasible on account of lack of personnel or volume of work to be done, one branch office can render services in two or more service center areas. All sectors must, however, open branches in all service centers as soon as possible.

232  *Delivery of Public Services in Asian Countries*

4) The district panchayat will designate a supervisor from among the personnel deputed in such service centers on the basis of status and seniority.

5) The functions of the designated supervisor will be as follows: to provide physical and technical assistance to the village panchayats for effective formulation and implementation of development plans; to regularly supervise development projects or programs within the areas served by the service center; to send other officials of the service center on official tours for a period of 7 days; to work as coordinator in maintaining links with the district panchayat and other line offices of the district; to conduct quarterly meetings regarding the projects implemented in the area. Such a meeting will be presided over by the district panchayat member representing the respective area and will include all class organization district committee members of the area and the Pradhan Panchas, vice Pradhan Panchas, and secretaries of the village panchayats in the respective areas.

In addition to the service centers already operating under the integrated regional development projects, the government has decided to establish service centers in the 14 districts that have been designated for intensive implementation of the Decentralization Act from the current fiscal year.[7] These fourteen districts have been selected according to the following criteria: five of the districts constitute the five developmental regional headquarters, while the remaining nine districts constitute the zonal headquarters.

**Conclusion and Recommendations**

It is too early to evaluate the effectiveness of the service centers, but the concept has been strengthened by the realization that the district machinery cannot adequately meet needs at the lower level; and it is further reinforced by the Decentralization Act that supports the process of institutionalization at the local level. Strengthening the local planning process is an ideological prerequisite of the partyless political system since only in local institutions can people participate without the intermediary of political organizations. That, in fact, is the primary objective of decentralization.

From the series of steps that the government is taking with regard to the enforcement of decentralization, the service centers will be immediately established in the 14 districts selected for intensive implementation. Their spread in the other 61 districts may be more gradual, depending on a number of accompanying variables, resource constraint being a major consideration. The performance of the service centers will not only have to be supported, but also carefully monitored. Hence, the following recommendations are made to facilitate the smooth functioning of the service centers on an experimental basis:

1) A basic infrastructure must be immediately developed and personnel deputed to work at the service center level.
2) Training centers in neighboring areas should be entrusted with the function of identifying training needs and conducting training programs for the manpower involved in service center operations.
3) The panchayats of the area should be more directly involved in the running of the service so that widespread participation on the part of the people is encouraged, and benefits derived from such participation.
4) Political commitment must be maintained to expedite the bureaucratic process of starting and expanding the service areas.
5) Special incentives should be provided to officials working at the service center level. Those that rank highest in terms of rendering services should be rewarded.
6) The performance of the district level office heads should be judged on the basis of their support of the service centers.
7) An active monitoring and evaluation wing should be created at the center that can analyze problems and take necessary steps to solve such operational problems.
8) Evaluations should be conducted periodically, and those at the highest level of decision-making should consider the evaluation results with a view to making policy changes, if necessary.
9) International attention should be solicited, to ensure that service centers are established under the guidance of experts in the field.

## Notes

1. For detailed discussion on rural development in Nepal see S.P. Adhikari, *Rural Development in Nepal, Problems and Prospects;* and K.N. Sharma, *Stray Thoughts on Rural Development in Nepal.*

2. For detailed information on the Panchayat see K.N. Sharma, *Panchayat System in Nepal: An Experiment in Partyless Democracy.*

3. For a precise summary of Planning in Nepal see Madhab Prasad Paudyal, "Planning in Nepal."

4. For an analytical discussion of the Referendum see K.N. Sharma, *Communication in a Crisis Situation; the 1980 Referendum.*

5. For more information on IRDP see S.P. Adhikari and Y.N. Ojha, *Integrated Rural Development in Nepal.*

6. For further discussion on decentralization see M.P. Kafle, *Decentralization in Nepal.*

7. The Decentralization Act has been declared operative from 29th December 1984 and planning in all 75 districts has to start on this basis for the next fiscal year.

**Appendix I**  The Organizational Structure of Local Panchayats

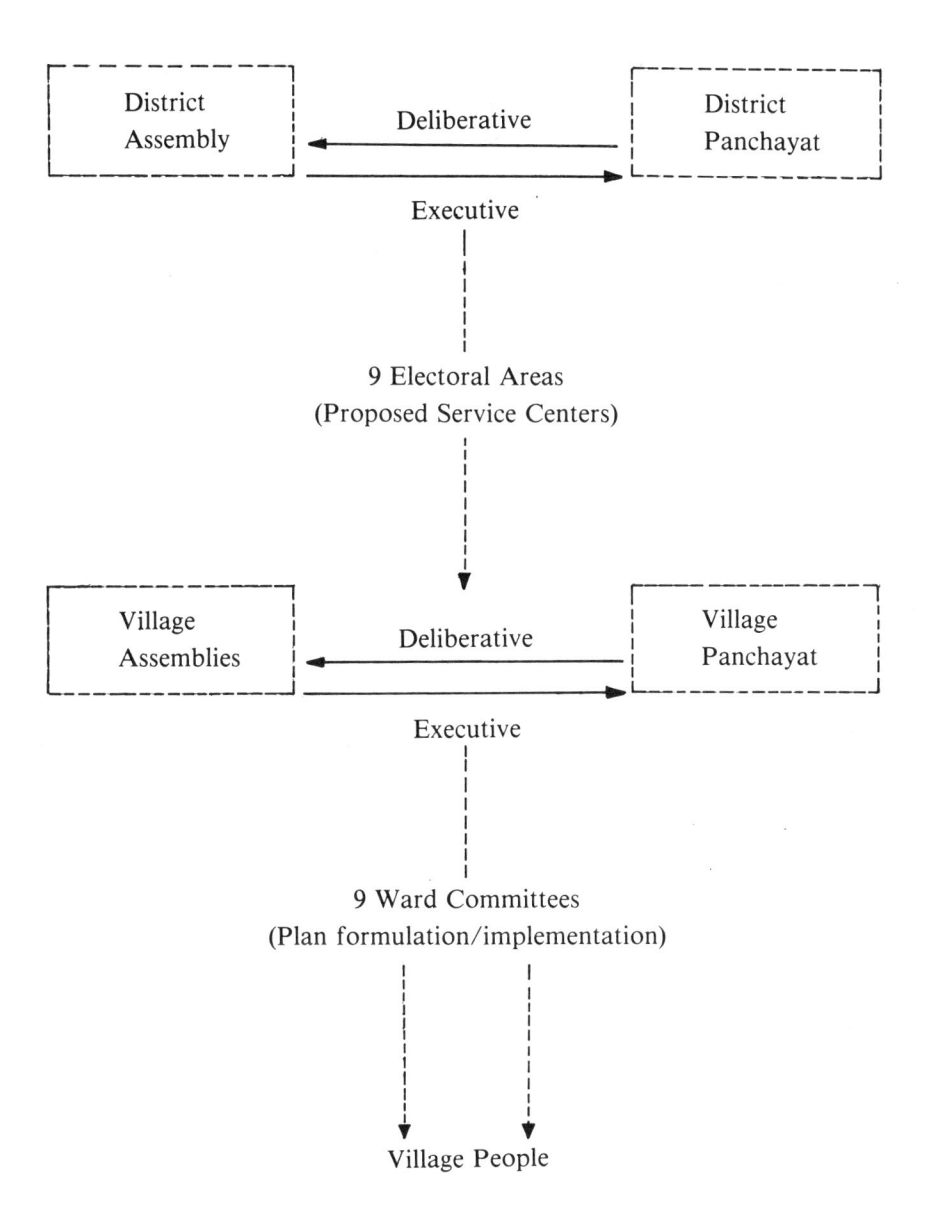

```
┌─────────────┐                      ┌─────────────┐
│  District   │    Deliberative      │  District   │
│  Assembly   │ ←─────────────────   │  Panchayat  │
│             │ ─────────────────→   │             │
└─────────────┘     Executive        └─────────────┘
                        │
                        │
                        │
                        ▼
                9 Electoral Areas
             (Proposed Service Centers)
                        │
                        │
                        ▼
┌─────────────┐                      ┌─────────────┐
│   Village   │    Deliberative      │   Village   │
│ Assemblies  │ ←─────────────────   │  Panchayat  │
│             │ ─────────────────→   │             │
└─────────────┘     Executive        └─────────────┘
                        │
                        │
                        ▼
                9 Ward Committees
          (Plan formulation/implementation)
                   │       │
                   ▼       ▼
                 Village People
```

236  *Delivery of Public Services in Asian Countries*

**Appendix II**  Existing Service Delivery System

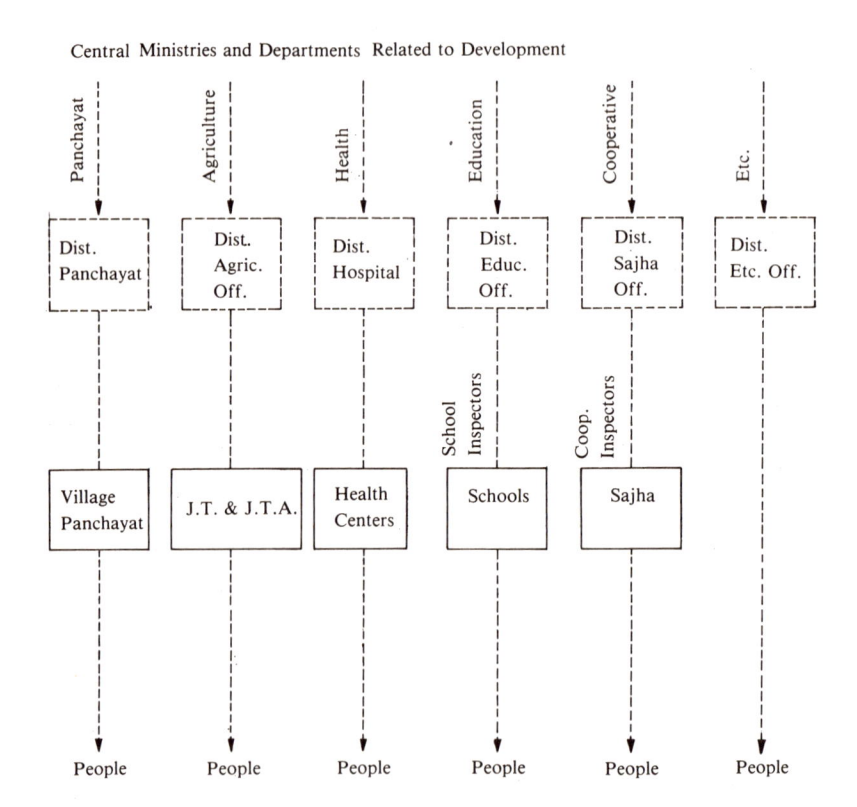

Central Ministries and Departments Related to Development

| Panchayat | Agriculture | Health | Education | Cooperative | Etc. |
|---|---|---|---|---|---|
| Dist. Panchayat | Dist. Agric. Off. | Dist. Hospital | Dist. Educ. Off. | Dist. Sajha Off. | Dist. Etc. Off. |
| Village Panchayat | J.T. & J.T.A. | Health Centers | Schools (School Inspectors) | Sajha (Coop. Inspectors) | |
| People | People | People | People | People | People |

*Service Centers in Nepal*

**Appendix III**  New Service Delivery System

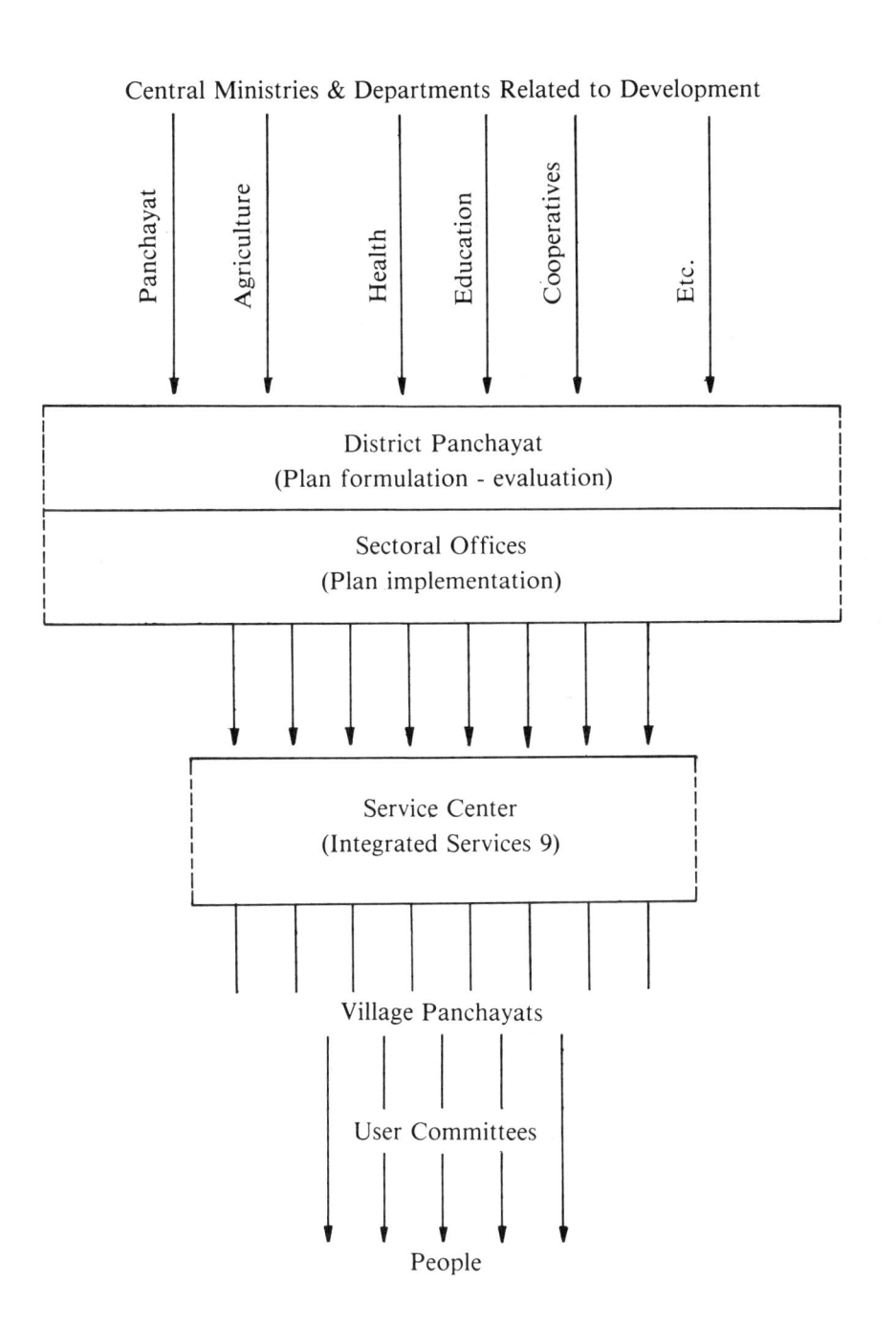

Central Ministries & Departments Related to Development

- Panchayat
- Agriculture
- Health
- Education
- Cooperatives
- Etc.

↓

District Panchayat
(Plan formulation - evaluation)

Sectoral Offices
(Plan implementation)

↓

Service Center
(Integrated Services 9)

↓

Village Panchayats

↓

User Committees

↓

People

# 11

# Toward Productivity and Excellence: A Comparative Analysis of the Public Personnel Systems in the ASEAN Countries

*Jon S.T. Quah\**

"Productivity" and "excellence" are two words which have gained wide usage in recent years. This is reflected in the recent explosion in the literature of books with these words in their titles.[1] Public personnel administration (PPA) is concerned with improving the productivity of civil servants and encouraging them to strive for excellence in the performance of their duties. More specifically, PPA refers to those activities conducted by the central personnel agencies or government departments, viz., recruitment, selection, classification, compensation, promotion, training, performance evaluation, disciplinary control and termination of civil servants. The public personnel system in a country consists of the central personnel agencies and government departments which perform the above personnel functions.

We begin our comparative analysis of the public personnel systems in the five ASEAN countries by ascertaining the size of their civil services, describing their legal framework, and identifying the central personnel agencies as a prelude to the discussion of the various personnel functions.

## SIZE OF CIVIL SERVICE

The size of the civil service is an important variable to consider here because it determines the nature and scope of the public personnel system in a country. The greater the size of a civil service, the greater the scope of activities of its public personnel system and the problems it encounters. Following Selcuk Ozgediz, we restrict our definition of the civil service to include "the institutions of the central (or federal) government and those of state, local, regional, and

---

\*National University of Singapore, Singapore.

provincial authorities."[3] This means that employees of statutory boards and public enterprises will be excluded.

If we compare the size of the civil service in the five ASEAN countries, we can discern a great deal of variation. In terms of the actual number of civil servants, Indonesia ranks first with 2,304,867 civil servants, followed by the Philippines (1,064,620 civil servants), Thailand (847,303 civil servants), Malaysia (665,265 civil servants), and Singapore, which has only 73,400 civil servants. More specifically, as Table 1 shows, the Indonesian Civil Service (ICS) is 31 times larger than the Singapore Civil Service (SCS), the Philippine Civil Service (PCS) is 14.5 times the size of the SCS, the Thai Civil Service (TCS) is 11.5 times larger than the SCS, and the Malaysian Civil Service (MCS) is 9.1 times the size of the SCS.

However, if we compare the ratio of the number of civil servants per 1,000 population, we find that MCS has the most favorable ratio of 45 civil servants per 1,000 population, while the ICS has the least favorable ratio of 15 civil servants per 1,000 population. The SCS, PCS and TCS have ratios of 29, 23 and 19 respectively. Similarly, if we calculate the ratio of the number of civil servants per square kilometer it can be seen that the SCS has the most favorable ratio of 118.7 civil servants per square kilometer on the one hand, and the ICS has the least favorable ratio of 1.2 civil servants per square kilometer on the other hand.

## Legal Framework of Civil Service

The legal framework of the civil services in the five ASEAN countries varies according to the former colonial heritage and constitutional provisions of the country concerned. In Indonesia, the legal basis of the ICS is not found in the 1945 Constitution but in Law No. 8 of Year 1974, which deals with "Fundamentals of Civil Service." This law provides the President with the authority to administer civilian public servants in Indonesia, and identifies the functions, tasks, rights and guidance of the latter.[4]

Unlike the ICS, the legal basis of the MCS is found in the Federal Constitution, which specifies the appointment, dismissal, reduction in rank, secondment, and protection of pension rights of civil servants. In addition, the Constitution also provides for the establishment of the five service commissions, with relevant details of their membership and functions. Other aspects of the conditions and terms of service and operational procedures of civil servants are governed

**Table 1  Size of the ASEAN Civil Services**

| Country | No. of civil servants | No. of times larger than the SCS | Population (millions) | Civil servants/ 1000 popn. | Land area (km$^2$) | Civil servants/ km$^2$ |
|---|---|---|---|---|---|---|
| Indonesia | 2,304,867 (1982) | 31.4 | 153.1 (1982) | 15 | 1,904,345 | 1.2 |
| Philippines | 1,064,620 (1979) | 14.5 | 46.7 (1979) | 23 | 300,000 | 3.5 |
| Thailand | 847,303 (1980) | 11.5 | 47.17 (1980) | 19 | 542,373 | 1.6 |
| Malaysia | 665,265 (1983) | 9.1 | 14.89 (1983) | 45 | 330,434 | 2.0 |
| Singapore | 73,400 (1984) | — | 2.53 (1984) | 29 | 618 | 118.7 |

Source:  Data on the number of civil servants in the five ASEAN countries are obtained from the following sources: Republik Indonesia, *Pidato Pertanggungjawaban* (Jakarta: Majelis Permusyawaratan Rakyat, 1983), p. 1373; *Annual Report of Personnel 1979* (Manila: Civil Service Commission, 1980), p. 3; *Public Services Department: Organization and Functions* (Kuala Lumpur: Information and Documentation Unit, Public Services Department, 1984), p. 13; Republic of Singapore, *Economic Survey of Singapore 1984* (Singapore: Ministry of Trade and Industry, 1985), p. 56. Data on the number of Thai civil servants were provided by the Civil Service Commission of Thailand. Data on population and land area are obtained from: *World Development Report 1981* (Washington, D.C.: The World Bank, 1981), pp. 134-135; *Economic Report 1984/85* (Kuala Lumpur: Ministry of Finance, 1984), p. iv; and *Singapore: Facts and Pictures 1984* (Singapore: Information Division, Ministry of Culture, 1984), pp. 1 and 5.

by the general orders issued by the Public Services Department (PSD) in accordance with Article 132(2) of the Federal Constitution.[5]

The PCS was reorganized after the proclamation of martial law by President Ferdinand E. Marcos on September 21, 1972. Three documents constitute the legal basis for the PCS. The first document was the Integrated Reorganization Plan (IRP) or Presidential Decree (P.D.) No. 1, which was enacted into law by President Marcos three days after martial law was declared. Part III of the IRP stressed that the personnel policies, programs, and procedures of the government should be geared toward strengthening the merit system and development of a more professionlized, efficient, and honest civil service. Furthermore, the IRP identified the Civil Service Commission (CSC) as the central personnel agency for setting standards and enforcing the laws and rules governing the selection, utilization, training and discipline of civil servants. The second document was the 1973 Constitution, which provided the basic framework for the establishment and operation of a civil service system. According to Article XII of the 1973 Constitution, the civil service should be administered by an independent CSC, which was required to create a career service and adopt measures to enhance morale, efficiency and integrity in the civil service. Finally, P.D. No. 807 was introduced on October 6, 1976 to help the government departments pursue programs consistent with national goals by reorganizing the CSC, decentralizing personnel actions, reaffirming the merit system, and creating the Career Executive Service (CES) to promote administrative efficiency and innovation.[6]

The legal basis of the SCS can be found in Part IV of the Constitution of Singapore, Articles 70-81. Article 71 excludes from the definition of "public office" all those persons whose remuneration is calculated on a daily rate. Article 73 specifies the size and membership of the Public Service Commission (PSC), and Article 78 describes its functions. The Constitution also spells out the general rules concerning the appointment and transfer of civil servants and the protection of their pension rights. The PSC was first entrusted with the function of taking disciplinary action against erring civil servants in 1956, but it only assumed full responsibility for disciplinary matters in 1963, when it was given executive power of disciplinary control over civil servants by the Constitution. Finally, civil servants are required to follow the administrative and financial procedures described in the five instruction manuals; failure to do so will result in disciplinary action against the offender.[7]

In Thailand, the legal framework of the TCS is the Civil Service Act of 1975 (B.E. 2518), which replaced the Civil Service Act of 1954 (B.E. 2497) on September 9, 1975. The implementation of the Civil Service Act of 1975 was a major administrative reform of the TCS because it led to the following changes. First, the traditional rank classification system was replaced by a modern position classification system. Second, to protect permanent officials from unjustified political interference, political officials were excluded from the Civil Service Act of 1975 since they were covered by the Political Official Service Act of 1975. Finally, the CSC was entrusted with the duty of making proposals and giving advice to the Council of Ministers on personnel administration policy and the management of the TCS.[8]

**Central Personnel Agencies**

The number of central personnel agencies in the five countries varies from one in the case of Indonesia to ten in the case of Thailand. There is also diversity in the scope of the functions performed by the various central personnel agencies.

The central personnel agency in Indonesia is the Institute of Public Personnel Administration (IPPA), which was formed in 1972 to replace the Bureau of Personnel Affairs created in 1950. The IPPA is responsible to the President and its *raison d'etre* is "to improve, maintain, and develop state civil administration so that the government machinery runs smoothly."[9] More specifically, the IPPA has four tasks to perform:

1) to plan the guidance of the Civil Service in accordance with Presidential policy;

2) to prepare regulations involving the civil service sector;

3) to administer personnel matters as well as a pension system; and

4) to provide supervision, coordination, and guidance to implement regulations in the Civil Service and the pension sector in the ministries and state institutions/nonministerial government institutions.[10]

In Malaysia, there are six central personnel agencies: the PSD and five service commissions. The PSD was established in 1970 as a result of the reorganization of the Federal Establishment Office. The PSD's aim is to "formulate, plan and implement policies to ensure that the civil service consists of personnel that are efficient, dedicated and trained to shoulder responsibilities in implementing all national policies and objectives."[11] The five service commissions are: the Public Services Commission (PSC), the Judicial and Legal Service Commission, the Police Force Commission, the Railway Service Commission and the Educational Service Commission. According to Article 144(1) of the Federal Constitution, each of the five service commissions is responsible for the "appointment, confirmation, emplacement on the permanent or pensionable establishment, promotion, transfer and exercising disciplinary control over members of the service or services over which they have jurisdiction."[12] However, it should be noted that of the six agencies, the PSD and PSC are the most important central personnel agencies in Malaysia.

In the case of the Philippines, the CSC, which was originally created in 1959 by the Republic Act No. 2260, was identified by P.D. No. 1 and the 1973 Constitution as the central personnel agency responsible for strengthening the merit system and for professionalizing the career service in government.[13] More specifically, the CSC has seven functions to perform:

1) to promulgate policies, rules, standards for the Civil Service, and adopt plans and programs to promote economical, efficient, and effective personnel administration in the Government;

2) to enforce the Civil Service Law and rules by post-auditing personnel actions in the departments and agencies, and applying appropriate sanctions whenever necessary;

3) to hear and decide administrative cases brought before it on appéal from the decision of the department or agency head;

4) to appoint the personnel, and exercise overall supervision and control over the activities of the Commission;

5) to advise the President on matters involving personnel management in the Government;

6) to assist in the improvement of personnel units and programs in the departments and agencies; and

7) to perform such other functions as may be provided by law.[14]

In 1978, the Merit Systems Board (MSB) was created by P.D. No.1409 to assist the CSC in attaining its objective of promoting and protecting the merit system in public office. The MSB performs such quasi-judicial functions as dealing specifically with administrative cases, complaints against personnel action, abuses, misfeasance, malfeasance, and nonfeasance, and other violation of existing civil service laws, rules and regulations, including the New Administrative Code.[15] In sum, the CSC and the MSB are the two central personnel agencies in the Philippines.

There are three central personnel agencies in Singapore. The oldest and perhaps also the most important central personnel agency for the SCS is the PSC, which was formed on January 1, 1951 to keep politics out of the SCS and to accelerate the latter's pace of localization.[16] Since the localization of the SCS was completed some time ago, the primary aim of insulating the SCS from political influences is still important because the purpose of the PSC's program is "to meet the staffing requirements of the Government in accordance with the merit principle."[17] The PSC's duty, according to the Constitution, is "to appoint, confirm, emplace on the permanent or pensionable establishment, promote, transfer, dismiss and exercise disciplinary control over public officers."[18]

The Legal Service Commission (LSC) is the second central personnel agency in Singapore. The LSC is responsible for the appointment, confirmation, promotion, transfer, dismissal and disciplinary control over officers in the Singapore Legal Service. Before 1972, the PSC shared the functions of personnel management with the Establishment Division of the Ministry of Finance, which was responsible for all civil service personnel matters not handled by the PSC. From 1972-1980, the functions of personnel management in the SCS were shared between the PSC (which was responsible for recruitment, selection, promotion, training, transfer, disciplinary control and dismissal), the Establishment Unit of the Prime Minister's Office (which dealt with the career development and training of Division I officers) and the Personnel Administration Branch (PAB) of the Budget Division in the Ministry of Finance (which took care of job classification and terms and conditions of service).[19] In April 1981, the function of career development and training of Division I officers was transferred from the Establishment Unit of the PMO to the PSC.

On the recommendation of the Management Services Department, the Public Service Division (PSD) was created on January 3, 1983 for the purposes of formulating and reviewing personnel policies in the SCS and ensuring that such policies would be consistently implemented in the various ministries. The PSD is now responsible for all personnel policy matters concerning appraisal, posting, training, schemes of service, service conditions and welfare. It also provides such central personnel services as conducting pay research and administering and holiday bungalow scheme. The PSD has taken over all the functions performed previously by the PAB and the PSC's role is now restricted to ensuring impartiality in the appointment, promotion and disciplinary control of civil servants, as stated in the Constitution. The Deputy Secretary of the PSD also serves as the PSC Secretary in order to enhance cooperation and coordination between the two organizations.[20] In short, the functions of personnel management in the SCS are now shared between the PSD and PSC, and to a lesser extent, the LSC.

Of the five countries, Thailand has the largest number of central personnel agencies. In addition to the CSC, which is the oldest and the most important agency, there are ten other central personnel agencies, viz., the Judicial Service Commission, the Teachers' Council, the Universities Officials Commission, the Public Prosecutor Service Commission, the Provincial Administration Commission, the Municipality Officials Commission, the Bangkok Metropolitan Officials Commission, the Legislative Body Officials Commission, the Sukhapiban (Sanitary District) Officials Commission, and the Police Officials Commission.[21] According to the Civil Service Act of 1975, the CSC is the personnel policy-making and standard setting body. More specifically, the CSC has a total of 18 duties to perform.[22] The more important duties include: giving advice on personnel matters to the Council of Ministers; job classification; conducting competitive examinations for entry into the TCS and for government scholarships; and to consider appeals against orders of discharge, dismissal or expulsion of civil servants. The CSC is assisted in the performance of its various functions by a Civil Service Sub-Commission (CSSC) in a ministry, department or province. The CSC ensures close coordination and a good working relationship between itself and the other ten central personnel agencies.[23]

Table 2 summarizes the above discussion on the central personnel agencies in the five ASEAN countries. It identifies clearly the various agencies involved in performing the different personnel functions in the civil services of these countries. The year of formation of each agency is also provided to indicate its age. In sum, as we move from Indonesia to Thailand, the number of central personnel agencies increases from one to two (Philippines), to three (Singapore), to six (Malaysia), and to ten.

## Table 2 Central Personnel Agencies in the ASEAN Countries

| Country | Central Personnel Agencies | Year of Formation | No. of Agencies |
|---|---|---|---|
| Indonesia | Institute of Public Personnel Administration | 1972 | 1 |
| Malaysia | Public Services Commission | 1957 | 6 |
| | Judicial and Legal Service Commision | 1957 | |
| | Police Force Commission | 1957 | |
| | Railway Service Commission | 1957 | |
| | Educational Service Commission | 1957 | |
| | Public Services Department | 1970 | |
| Philippines | Civil Service Commission | 1959 | 2 |
| | Merit Systems Board | 1978 | |
| Singapore | Public Service Commission | 1951 | 3 |
| | Legal Service Commission | 1951 | |
| | Public Service Division | 1983 | |
| Thailand* | Civil Service Commission | 1928 | 10 |
| | Judicial Service Commission | 1934 | |
| | Teachers' Council | 1945 | |
| | Universities Officials Commission | 1959 | |
| | Public Prosecutor Service Commission | 1960 | |
| | Provincial Administration Commission | 1966 | |
| | Municipality Officials Commission | 1967 | |
| | Bangkok Metropolitan Officials Commission | 1973 | |
| | Legislative Body Officials Commission | 1975 | |
| | Police Officials Commission | 1978 | |

Source: Amara Raksasataya and Heinrich Siedentopf (eds.), *Asian Civil Services: Developments and Trends* (Kuala Lumpur: Asian and Pacific Development Administration Center, 1980), pp. 137, 262, 270, 367-372, 442-445, and 541-548.

*Note: There are actually eleven central personnel agencies. The Table omits the *Sukhapiban* (Sanitary District) Officials Commission created in 1977 *(editors' note).*

## Recruitment and Selection

*Recruitment and Selection Criteria.* The recruitment and selection process in the civil service is crucial to the successful implementation of personnel policies and programs because it determines the *quality* of individuals who apply for positions in the civil service and who enter the civil service after meeting the various criteria imposed by the central personnel agency. Given the choice between merit and patronage in recruiting and selecting candidates for civil service positions, all the five ASEAN civil services have opted for the merit principle rather than patronage. However, the operationalization of this merit principle in terms of specific criteria varies according to the civil service concerned.

In Indonesia, Article 16 of Law No. 8 of Year 1974 states that "the recruitment of civilian public servants must be based purely on objective requirements already stipulated, and may not be based on religion, group, or region."[25] More specifically, an applicant for a civil service position must satisfy 11 criteria and failure to meet any criterion will result in the rejection of his application. The criteria are: (1) citizenship; (2) age limit from 18-40 years; (3) no prison record; (4) non-involvement in subversive movements against the government and Constitution; (5) no record of ignominious dismissal by a public or private organization; (6) not currently employed as a public servant or as a prospective civilian public servant; (7) possession of necessary educational qualifications, capability or skills; (8) possession of a local police certificate to indicate the applicant's good record of conduct; (9) medical fitness, as certified by a doctor's certificate; (10) willingness to be posted anywhere in Indonesia or in another country as decided by the government; and (11) the residual category of "other special terms determined by the relevant agency."[26] Although civil servants are allowed to have second jobs (because of the low salaries), they are not allowed to have both jobs with the ICS as this would deprive others of the opportunity to work in the ICS. Thus, the sixth criterion exists to prevent such "moonlighting." The tenth criterion is also necessary as most applicants prefer to work in Jakarta and other major cities rather than in the provinces or rural areas.

In Malaysia, the merit principle has not been adhered to fully, especially in the case of recruitment and selection to the Administrative and Diplomatic Service (ADS), where a quota system of 4 Malays to 1 non-Malay has been practiced since 1952. According to the Constitution, there should be no discrimination against citizens "on the ground only of religion, race, descent or place of birth ... in the appointment to any office or employment under a public authority" except in the case of the reservation of positions in the ADS for the indigenous group, i.e., the Malays or Bumiputras.[27] Thus, the quota system not only gives rise to "protective discrimination" for the Bumiputras but also ensures that they will be recruited in adequate numbers in the MCS. Article 136 of the Constitution further states that all persons of whatever race in the same grade in the service of the Federation "shall subject to the terms and conditions of their employment, be treated impartially."[28] All appointments to the MCS are made in accordance with the required qualifications stipulated in the specific schemes of service determined by the PSD. Almost all appointments to the MCS come under the purview of the PSC since it is responsible for recruiting and selecting candidates for the MCS. More specifically, the PSC relies on interviews to assess whether candidates are suitable for appointment to the MCS according to the following criteria: (1) qualification; (2) age; (3) experience; (4) personality; (5) general knowledge; (6) appearance; (7) judgement; (8) referees' comments and confidential reports; and (9) other factors which it considers to be relevant.[29]

In the case of the Philippines, Article 12 of the 1973 Constitution specifies that all appointments in the PCS; with the exception of those which are policy-determining, primarily confidential, or highly technical in nature, are made only according to merit and fitness, which are determined as far as possible by competitive examinations. Recruitment and selection in the PCS is decentralized as each department or agency evolves its own screening process, which includes tests of fitness in accordance with standards and guidelines set by the CSC. Admission to entrance examinations for the first and second levels of the Career Service is restricted to Philippine citizens between 18-50 years. However, a candidate will be disqualified if he (1) lacks any of the minimum qualifications; (2) is physically or morally unfit for the position; (3) is found "guilty of a crime involving moral turpitude, or of infamous, disgraceful, or immoral conduct, or of dishonesty or drunkenness or addiction to narcotics"; or (4) has been dismissed from the service for cause.[30] Finally, "no discrimination shall be exercised, threatened or promised against, or in favor of, any person examined or to be examined because of his political or religious opinions or affiliations."[31]

In Singapore, the PSC's major function is the recruitment and selection of candidates for Divisions I and II appointments. It relies solely on interviews for selecting qualified candidates for the SCS. To be eligible for appointment to the SCS, a candidate must satisfy the following six criteria: citizenship,[32] age, education, experience, medical fitness and character (i.e., no criminal conviction, no record of corruption, and not a security risk). Candidates for Divisions I and II appointments who meet such criteria are interviewed by the PSC members. Letters of appointment are only issued to the successful candidates if they pass their medical examination and security screening (by the Internal Security Department, the Corrupt Practices Investigation Bureau and the Criminal Record Office) and after their educational certificates and relevant documents have been verified. The PSC thus serves as the gatekeeper to the SCS by ensuring fair play and impartiality in recruiting and selecting candidates for appointments to Divisions I and II on the basis of merit. Indeed, the PSC controls the quality of personnel entering the SCS by "keeping the rascals out" and attracting the best qualified candidates to apply for entrance to the SCS.[33]

In Thailand, the CSC is responsible for recruiting and selecting candidates for the TCS. The various competitive examinations are conducted by the CSC's Examination Division.[34] Section 24 of the Civil Service Act of 1975 identifies the 14 criteria for a person to become a civil servant, viz., (1) Thai citizenship; (2) at least 18 years old; (3) belief in the democratic form of government under the Constitution; (4) not a political official; (5) physically and mentally fit; (6) not suspended or discharged from government service; (7) not morally defective; (8) not insolvent; (9) never declared bankrupt; (10) never imprisoned; (11) not penalized by discharge or dismissal from a state enterprise; (12) never penalized by discharge or dismissal for a disciplinary offense; (13) never penalized by expulsion for a disciplinary offense; and (14) has not cheated in a government service entrance examination.[35]

*Selection Methods.* The two major selection methods of competitive examinations and/or interviews have been used by the central personnel agencies in the five ASEAN countries for selecting suitable candidates for the civil services. Indonesia, Malaysia and Thailand employ a combination of competitive examinations and interviews in recruitment and selection. On the other hand, both the Philippines and Singapore rely solely on a single method (either examination or interview) to select candidates for the PCS and the SCS, respectively.

For entry into the ICS, candidates must pass written examinations which test their general knowledge on Indonesia, their technical knowledge about the positions applied for, and their writing ability and style of language. If necessary, an oral examination may be held to supplement the written examination. Furthermore, a skills examination is required for those applying to become typists or drivers of motor vehicles. In some cases, candidates must also undergo a psychological test. To ensure objectivity, examination papers are graded by at least two examiners and oral examinations are conducted by at least two examiners also. A list of the eligible candidates is prepared in order of merit, and this list is submitted by the examination committee to the relevant agency to be used accordingly.[36]

Until recently, selection to the MCS was by interviews only and candidates were assessed on the basis of their performance during the interviews. However, in 1977, the government stopped direct recruitment to the ADS and candidates were appointed on a temporary basis as cadet ADS officers to undergo a one year intensive training course at the National Institute of Public Administration (INTAN) before being appointed as probationary ADS officers.[37] In other words, entry to the ADS is based on successful performance during the interviews and passing the examinations conducted by INTAN.

In the case of Thailand, the combined use of examinations and interviews for selecting candidates to the TCS can be more clearly seen. The Examination Division of the CSC first reviews all the applications submitted to identify eligible candidates as well as to eliminate unqualified candidates. The eligible candidates are required to take a written examination consisting of two parts: (1) the general ability part, which tests the candidate's general mental ability and his proficiency in the Thai language; and (2) the specific ability part, which assesses the candidate's aptitude, skill or knowledge appropriate to the position applied for. The final step in selection is the qualification appraisal interview, which is designed to examine whether the candidate possesses the qualifications required for the position and to assess such personal characteristics as his poise, attitude, adjustment, motivation and human relations.[38]

*Traditional or Realistic Recruitment?* In his book, *Organizational Entry: Recruitment, Selection, and Socialization of Newcomers,* John P. Wanous introduced the distinction between traditional recruitment and realistic recruitment. Traditional recruitment refers to the approach of "selling" the organization to outsiders by presenting only positive information and distorting information presented to emphasize the positive aspects. According to Wanous,

> This selling of the organization involves two actions: (1) only positive characteristics are communicated to outsiders rather than those things insiders find dissatisfying about the organization, and (2) those features that are advertised may be distorted to make them more positive.[39]

In short, traditional recruitment is designed to attract as many candidates as possible. On the other hand, realistic recruitment does not attempt to "sell" the organization, but provides "outsiders with *all pertinent* information *without distortion.*"[40] Wanous contends that realistic recruitment is superior to traditional recruitment because realistic recruitment not only increases job satisfaction, but also "reduces subsequent unnecessary turnover caused by the disappointment of initial expectations inflated by traditional recruitment."[41]

If we examine the five ASEAN countries in terms of their approach to recruitment, we will find that they emphasize traditional recruitment rather than realistic recruitment. This focus on traditional recruitment is understandable given the fact that the civil service is the largest employer in these countries; it relies on traditional recruitment to lower the selection ratio ("the proportion of job candidates who are hired") and to justify the budget of the central personnel agencies. Another advantage is that the low selection ratio gives the impression that only the "best" candidates are chosen since only a small proportion of those who apply are actually hired.

Furthermore, given the low salaries in the public sector (especially in Indonesia, the Philippines and Thailand), it is not difficult to understand why the civil services in these countries rely on traditional recruitment to attract as many applicants to apply for civil service jobs. The relatively higher salaries in the private sector in all the five countries also means that there is constant competition between the public and private sectors for the best candidates. The traditional approach to recruitment is employed by the central personnel agencies in the five countries to enable them to compete with the private sector for competent personnel and to minimize the less attractive aspects of working in the civil service (i.e., low salaries, red tape, etc.).

While the emphasis on traditional recruitment in the five countries is understandable, nevertheless, the time is now opportune for these countries to reconsider their approach to recruitment. From the figures given on the size of the five civil services in Table 1 above, we can say that there is no serious shortage of civil servants in these countries. Traditional recruitment is more expensive in the long run if turnover is high. On the other hand, realistic recruitment will help to reduce turnover, as candidates recruited by this method tend to stay longer in the organization than those recruited by the traditional method.[42]

## Classification

The five ASEAN countries have either adopted the British system of rank classification or the U.S. system of position classification, or a combination of both. More specifically, Malaysia and Singapore (being former British colonies) have retained rank classification; Thailand has shifted from rank classification to position classification on the advice of U.S. consultants; and Indonesia and the Philippines have adopted a combination of rank classification and position classification.

In Malaysia and Singapore, the system of rank classification is originally based on the 1947 Trusted Commission's recommendation that the civil service be reorganized and divided into four divisions according to the duties and salaries of its members. Division I consisted of those in the administrative and professional grades, Division II the executive grades, Division III the clerical and technical grades, and Division IV, which includes those performing manual tasks.[43] The SCS today still retains the fourfold division of work suggested 38 years ago by the Trusted Commission. However, in Malaysia the Suffian Salaries Commission recommended in 1967 the replacement of Divisions I-IV with Categories A-D, with appropriate revisions of the salaries in each category. Category A, the Managerial and Professional Group includes those earning more than M$1,250 a month. Category B, the Executive and Sub-Professional Group, consists of those with monthly salaries between M$700 and M$1,250. Category C, the Clerical and Technical Group, covers those with monthly salaries between M$250 and M$700. Industrial and manual workers come under Category D since they earn less than M$250 a month.[44]

In Thailand, the traditional rank classification system was employed from 1928 to August 1975 as the basis for the compensation of civil servants. However, with the government's increased emphasis on national development programs and the resulting expansion of the public bureaucracy in the 1960s, the rank classification system "became a serious barrier to efficient management."[45] In March 1946, E.J. Barbour, an American consultant, wrote a paper on "The Needs of the Thai Civil Service System" to identify the most basic needs of the TCS and to make recommendations for meeting these needs. He identified the ten most vital needs of the TCS and made a total of 35 recommendations. One of the vital needs was "a more effective system of classifying positions on the basis of their duties, responsibilities and qualification requirements." To meet this need, he recommended the establishment of a system of position classification to replace the traditional rank classification system.[46] On

November 20, 1964, a Civil Service Improvement Committee was formed with the aim of improving the effectiveness of personnel management in the TCS. This Committee recommended the adoption of a position classification system in the TCS. The Cabinet approved this recommendation on December 21, 1965, and the United States Operations Mission of Thailand provided technical assistance to the TCS from June 1965 to June 1971 for the development and installation of the position classification system. Implementation of the position classification plan began on April 28, 1971; full implementation throughout the TCS was finally completed on September 9, 1975. Today, the TCS has a position classification system which divides the civil servants into eight occupational groups and 246 classes.[47]

In Indonesia, a combination of rank classification and position classification is used since civilian public servants are first ranked according to 17 levels, from the lowest rank (Junior Clerk) to the highest rank (Senior Administrator). The 17 levels are then divided into four groups, depending on the duties, responsibilities and educational qualifications. Levels 1-4 constitute Group I, which consists of the clerical workers. Group II (Levels 5-8) includes the supervisors, Group III (Levels 9-12) covers the superintendents, and the administrators come under Group IV (Levels 13-17).[48]

Similarly, in the Philippines both rank classification and position classification are used in the PCS. However, it should be noted that before the restructuring of the PCS under the Integrated Reorganization Plan (IRP) in 1972, only position classification was used.[49] The PCS is divided into the Career Service and the Non-Career Service (for political appointments). Within the Career Service, there are three levels:

1. *First Level* -- includes personnel in the clerical, trades, crafts, and custodial positions who perform non-professional or sub-professional work in non-supervisory or supervisory capacity and requires less than four years of college work.

2. *Second Level* -- includes personnel in the professional, technical, and scientific positions who perform non-supervisory or supervisory duties and requires at least four years of college up to Division Chief Level; and

3. *Third Level* -- includes positions in the Career Executive Service (CES).[50]

The Career Service of the PCS has a mixed classification system because its first two levels are based on position classification, while the third level (CES) employs rank classification.

**Compensation**

Compensation for civil service jobs in the five countries ranges from very low (Indonesia), to low (Philippines and Thailand), to adequate (Malaysia), and to high (Singapore). Low civil service salaries make it difficult for the central personnel agencies to compete in the labor market for competent and talented personnel. Low salaries also make the civil servants more vulnerable to corrupt activities and other forms of unethical behavior. On the other hand, the ability of each government to improve civil service salaries would depend on the country's level of economic development and the availability of funds for such an expensive undertaking.

Some scholars have argued that bureaucratic corruption becomes a serious problem in a society where the civil servants are generally paid very low wages and where there is an unequal distribution of wealth.[51] The linkage between low salaries and bureaucratic corruption is best illustrated in Indonesia, where civil servants receive among the lowest salaries in the world. Each civil servant receives a basic salary and allowances for himself, his wife and children.[52] The basic salary of the most junior civil servant (a newly appointed Junior Clerk) is Rp. 12,000 (US$19.50) per month, while the most senior civil servant (a Senior Administrator with 24 years of experience) receives a monthly basic salary of Rp. 120,000 (US$195).[53] The ratio of the monthly basic salary of the most senior civil servant to the most junior is thus 10:1. Thus, even though civil servants also receive a rice allowance and a functional allowance, it is difficult, if not impossible, for them to survive on their salaries and allowances because the latter amount to about one-third of the amount needed by them to sustain their families' standard of living.[54] A survey of regional officials in Indonesia by an American scholar has indicated that these officials consider low salaries to be the most important factor responsible for corruption.[55]

A second consequence of the low salaries of the Indonesian civil servants is that many, if not all, have a second job. In fact, since the government has not been able to raise the salaries of civil servants in recent years, the working hours of civil servants have been adjusted to allow them to work elsewhere after their office hours. For example, for civil servants based in Jakarta, their working hours are: Monday to Thursday, 0800-1500; Friday, 0800-1130; and Saturday, 0800-1400. Thus, during each week they are required to spend 37.5 hours on their first job.[56] However, the necessity of holding more than one job by the Indonesian civil servants means that their time and energies must be divided between their various jobs. This might lower their productivity and even commitment to their primary jobs, especially when their secondary jobs pay better. According to Clive Gray, "In Indonesia's public service many people hold two or more jobs, but those who put in the contractual time on each of one or more public sector appointments constitute a minority of dedicated souls."[57]

Civil servants in the Philippines and Thailand also receive low salaries, but their salaries are much higher than those of their Indonesian counterparts. In the Philippines, P.D. No. 985 reduced the original 75 salary ranges and 5 salary steps formulated in 1957 to 28 salary grades with 8 steps for each grade in 1976.[58] The monthly salary of the most junior civil servant (Salary Grade 1, Step 1) is P286 (US$36) and the monthly salary of the most senior civil servant (Salary Grade 28, Step 8) is P5935 (US$747). The ratio of the monthly salary of the most senior civil servant to the most junior is 21:1.[59] For those civil servants whose basic salary is low, substantial living allowances such as allowances for clothing, transport, children and representation expenses are given to help them cope with inflation. Also, overtime pay and partial coverage for hospitalization and medical fees are provided.[60]

In his study of the TCS, Kasem Suwanagul highlighted the problem of low salaries of the civil servants during the post-war period and contended that such low salaries had contributed to an increase in bureaucratic corruption. Civil servants' salaries could not keep pace with the rising cost of living after the war and were also lower than the salaries offered in the private sector.[61]

According to the Schedule of Civil Service Salaries (No. 3), 1980, the monthly salary of the most junior civil servant (Level 1, Step 1) is B1,255 (US$46) and the monthly salary of the most senior civil servant (Level 11, Step 9) is B17,745 (US$657). The ratio of these two salaries is 14:1.[62] Since the salaries are inadequate to meet inflation, civil servants are provided with other benefits and services. Employee benefits given include retirement benefits, cost-of-living allowances, health benefits, children's allowances, special allowances and leave with pay. The services provided to civil servants include housing facilities for provincial officials, medical services, educational assistance, and social and recreational programs.[63]

In contrast to the three countries discussed above, civil servants in Malaysia enjoy much higher salaries. Following the salary revision recommended by the Cabinet Committee Report II in July 1980, the monthly basic salary for the most senior position is M$6350 (US$2886) and the corresponding salary for the most junior position is M$250 (US$114). The resulting ratio of both salaries is thus 25:1.[64] Malaysian civil servants also receive such fringe benefits as eligibility for government housing, medical benefits and car loans.[65]

Civil servants in Singapore have the highest salaries among the five countries. When the People's Action Party (PAP) government assumed power in June 1959, it was determined to eradicate corruption in general and in the SCS in particular. Apart from taking various anticorruption measures,[66] the government also minimized the need to be corrupt among civil servants by constantly improving their salaries and working conditions. Another important reason, which surfaced subsequently, for improving the salaries and working conditions in the SCS was the need to stem the outflow of competent senior civil servants to the private sector by offering competitive salaries and fringe benefits to reduce the gap between the public and private sectors.[67] Accordingly, the salaries of civil servants were revised in 1972, 1973 and 1979. In 1981, a survey on the employment and earnings of 30,197 graduates found that graduates in the private sector earned, on the average, 42 percent more than those in the public sector.[68] At the same time, figures provided by the PSC showed that many senior civil servants had left the SCS for more lucrative jobs in the private sector.[69]

To deal with the twin problems of wide disparity in pay between graduates in the public and private sectors and the serious brain drain of senior civil servants from the SCS to the private sector, the government further revised the salaries of those in the Administrative Service and other Professional Service in April 1982. Consequently, the monthly consolidated salary for the most senior position (Staff Grade III) is S$21,700 (US$9,864). If the National Wages Council (NWC) allowance is included, the total salary would be S$25,112 (US$11,415) per month. At the other extreme of the scale, the most junior position (Bilal) carries a monthly salary of S$380 (US$173).[70] The ratio of the highest salary to the lowest salary is 57:1. In addition to their monthly basic salary, civil servants also receive a NWC allowance and such fringe benefits as housing loans, car loans and microcomputer loans. Senior civil servants such as permanent secretaries are provided with a Mercedes Benz each for their use, and they are also appointed as directors of various government companies.

## Promotion

As in the case of recruitment and selection, the five ASEAN countries subscribe to the merit principle in promotion, but the actual criteria used for promotion vary according to the country concerned.

In Indonesia, the promotion in rank of a civilian public servant is considered once in four years. More specifically, there are four criteria which are considered for promotion, viz., (1) four years service in the substantive rank; (2) a good work performance assessment by his superior; (3) the function makes this possible, i.e., with the same echelon; and (4) successful completion of the service test for promotion from one group to another group.[71]

In Malaysia, a promotion exercise is carried out when there is a vacancy in a higher grade in a specific scheme of service. All promotion exercises are conducted by the appropriate Department Promotion Board. The interview method is used to assess a candidate's suitability for promotion. The candidate's annual performance on the job and "special confidential" reports on his performance are also taken into consideration. Before 1957, seniority was much more important than merit in the promotion of civil servants. However, during the 1960s and 1970s, merit became "the primary, if not the main, criterion for promotion."[72] According to General Order 50, Chapter A, merit is defined in terms of "efficiency shown by a person in the performance of his duties; and personal qualities including integrity as well as qualifications and experiences appropriate to the post to be filled."[73] In 1976, the performance during training of ADS officers was introduced as another criterion for assessing the suitability of these officers for promotion. Accordingly, INTAN conducted a training course with this objective in mind for a group of ADS officers due for promotion from senior timescale to superscale G. Since then such training courses have become standard procedure for promotion to that grade. In terms of weight given to the various criteria for promotion of ADS officers, 33 percent is given to the performance in the training course, another 33 percent is allocated to annual and special confidential reports, and the remaining 33 percent is set aside for the candidate's performance during the interview by the Promotion Board.[74]

In the Philippines, the PCS practises "merit promotion" rather than the traditional seniority rule. Preference in promotions is given to an employee occupying a next-in-rank position if he is competent and qualified, has civil service eligibility, and if he fulfils the other conditions for promotion to the higher position when it becomes vacant. To determine the degree of competence and qualification of a civil servant, five criteria are employed: (1) performance; (2) education and training; (3) experience and outstanding accomplishments; (4) physical characteristics and personality traits; and (5) potential.[75]

In Singapore, civil servants are promoted by the PSC on the basis of official qualifications, experience and merit.[76] Eligible candidates for promotion are interviewed by PSC members and selection boards. The actual procedure for the promotion of serving officers has five stages: (1) invitation to apply for promotion; (2) testing the eligibility of applicants by reviewing their applications; (3) selecting the most suitable applicants by means of the interview method; (4) approval of the promotion; and (5) informing the officer of promotion, salary and conditions of service in the new appointment.[77]

Finally, in Thailand, civil servants must meet the requirements of minimum qualifications for the positions before they can be considered for promotion. Furthermore, such criteria as knowledge, ability, conduct, service record of the candidate and his salary step, also influence his prospects for promotion. For promotion from level 1 to level 6, candidates are required to pass promotion examinations. However, for promotion to more senior positions from level 6 to level 11, no written examinations are required. The Director of the Personnel Policies and Standards Division of the CSC has identified two problems regarding the promotion of Thai civil servants: emphasis on intra-departmental promotion rather than inter-departmental promotion (except for senior posts); and lack of systematic assessment of the job performance of incumbents for promotion.[78] Moreover, there is also dissatisfaction with how promotions are conducted at the municipal level and this has resulted in the writing of anonymous letters as a sign of protest.[79]

Perhaps the most serious problem concerning promotion in the TCS was pointed out some years ago by Likhit Dhiravegin in his study of the Thai bureaucratic elite. He found that promotion in the TCS was based not only on merit, as indicated above, but also on favoritism. He wrote:

> In a civil bureaucracy in which internal politics and the politicking skill are part of the game, favoritism is unavoidable despite the expressed policy of emphasizing merit as the prime criterion for promotion. And actually in any case, the official reason for special promotion is always given in the name of merit regardless of whether it is really due to merit or whether one happens to be successful in "snowing" one's boss.[80]

On the basis of the observations made by experienced Thai bureaucrats, Likhit provides an interesting catalogue of the various types of gifts and services which the Thai civil servant must provide or perform for his superior officer in order to gain his favor.[81] However, favoritism is not confined to "pleasing the boss with gifts and servile services," but also includes supporting the boss in his "empire-building" efforts within the bureaucracy.[82] In short, to be successful in the TCS, a civil servant must be pulled by his superiors, pushed by his subordinates, and supported by his equals.[83]

## Training[84]

Of the five countries under discussion, the Philippines was the first country in Asia to establish an institute of public administration in 1952, when the Philippine Institute of Public Administration (PIPA) was created with technical and financial assistance from the U.S. government.[85] The PIPA's task was to improve the study and practice of public administration in the Philippines by initiating research projects on various aspects of Philippine public administration, and by training qualified personnel for the PCS. In October 1966, the PIPA was renamed the College of Public Administration (CPA) at the University of the Philippines. The CPA has been quite successful in promoting research and training civil servants.[86] Apart from the CPA, the CSC, the Development Academy of the Philippines, the National Defense College of the Philippines, and the Civil Service Academy are also involved in the training of Filipino public officials.

In Thailand, training of civil servants is conducted by the National Institute of Development Administration (NIDA) and the CSC. NIDA was originally known as the Thai Institute of Public Administration (TIPA), which was formed as part of Thammasat University in September 1955 with the arrival of four U.S. experts in public administration from Indiana University.[87] In April 1966, TIPA was reorganized to form the NIDA. NIDA is different from TIPA in two respects. First, NIDA was created as a separate institution and not as part of Thammasat University. Second, NIDA's program has been broadened to include not only public administration courses, but also courses in business administration, development economics, and applied statistics.[88] In 1974, the CSC established a training center to conduct appropriate courses, seminars and training activities for the TCS.[89]

Indonesia is the third ASEAN country to set up an institute of public administration for the training of civil servants. On May 5, 1958, the National Institute of Administration (LAN) was established to perform the following functions:

(1) to act as the management consulting agency of the ICS; (2) to act as administrative research center for the country; (3) to act as the in-service training center for the ICS; and (4) to disseminate the art and science of public administration in Indonesia.[90] In 1971, LAN was reorganized and, according to Article 2 of the Presidential Decree of the Republic of Indonesia No. 5 of 1971, its function now is:

> To assist the President in improving, maintaining, increasing and developing the efficiency and success of the State Administration so that the smoothness of the running of the Government in the widest meaning is achieved.[91]

Apart from the training of civil servants, LAN also submits proposals for administrative reform to the President, conducts research and provides consulting service in public administration, as well as developing and advancing the science of public administration in the country.

In the case of Malaysia, the Staff Training Center (STC) was formed in 1963 as part of the New Zealand/Colombo Plan assistance program.[92] In 1965, two U.S. public administration experts, John D. Montgomery and Milton J. Esman, were hired by the Malaysian government to examine Malaysia's administrative system and to make recommendations for improving its capacity for development administration. At the end of their four week "parachute drop" into the MCS, Montgomery and Esman submitted a 23-page report which recommended, *inter alia,* the creation of a Development Administration Unit (DAU) in the Prime Minister's Department to plan and guide the major programs of administrative improvement.[93] The Montgomery-Esman Report was accepted by the Malaysian government and the DAU was set up on July 1, 1966 with assistance from Harvard University. After conducting a joint evaluation of training programs offered by the central and state governments in 1967, the STC and DAU recommended, among other things, the "radical expansion and upgrading" of the STC to form a National Institute for Development Administration.[94] The STC-DAU Report was accepted by the Malaysian Cabinet in 1970. Accordingly, a National Institute of Public Administration or its Malay equivalent, Institut Tadbiran Awam Negara (INTAN), was formed in September 1972 for the purpose of providing "government employees with the knowledge and skills required in the management of public policies and programs.[95] More specifically, INTAN has three broad objectives to fulfil:

1) to increase the capacity and effectiveness of public agencies at all governmental levels (federal, state, and local) in the formulation and implementation of the country's policies and development programs;

2) to develop the Civil Service in Malaysia to became progressive, dedicated, motivated, and responsive to the needs of the country; and

3) to instill the right attitude among the civil servants toward their role in the Malaysian society and the implications of the Government's action on the socio-economic and political systems of the country.[96]

INTAN has been quite successful in its training activities, and from 1973 to August 1978, it had organized a total of 1,372 courses involving 25,117 civil servants.[97] Indeed, a World Bank consultant has described it as a "case of successful training strategy" in his survey of the trends, development, and problems in public administration and management training in developing countries.[98]

Singapore is the last of the five countries to set up a training institute for its civil servants. The Staff Training Institute (STI) was established in March 1971 to rectify the inadequacy of on-the-job-training in the SCS and to produce well-trained and efficient civil servants equipped with a knowledge of modern management concepts and techniques.[99] It should be noted that the STI was not an institute of public administration since it was merely a training institution and did not have a research program. It provided training courses for civil servants in five areas, viz., induction training, management training, specialized and vocational training, language training, and leadership training.[100] In April 1976, the STI was renamed the Civil Service Staff Development Institute (CSSDI). Three years later, the CSSDI's name was changed again to the Civil Service Institute (CSI).

The delay in the creation of INTAN and STI can be attributed to the former British colonial heritage of Malaysia and Singapore, which did not place much emphasis on training other than on-the-job-training. However, this "resistance" to training for development administration has been eroded much more rapidly in Malaysia than in Singapore because of the Montgomery-Esman Report. Furthermore, more Malaysians have gone on government scholarships to the U.S. for training in public administration than Singaporeans, who are usually sent to the Commonwealth countries for training in engineering and medicine, rather than public administration.[101]

Given the Singapore government's emphasis on upgrading the skills of the population and on improving productivity, it is difficult to understand why training has not received the attention it deserves in the SCS. The CSI has 49 staff members but only 17 members perform training functions. With such limited manpower and a budget of S$2.2 million, it is expected to satisfy the training needs of the SCS and the various statutory boards.[102] In short, paying lip-service to training is not enough; the training of civil servants in Singapore can only be improved if the CSI is given more staff and resources to enable it to perform its functions more effectively.

**Performance Evaluation**

In Indonesia, each civilian public servant is evaluated by his direct superior in terms of six criteria and a service test for appointment in certain ranks. The six criteria are: (1) work capability; (2) diligence; (3) work discipline; (4) cooperation; (5) initiative; and (6) leadership.[103] The report on the performance and personal qualities of a civil servant and the service test are traditional methods of performance evaluation, and are therefore more vulnerable to the various rating errors.[104]

Similarly, traditional methods of performance evaluation are also used in the MCS, TCS, and SCS. ADS officers in Malaysia are evaluated for promotion on the basis of their performance during training and during the interviews by the promotion board as well as the assessment of their superior officer as reflected in the annual and special confidential reports. In Thailand, the consideration of annual salary increments and the promotion of civil servants are at the discretion of the appointing authority and are based on a man-oriented assessment. As in the case of promotion, both favoritism and merit are important criteria in assessing the performance of Thai civil servants.[105]

The SCS relies on traditional methods of performance appraisal for assessing its members. The Shell staff appraisal scheme which has been incorporated in the Staff Performance Report (SPR) is confined to members of the Administrative Service. Part II of the SPR, which seeks to identify the personal qualities and performance of the officer being evaluated, is basically a graphic rating scale and it is therefore vulnerable to rating errors. Similarly, the bulk of the Staff Confidential Report (SCR) G259, which is used for the Professional grades, is based on the traditional graphic rating scale. The remaining Division I and II officers are assessed by the SCR G205, while all Division III and IV civil servants are evaluated by the SCR G206. Both the SCR G205 and SCR G206 also use the graphic rating scale and are therefore not immune to rating errors.[106]

The Philippines is the only country among the five under study to adopt a modern method of performance evaluation. After nearly two years of study among five pilot agencies in 1976, a Performance Appraisal System (PAS) was developed to minimize subjectivity in performance evaluation. From January 1979, the PAS was used to assess the performance of Filipino civil servants. It replaced the old traditional rating system of 70 percent personality factors and 30 percent performance factors. In the PAS, emphasis has been placed on output results rather than input or character traits. The weight is now 75 percent for output factors (quantity, quality and timing of results) and 25 percent for input factors (public relations, punctuality and attendance, and potential).[107] The PAS is a modern method of performance appraisal because it is based on the concept of Management by Objectives (MBO).[108] According to a member of the CSC, the PAS has improved the quality of performance evaluation in the PCS in three ways: it promotes constant dialogue between supervisors and supervisees thus providing feedback; it improves efficiency; and it also enhances employee motivation.[109]

The ICS, MCS, SCS and TCS should follow the example of the PCS in adopting the PAS. Instead of relying on traditional methods, more modern methods like MBO, Behaviorally Anchored Rating Scales (BARS) and the Assessment Center Technique, could be suitably modified for use by these civil services. Modern methods are expensive to develop, but are much more accurate than traditional ones. Between using a cheap but inaccurate method of performance evaluation and an expensive but accurate method, there is really no choice at all if the concern is to improve the quality of performance appraisal in the ICS, MCS, SCS and TCS.

**Disciplinary Control**

In the ICS, a civilian public servant who has infringed the disciplinary provisions will be punished according to the severity of the offence. There is a range of eight types of penalties from a written reprimand to dismissal as a civilian public servant. A civil servant accused of indiscipline can submit a written appeal against the sentence to an Appeals Committee for a review of the case.[110] According to a U.S. consultant, the lack of discipline is a serious problem in the ICS.[111]

In Malaysia, the Federal Constitution ensures that a civil servant shall not be dismissed or reduced in rank without a reasonable opportunity of being heard. According to Chapter D of the General Orders, eight types of disciplinary offences are identified and the punishment for each offence specified, ranging from a warning to dismissal. There is also an Appeals Board over every level of Disciplinary Board. The PSD and PSC constitute the highest level of Disciplinary Board and Appeals Board, respectively.[112] Discipline in the MCS was a problem before Datuk Seri Dr. Mahatir Mohamad became Prime Minister in July 1981. Dr. Mahatir is serious about administrative reform and eradicating bureaucratic corruption and problems of discipline in the MCS. To reduce absenteeism and to ensure that all civil servants, including senior officials, keep office hours, the Clock-In System was introduced soon after he assumed office as Prime Minister.[113]

In the Philippines, P.D. No. 807, October 1975, has identified 30 general grounds for disciplinary action against civil servants, ranging from dishonesty to nepotism.[114] In addition, other specific grounds for disciplinary action can be found in several administrative rules and regulations. There are seven types of penalties, varying in descending order of severity from dismissal or removal from service to reprimand.[115] The MSB deals with complaints against any officer arising from abuses, personnel actions, and violation of the merit system. Discipline was also a serious problem in the PCS before the advent of martial law in 1972. After martial law was proclaimed, the situation improved somewhat, especially after the summary dismissal of 1,500 civil servants in early 1973.[116] However, the problem of discipline remains with the PCS in spite of the purges.

In Singapore, the PSC is also responsible for taking disciplinary action against civil servants found guilty of any of the 18 offences listed in the Schedule to the Public Service (Disciplinary Proceedings--Delegation of Function) Rules, 1970.[117] If a civil servant is found guilty of a disciplinary offence, the PSC can either dismiss, demote, impose some lesser penalty (stoppage or deferment of salary increment, fine or reprimand, or a combination of such penalties) or retire him, depending on the seriousness of the offence.[118] Allegations of corrupt behavior by civil servants are referred by the PCS to the Corrupt Practices Investigation Bureau for further investigation and action. Discipline is not a serious problem in the SCS: there were only 169 disciplinary cases in 1982, which constituted only 0.2 percent of the 68,677 civil servants.[119] Indeed, the strict discipline of the SCS is one of the major reasons for its high level of efficiency.

Finally, in the case of Thailand, the Civil Service Act of 1975 stipulates what the civil servants must and must not do. There are six types of penalties for disciplinary offences: reprimand, reduction in salary, demotion in salary step, discharge, dismissal and expulsion. The type of penalty meted to the offending civil servant will depend on the severity of the offence. If there are grounds for investigation, the appointing authority will form a committee of inquiry which should complete its investigations within 30 days. If the CSC finds that the penalties recommended are not appropriate, it can advise the Prime Minister to ask the relevant department to make the necessary adjustment. A civil servant wishing to appeal against the reprimand, reduction in salary, or demotion in salary step, can do so to the supervisor who issued the order. For cases involving more severe penalties, appeals must be submitted to the Civil Service Special Sub-Commission, which acts on the CSC's behalf.[120] In 1980, 1,289 civil servants were disciplined. This number constitutes 0.56 percent of the 230,431 civil servants.[121]

## Conclusion

We have described the public personnel systems in Indonesia, Malaysia, the Philippines, Singapore and Thailand in terms of the various personnel functions. Moreover, the similarities and differences in recruitment and selection, classification, compensation, promotion, training, performance evaluation and disciplinary control in the five countries have also been identified. It only remains for us to identify the strengths and weaknesses of the public personnel system in these countries as this will enable us to assess the extent to which they have attained the goals of productivity and excellence.

The record of the five public personnel systems in attaining the goals of productivity and excellence is a mixed one. On the one hand, countries like Indonesia, the Philippines and Thailand appear to be facing problems in meeting these goals. The Indonesian public personnel system has the heaviest burden since the ICS is the largest civil service in the five countries. Furthermore, the salaries of civil servants are extremely low, thus giving rise not only to corruption, but also to moonlighting, inefficiency and lack of job commitment. Low salaries do not promote productivity or excellence. Traditional methods are employed in recruitment and performance evaluation. Discipline is also a problem in the ICS. Even though the classification system is mixed, there is little or no job analysis in the ICS.

The TCS is similarly plagued with the problems of corruption, low salaries, traditional recruitment, traditional methods of performance evaluation, and discipline. While training is not a serious problem in the TCS, it should be noted that promotion of civil servants is based on merit and favoritism. In the same way, the PCS suffers from low salaries, widespread corruption, reliance on traditional recruitment, and problems of discipline. To compensate for these weaknesses, the PCS encourages job analysis, has a good training record, and uses a modern method of performance evaluation.

On the other hand, Malaysia and Singapore appear to be more likely to meet the goals of productivity and excellence. Apart from being smaller countries, both are not affected by low salaries or corruption. However, both the MCS and SCS rely on traditional recruitment and traditional methods of performance evaluation. Since both personnel systems use the rank classification system, there is little or no job analysis. While INTAN has succeeded in its training activities, the CSI requires more personnel and funds to increase its effectiveness. The quota system used in the ADS has reduced the chances of non-Malays to enter the ADS and created problems of morale among them. There is no serious problem of discipline in the SCS. In Malaysia, disciplinary problems were more serious before Dr. Mahatir assumed office as Prime Minister in July 1981. Given the SCS's extremely high salaries, the SCS should not rely mainly on financial incentives to attract, motivate and retain talented people in the public bureaucracy. Non-financial rewards (giving letters of appreciation, recognition for work well done) can help to increase the civil servant's commitment to his job and the organization.

In sum, the public personnel systems in the five countries should focus on realistic recruitment rather than traditional recruitment. With the exception of the Philippines, traditional methods of performance evaluation should be replaced by modern methods whenever possible. Indonesia, the Philippines and Thailand have public personnel systems which have been adversely affected by low salaries and the widespread corruption and moonlighting that results. Finally, more job analysis should be introduced especially in Malaysia and Singapore, which have the rank classification system.

**Notes**

1. See for example: W.L. Balk, *Improving Government Productivity* (Beverly Hills: Sage Publications, 1975); David Bain, *The Productivity Prescription* (New York: McGraw-Hill Book Co., 1982); Michael LeBoeuf, *The Productivity Challenge* (New York: McGraw-Hill Book Co., 1982); T.J. Peters and R.H. Waterman, Jr., *In Search of Excellence* (New York: Harper & Row, 1982); C.R. Hickman and M.A. Silva, *Creating Excellence* (London: George Allen & Unwin, 1984); and Tom Peters and Nancy Austin, *A Passion for Excellence* (New York: Random House, 1985).

2. Brunei, the sixth member that joined ASEAN in January 1984, is excluded for two reasons: it was not in ASEAN when the study was conducted, and published data on its public personnel system are scarce. See the relevant chapters in Amara Raksasataya and Heinrich Siedentopf (eds.), *Asian Civil Services* (Kuala Lumpur: APDAC, 1980).

3. Selcuk Ozgediz, *Managing the Public Service in Developing Countries* (Washington, D.C.: World Bank Staff Working Papers No. 583, 1983), p. 2.

4. Cyrus Manurung, "The Public Personnel System in Indonesia," in Raksasataya and Siedentopf (eds.), *op. cit.,* pp. 137 and 139.

5. Elyas bin Omar, "The Civil Service Systems in Malaysia," in *ibid.,* pp. 255-257.

6. Filemon U. Fernandez Jr., "The Civil Service System in the Philippines," in *ibid.,* pp. 366-367.

7. See Republic of Singapore, *The Constitution of the Republic of Singapore* (Singapore: Singapore National Printers, 1980); Lee Boon Hiok, "The Public Personnel System in Singapore," in Raksasataya and Siedentopf (eds.), *op. cit.,* pp. 442-443; and Jon S.T. Quah, "The Public Bureaucracy and National Development in Singapore," in K.K. Tummala (ed.), *Administrative Systems Abroad* (Washington, D.C.: University Press of America, 1982), pp. 50-52.

8. See "Civil Service Act of 1975 (B.E. 2518)," (Bangkok: Office of the CSC, January 1979), mimeo.; and Udol Boonprakob, "The Civil Service System in Thailand," in Raksasataya and Siedentopf (eds.), *op. cit.,* pp. 543-544.

9. Manurung, *op. cit.,* p. 139.

10. *Ibid.,* p. 139.

11. Omar, *op. cit.,* p. 260.

12. *Ibid.,* p. 262.

13. For details of the origins and evolution of the CSC in the Philippines see Jose P. Leveriza, *Personnel Administration in the Government* (Metro-Manila: National Book Store, 1980), pp. 17-25.

14. Quoted in Fernandez, *op. cit.,* p. 369.

15. *Ibid.,* p. 370.

16. See Jon S.T. Quah, "Origin of the Public Service Commission in Singapore," *Indian Journal of Public Administration,* Vol. 18, No. 4 (October-December 1972), p. 564.

17. Republic of Singapore, *The Budget for the Financial Year 1984/85* (Singapore: Singapore National Printers, 1984), p. 70.

18. Republic of Singapore, *The Constitution of the Republic of Singapore,* p. 43.

19. Lee, *op. cit.,* pp. 442-443.

20. Veronica Quek, "The Public Service Division," *Management Development,* No. 38 (January-March 1983), p. 3.

21. Boonprakob, *op. cit.,* p. 542. Boonprakob's list does not include the *Sukhapiban* (Sanitary District) Officials Commission *(editors' note).*

22. For a list of these 18 duties, see *ibid.,* pp. 545-546.

23. *Ibid.,* pp. 543-544.

24. For further details, see the relevant chapters on the five countries in Raksasataya and Siedentopf (eds.), *op. cit.*

25. Manurung, *op. cit.,* p. 146.

26. *Ibid.,* pp. 146-147.

27. Quoted in Omar, *op. cit.,* p. 256.

28. Quoted in *ibid.,* p. 256.

29. Ahmad Takiyuddin bin Shaari, "Recruitment and Selection in the Malaysian Public Service," in Amara Raksasataya and Heinrich Siedentopf (eds.), *Asian Civil Services Technical Papers,* Vol. 2 (Kuala Lumpur: APDAC, 1980), p. 29.

30. Fernandez, *op. cit.,* pp. 380-381.

31. *Ibid.,* p. 382.

32. Where there are no suitable citizens to fill the vacancies or where non-citizens are better qualified than citizens, the PSC has appointed Malaysians and other expatriates to Divisions I and II posts.

33. Quah, "The Public Bureaucracy and National Development in Singapore," in Tummala (ed.), *op. cit.,* p. 51.

34. Boonprakob, *op. cit.,* p. 551.

35. "Civil Service Act of 1975 (B.E. 2518)," pp. 11-12.

36. Manurung, *op. cit.,* pp. 149-151.

37. Omar, *op. cit.,* pp. 264, 274-275 and 289.

38. For a detailed description of recruitment and selection in the TCS, see Wilars Singhawisai, "Recruitment and Selection in the Thai Civil Service," in Raksasataya and Siedentopf (eds.), *Asian Civil Services Technical Papers,* Vol. 2, *op. cit.,* pp. 68-137.

39. John P. Wanous, *Organizational Entry* (Reading, Mass.: Addison-Wesley Publishing Co., 1980), pp. 34-35.

40. *Ibid.,* p. 37.

41. *Ibid.,* p. 41.

42. *Ibid.,* pp. 42-43.

43. *Report of the Public Services Salaries Commission* (Kuala Lumpur: Government Printing Office, 1947), paragraph 44.

44. Omar, *op. cit.,* p. 257.

45. Boonprakob, *op. cit.,* p. 548.

46. E.J. Barbour, "The Needs of the Thai Civil Service System," Paper written for the Public Administration Division, United States Operations Mission of Thailand, March 25, 1964, pp. 2 and 18.

47. Boonprakob, *op. cit.,* pp. 548-550.

48. Manurung, *op. cit.,* pp. 144-145.

49. Fernandez, *op. cit.,* p. 378.

50. *Ibid.,* p. 379.

51. Ralph Braibanti, "Reflections on Bureaucratic Corruption," *Public Administration* (London), Vol. 40 (Winter 1962), pp. 357-372.

52. For the best treatment of the subject, see Clive Gray, "Civil Service Compensation in Indonesia," *Bulletin of Indonesian Economic Studies,* Vol. 15, No. 1 (March 1979), pp. 85-113.

53. Manurung, *op. cit.,* p. 162.

54. Theodore M. Smith, "Corruption, Tradition and Change," *Indonesia,* Vol. 11 (April 1971), p. 29.

55. *Ibid.,* pp. 30-31.

56. Buchari Zainun, "Effective and Efficient Utilization of Civil Service Working Time: Indonesian Case," *Indian Journal of Public Administration,* Vol. 28, No. 3 (July-September 1982), p. 453.

57. Gray, *op. cit.,* p. 92.

58. Fernandez, *op. cit.,* pp. 389-392.

59. The salary figures are taken from *ibid.*, p. 422. The conversion of pesos into US$ is based on the 1980 exchange rate.

60. *Ibid.*, pp. 393-394.

61. Kasem Suwanagul, *The Civil Service of Thailand* (Ph.D. Dissertation, New York University, 1962), pp. 79-80.

62. The salary figures are taken from "Civil Service Act of 1975 (B.E. 2518)," p. 46. The rate of conversion into US$ is based on the 1980 exchange rate.

63. Boonprakob, *op. cit.*, pp. 555-557.

64. The salary figures are taken from *Public Services Department: Organization and Functions* (Kuala Lumpur: Information and Documentation Unit, PSD, 1984), p. 36.

65. Omar, *op. cit.*, p. 267.

66. See Jon S.T. Quah, "Administrative and Legal Measures for Combatting Bureaucratic Corruption in Singapore," (Singapore: Department of Political Science, University of Singapore, Occasional Paper No. 34, 1978).

67. Jon S.T. Quah, "The Public Bureaucracy in Singapore, 1959-1984," in You Poh Seng and Lim Chong Yah (eds.), *Singapore: Twenty-Five Years of Development* (Singapore: Nan Yang Xing Zhou Lianhe Zaobao, 1984), p. 296.

68. *Sunday Times,* February 21, 1982, p. 1.

69. *Sunday Times,* February 28, 1982, p. 1.

70. Republic of Singapore, *The Budget for the Financial Year 1984/85,* pp. 509-511.

71. Manurung, *op. cit.*, p. 160.

72. Omar, *op. cit.*, p. 266.

73. Quoted in *ibid.*, p. 266.

74. *Ibid.*, pp. 268-269.

75. Fernandez, *op. cit.*, p. 387.

76. S. Jayakumar, *Constitutional Law* (Singapore: Malaya Law Review, Faculty of Law, University of Singapore), p. 101.

77. Government of the Republic of Singapore, *Instruction Manual No.2 Staff (except daily-rated staff appointments)* (Singapore: Ministry of Finance, 1972), Section E Appointment--by promotion, paragraph 16.

78. Boonprakob, *op. cit.*, p. 554.

79. Ronald L. Krannich, "The Politics of Personnel Management: Competence and Compromise in the Thai Bureaucracy," *Hong Kong Journal of Public Administration,* Vol. 3, No. 1 (June 1981), pp. 46-49.

80. Likhit Dhiravegin, *The Bureaucratic Elite of Thailand* (Bangkok: Thai Khadi Research Institute, 1978), p. 132.

81. *Ibid.,* pp. 137-146.

82. *Ibid.,* pp. 148-149.

83. *Ibid.,* p. 150.

84. For further details, see Jon S.T. Quah, "The Study of Public Administration in the ASEAN Countries,"*International Review of Administrative Sciences,* Vol. 46, No. 4 (1980), pp. 355-359.

85. Gregorio A. Francisco, Jr. and Edwin O. Stene, "The Philippine Institute of Public Administration," *Philippine Journal of Public Administration,* Vol. 2, No. 2 (April 1958), p. 134.

86. Quah, "The Study of Public Administration in the ASEAN Countries," *op. cit.,* p. 356.

87. Joseph L. Sutton, "The Institute of Public Administration in Thailand," *Philippine Journal of Public Administration,* Vol. 2, No. 2 (April 1958), p. 121.

88. Amara Raksasataya, "Preparing Administrators for National Development: Thailand Experience," in Hahn-Been Lee and Abelardo G. Samonte (eds.), *Administrative Reforms in Asia* (Manila: EROPA, 1970), pp. 221-222.

89. Boonprakob, *op. cit.,* pp. 553-554.

90. Sondang P. Siagian, "Improving Indonesia's Administrative Infrastructure: A Case Study," in Lee and Samonte (eds.), *op. cit.,* p. 118.

91. Quoted in Manurung, *op. cit.,* p. 157.

92. Y. Mansoor Marican, *Public Personnel Administration* (Singapore: ISEAS, 1979), p. 10.

93. Milton J. Esman, *Administration and Development in Malaysia* (Ithaca: Cornell University Press, 1972), pp. 140-144.

94. *Ibid.,* pp. 185-191.

95. Marican, *op. cit.,* p. 11.

96. Omar, *op. cit.,* p. 265.

97. *Ibid.,* p. 266.

98. Samuel Paul, *Training for Public Administration and Management in Developing Countries: A Review* (Washington, D.C.: World Bank Staff Working Papers No. 584, 1983), pp. 100-105.

99. *Straits Times,* March 16, 1971, p. 17.

100. John Tan, "Review of Activities of Staff Training Institute," *Management Development,* No. 1 (September 1973), p. 8.

101. Quah, "The Study of Public Administration in the ASEAN Countries," *op. cit.*, p. 359.

102. Quah, "The Public Bureaucracy in Singapore, 1959-1984," *op. cit.*, p. 309.

103. Manurung, *op. cit.*, p. 164.

104. See J.L. Gibson, et al., *Organizations: Behavior, Structure, Process*, 3rd ed. (Dallas: Business Publications, 1979), Chapter 13.

105. Boonprakob, *op. cit.*, p. 559.

106. Quah, "The Public Bureaucracy in Singapore, 1959-1984," *op. cit.*, p. 308.

107. Fernandez, *op. cit.*, p. 396.

108. For the best description of the PAS, see *Performance Appraisal: A Key to Success in Your Career* (Manila: Office of Performance and Promotions Systems, CSC, 1980).

109. Fernandez, *op. cit.*, pp. 396-397.

110. Manurung, *op. cit.*, p. 165.

111. Theodore M. Smith, "A Tentative Report Concerning Indonesia's Administrative System, Its Capacity and Problems in Connection with Economic Development," (Jakarta, unpublished report, January 1970), p. 9.

112. Omar, *op. cit.*, p. 269.

113. Vasantha D.R. Charles, "Clock-In System," *Perintis*, Vol. 6 (September 1984), p. 15.

114. See Fernandez, *op. cit.*, pp. 426-427, Appendix 8 for a list of these grounds.

115. *Ibid.*, p. 399.

116. Lediviña V. Cariño, "Personnel Policies and Bureaucratic Behavior under Martial Law," *Philippine Journal of Public Administration*, Vol. 21, Nos. 3 and 4 (July-October 1977), p. 313.

117. For a listing of these offenses, see Quah, "Administrative and Legal Measures for Combatting Bureaucratic Corruption in Singapore," *op. cit.*, p. 21, fn. 18.

118. *Ibid.*, p. 7.

119. Jon S.T. Quah, "Public Administration in a City-State: The Singapore Case," in Keiso Hanaoka (ed.), *Comparative Study on the Local Public Administration in Asian and Pacific Countries* (Tokyo: EROPA Local Government Center, 1984), p. 211.

120. Boonprakob, *op. cit.*, p. 560.

121. Data obtained from the CSC of Thailand.

# 12

# Toward Effective Delivery of Public Services: An Analysis of the National Budgetary System and Reforms in Sri Lanka*

## C.T. Elangasekere**

National budgeting is a procedure which seeks to estimate the income and expenditure of a country over a particular period (usually a financial year). For this purpose the past performance of key economic and financial variables is examined, and attempts are made to forecast future patterns of financial and economic activities within the country, as well as to estimate overall income-expenditure magnitudes. Thereafter, resources are allocated to different sectors on the basis of predetermined developmental goals and priorities. In other words, the budget is not intended to be a mere annual financial statement of a government. It has, on the contrary, a wider role to play in that it charts a plan of action directed toward achieving certain national development goals of the government in power.[1]

Although it is primarily concerned with financing governmental activities, including the provision of public services, the national budget is also an instrument for managing the total economy and for translating national development goals and plans into action through numerous implementing agencies and public service delivery systems. In this sense, it is an annual operational plan. It is also a device which the government uses to participate in and coordinate the total national effort. On account of its pervasive influence on almost all administrative action, the national budget forms an integral part of the total management system of the central government.

Today, the financial organization of democratic societies has resulted in the budgetary system becoming a device for ensuring fundamental constitutional safeguards within those societies. Thus, the annual budget is now considered a means of asserting legislative control over the Executive by ensuring that

---

\* Abridged from the original Conference paper by Captain Sumaet Punyaratabandhu.
\*\* Sri Lanka Institute of Development Administration (S.L.I.D.A.), Colombo, Sri Lanka.

the Legislature (consisting of elected representatives of the people) decides annually the purposes and allocations of expenditure, as well as the method of collecting revenue to finance expenditure to be incurred by the central government.

### The Financial Organization of Sri Lañka

*Role of the Legislature and the Cabinet.* According to the Constitution of Sri Lanka (1978), Parliament is supreme as regards matters relating to public finance because, "Parliament shall have full control over public finance; no tax, rate or any other levy shall be imposed by any local authority or any other public authority except by or under the authority of a law passed by Parliament or of any existing law." Within Parliament - as in the United Kingdom - financial initiative and executive authority rest with the Cabinet, and only a Cabinet minister may propose a "money bill" such as the Annual Appropriation Bill (i.e., the Budget). Next to Parliament and the Cabinet, the highest financial authority is the Minister of Finance and Planning, to whom the Cabinet has delegated executive authority to implement financial policies and annual financial plans of the government which have been approved by the legislature. As in the case of the United Kingdom, control by Parliament of public financial operations is facilitated by the "Consolidated Fund," which was created in 1946.

Legislative control over the annual budget is directly exercised through a number of mechanisms. First, there is the examination by Parliament (during the Budget Debate and the Committee Stage Discussions) of revenue targets and financial provisions included in the Draft Estimates of Revenue and Expenditure and the Budget Proposals submitted to Parliament by the Minister of Finance. This provides an opportunity for Members of Parliament to critically examine the performance of the entire public service delivery system, and to air their grievances relating to specific projects or services undertaken within their respective electorates. Second, there is the report of the Auditor-General who is expected to critically examine the performance of public sector agencies and submit his findings and observations to Parliament within ten months after the close of a financial year. The third mechanism is the review of financial operations of ministries, departments; and public corporations by the Parliamentary Committee on Public Accounts, and by the Parliamentary Committee on Public Enterprises. These reviews undertaken by the Auditor-General and the Parliamentary Committees also provide an opportunity to examine the manner in which funds have been spent on public sector projects and public services during the previous financial year.

*The Minister of Finance.* The Minister of Finance exercises supervisory control by prescribing standards through regulations and circulars for adoption and compliance by all government agencies engaging in financial transactions, and by reserving certain specific items for Treasury approval, on account of their financial implications. He also exercises control over the Annual Budget. As he is primarily responsible for finding financial resources to implement the expenditure proposals in the Annual Budget, his ministry must examine those proposals prior to their inclusion in the Annual Budget Estimates. Furthermore, the Minister of Finance is directly responsible for selecting the package of proposals to be included in the Budget Speech which he delivers in Parliament. This necessitates a process of policy analysis and strategy determination which involves an examination and evaluation of both the quantity and quality of public services to be provided, and social welfare measures to be adopted in the ensuing financial year.

*Treasury Control of Financial Administration.* The central coordinating function relating to all fiscal and financial operations is the responsibility of the Ministry of Finance and Planning and its most important department, the Treasury. The Ministry of Finance derives its authority not only from the Constitution, the Legislature, and the Executive, but also from other legislation, financial regulations, and circulars relating to the conduct of the Government's financial operations.

The concept of "Treasury control" is based on the assumption, borrowed from Whitehall, that from the point of view of national development and efficiency, the total impact of the Government's financial operations must be subjected to continuous examination and centralized coordination. For this purpose, the Treasury formulates financial regulations and issues circulars, on the authority of the Minister of Finance, to ensure uniformity and fairness in public financial management and more particularly in respect of budget formulation and execution. The chief function of the Treasury is therefore to control and supervise government finances on behalf of the Minister of Finance, to ensure timely successful completion of projects, as well as the effective provision and delivery of public services.

*Allocation of Financial Resources.* Parliament and the Cabinet are responsible for making macro-level decisions relating to the allocation of resources through the Annual Budget (for both capital and recurrent expenditure) to various programs, projects, and activities. These decisions are based on recommendations submitted by the Minister of Finance and Planning, Presidential Commissions of Inquiry, and various official committees. At the next level, the sectoral and line ministries determine the manner in which funds channelled to them are allocated to various departments and other public sector agencies. Thereafter, the heads of project ministries, departments, and other public agencies decide how the financial resources allocated to them are to be distributed among various programs, projects, and activities. In the case of district ministries, as the annual grants channelled to these agencies are an aggregate of electoral allocations (i.e., approximately Rs. 5 million per electoral district), the respective Members of Parliament who represent these districts tightly control the allocation of funds for various projects and public services to be funded during the ensuing financial year. These Members of Parliament may, however, be influenced by the District Minister, public officials, or by representations made by constituents, local government bodies, or people's organizations.

When financial and other resources are provided by a multilateral or other external agency for rural development projects, the selection of component projects and services is usually determined on the basis of preliminary resource and needs surveys conducted by the funding agencies, together with related studies undertaken by local and foreign experts. The World Bank and the Swedish International Development Agency (NORAD) are two examples of external funding agencies.

*The Integrated Planning and Financial System.* Since 1977, the planning and financial functions of the Government of Sri Lanka have been integrated both functionally and organizationally in a single agency - the Ministry of Finance and Planning - under a senior Cabinet minister. This organizational linkage has fostered a close relationship between the planning and financial-cum-budgeting functions of the Government. This is in sharp contrast to the mutually suspicious (and often adversary) attitude which prevailed earlier between ministries when these crucial functions of the Government were handled by separate ministries. It has also helped considerably to eliminate many institutional problems, such as a lack of coordination and total absence of a continuing dialogue between major components of the public administration system.

## The National Budgeting System

*The Annual Budget Cycle.* The national budget process in Sri Lanka involves a series of operations which are basically cyclical in sequence. Inherent in this is the continuity and repetitive character of the budget process. Budgeting is thus not considered a discrete annual exercise but a continuous, inter-linked process with specific identifiable phases, as follows:

1. Preparation of the Budget - undertaken by the line ministries, the Ministry of Finance, and the Treasury.
2. Submission of the Budget to Parliament by the Minister of Finance:
    a) first reading (tabling of draft estimates),
    b) second reading (Budget Speech).
3. Examination of the Budget by Parliament:
    a) Budget Debate,
    b) Committee stage discussion (third reading).
4. Parliamentary approval of the Budget.
5. Budget implementation by line agencies.
6. Performance monitoring and progress control by the Treasury, line ministries, and the Ministry of Plan Implementation.
7. Budget evaluation by the Auditor-General and Parliament.

The concept of the budget cycle also implies a flow-down and flow-up of decisions, data, information, and suggestions. Policy and program decisions are made at the higher levels and move down to the operating level, while data and information generated at the operating level and decisions taken at this level are transmitted up through the organizational hierarchy to influence budget decisions at national level.

*Budget Format.* Until the early 1970s the Annual Estimates of Expenditure were prepared on the basis of the traditional "line-item system" of budget classification and preparation. These budget estimates were made up of aggregates of provisions, listed under certain pre-determined votes and a number of standardized (or special) sub-heads, and were not identified in respect of different programs, projects, or activities undertaken under a particular head of expenditure. From such a budget format, it was not possible to extract the total estimated cost of a particular activity, as it was not designed to provide such information. This was a serious drawback of the traditional budget estimates. Another major disadvantage of the traditional budget system was that the objectives or the purposes for which funds were provided by the legislature were not clearly spelt out in the estimates of expenditure.

In the early 1960s there developed a growing realization that improvements in budget presentation were necessary to obtain realistic costs with regard to various programs being undertaken and services provided by the Government. The result was the introduction of program and performance budgeting procedures in the early 1970s, which shifted the emphasis from the things which the Government "bought" to things which the Government "did." Performance budgeting was considered extremely useful in enabling the Legislature and the Executive to manage the national economy more effectively and - in particular - to decide which program, project, or service deserved priority over others in the allocation of scarce national resources.

Furthermore, by identifying objectives and targets of accomplishment it provided a certain orientation to policy and project implementation, which was expected to result in improved performance and the effective provision of various public services. It also made it possible to evaluate and review projects and services by comparing the anticipated performance goals or targets with actual accomplishment - and thereafter its intended impact on beneficiaries with actual impact (or sometimes unintended impacts).

*Components of the Budget System.* There are five principal components which are distinguishable in the budget system of Sri Lanka. They are:

1. The macro-level National Budget presented in Parliament annually by the Minister of Finance and Planning.
2. Budgets of centralized public agencies:
    a) sectoral/line ministry budgets;
    b) line department budgets.
3. District level budgets:
    a) district (ministry) budgets:
        i. district level decentralized budget,
        ii. district development council budget;
    b) district integrated rural development project budget.
4. Budgets of public sector agencies:
    a) budgets of public corporations and statutory boards;
    b) budgets of local authorities (i.e. municipalities, *gramodaya mandalayas*).
5. Budgets of non-governmental organizations:
    a) budgets of multilateral organizations operating in Sri Lanka;
    b) budgets of foreign and local donor agencies.

Budgets grouped under categories (2) - (5) above are wholly or partly funded through the National Budget. For example, even in the case of district integrated rural development projects implemented with external financial assistance, certain items of operational expenditure (e.g., salaries of local civil service personnel) are met directly from the allocations set apart in the annual budget to meet such counterpart costs. Provision of public services is generally entrusted to organizations which are identified under categories (2) - (4). Nevertheless, it has to be conceded that numerous multilateral, private, and voluntary agencies - referred to under (5) - undertake many development projects and provide a variety of services to the public utilizing their own resources.

*Decentralized Budget.* The formulation and implementation of the annual budget was for a long time a central government exercise, confined largely to the Ministry of Finance and other line ministries. During the past few decades, there has been a growing awareness of the need to decentralize the budget process with a view to:

1. ensuring greater popular participation in the development process, especially at the grassroots level;
2. minimizing regional imbalances in development by increasing production and implementing projects which will generate employment, based on regional and electoral needs and priorities, as well as their resource base;
3. eliminating the urban bias in development planning and national budgeting by restricting the magnitude of resources flowing to the urban areas, which sustain only 30 per cent of Sri Lanka's population;
4. encouraging more meaningful local level planning based on realistic and accurate information and data, relating to local conditions and resources;
5. securing the cooperation and participation of the Members of Parliament for ensuring expeditious and successful completion of development projects and efficient delivery of public services in the respective electoral districts.

In order to support and expedite the process of decentralization of the administration already under way, a proposal was made in the latter half of the 1960s to decentralize the budget on a district basis. Such a measure was expected to accelerate regional development. Consequently in October 1973, a District Political Authority (who was a member of the Legislature) was appointed for each district, to oversee the delivery of public services and coordinate the implementation of district-level development projects. This step paved the way for the introduction of a decentralized system of budgeting in 1974, through which each district was given an allocation based on the number of electorates within the district. During this early phase, each electorate was given a flat annual allocation of one million rupees, which was later increased to Rs. 2.5 million.

These funds of the decentralized budget were intended to meet the cost of local or district level projects, including social welfare programs. The decentralized budgeting procedure was also expected to generate increased employment opportunities in the districts by speeding up the national development process, while strengthening the public service delivery infrastructure. This was also believed to be a more meaningful and realistic approach to regional development, as key decisions were expected to be taken at the local or district level, on the basis of more reliable data relating to the particular operational environment.

*District Ministries and District Budgets.* With the establishment of the "district ministries" in 1979, a system of district budgeting was initiated, whereby each district was granted an allocation from the aggregate decentralized budget. This procedure enabled the district level agencies to formulate, appraise, select, and implement capital works of a local nature in respect of approved projects, on the basis of local priorities. This system was evolved to generate increased production and employment in the rural sector by enlisting the participation of the local people in planning and implementing development projects and improving the delivery network at village level. The Members of Parliament within a district were expected to assume responsibility for the proper utilization of funds and the completion of projects in their respective electoral districts, while encouraging the people to participate directly in the implementation of these activities. These district allocations were also determined within a budget of Rs. 2.5 million per electoral district. To ensure better management and utilization, these funds were made transferable among projects.

No specific guidelines were issued for strict compliance when determining priorities among projects, as priorities were left to vary from district to district. In consequence, of Rs. 468 million allocated under the Decentralized Budget of 1984, 81 percent (Rs. 378 million) was spent on "new works," while only 19 percent (Rs. 90 million) was spent on "continuation works." This indicates the relative preference shown by district level decisionmakers (especially

Members of Parliament) for new infrastructural development projects (e.g., electrification, construction of roads, school buildings, rural hospitals), resulting in a significant improvement in, or extension of, the public service delivery system during the last decade.

This system of budgeting has enabled district level needs to be looked into promptly, especially in respect of social overhead infrastructure projects, which are accorded low priority by the line ministries. These district level projects funded from the Decentralized Budget have also generated increased employment opportunities to those residing in the affected districts, largely because the projects are undertaken using local skills and labor.

*District Development Council Budgets and District Plans.* District development councils, which were established in 1981 under the District Development Council Act, took over the functions earlier handled by some local authorities (town councils and village committees). As a result, development activities at village and district level were increased, based on a "District Plan" and a "District Budget." More funds were allocated to district development councils to initiate development activities and to improve and maintain the public service infrastructure at district and rural levels.

Thus, apart from the funds allocated to each district ministry under the Decentralized Budget, a separate matching grant (of Rs. 420 million in the 1985 Budget estimates) was established, to be allocated among development councils for local level development activities. The Ministry of Local Government and Housing was originally entrusted with the responsibility for distributing this block allocation among various district development councils on the same basis as the decentralized budget funds (i.e., Rs. 2.5 million per electoral district). At present, however, the Treasury releases funds on a quarterly basis, taking into account the volume of work undertaken and accomplished by each district ministry in the previous quarter. When funds are released to the districts, as in the case of the decentralized budget funds, it is the respective Member of Parliament who determines the manner in which such funds are utilized.

*Integrated Rural Development Programs at District Level.* Since 1978, integrated rural development (IRD) has become a very popular development strategy in Sri Lanka, with 11 districts being included in the programs. Funding is mainly through multilateral organizations and donor countries or agencies. Originally, these IRD programs were aimed at correcting regional imbalances in development and improving the regional infrastructure of certain districts which were not expected to benefit from major development projects (e.g., the Mahaweli Development Project) which were undertaken by various line ministries.

The IRD programs incorporated a group of complementary projects which were expected to raise rural incomes and living standards by generating additional employment opportunities. The programs were also designed to improve the existing rural infrastructure, including the necessary institutional facilities at the grassroots level. IRD project plans were generally based on detailed base-line studies and in-depth analyses of district-level needs, resource endowments, prospects for development, and implementation capacities. The most noticeable difference between the other district budgeting systems and IRD projects is that sectoral programs and priorities are clearly indicated in respect of the IRD project plans by a project steering committee (in consultation with the donor agency). This eliminates the possibility of low priority projects being incorporated into the overall IRD program at the request of persons with vested interests.

*Budget Examination by the Legislature.* After formal submission of the Annual Budget to Parliament by the Minister of Finance and Planning, the Members of Parliament examine the policies and programs of the Government, the financial provisions included in the Annual Budget Estimates (relating to both recurrent and capital expenditure), revenue measures, and other proposals contained in the Budget Speech. This exercise involves both a reappraisal of past performance and an attempt to discern the emerging socioeconomic scenario. During the Committee Stage discussions which cover a wide range of issues, the Members of Parliament are able to analyze the probable impact of the Budget on the total economy and particularly, on the quality of life of the average citizen. Furthermore, they can air the grievances of constituents, especially with regard to the scope, adequacy, and effectiveness of public services undertaken by the Government. Such representations tend to focus attention on the availability of public services and the efficiency of delivery systems. Finally, Members of Parliament can examine the adequacy and utilization of funds allocated to the Government for the provision of public services.

In response to observations made and issues highlighted by Members of Parliament, the Government may agree to revise the Draft Budget Estimates by introducing "Committee Stage Amendments," in order to increase or decrease allocations made under various heads of expenditure. Budget debates and committee stage discussions also perform an important democratic function by enabling legislators to represent their constituents and to focus on weaknesses of the public administration apparatus (including its delivery systems) and any other shortcomings of government policies or strategies.

*Budget Implementation and Public Services.* Implementation of the budget is directly or indirectly handled by various line ministries, departments, district ministries, district development councils, *pradeshiya/gramodaya, mandalayas,* local bodies, statutory bodies, public corporations, as well as some private agencies, in terms of guidelines and instructions issued by the Ministry of Finance or any other body empowered to do so by the Cabinet. Besides official responsibility for implementing programs contained in the annual estimates, the Cabinet - together with district and project ministers in charge of their respective ministries - must maximize goal attainment while minimizing wastage and delays.

*Program Control and Evaluation of Budget Implementation.* The primary responsibility for monitoring and assessing the effectiveness of programs and public services rests with the respective ministries and departments. However, the Ministry of Finance and Planning - through the Treasury - also attempts to keep a close watch on programs, projects, and activities funded through the national budget. Furthermore, the Ministry of Plan Implementation separately monitors the annual work programs of all public sector organizations.

Although Parliament appropriates funds to the Government through the Annual Budget during a financial year, it is the Executive which uses the funds so allocated by the Legislature. Hence, in order for the Legislature to ascertain whether projects as implemented by the Executive are in accordance with its directives and guidelines, an independent public officer - the Auditor-General - has been appointed to examine and audit the accounts of all ministries and departments, local authorities, public corporations, and other government agencies. The Auditor-General is required to submit a report to Parliament containing his observations on financial operations and overall performance of the government agencies referred to above.

When the Auditor-General submits his annual report to Parliament along with the appropriation accounts of the Government, it is referred by the Legislature to the Public Accounts Committee, which consists of a few Members of Parliament drawn from both sides of the House. This committee is elected by Parliament to examine the Auditor-General's report and to submit its observations and recommendations concerning excesses and irregularities in expenditures incurred by various public sector agencies when undertaking projects and services. During the course of its sittings, the Public Accounts Committee (which is assisted by the Auditor-General and the Finance Division of the Treasury) issues reports and comments on the explanations submitted by ministries and departments.

A similar exercise relating to public corporations and statutory bodies (which are responsible for the provision of many public services in Sri Lanka) is undertaken by the Parliamentary Select Committee on Public Enterprises. This committee reviews the financial operations and annual work programs of these public sector organizations, taking into consideration the Auditor-General's observations in respect of the activities handled by those organizations. The committee is assisted by the Public Enterprises Division of the Treasury.

The examination by the Auditor-General and Parliamentary Select Committees of financial operations and overall performance of all public sector organizations constitutes the final evaluation of the financial stewardship of various accounting officers in respect of financial provisions allocated to them for the provision of public services assigned to those organizations. The Treasury often accepts the comments and suggestions made by the Auditor-General and the Parliamentary Select Committees. Subsequently, these may be communicated to the ministries, departments, and public corporations in the form of Treasury directives. All public sector organizations are expected to comply with these rulings and procedures, which are specific instructions issued by the Treasury, intended to improve the quality of public financial management and ultimately the effectiveness of the total public administration system and its delivery mechanisms.

**National Budgeting and the Delivery of Public Services: An Overview of Some Key Problem Areas**

*The Inadequacy of Resources.* One of the most formidable problems faced by Sri Lanka is the inadequacy of resources to meet the needs of her growing economy. Although the annual budget is expected to provide funds to implement various development programs and to ensure basic welfare services, it has not been able to generate the necessary fiscal resources to achieve these objectives on account of the restricted tax base which is a result of the relatively low per capita income in Sri Lanka. Furthermore, public sector agencies responsible for revenue collection are often content with collecting the minimum revenue with the least effort. In a situation of resource scarcity it is the public services, especially the public utilities sector, which is denied adequate resources to even meet day-to-day expenditure - with adverse effects on delivery mechanisms.

There are other unpredictable external and internal factors which have contributed to the depletion of resources available to finance projects. Some of these unfavorable external factors are the increasing cost of fuel, declining prices of major exports, rising costs of imports, the gradual depreciation of the Sri Lankan rupee vis-à-vis major world currencies (and consequential inflationary pressures), and protectionism in the developed countries. This deteriorating resource situation has been further aggravated by ethnic disturbances which occurred in 1983, and the consequential destabilization and dislocation in certain crucial revenue-generating or foreign exchange-earning sectors and increasing expenditure on defense and anti-terrorist operations which has increased from about two to ten percent of the annual budget in recent years.

It has been observed that whenever there is any significant reduction in anticipated resources due to some unforeseen circumstance, the first casualties of subsequent budget cuts are the social overhead projects or public service activities, as these are usually assigned a lower priority by development planners even though such budget cuts would adversely affect the average citizen almost immediately. Such cutbacks in budgeted expenditure adversely affect the economically and socially disadvantaged groups.

*The Over-Centralized Budget System and Inappropriate Development Goals.* National budgeting in Sri Lanka still remains a highly centralized exercise based on the British Whitehall model, with all major decision-making operations confined exclusively to the central planning office (i.e., the Treasury) in the Ministry of Finance and Planning. Development goals and investment guidelines which invariably determine the scope and content of the Annual Budget are, on the whole, unilaterally decided in Colombo. The overwhelmingly centralized nature of national planning and budgeting operations in Sri Lanka is further aggravated by a lack of awareness on the part of key decisionmakers at the center of local level needs and aspirations. Macro-level priorities and investment criteria are often determined by officials who, on account of their predominantly urban background and work experience, tend to be ignorant of rural lifestyles and needs.

*The Urban Bias in Resource Allocation.* A strong urban bias is noticeable in the allocation (through the Annual Budget) of resources for capital expenditure. This inevitably results in rural areas (which sustain over 70 percent of Sri Lanka's population) being inadequately served with public services (e.g., schools, dispensaries, family planning clinics, electricity, drinking water, post offices, etc.) and extension facilities (e.g., agricultural credit). Although the rural infrastructure, including the public service delivery system, has benefited from the introduction of a decentralized budget, district development council grants, and integrated rural development projects, a closer examination reveals that the total amount of financial resources which are channelled directly to the districts represents only three percent of the Annual Budget.

*Absence of an Effective Mechanism for Program Control and Impact Analysis.* The present system of public administration lacks a well-established control mechanism to provide relevant operational data and information, not only for day-to-day decision-making, but also for macro-level policy formulation (i.e., national planning and budgeting). The absence of such a mechanism makes a systematic performance appraisal virtually impossible; neither can there be any impact analysis in respect of the Annual Budget implementation process (which includes the operations of the entire public service delivery system). This lacuna prevents mid-course corrective action to avoid or mitigate the effects of undesirable or unanticipated outcomes. It also deprives policy makers of a valuable feedback channel, which is a prerequisite for policy analysis, development, and refinement. Systematic policy analysis may lead to a reappraisal of strategies and operational procedures relating to the service delivery system, with a view to making it more accessible to clients.

*Outdated Financial System and Practices.* Most budgeting and accounting procedures currently in use in Sri Lanka originated during the British colonial period. Although some of these have already been discarded in the United Kingdom itself, they continue to be rigidly applied in Sri Lanka. Many of these procedures have been incorporated in the *Financial Regulations,* which is the authoritative manual of public financial management in Sri Lanka. These outmoded pratices are time consuming, costly, and have mitigated against the development of a less cumbersome and result-oriented accounting system. The excessive controls which characterize the present system have not only delayed budget execution, but have also vitiated the beneficial impact of many public services provided by the Government. During the colonial era, these inflexible and stringent procedures involving a complicated system of checks and balances were adopted because the British were suspicious of the "natives" who made up the country's bureaucracy. However, it is anachronistic to continue with these practices, without appropriate adaptation and modification.

*Financial Indiscipline.* There is at the budget implementation stage a noticeable absence of administrative accountability and cost consciousness on the part of public sector agencies. This is evidenced by a disregard for proper procurement procedures and materials management practices, frequent delays in project execution, blatant misuse of public property, no supervision of public service deliveries, etc. This amounts to a mismanagement of public funds allocated by the Legislature for specific public service activities.

Furthermore, some public sector agencies are unable to utilize budgetary allocations made to certain projects, resulting in under-expenditures of 20-40 percent at the end of a financial year. This may be due to the over-estimation of project costs, unanticipated implementation bottlenecks, or inefficient project management. Such non-utilization of scarce resources entails an opportunity cost, in that it prevents such resources from being channelled into alternative projects - for example, to undertake a new community development project or public service, or to expand the scope of an existing service delivery system.

*Difficulty of Access to Public Services.* Another recurring and related complaint which public administrators have to contend with is the "access problem." This may arise mainly on account of physical factors such as the unfavorable location of a particular service delivery outlet. On the other hand, it may be the procedural hurdle (i.e., bureaucratic red tape) which a client encounters when trying to obtain goods, services, or information from a government functionary or a service extension outlet. Access to certain public services may also be seriously hampered by the absence of communications facilities at service outlets. Most of these access problems can be attributed to either inadequacy of budgetary provisions, or unsatisfactory organizational arrangements.

*Absence of a Manpower Development Strategy.* In spite of an adult literacy rate of over 90 percent and an education system which guarantees a free education from kindergarten through university, the budget implementation process and the effectiveness of the public service delivery system in Sri Lanka have been adversely affected by a persistent inadequacy of high-level manpower and skills. There has, however, been no serious attempt so far to assess or to make an inventory of the manpower resources available within Sri Lanka. In the absence of such basic manpower data, it is not possible to formulate a manpower development strategy which will lay down the broad guidelines relating to recruitment, deployment, training, and development of the country's manpower resources.

Furthermore, in the public sector at present, policies with regard to compensation, promotion, and training do not attract the educated sectors of the population. This situation has been further aggravated by the highly politicized nature of the work environment, resulting in frequent interference, unfair transfers and promotions, etc. There are also numerous instances where persons trained in specialized fields are given civil service assignments which are not related to their fields of specialization or prior experience, while elsewhere in the public sector, various development projects and agencies are languishing for want of those identical skills. The reluctance on the part of skilled personnel to move out of urban areas is largely due to the lack of basic facilities (i.e., suitable official quarters, satisfactory medical facilities, good schools, etc.) and uncongenial working conditions (i.e., poor communications facilities, inadequacy of office space, equipment, and furniture). Many of these problems result from the ineffective way in which resources are channelled through the annual budget to the rural areas.

*Internal and External Brain Drain.* At the same time, there is an internal as well as external brain drain from the public sector, which has further depleted the limited manpower resources available to maintain the public service delivery system. The internal brain drain has been to the private sector, which has merely offered a more attractive remuneration package. The external brain drain has been due to not only higher salaries abroad, but also to more satisfying job environments. As referred to earlier, recurring budgetary constraints have prevented the Government from offering a reasonable compensation package to retain Sri Lankan professionals and scientists. A consequence of the brain drain has been that over the past few decades the Government has been faced with a collapse of the public service delivery system in rural areas.

*Absence of Participation by Beneficiaries in Public Sector Decision-Making.* It should be noted that there is virtually no direct involvement by beneficiaries in the public sector decision-making process, especially at grassroots level. On the contrary, projects launched and services provided at village level are based on the perceptions of either outsiders or the rural elites, whose views are considered to reflect the views of an entire village. This form of pseudo-community participation in decision-making is a total farce because projects launched and public services provided - presumably to satisfy the needs of villagers - not only enable the rural vested interests to further strengthen and consolidate their prevailing dominant position, but also help them to continue their exploitation of the rural economy, by manipulating the public service delivery system to serve their particular needs.

The foregoing is by no means a comprehensive survey of the problems which are encountered when formulating and implementing the national budget and operating a public service delivery system in Sri Lanka. It is merely intended to provide a backdrop against which major issues can be identified and viewed in their proper perspective.

## Toward a More Effective National Budget and Public Service Delivery System: An Agenda for Action

Any government attempting to reduce poverty and inequality must identify an appropriate mix of policies and strategies which is capable of responding to the dynamics of the operational environment. In this context, some possible interventions will be examined which may improve the effectiveness of two critical components: the national budget and the public service delivery system of Sri Lanka.

*Determining Appropriate Development Goals.* A national budget should reflect the development goals and priorities of a government. In the context of Sri Lanka, policy makers should adopt a balanced approach to development, involving both macro-level and micro-level considerations. There should be a move away from urban-oriented investments and large-scale, spectacular projects, to small-to-medium scale public utility projects or social welfare activities which will have an immediate impact on the quality of life of rural inhabitants, who make up the bulk of Sri Lanka's population. National planning agencies which formulate guidelines for the annual budget should recognize the prevailing urban bias and re-orient their goals, priorities, and strategies to benefit the rural population.

*A More Equitable Allocation of Resources.* To avoid urban bias in resource allocation, more funds should be appropriated to improve the infrastructure in rural areas, which have in the past generally been accorded a very low priority by development planners, due to either an insensitivity to or an unawareness of the needs and aspirations of people living in those areas, compounded by an ignorance of the resources available at the grassroots level. In short, rapid infrastructure development in peripheral areas should be the main thrust of the national development effort. A serious effort should be made to channel financial resources to local government units, instead of the token allocations granted at present. In this way, policy makers and service providers at the district and rural levels will be able to make decisions which can really benefit people living in those areas.

*The Integration of the District Plan and District Budget.* Although a decentralized budget system was introduced in the early 1970s and formally instituted with the establishment of the District Budgeting System in the 1980s, operational procedures have still to be streamlined, in order to make the best possible use of funds and other resources available at local level. To this end, increased financial authority has to be delegated to policy makers at local levels to determine their priorities, on the basis of local needs and resources. Greater discretion should also be allowed to enable them to allocate resources to projects and services which benefit the people living within a particular district - and not projects recommended by planning offices at the center. This would involve a strengthening of the institutional framework for genuine participation by the people in decision-making at grassroots level - examples being the *Pradeshiya* and *Gramodaya Mandalayas*.

Ideally, all funds being channelled to a district should flow into a district development fund, from which allocations can be periodically released, based on an integrated district development plan designed to improve the quality of life of the average citizen living in a district. An operational annual budget should be formulated on the basis of such a plan to undertake not only directly productive investment, but also to improve and expand the public services and social welfare activities within a district. Administrative support should be provided to enable such service outlets to be efficiently operated and managed.

*Structural Reorganization and Streamlining Procedures.* Mere allocation of additional financial and other resources will not lead to rapid development at the district, divisional, and village levels without institutional and administrative support systems which will ensure the delivery of goods and services to the intended beneficiaries. Such a support system may need, *inter alia,* the following:

1. rationalization of organizational structures and internal authority relationships, to avoid duplication of effort and excessive hierarchic layers which hamper decision-making and coordination of projects and public services;
2. simplification and streamlining of cumbersome and rigid operational systems and procedures, in order to eliminate bureaucratic bottlenecks and expedite the implementation of projects and delivery of services;
3. supervision of development projects and public services by public sector agencies. In this connection, it may be most cost effective to have a single official directly responsible for the overall management of a particular project, or delivery of a specific public service. If so, that official should also be made accountable for the proper disbursement of financial provisions allocated to that activity.

Cost consciousness should be inculcated among those who are in the top management or supervisory positions, to make them sensitive to expenditure which does not contribute to effective delivery of public services or desirable project outcomes.

*Progress Control and Periodic Impact Analysis.* A mechanism should be established to provide progress control, information, and data, while periodic impact analyses should be undertaken to determine whether there is any consistency between anticipated goals and actual outcomes. Any significant discrepancy between goals and outcomes should be analyzed with a view to identifying the causal factors. Such an exercise is bound to provide information which will help an organization avoid such problems in the future.

*Improving Access to Public Services.* To ensure quick and unhampered access to public services, delivery outlets should be conveniently located, to be within easy reach of intended beneficiaries. Action should be taken to guarantee basic community needs (i.e., food, shelter, and clothing), and critical factors of production (i.e., water and land) and other facilities (e.g., extension services, electricity, communications systems). As mentioned earlier, procedures should also be made explicit to the public; and they should be simplified and streamlined to prevent malpractices and corruption by unscrupulous government functionaries. There is also a need to further decentralize the delivery system, which has hitherto been concentrated in Colombo. Although various institutional devices (such as district development councils, *pradeshiya/gramodaya, mandalayas*) have been set up in this decade, it appears that the original intentions have not been fulfilled, on account of numerous organizational inadequacies.

*The Provision of Necessary Manpower.* Since manpower is an indispensable resource for operating the public service delivery system, action should be taken to implement a national manpower development strategy and formulate a set of public personnel policies in Sri Lanka, which would help to procure and retain competent personnel. To ensure the availability of sufficiently qualified personnel to support a widely dispersed public service delivery network, sufficient budgetary resources should be allocated to recruit the required personnel, provide them with an adequate remuneration, and also improve basic facilities (e.g., housing, communications, schools) to enable such personnel to work in remote rural areas without undergoing undue privations. It may even be justifiable to pay a special monthly allowance to persons who are assigned to serve in "difficult areas." It has also been suggested that central personnel agencies should require civil service personnel to serve in the so-called "difficult areas" for a certain number of years before becoming eligible for promotions, scholarships for study abroad, and transfers to more congenial posts. At present, on account of the prevailing shortages of qualified personnel in fields such as medicine, engineering, and teaching, it is necessary for central personnel agencies to devote greater attention to these manpower categories, with a view to preventing a breakdown of public services in peripheral areas.

**Conclusion**

The national budget is an instrument used by many governments to accelerate the pace of development, especially economic and social development, in a country. It may be viewed as a contract entered into annually by the executive and legislative branches of the government, which allows various executive agencies and departments to raise and spend public funds in certain specified ways during a financial year. It is also an economic-cum-legal document that facilitates the exercise of fiscal control by the elected representatives of the people over the sub-national units of government.

Governments seek to use the national budget as a device to provide certain essential services to the public, by identifying the institutional structure and administrative support systems required, and by channelling the necessary resources to create and maintain them. The budget may also provide funds to improve the efficiency of delivery facilities. However, it should be noted that there is no one best policy package which can be recommended to improve the overall performance of the national budgetary processes or the public service delivery systems. There are no permanent panaceas for any given country, sub-national unit, or public sector agency. Every component of a particular course of action or policy package needs to be constantly examined and evaluated, with a view to modifying, updating, and refining it to suit the ever-changing conditions of the operational environment. The search for the most appropriate system or set of procedures will always remain an unfinished task with a constantly changing agenda for action.

## Note

1. This Chapter is based upon the following documentary sources: G. Abeysekera, *Resource Mobilization for the National Budget,* memo, Sri Lanka Institute of Development Administration (SLIDA), 1984; S. Balasingham, *Parliamentary Control of Finance* (Colombo: Government Press, 1968); J. Burkhead, *Government Budgeting* (New York: J. Wiley Co., 1967); Central Bank of Sri Lanka, *Annual Report* (Colombo: Government Press, 1984); R.J. De Mel, *Budget Speech* (Colombo: Government Press, 1984); R.J. De Mel, *Budget Speech* (Colombo: Government Press, 1985); C.T. Elangasekere, "The Budgetary Process in Sri Lanka," in V.T. Navaratne (ed.), *Public Administration in Sri Lanka: A Symposium* (Colombo: SLIDA (forthcoming)); C.T. Elangasekere, "The Planning System in Sri Lanka," *ibid.;* Government of Sri Lanka (GOSL), *Constitution* (Colombo: Government Press, 1978); GOSL, *Financial Regulations* (Colombo: Government Press, 1960); GOSL, *Annual Estimates of Revenue and Expenditure* (Colombo: Government Press, 1985); GOSL, *District Development Councils Act* (Colombo: Government Press, 1981); Sri Lanka Institute of Development Administration (SLIDA), *Social Development Planning in a Few Selected Districts - An Evaluation* (Colombo: SLIDA, 1985 (forthcoming)); SLIDA, *A Study of the District Minister Scheme* (Colombo: SLIDA, 1984).

# 13

# Delivery of Public Services: Framework for Policy Analysis and Strategy Recommendations

*The Editors*

> A means-end relationship is an empirical proposition, a hypothesis. If we break its contextual limits, we not only transform the hypothesis into sheer speculation, but we lose the opportunity to observe consequences and, hence, to build the knowledge that is needed. Effective development strategies depend, therefore, on accurate descriptions of systemic conditions and upon the construction of means-ends arrangements that are contextually or systemically relevant.
>
> Martin Landau[1]

The burden of construction and implementation of means-ends arrangements for the delivery of public services in developing countries has fallen almost exclusively upon the public administration. Its task has hardly been an easy one. Commenting on this, Naomi Caiden and Aaron Wildavsky are quite direct: developing countries "lack more than money; they lack capable manpower, useful data, and governmental capacity to mobilize existing resources."[2] Unlike rich countries, poor countries lack "the redundancy of men, money, and institutions which let organizations function smoothly and reliably in performing complex tasks."[3] Worse still, given their paucity of resources, developing countries can ill afford the luxury of making mistakes, for under conditions of scarcity, even the smallest error is costly. Which is precisely why it is so essential for planners and those responsible for implementation of plans and programs to possess the relevant knowledge premises about systemic conditions and contextual factors that critically affect program outcomes. As Chee Meow Seah acknowledges in his study of urban transportation in Singapore, the delivery of public services is not a simple exercise in logistics, but is influenced by a variety of contextual factors.

There is as much, if not more, to be learned from past failures as there is from successes -- which is just as well, considering that the overall record has been one of expectations far outstripping actual results. Although the case studies in this book document strategies that have worked, theirs is also a tale of failed expectations, of achievements falling markedly short of targeted outcomes. The question is immediately raised, "Why?" Our cases suggest several answers. In brief, problems are identified within the administrative system, but more importantly, key factors are identified in the political, economic, social and cultural environment which significantly affect program implementation and development outcomes.

The case studies are instructive. Taken together they suggest certain systemic and contextual similarities which many of the Asian developing countries share in common. Our concluding chapter performs in effect an extractive function, by drawing out and calling attention to systemic properties which should inform decision making with respect to the delivery of public services. Accordingly, in the discussion which follows, we shall first consider the contextual variables that constitute, as it were, a common denominator in the external environment of public service delivery systems. We then describe briefly key administrative system variables that are said to affect service delivery, after which we examine the implications for strategies and structures. The final section, "Future Directions," reviews the options available to government and discusses the need to pay attention to administrative aspects of policy implementation.

## Contextual Variables

By contextual variables we mean those factors in the external environments of organizations responsible for the delivery of public services, that significantly affect program implementation and program outcomes and impacts.[4] Since these variables are exogenous to delivery systems, they are assumed to be nonmanipulable by the delivery system (at least in the short term). From the perspective of planners and administrators, therefore, they should be treated as givens. Contextual variables may facilitate, or they may impede, public service delivery. Obviously, contextual variables are specific to each service delivery system. Factors that influence public service delivery in one area may have a negligible impact on delivery in another area. Even in the same public service sector different sets of variables are operative in different country contexts. Nevertheless, our case studies indicate that certain kinds of variables seem to have significant impact, irrespective of public service sector or national culture. Although we would be the first to admit the hazards of generalizing across problem contexts, it would be a disservice to the discipline of public administration if we failed to derive the appropriate inferences from the insights yielded by the case studies.

*Political System Variables.* The case studies indicate that four major classes of political system variables significantly affect public service delivery. First, the greater the acceptance of public authority in the political culture, the more likely it is that decisions taken unilaterally by the public sector will go unquestioned, as the Singaporean and Korean case studies demonstrate. Several of the studies indicate, however, that there are limits to the acceptance of public authority, and that these boundaries vary from policy sector to policy sector. In Korea, rural inhabitants have been generally acquiescent with respect to public health decisions, but this has not been true in the case of the pricing of agricultural products, for example. In Thailand, state interventions in the area of housing and land use policy have traditionally been rare. Should the state suddenly decide to assume an interventionist role in this policy area, there are no grounds for assuming that its decisions will go unchallenged.

A second variable pertains to the type of policy making model that is modal to a given situation. The more elitist the character of decision making, the more likely that the value premises which inform the selection of public service programs will diverge from the preferences of the public at large. This is true of primary health care services both in Korea and in the Philippines. When public services are provided in accordance with elitist perceptions of the public's "needs," it should hardly come as a surprise when the intended beneficiaries' response is less than enthusiastic. The task for the analyst is to identify under what conditions decision making is or is not elitist. In this regard, the Singapore case is informative: it instructs that elitism can break down when the ruling power coalition is ambivalent or divided with respect to a given policy issue. Under these circumstances, a wider appeal is made to the public, which then enters into the decision process.

The third variable concerns the presence or absence of vested interests, i.e., groups which favor or oppose specific types of policies and policy options. As the study on low income housing in the ASEAN countries shows, until recently eviction and resettlement, rather than upgrading, were the dominant features of housing policy, primarily owing to powerful protagonists who favored these policy options because of the land value of inner city slums and squatter settlements.

A fourth factor has to do with policy priorities, or "political will." The higher the priority, the greater the political will, the more likely the success of implementation. For example, Korea's recent emphasis on health policies has led to the enactment of a Special Law for Rural Health Care Service. At the same time, Korea has accorded relatively low priority to the provision of urban shelter, preferring instead to concentrate on the development of key industries. By contrast, housing has been a high priority in Singapore, while public transportation has received less attention. Policy priorities are linked to perceived severity of problems. Housing has been a less severe problem in Thailand and Malaysia than in the Philippines and Indonesia; it has possibly been most severe in Singapore.

Political will implies commitment at all levels of government. In centralized systems, commitment of the national government is a necessary but not sufficient condition to ensure adequate delivery levels. What is equally critical to program success, as the Philippines study indicates, is the involvement and dedication of local leadership.

Related to the issue of policy priorities and political will is the stability of governments. The more stable a government, the greater the continuity of policies, the more likely it is that policy priorities will remain fairly constant over time -- thus enhancing the chances of effective implementation.

*Socioeconomic Variables.* These pertain generally to characteristics of target populations and include factors such as education and income levels, and demographics such as age, sex, and place of residence (urban or rural). The data cited by In-Joung Whang show that the lower the age, the higher the income, the greater the contact ratio in the case of primary health care in Korea. Also, the higher the education level, the greater the contact ratio. Rural populations tend to be older, less educated, and less well off than urban populations -- which is why they are less likely to seek assistance in matters connected with primary health care. In the Philippines, low income levels are a major cause of low participation in primary health care activities. In the study conducted by Victoria Bautista and Josie de Leon, the chief reason respondents gave for not participating in the primary health care program was lack of time, owing to their preoccupation with earning a living.

*Sociocultural Factors.* Unlike socioeconomic variables which tend to exhibit considerable within-country variation, sociocultural factors tend to be more uniformly distributed within a given country or region. Their presence may either limit public acceptance of certain types of services, or else facilitate the implementation of programs. The case studies provide several interesting examples. In the field of primary health care, the Korean culture undermines the success of the program which places heavy reliance on community participation. This is because the Korean tendency is to view health problems as a purely private affair, one that is strictly up to the individual to resolve. Moreover, the traditional male-dominated Korean culture has been a contributing factor in the public's reluctance to accept the all-female community health practitioners. In the area of public housing, to take another example, the provision of walk-up apartments has met with notably poor results in many of the ASEAN countries, because indigenous lifestyles are ill-adapted to low rise habitation. In Nepal, the distribution of the benefits of development has been directly affected by the caste system. The higher the caste, the wealthier, and the more likely to absorb the bulk of developmental inputs. There has been little "trickle-down" of development to the mainly illiterate and impoverished lower castes.

Lest it be concluded that all sociocultural factors work to the impediment of public service delivery, we should point out that there also exist certain norms, specific to each national context, that operate to the advantage of public service delivery. For example, the Singaporean study on public transportation notes that in Singapore, public interest norms have effectively served to deter potential opposition to government measures.

*Physical Factors.* Physical factors affect delivery of public services. The more remote and inaccessible the area, or the more difficult the topography, the more problematic the implementation of public services. The mountainous terrain of Nepal, where fifty percent of the population lives, inhibits the growth of services. Transportation and marketing are two of the more vital areas affected. The Philippine islands also suffer from similar problems of inaccessibility.

*Interrelationships Among Contextual Variables.* We have identified most of the contextual variables mentioned in the case studies, that appear to be cross-culturally salient. What the case studies have not done sufficiently, however, is to discuss the interrelationships among contextual variables and their impact on delivery of public services. This is a line of inquiry that warrants further investigation. For planners and practitioners, to know that certain factors significantly affect delivery systems is not enough. For policymaking purposes, what is required is both knowledge and understanding of degree or magnitude *(How much of an effect?),* as well as knowledge of conjoint influence and interaction among any given set of independent variables *(When A and B appear together, does this have a greater effect than the simple sum of the effect of A plus the effect of B?,* for example). In short, we want to know if and how political system variables relate to socioeconomic and sociocultural factors. Are the relationships linear and additive, or are they perhaps multiplicative in nature?

Chee Meow Seah suggests, but does not elaborate, the hypothesis that acceptance of authoritarianism is inversely related to education levels. This implies that the higher the education, the less likely the acceptance of authoritarianism and the more likely that the actions of political leaders will be questioned. Were we to extend this hypothesis further, we might note that rural populations tend on the whole to be less educated than urban dwellers; from this it follows that one would expect rural populations to be more accepting of authoritarianism and less questioning of the actions of political leaders. Even if this hypothesis were empirically valid, the evidence from the Philippines and Korean primary health care studies suggests, however, that acceptance of authoritarianism does not necessarily imply high levels of participation and cooperation on the part of target populations. It merely implies that government measures will not be resisted. Chee Meow Seah has remarked that most policies contain assumptions that client groups will change their behavior patterns in response to a policy output. His query, and ours: Is this a realistic assumption?

These are the kinds of conceptual linkages that have to be made -- and substantiated empirically -- in order for planners and practitioners to select correctly from among alternative implementation strategies with respect to the provision of public services. Public administration is, if anything, the management of complexity, and the complexity of the external environment has to be modelled faithfully if it is to serve managerial purposes. Moreover, linkages between contextual variables and administrative system variables must further be specified. In particular, to what extent do political system variables exert an influence on administrative structures? From casual observation, it appears quite frequently to be the case that the more elitist the political decision making system, the more centralized the administrative apparatus that is charged with carrying out policies. The question arises, is this a necessary (i.e., causal) association, or is it a purely fortuitous observed connection?

## Administrative System Variables

The problems raised by the case studies are familiar ones: substandard personnel, inadequate budgets, and, almost universally, overcentralized administrative structures leading to further complications in management and coordination. In his comparison of personnel systems in the ASEAN countries, Jon S.T. Quah takes note of poor performance levels and a general inability to attract the best candidates in recruitment to the civil service. The explanation for this is attributed to inadequate salary structures (with the exception of Singapore), outmoded recruitment and selection procedures, and bureaucratic norms which sanction, among others, corrupt practices, personalistic modes of conduct, and violations of formal regulations prescribing promotion on the basis of merit. The quality of personnel and the prevailing bureaucratic ethos are detrimental to interactions with the recipients of public services. The Korean case study on primary health care notes the arrogant and bureaucratic behavior of doctors toward their patients. In Nepal, qualified personnel prefer to stay away from rural areas. The problem is further compounded by the social distance between educated officials and illiterate villagers. The Korean and Nepalese case studies are not isolated examples; they are illustrative of a general phenomenon that is common to most of the Asian developing countries.

Nearly all of the case studies document problems arising from highly centralized administrative structures. Centralization occurs with respect to policies, budgets, and personnel. When all decision making takes place in the central ministries, linkages extending down to the local level are sometimes overlooked or simply ignored. For example, development sectors in Nepal have no formal links with local institutions, except for the Panchayat sector, and there is no local participation in decision making. Even where participation of local institutions is formally an integral part of decisional processes, theory and practice often remain poles apart. Primary health care in the Philippines provides a case in point: power is denied to local government, with the result that local development councils are turned into "talking forums" rather than action-oriented bodies. Moreover, the central administration can weaken local institutions in a number of different ways. The case of Malaysia has seen the refusal on the part of State governments to let local authorities fill in their personnel vacancies, on grounds of insufficient budgetary resources.

Budgets, or rather the lack thereof, play a crucial constraining role in developmental efforts. C.T. Elangasekere points out the resource inadequacy to meet developmental needs, which is due primarily to a restricted tax base. His paper deals with budgeting as the allocation of governmental resources to the different sectors, with the budget document as a plan of action directed toward achieving national developmental goals. In Sri Lanka, the introduction of decentralized District budgets has had a significant impact on public services, insofar as it has resulted in an increase in social infrastructure services in response to local demands -- such services had not been a high priority for the central government. Nevertheless, Elangasekere also documents problems in budgeting that, while common to many developing as well as developed countries, are soluble within the administrative framework. These are: the lack of performance monitoring to assist management decisions; an outdated financial system and practices; and absence of administrative accountability and cost consciousness. More importantly, Elangasekere draws attention to the role of external donor and lending agencies such as the World Bank and the Swedish International Development Agency (to these we might add a long list, e.g., the United States Agency for International Development, Japan's OECF, Canada's CIDA, and so forth). There is no denying the role that these agencies have played in the identification of needs and setting of developmental priorities, as well as the selection of projects and services to be provided, including modes of implementation. While their contributions should not be belittled, it is generally recognized nowadays that donor agency perceptions, however well intentioned, have not always been congruent with local priorities. As many of our case studies suggest, when developmental programs do not correspond to local felt needs, problems in implementation arise.

The task of implementing programs is rendered more complex when there exist interdependencies among public agencies. The Indian, Thai, Singaporean, and Korean case studies draw attention to multiple, overlapping jurisdictions, crossed lines of authority, and fragmented authority structures at the center. The universal call is for more coordination. On this issue, however, the editors take a divergent view. In our perspective, "More coordination!" is an empty prescription, unless specific mechanisms and procedures can be identified. None of the case studies, however, provides satisfactory answers. The Philippines study demonstrates that creating successive tiers of coordinating committees serves little purpose. Agencies tend to be preoccupied with their own concerns. Agency goals take priority – a quite unsurprising finding. Finally, "coordination" often entails an additional workload in the absence of reward or other incentives.

The problem is compounded in highly centralized systems when control over local authorities is exercised through cumbersome reporting and authorization procedures and a communications network that can assume truly labyrinthian proportions. The Philippines case study points out the obvious consequence: officials in the field are overloaded with paperwork and filling out the various reporting, monitoring, and evaluation forms. Yet the fruits of their labor are largely lost, given the length of the communications and decision making chain and the incapacity of the system to process information.

## Strategies and Structures: Comments and Recommendations

Having made reference to problems pertaining to the administrative system and having identified contextual factors which generally serve as constraints in the delivery of public services, the case studies suggest solution alternatives with respect to administrative strategies and structures. Some of the suggestions are quite pragmatic; they are based on observation of what has actually worked, and they are easily implementable in the sense that the administrative system can carry them out without reference to external conditions. The Korean primary health care study, for example, suggests that when a new program is attached (or "piggy-backed" on) to an ongoing program whose success has been proven, its chances of success significantly improve. The Singapore study on public transportation warns that where a function is located (i.e., in which agency) is an important determinant of whether it will receive priority. In the case of Singapore, public transportation was initially accorded low priority because it was made the functional responsibility of an agency whose primary concern was in the area of housing. The moral to be drawn from this is, do not place new programs in agencies that are going to give them low priority.

Other suggestions from the case studies show sound common sense by taking selected components of the task environment into account. Jürgen Rüland cautions against the uniform imposition of strategies: given heterogeneous social groups, existing strategies should be applied in a selective and flexible way to different target groups. Patom Manirojana also sounds the same theme when he advises that distinction be made among the different target or client groups. Chee Meow Seah takes an incremental approach while advocating multiple, complementary strategies, each strategy contributing to a marginal reduction in the problem. Moreover, options appear more attractive to decision makers when they can be made to serve more than one objective -- as in the case of Singapore's Mass Rapid Transit Stations which also serve a defense purpose by doubling as air-raid shelters. In-Joung Whang's study suggests that when examining the feasibility of implementation of any given policy alternative, attention should be paid to legal statutes and administrative regulations to distinguish what can be done within the existing legal framework, and what requires new enactments or laws. It is the case quite often that the more complicated the legal process, the greater the delay in implementation, and the poorer the chances of success.

With respect to structural changes, most of the case studies focus on the problem of centralization of authority. An operative rule for bureaucracy appears to be, "When in doubt, centralize." As Manirojana observes, bureaucrats prefer centralized forms of administration -- centralization creates certainty with respect to power and responsibility, it clearly defines authority and the limits of authority, and most importantly, it enables the central administration effectively to control lower tiers of administration. We note, in addition, that proponents of centralized planning and control in public services base their argument on another set of grounds. Their assertion is that centralization and hierarchical control alone can curb the tendencies of agencies to pursue narrow sectarian or parochial interests. Services that benefit socially and economically heterogeneous populations are possible only in structures where special interests are held tightly in check.[5] When policies are concerned primarily with considerations of social equity and the equitable distribution of benefits, these can be obtained only through centralized administrative structures. Even though centralization may be a necessary condition, however, it is hardly a sufficient one. K.N. Sharma's study notes the uneven distribution of the benefits of development that has occurred under the highly centralized Nepalese administrative system.

The problem, of course, is that centralization seldom works. The means-ends linkages have failed to be substantiated, either empirically or in theory. In fact, organization theorists have long argued that centralized systems are inappropriate in situations where goals are ambiguous, techniques uncertain, and environmental conditions constantly changing.[6] Our case studies offer ample evidence of the truth of this. Some authors propose, as a solution, a greater degree of administrative decentralization or deconcentration. Advocates of this perspective generally base their arguments on the grounds that decentralized systems permit greater adaptiveness to local needs and greater innovativeness in regard to program implementation, in virtue of their greater flexibility. They are therefore viewed as a more efficient means of utilizing (and allocating) societal resources.[7]

The question the editors wish to raise at this juncture is, Given political system contextual variables that tend toward authoritarian forms of government and elitist decision making, how realistic is it to expect the administrative system to transform itself into a decentralized entity? Any decentralization or deconcentration of authority entails a redistribution of power among the tiers of government, and this is clearly a political issue. Shamsuddin Kassim notes in this connection, "Given the realities of the federal system, such a suggestion would be impractical and unrealistic." His reference is to the Malaysian system, but it is equally applicable to the rest of the studies in this volume. By extension, recommendations regarding increased people's participation at the grassroots level are also subject to the same doubts. Such participation is a function of the political system; it is not an administrative solution -- as, indeed, is shown by Bautista and de Leon's study.

The case studies illustrate the complexity of public service delivery. More often than not, we find ourselves in a Catch-22 situation. Which is to say, implementation of public service delivery devolves upon the public sector because (historically, at least) it has been in the best position to mobilize the resources necessary to the task of development. Historically also, determination of the path of development, including specification of the types of public services to be provided and their scope, has been virtually the sole prerogative of the public sector. As a natural consequence, perhaps, the proliferation of public services has been accompanied by the growth of public bureaucracies -- a growth that one is tempted to say has been exponential in character. In turn, the need to control an increasingly complex and differentiated administrative system has led to even greater hierarchy and centralization. The catch, however, is the following one. Given enormous complexity and uncertainty in the external environment, centralized decision systems tend to fail because of structural weaknesses and a built-in incapacity to process information in a timely fashion. At the same time, the centralized decision apparatus is simply not designed to accommodate decentralized forms within its system. All the much-vaunted claims concerning well-balanced combinations of "top-down" and "bottom-up" decision making within the same planning or implementation system usually turn out upon inspection to be more fantasy than fact, more imaginary than real.

Yet governments in the developing countries are loath to sit back and let nature, or more correctly, the forces of the market, take their course. As Chung-Hyun Ro points out, governmental neglect of potential problems can lead to disruptive social tensions in the long run. Under the circumstances, then, what strategies might one sensibly recommend? If the case studies suggest anything, it is that there are no tailor-made solutions. There are no universal panacea to be prescribed. Strategies must be devised in accordance with contextual imperatives; it would be folly to disregard the contextual variables that are specific to each problem context. Nevertheless, some general guidelines in the selection of strategies are possible. Based upon our reading of the case studies in this book, we offer the following prescriptions.

First, identification of appropriate solutions depends in large measure upon correct initial specification of the problem. In this connection, we note that problem specification implies the identification of root causes, extending to assessment of which of the root causes are capable of solution and which are not. Incorrect problem specification results inevitably in the selection of "wrong" solutions. This may sound so obvious as not to warrant mention, but the rather sad fact of the matter is that quite often it is the obvious that is overlooked when it comes to specification of policy options and strategies. The so-called housing problem in urban areas quite often turns out not to be a shelter problem at all, but rather one of land use, as Rüland's study correctly points out. To solve the land use problem indirectly by means of housing policy may, of course, be feasible. But the route is rather circuitous, and it is likely that salient factors will be omitted from the calculations, simply because they do not appear to be relevant in the context of housing.

Even when the initial problem specification and identification of root causes is essentially correct, in considering which policy options to pursue, policymakers also have to take into account side effects and the interaction between substantive policy areas. Solving a problem in one policy area may create new problems in other policy areas. To the extent that side effects, both positive and negative, are anticipated, steps may be taken to prevent deleterious outcomes and to ensure that maximum benefits are yielded.

Our second suggestion concerns the utility of classifying problems in terms of the extent to which they depend on external factors for their solution. Depending on the number and nature of the contextual variables, it is likely that solutions will become progressively more difficult to obtain, the greater the influence of external factors. One strategy that may be worthwhile pursuing is to select options that are relatively manageable in terms of implementation -- i.e., options that are *least* subject to external influences.

In this regard, we venture the somewhat heretical suggestion that administrative reform is less a profitable strategy than it is a costly undertaking that runs an extremely high risk of failure. For successful reform of administrative structure depends, in the first instance, and indeed some may say paradoxically, on a political environment that is supportive of -- no, that *demands* -- reform. Unless the political will is present, comprehensive administrative reform is almost doomed to failure from the start. Our Malaysian study of local government reform is a case in point: nearly a decade after local government was restructured with the "aim of improving the capacity of local authorities in providing services to the people... there has been no improvement in the capacity to deliver services." Our case studies indicate that structural reforms invariably lead to even more problems, and create the potential for conflict among agencies. Chee

Meow Seah's study on public transportation in Singapore points out that it is possible to take on new functions with old structures; provided that there is sufficient administrative flexibility, it is simpler to modify standard operating procedures than to tamper with administrative structures.

Our own assessment is that structural reform is much like going from a two-way to a one-way traffic system: it should be attempted as a last resort, when all other possibilities have been exhausted. A great deal more uncertainty is involved, however, than in the case of traffic. There are no *a priori* grounds for assuming that structural reform will result in desired outcomes. After reviewing the literature, Christopher Hood and Andrew Dunsire come to the conclusion that, "Evidence linking organisational structure with effectiveness is at best tenuous and circumstantial;" moreover, "even fairly systematic studies seeking to explore relationships between structure, environment, and performance have not arrived at clear-cut results."[8] If, however, despite the paucity of theoretical (and empirical) support for structural reform as a means of securing more effective performance, advocates were to persist in their demands for such reform, then they should be quite specific with respect to the dimensions to be affected. Pugh et al., for example, have identified at least five primary structural dimensions: specialization, standardization, formalization, centralization, and configuration.[9] There are doubtless other dimensions that are salient to the discussion.

A third suggestion has to do with identification of policies that require active participation from the people (e.g., from intended beneficiaries), and those that do not. With respect to the former case, where the success of a program depends on contributions from the client population, there seems to be little point in investing resources in projects that target groups are uninterested in, or in selecting methods of implementation that are unacceptable to the people. The two primary health care studies as well as the study on ASEAN public housing provide evidence of this. Rüland's observation is pertinent: "The poor quite often have different perceptions of what is considered to be social injustice than foreign observers, domestic intellectuals, or governments." The strategy that we recommend is to identify areas where people's cooperation is likely to be obtained and to select projects and modes of implementation that will maximize cooperation. Bautista and de Leon make a similar recommendation in concluding that, given the fact that "non-health related activities take precedence over health concerns in the community, a rethinking may be made in terms of the entry point within which community-based activities are pursued."

## Future Directions: Delivery Options and Implementation Issues

While the case studies direct attention to strategies that work as well as those that do not, they leave open the question of the kinds of delivery options that governments might profitably pursue. Manirojana has pointed out, following Caiden, that public service delivery "can be handled by combinations of seven different systems, namely, voluntary organizations, the market place, external suppliers, other domestic governments, public enterprises, private contractors, and third sector organizations." With respect to any public service undertaken by government, the available options are either for the government to assume sole responsibility or to assume joint responsibility with other organizations in some form of joint delivery or to contract service delivery out to other organizations. These are options that require serious investigation before embarking upon the delivery of any given service. It is quite possible that for each type of public service there are alternative policy options which are optimal to a given situation. Consideration of optimal alternatives is beyond the scope of this book, but it most certainly constitutes a fruitful topic of inquiry for future research.

A prior consideration, of course, concerns whether or not any particular service should be undertaken at all by government. In Asian societies political power has traditionally been tied to moral and social considerations. Although the *scope* of activities to be undertaken by the state finds little basis in philosophical principle, there is ample historical precedent for public service delivery, especially in the post-World War II period. In accordance with the requirements of development administration (and its implications regarding the role of government as "change agent"), the tendency has been for modern-day governments themselves to define their role, which includes definition of scope with respect to provision of public services. In retrospect, it appears that in many instances governments have overextended themselves. Given unavoidable resource limitations, as well as having to face a multitude of administrative constraints, governments would do well to consider which types of "public" services can be handled by nongovernmental organizations (for instance, private, voluntary associations) or by the private sector, without having to rely on public sector assistance or initiatives. In this regard, future policy research that takes into account the relevant contextualities may make a significant contribution in identifying the options available to government.[10]

Obviously, public service delivery does not terminate with the selection of policy alternatives or with stipulation of strategies and structures for carrying out public services. *Implementation* remains a critical issue, one which ought to be addressed when considering options and strategies. The term implementation has a fairly standard meaning. It refers to "a process of interaction between the setting of goals and *actions geared to achieving them.*"[11] Phrased somewhat differently, successful implementation depends upon the correct "construction of means-ends arrangements that are contextually or systemically relevant" -- the phrase is taken from the quotation from Landau that appears at the beginning of this chapter. The process of constructing means-ends linkages must of necessity take into account all the relevant factors, both in the internal organizational or administrative system, as well as in the external environment. The literature on implementation abounds, especially in the field of public policy and policy analysis. We hardly propose to embark upon an in-depth discourse on this topic at this juncture. We simply wish to make the point that consideration of policy options and strategies without considering implementation is equivalent to thinking about *what* to do without thinking about *how* to do it -- which for most practical purposes is rather useless.

Despite technological advances and an expanding repertoire of sophisticated techniques, the ever-increasing complexity in the external environment has made the task of public administration commensurately problematic. Many administrative structures and strategies that served quite well in the past may no longer be suitable. This has given rise to a phenomenon with which we are all too familiar: the quest for remedies and solutions. Now there is nothing wrong with going after solutions. The enterprise as such is both recommended and entirely commendable. A problem arises, however, in the way we proceed in search of answers. For example, it is quite customary for books on development administration to start out with a preferred solution (e.g., "decentralization," or, "privatization," which are both very much in vogue currently) and then to proceed to examine instances of their application in selected countries. But this volume has not done so, and for good reason. Too often others have tended to put the cart before the horse. Time and time again they have made the mistake of prescribing a preferred solution before correctly diagnosing the problem. If our case studies suggest anything at all, it is that there are neither standard cures nor all-purpose solutions to be found in the delivery of public services. If solutions and their implementation are to be effective, attention must be paid to the contexts. The first procedural step in the search for solutions is correct specification of the external environment. The external environment provides facilitating as well as limiting conditions on public service delivery. To understand the external environment, therefore, is to know whether a proposed solution is feasible or not in a given time and place and within a specific administrative context.

Moreover, for any given problem and its context, there may exist more than one solution. So the task of the investigator is to identify alternative solutions, some of which may turn out to be substitutes for one another, while others may turn out to be complementary. The precise character of a solution (or set of solutions), however, is left "open-ended," to be determined by specific political, economic, social, cultural, and administrative contexts. We decide to decentralize, for example, only when it is appropriate (i.e., instrumental) to do so. And appropriateness or means-ends instrumentality is contextually determined.

Since solutions are not to be prescribed in advance, how are we to know what works and what does not? Our reply: by experimentation and experimentation alone will we accept or reject our hypotheses. The task of development administrators is largely a problem in management. In the absence of powerful theories or proven technologies, the public administrator must not only proceed pragmatically, he must also play the role of experimental scientist. It is only through experimentation -- used here in the scientific sense, which includes adherence to the principles of experimental design -- that we will learn with a greater degree of certainty what works, what doesn't, and why. Experimentation is *not* "muddling through" (with all due respect to Charles Lindblom[12]); if it is trial and error, it is systematic trial and error, carrying with it the implication that learning occurs with each experience or "trial."

The studies that appear in this book should be viewed as descriptions of events that could potentially provide the basis for experimentation. As we learn (or ought to learn) from our own past experience, so do we also learn by analogy from the experience of others. Our case studies represent the beginning of a search for more effective public service delivery systems. Much more investigative research is needed before we can claim to have solved the puzzle. At the very least the cases in this book direct attention to factors that should prove salient to the task at hand. If we pay attention to the analysis of what is already known, if we spend the time to synthesize and to draw the appropriate inferences from our experiences in development administration, then from a multitude of seemingly disparate cases and seemingly disjointed and albeit somewhat circumstantial evidence, we may piece together the whole, which turns out in the event to be greater than the sum of its individual parts.

**Notes**

1. Martin Landau, "Linkage, Coding and Intermediacy," in Joseph W. Eaton (ed.), *Institution Building and Development: from Concepts to Application* (Beverly Hills: Sage Publications, 1972), p. 109.

2. Naomi Caiden and Aaron Wildavaky, *Planning and Budgeting in Poor Countries* (New Brunswick: Transaction Books, 1980), Introduction, p. vii.

3. *Ibid.*

4. The terms "contextual variables," "external environment," and "task environment" are sometimes used as if they were interchangeable. In a broad sense, perhaps they are. In the literature on this subject, however, one finds that there is no standard usage. Some theorists employ the terms interchangeably; others do not. J.D. Thompson, for example, defines the task environment of organizations to consist of four components: clients, competitors, suppliers, and regulators (see *Organizations in Action* (New York: McGraw Hill, 1967)). D.S. Pugh, et al. have conceptualized seven contextual variables: origin and history; ownership and control; size; charter or purpose; technology; location; and dependence on the environment (see "A Conceptual Scheme for Organizational Analysis," *Administrative Science Quarterly,* Vol. 8, No. 3 (Dec. 1963), pp. 289-315).

5. H. Aldrich, "Centralisation versus Decentralisation in the Design of Human Service Delivery Systems: A Response to Gouldner's Lament," in O. Grusky and G.A. Miller (eds.), *The Sociology of Organizations* (New York: The Free Press, 1981), pp. 373-382.

6. *Ibid.,* pp. 383-391. See also, Russell Stout, Jr. and Martin Landau, "To Manage Is Not To Control: Or the Folly of Type II Errors," *Public Administration Review,* Vol. 39, No. 2 (March/April 1979), pp. 148-156. For alternatives, see, e.g., Martin Landau, "Redundancy, Rationality, and the Problem of Duplication and Overlap," *Public Administration Review,* Vol. 29, No. 4 (Aug. 1969), pp. 346-358.

7. Aldrich, *op. cit.,* pp. 373-382.

8. Christopher Hood and Andrew Dunsire, *Bureaumetrics: The Quantitative Comparison of British Central Government Agencies* (University, Alabama: The University of Alabama Press, 1981), p. 22.

9. C.R. Hinings and Gloria L. Lee, "Dimensions of Organization Structure and Their Context: A Replication," in D.S. Pugh and C.R. Hinings (eds.), *Organi-*

*zational Structure: Extensions and Replications* (Great Britain: Saxon House, 1976), p. 3.

10. E.S. Savas in *Privatizing the Public Sector: How to Shrink Government* (Chatham, N.J.: Chatham House, 1982) gives an exceptionally lucid exposition on how to reduce the size and scope of government while increasing the level and quality of public services. Anyone embarking on future policy research on this topic would do well to take Savas' book as his starting point.

11. Jeffrey L. Pressman and Aaron B. Wildavsky, *Implementation* (Berkeley: University of California Press, 1974), Preface, p. xv, emphasis added.

12. This paragraph is excerpted from Suchitra Punyaratabandhu-Bhakdi, "Development Administration in Thailand: Changing Patterns?", pp. 22-23, paper given at the Panel on Changing Patterns of Development Administration in Asia, Annual Meeting of the American Society for Public Administration, Anaheim, California, April 13-16, 1986. The reference to Lindblom is of course to his seminal article, "The Science of Muddling Through," *Public Administration Review,* Vol. 19 (1959), pp. 79-88.

# List of Abbreviations and Acronyms Appearing in the Text

| | | |
|---|---|---|
| ADS | - | Administrative and Diplomatic Service (Malaysia) |
| ARD | - | Accelerated Rural Development (Thailand) |
| ASEAN | - | Association of Southeast Asian Nations |
| BAAC | - | Bank for Agriculture and Agricultural Cooperatives (Thailand) |
| BHS | - | Barangay Health Station (Philippines) |
| BHW | - | Barangay Health Worker (Philippines) |
| BPHCC | - | Barangay Primary Health Care Committee (Philippines) |
| CBD | - | Central Business Area (Singapore) |
| CHP | - | Community Health Practitioner (Korea) |
| CSC | - | Civil Service Commission (Philippines, Thailand) |
| CSI | - | Civil Service Institute (Singapore) |
| DAE | - | Department of Agricultural Extension (Thailand) |
| DISPHCAG | - | District PHC Action Group (Philippines) |
| E.O. | - | Executive Order (Philippines) |
| ESCAP | - | Economic and Social Commission for Asia and the Pacific |
| ICS | - | Indonesian Civil Service |
| IEC | - | information/education/communication (Philippines) |
| INTAN | - | Institut Tadbiran Awam Negara (Malaysia) (National Institute of Public Administration) |
| IPHO | - | Integrated Provincial Health Office (Philippines) |
| KIPH | - | Korea Institute of Population and Health (Korea) |
| KIPH | - | Korea Institute of Public Health (Korea) |
| KNHC | - | Korea National Housing Corporation (Korea) |
| LAN | - | National Institute of Administration (Indonesia) |
| LPH | - | Laguna Provincial Hospital (Philippines) |
| LSC | - | Legal Service Commission (Singapore) |
| MCH | - | Maternal and Child Health (Korea) |
| MCS | - | Malaysian Civil Service |
| MOAC | - | Ministry of Agriculture and Cooperatives (Thailand) |
| MOC | - | Ministry of Construction (Korea) |
| MOF | - | Marketing Organization for Farmers (Thailand) |

| | | |
|---|---|---|
| MOH | - | Ministry of Health (Philippines) |
| MOHA | - | Ministry of Home Affairs (Korea) |
| MRT | - | Mass Road Transit (Singapore) |
| MSB | - | Merit Systems Board (Philippines) |
| NESDB | - | National Economic and Social Development Board (Thailand) |
| NFWC | - | National Federation of Women's Club (Philippines) |
| NHA | - | National Housing Authority (Thailand) |
| NIDA | - | National Institute of Development Administration (Thailand) |
| NTUC | - | National Trade Union Congress (Singapore) |
| PAB | - | Personnel Administration Branch (Singapore) |
| PCF | - | Population Center Foundation (Philippines) |
| PCS | - | Philippine Civil Service |
| P.D. | - | Presidential Decree (Philippines) |
| PDC | - | Provincial Development Council (Philippines) |
| PHC | - | Primary Health Care (Philippines) |
| PHDS | - | Public Health Delivery System (Korea) |
| PHO | - | Provincial Health Office (Philippines) |
| PMO | - | Prime Minister's Office (Singapore) |
| PROPHCAG | - | Provincial PHC Action Group (Philippines) |
| PSC | - | Public Service Commission (Malaysia) |
| PSC | - | Public Service Commission (Singapore) |
| PSD | - | Public Services Department (Malaysia) |
| PSD | - | Public Service Division (Singapore) |
| PWD | - | Public Works Department (Singapore) |
| RHDS | - | Rural Health Delivery System (Korea) |
| RHU | - | Rural Health Unit (Philippines) |
| RIC | - | Rural Information Council (Philippines) |
| RTAC | - | Road Transport Action Committee (Singapore) |
| SBS | - | Singapore Bus Service |
| SCS | - | Singapore Civil Service |
| TCS | - | Thai Civil Service |
| UNDP | - | United Nations Development Program |
| UP-CCHP | - | University of the Philippines Comprehensive Community Health Program |

# Index of Names

Abeysekera, G., 293n.1
Abrams, C., 141, 155n.27
Adhikari, S.P., 234nn.1,5
Aldrich, H., 310nn.5,7
Alfiler, Ma. Concepcion, 102n.10, 103n.33
Ancog, A., 155n.18
Angel, S., 152, 154nn.1,6, 156n.35, 157nn.49-51,58
Aristotle, 7, 8
Asoka the Great, King, 4
Augustine, 8
Austin, James E., 27
Austin, Nancy, 267n.1

Bacon, Francis, 174
Bain, David, 267n.1
Balasingham, S., 293n.1
Balk, W.L., 267n.1
Ban Lee Goh, (see Goh Ban Lee)
Banzon, Amporo, 101nn.3,4
Barbour, E.J., 252, 269n.46
Barker, Ernest, 10, 11, 19nn.23-30
Baross, P., 156n.35, 157n.59
Bautista, Victoria, 103n.36, 297, 304, 306
Beers, B.F., 18n.5
Benson, C.S., 50
Bentham, Jeremy, 10, 19n.22
Bismarck, Otto von, 12
Blaise, H., 128n.12
Bodin, Jean, 9, 10
Bollens, John C., 23, 48n.5
Boonprakob, Udon, 267n.8, 268nn.21-23,34, 269nn.45,47, 270nn.63, 78, 271n.89, 272 nn.105,120
Boonyabancha, Somsook, 138, 154nn.6,8,9,12,13
Braibanti, Ralph, 269n.51
Briones, L.M., 155nn.23,24
Bruno, E., 155n.32, 156n.35
Buddha, the, 4
Burgess, R., 145-147, 149, 155n.32, 156nn.37, 42,43,48

Burkhead, J., 293n.1
Caiden, Gerald E., 23, 48nn.2,3
Caiden, Naomi, 294, 307, 310n.2
Callis, H.G., 18n.4
Cariño, Ledivina, 101n.7, 103n.32, 272 n.116
Chan, P., 154n.16
Chandarasorn, Voradej, 49n.14
Charles, Vasantha D.R., 272n.113
Chaturvedi, T.N., 65
Chee Meow Seah (see Seah Chee Meow)
Cheema, S.R., 157n.60
Chirathamkijkul, T., 152, 157n.58
Chung-Hyun Ro, 174nn.5,6,11, 304
Cicero, 8, 9
Clyde, P.H., 18n.5
Cook, Thomas J., 19n.17

Datuk Athi Nahappan, 204
Datuk Seri Dr. Mahatir Mohamad, 264, 266
de Guzman, Raul P., 103nn.40,41
de Leon, Josie, 297, 304, 306
De Mel, R.J., 293n.1
De Voy, R.S., 157nn.49,55
Dhiravegin, Likhit, 258, 271nn.80-83
Diamond, J., 154n.10
Doebele, W., 154n.1
Dubhashi, P.R., 63, 68
Dunsire, Andrew, 306, 310n.8

Eaton, Joseph, 128n.12, 310n.1
Elangasekere, C.T., 293n.1, 300, 301
Esman, Milton J., 128n.12, 260, 271nn.93,94

Fernandez, Filemon U., Jr., 267n.6, 268nn.14, 15,30,31, 269nn.49,50,58, 270n.75, 272nn. 109,114,115
Fesler, James W., 17n.1, 19n.36
Fichter, R., 155
Francisco, Gregorio A., Jr., 271n.85
Frederick William I, 13

*315*

Fromm, Gary, 48n.1
Galbraith, J.K., 50
Gandhi, Indira, 65
Gant, George, 25, 48n.8
Gibson, J.L., 272n.104
Goh Ban Lee, 150, 157n.52
Goodman, L.J., 174n.3
Gray, Clive, 255, 269nn.52,57
Grimes, O.F., 155n.20
Grusky, O., 310n.5
Gtotz, Gustave, 18nn.6,8

Hagensiek, C.A., 150, 157n.53
Hampel, R., 154n.15
Hang Koo Cho, 174nn.3,8
Harbert, Jacob, 50
Harmon, M. Judd, 7, 10, 18nn.9-16, 19nn.19-21
Harrison, Brian, 15, 19nn.33,34
Herrle, P., 155n.19, 156n.44
Hickman, C.R., 267n.1
Hinings, C.R., 310n.9
Hobbes, Thomas, 10, 19n.22
Hoad, Christopher, 306, 310n.8
Hunter, Guy, 53

In-Joung Whang (see Whang In-Joung)

Jakobson, L., 154n.4
Jayakumar, S., 270n.76
Jimènez, E., 154n.4
John of Salisbury, 9

Kafle, M.P., 234n.6
Kammeier, D., 157n.56
Kassim, Shamsuddin, 303
Kee Check Cheong, 157n.52
Keyes, W.J., 156n.33
Keynes, John Maynard, 16
Kim Dong Hee, 128nn.20,23
Kim Jin-soon, 128n.17
Kim Young-sik, 128n.23
Krannich, Ronald L., 270n.79
Kulp, Earl M., 23, 24, 48nn.4,6,7
Kung-tzu, 5

Ladavalya, Bhansoon, 130
Landau, Martin, 128n.12, 294, 308, 310nn.1,6
Laquian, A., 141, 154n.4, 155n.27
Laslett, Peter, 19n.22
Lasmiswaramma, M., 65
Lasswell, Harold, 50
LeBoeuf, Michael, 267n.1
Lee Boon Hiok, 267n.7, 268n.19
Lee, Gloria L., 310n.9
Leveriza, Jose P., 268n.1
Lim, W.S.W., 149, 157nn.50,51,54
Lindblom, Charles, 309
Lloyd, P., 154n.14
Lübbe, P., 155n.19
Lund, P., 50

Machiavelli, 9, 19n.18
Makepeace, Walter, 200n.1
Makil, P., 154n.7
Mangin, W., 141, 155n.27
Manirojana, Patom, 49nn.16,17, 302, 303, 307
Manu, 4
Manurung, Cyrus, 267nn.4,9,10, 268nn.25,26, 269nn.36,48,53, 271n.91, 272nn.103,110
Marcos, Ferdinand E., 241
Marican, Y. Mansoor, 271nn.92,95
Mathur, Kuldeep, 65
Mathur, O.P., 157n.56
Meng-tzu, 5
Miller, G.A., 310n.5
Mollett, J.A., 65
Montgomery, John D., 129n.30, 260
Moore, C.A., 18nn.2-5
Mosher, Arthur, 48n.6
Myung Chan Whang, 174n.4

Nam Jae-bong, 113
Napoleon, 13
Navaratne, V.T., 293n.1
Neher, Clark D., 14, 15, 19nn.32,35
Noranitipadungkarn, C., 150, 157n.53
Norris, Malcolm, 215n.1

Oberndörfer, Dieter, 130, 144, 147, 155nn.26, 31, 156n.45
Ocampo, Romeo, 94, 103nn.34,35, 155n.18
Ojha, Y.N., 234n.5
Ozgediz, Selcuk, 238, 267n.3
Omar, Elyas bin, 267nn.5,11,12, 268nn.27,28, 269nn.37,44, 270nn.65, 72-74, 271nn.96,97, 272n.112

Panganiban, Elena, 94, 103nn.34,35
Paudyal, Madhab Prasad, 234n.3
Paul, Samuel, 271n.98
Peters, T.J., 267n.1
Pfister-Gaspary, B., 155n.26
Plato, 7, 8
Polybius, 8
Prakesh, V., 154n.4
Pressman, Jeffrey L., 311n.11
Price, James, 129n.31
Pugh, D.S., 306, 310n.4,9
Punyaratabandhu-Bhakdi, Suchitra, 311n.12

Quah, Jon S.T., 201n.4, 267n.7, 268 nn.16,33, 270nn.66,67, 271nn.84, 86, 272nn.101,102, 106, 117-119, 299
Quek, Veronica, 268n.20

Raffles, Sir Stamford, 177, 178, 190
Raksasataya, Amara, 246, 267nn.2,4-8, 268 nn.24,29, 269n.38, 271n.88
Reforma, M., 155nn.23,24
Reischauer, Edwin O., 18n.5
Ro Chung-Hyun (see Chung-Hyun Ro)
Rodronguang, C., 157nn.49,55
Rogers, E., 127n.3
Rondinelli, D.A., 157nn.57,60
Roosevelt, Franklin D., 16
Rösel, J., 155n.19
Rüland, Dorothea, 130
Rüland, J., 154nn.2,3,5,15,17, 155n.26, 156n. 34, 305, 306

Santos, Narcisa, 103nn.42,43
Sarin, M., 147, 156n.46
Savas, E.S., 311n.10
Schmandt, Henry J., 23, 48n.5

Seah Chee Meow, 200n.2, 201nn.8-10, 294, 299, 302, 305, 306
Seneca, 8
Seshadhari, K., 65
Shaari, Ahmad Takiyuddin bin, 268 n.29
Sharma, K.N., 234nn.1,2,4, 303
Siagian, Sondang P., 271n.90
Siedentopf, Heinrich, 246, 267nn.2,4-8, 268nn. 24,29, 269n.38
Siffin, William J., 16, 19n.36
Silas, J., 145, 156n.35
Silva, M.A., 267n.1
Singh, S.P., 51
Singhawisai, Wilars, 269n.38
Skinner, R., 146, 156n.40
Smith, Theodore M., 269nn.54,55, 272n.111
Smith, Wallace F., 174n.1
Socrates, 7
Song Keun-yong, 108-113, 120-123, 127n.9, 128nn.10,21,22, 129n.32
Steinberg, F., 146, 147, 156nn.36,39,41
Stene, Edwin O., 271n.85
Stout, Russell, Jr., 310n.6
Sudan, M.L., 65
Suh Sang-mok, 128n.25
Suka, 4
Sung Do Jang, 174nn.3,8
Sung-woo Lee, 127nn.5,8
Sutton, Joseph L., 271n.87
Suwanagul, Kasem, 255, 270n.61
Swan, P., 157n.56

Tan, John, 271n.100
Taubman, Paul, 48n.1
Taylor, A.E., 18n.11
Thomas Aquinas, Saint, 9
Thompson, J.D., 310n.4
Tiwari, R.K., 65
Trimmer, G., 178
Tummala, K.K., 267n.7
Turner, J., 141, 155n.27

Venkatappiah, B., 55
Venkataraman, Shri R., 65
Verma, B.M., 65

Verwilgen, A.F., 18n.5
Von Hauff, M., 155n.26

Wang Gung-hsing, 6, 18n.5
Wandus, John P., 250, 251, 269nn. 39-42
Ward, P.M., 156nn.37,38,40
Wardlow, H., 201n.5
Waterman, R.H., 267n.1
Weidenbaum, Murray, 48n.1

Whang In-Joung, 127n.1, 129nn.26,28,31, 297, 302
Wildavsky, Aaron, 294, 310nn.2,11
Wu Teh Yao, 200n.2

Yeon Ha-cheong, 129nn.27,29

Zainun, Buchari, 269n.56
Zimmern, Alfred, 18n.7

# Index of Subjects

Administrative accountability
   absence of in Sri Lanka, 286
Administrative coordination
   lack of in Korean housing construction, 168-169
Administrative costs
   in public housing, 145
Administrative flexibility
   necessity for in problem solving, 191
Administrative hierarchy
   major structural defect of India, 70
Administrative reforms
   conditions for success, 305
   and effective performance, 306
   as a last resort, 306
   and perceptions of intended beneficiaries, 306
Administrative (structural) reform
   not a profitable strategy, 305
Administrative structure in Singapore
   inadequacy of in handling transportation problems, 183
Administrative structure, strong. *See* Structure, strong administrative
Administrative structures
   problems of in Nepal, 222-223
Administrative system, horizontally decentralized in Korea, 164
Administrative system, national, 24. *See also* Central administration
   defined, 24
Administrative system, public
   structural arrangement of in Thailand, 36
Administrator, agricultural
   prime task of, 53-54
Administrators, development
   managing problems as a major task of, 309
Administrators, public
   citizens as, 7
Agencies, central personnel
   in Indonesia, 242

   in Malaysia, 242-243
   in the Philippines, 243-244
   in Singapore, 244-245
   in Thailand, 245
Agencies, external donor and lending
   role of, 301
Agencies, private
   and politicization of the citizenry in the Philippines, 95
Agencies, public housing
   and overstatement of capacity, 143
Agricultural administrator. *See* Administrator, agricultural
Agricultural credit in India
   multi-institutional approach to, 53
   need for, 67
Agricultural development, 20
   firm basis for, 53
   major difficulties in Thailand, 21
   parties involved in, 28
   reasons for, 20
   in Thailand, 23, 28-29
Agricultural production
   required inputs for, 51-53
Agricultural sector, the
   classification in terms of two economic categories, 26
   conceptualization of, 26
   core services in, 23
   and necessity for community development-type strategies, 20
   peripheral services in, 23
   sub-sectors of in Thailand, 26
Agricultural sector, Indian
   weakest aspect of, 64
Agricultural sector, progressive
   goals of, 38
Agricultural sector, rural
   role of government in, 25
Agricultural sector, subsistence
   goals and objectives of in Thailand, 38, 40

Agricultural sector, Thai, 28
   restructuring of, 41-44
   structural elements in fundamental to the viability of the service delivery system, 39-41, 43-44
   system boundaries of, and effects on policies and plans, 40, 43
Agriculture, Indian
   basic characteristic of, 53
   crucial deficiencies in, 53
   development of the delivery system in, 54-57
   institutional credit in, 58-62

Basic minimum needs
   of farmers, 25
Basic needs development strategy, 142
Block-level planning
   weaknesses of in India, 70
Brahminism, Vedic, 3
Buddhism
   antithetical to Brahminism, 4
   precepts of kingship in, 5
   spread of, 4-5
Budget, the
   functions of, 273, 292, 300
Budget, the annual
   as a central government exercise in Sri Lanka, 279
   legislative control over in Sri Lanka, 274-275
   as a means of asserting legislative control by the Legislature over the Executive, 273-274
   problems pertaining to in Sri Lanka, 284-285
Budget execution in Sri Lanka
   excessive controls on, 286
Budget format
   changes in, in Sri Lanka, 278
   disadvantages of the traditional system in Sri Lanka, 277-278
Budget implementation
   handling of in Sri Lanka, 283
Budget system of Sri Lanka, the
   awareness of the need to decentralize, 279
   five principal components of, 278

Budgetary system, the
   as a device for ensuring fundamental constitutional safeguards in democratic societies, 273
Budgeting
   as the allocation of government resources to different sectors, 273, 300
Budgeting in Sri Lanka
   as a continuous process with identifiable phases, 277
Budgeting, decentralized district
   initiated in Sri Lanka to increase rural production and employment, 280
   power of Sri Lankan Member of Parliament in, 281
Budgeting, national
   highly centralized in Sri Lanka, 285
Budgets
   crucial constraining role of in development efforts, 300

Cabinet, the
   in Thailand, 32
Caste system, the
   and effect on socio-economic development in Nepal, 222
Central administration in Thailand, 30-32
   proposed improvements to, 43
Centralization
   failure of, 303
   as a necessary but not sufficient condition, 303
   necessity for according to Bodin, 10
   as operative rule for bureaucracies, 302-303
   when inappropriate, 303
Centralized decision systems
   failure of due to structural weaknesses, 304
   negative effects of in Sri Lanka, 285
Checks and balances
   system of, 8
   in Sri Lanka, 286
Chief district officer
   role of in Nepal, 224

Cities, primate
  and industrialization policies, 150
  as an outcome of the colonialist economic system, 15
Civic consciousness
  and the provision of social services, 12
Civil service, the
  defined, 238-239
  importance of the recruitment and selection process, 247
  position classification in, 252
  rank classification in, 252
  size of as an important variable, 238
Civil service in ASEAN, the
  compensation in, 254-256
  disciplinary control in, 263-265
  legal framework of, 239-242
  performance evaluation in, 262-263
  promotions in, 257-259
  recruitment into in Indonesia, 247
  recruitment into in Malaysia, 247-248
  recruitment into in the Philippines, 248
  recruitment into in Singapore, 248-249
  recruitment into in Thailand, 249
  selection methods for recruitment into, 249-250
  size of, 239
  training in, 259-262
Colonialism
  effect of, 14-15
  and nationalism, 15
Commercial sector, the
  public services in, 25
Committee Stage Amendments
  purpose of in Sri Lanka, 282
Communication channels
  and the adequate representation of interests in Singapore, 199
Communication gaps
  in India, 71
Communities, poor urban
  diversity of, 132-134
Community development
  objectives of, 20

Commuting, methods of
  in Singapore, 182-183
Concept Plan, the
  as a guideline for town planning in Singapore, 180-181, 188-189
Confucian school of thought, 5
Congruence of interests
  importance of in problem solving, 191
Consumer, the
  and cost of services, 1
Contextual problems
  time as a major variable in, 182
Contextual variables. See Variables, contextual
Control, hierarchical
  as a curb on narrow sectarian or parochial interests, 303
Conurbation, trend of
  reinforced by relocation, 136
Cooperative movement, Indian, 63
  establishment of, 54
  purpose of, 63-64
  weaknesses of, and suggested improvements to, 67-68
Coordination
  problems of compounded in highly centralized systems, 301
Core services
  defined, 23
  distinguished from peripheral services, 23
Cost recovery
  based on unrealistic expectations, 144, 145
  not vital to low-cost housing projects, 152
  rationale for, 143
  when successful, 152
Credit, agricultural
  provision of in India, 62-64
Credit, institutional
  in rural areas of India, 58-62
Credit needs of Indian cultivators
  determination of, 62
Credit needs of low-income urban families, 153
Credit systems in India
  institutional, 63
  non-institutional, 62

Crisis, major economic
　effects on low-cost housing services of, 148
Criteria, quantitative and formal
　required to gauge success of projects, 145
Crop loan system
　and credit needs in India, 62
Crops
　problems of, 21
Culture, Aryan, 3

Decentralization, 2. *See also* Strategies
　aims of in India, 71
　of development functions in Nepal, 227-228
　entails a redistribution of power, 303
　as a more efficient means of utilizing and allocating societal resources, 303
　and self-help, 146
Decentralization of the budget in Sri Lanka
　to accelerate regional development, 279
　development of, 289-290
　represents only three per cent of the annual budget, 286
Decision-making, participatory
　lack of in the Philippines, 94-95
Deconcentration. *See* Decentralization
Delivery of public services. *See* Public service delivery
Delivery process in India
　problems of, 65-66
　stages of, 66
Delivery system, the
　access to in Nepal, 222
　advantages of at sub-district level in Nepal, 229-230
　basic objective of, 51
　conditions for success, 51
　defined, 50, 104-105
　factors affecting efficiency of in India, 69-72
　flaws of in Nepal, 229
　historical development of in India, 54-62
　improvements of in India, 67
　preconditions for change in India, 71-72
　of rural health service in Korea, 104, 112-119

Delivery system, agricultural
　major focus of in India, 67
Delivery system, effective
　conditions for establishment of in India, 71-72
Delivery system, public
　collapse of in rural areas of Sri Lanka, 288
　importance of in combating rural poverty, 64, 68-69
　problems of in India, 66
Departmentalization, functional
　of agencies responsible for agriculture in Thailand, 40-41
Departments
　in the Thai bureaucracy, 30
Development
　social aspects of in India, 66-67
Development agencies
　at district level in Nepal, 223
Development councils
　role of in a community-based approach to service delivery in the Philippines, 99-100
Development fund, district
　required in Sri Lanka, 290
Development, guided
　in the village development program of Nepal, 220
Development in Nepal
　constrained by transportation problems, 221-222
Development, infrastructure
　inherent contradictions in, 176
　necessity for in Sri Lanka, 289
　and rationale for cost recovery, 143
　and role of the panchayat sector in Nepal, 220
Development, intense
　corridors of in Singapore, 181
Development, local
　different conceptions of in Nepal, 220
Development, participatory
　in the panchayat development program of Nepal, 220

Development policy
  provision of low-cost housing services a late-comer in, 151
Development program, panchayat
  in Nepal, 219-221
Development program, village
  in Nepal, 219-220
Development, regional
  accelerated in Sri Lanka by budget decentralization, 279
Development regions
  in Nepal, 223
Development, rural. *See* Rural development
Development schemes, rural
  in India, 52
Development strategy, 20
  in India, 65
Development strategy, manpower
  absence of in Sri Lanka, 287
  necessity for in Sri Lanka, 291-292
Development, technological
  inherent contradictions in, 176
Development, urban
  and role of international organizations, 142
Dimensions, structural
  and effective performance, 306
Disparities, socioeconomic
  dangers of a 'growth first, redistribution later' policy on, 148
District councils
  classification of in Malaysia, 205
Distributive justice
  objective of, 66
  and problems of inequality, 50
Distributive system
  effect of structural deficiencies in, 148
Dualism, 29

Economic growth, sustained
  effect on future housing policies of, 148
Economic justice, 9
Economic system, colonialist
  as fostering the growth of primate cities and dual economies, 15
Economic welfare, 10

Economics, free market
  right of landownership a sensitive issue in, 149
Economy, dual-
  as an outcome of the colonialist economic system, 15
Economy, informal sector
  importance of, 153
  and linkages with the modern economy, 153
Economy, mixed
  and complexity of the delivery system, 21
Economy, modern
  and linkage with the informal sector economy, 153
Economy, subsistence
  goals of, 38
Education
  and the state, 13
  in England, 13
  in France, 13-14
  in Germany, 13
Education, primary
  in England, 13
  in France, 13
  in Germany, 13
Education, public
  emergence of in the West, 14
  importance of as a public service, 13
Efficiency of the delivery system
  factors affecting in India, 69-71
Emperor, Japanese
  mandate to rule of, 6
England
  administration of poor relief in, 10-11
Equity, social, 303
Experimentation, 309. *See also* Solutions
Evictions
  as an important measure in coping with rapid urban growth, 138
  minimization of to conserve housing stock, 142
  undesirable socio-economic effects of, 135
Eviction, threat of
  causes politicization of the urban poor, 139

Factors, key
  which affect program implementation, 295
Factors, physical. *See also* Variables, contextual
  affecting public service delivery, 298
Farmers
  basic minimum needs of, 25
  contemporary perspectives on, 23
  participation of in India, 67
  requirements of in Thailand, 37
Feedback channel
  as a prerequisite for policy analysis, development, and refinement, 286
Framework, legal, 302
Framework, policy
  and delivery system efficiency, 69-70
France
  administration of poor relief in, 11

*General Theory of Employment, Interest and Money*
  as an influence on Roosevelt's New Deal, 16
  as theoretical justification for government intervention, 16
Germany (Prussia)
  administration of poor relief in, 11
  corn depots to control cost of living in, 11
Government
  Seneca's view of, 8
Government, big
  failure of, 1
Government, good
  principles of, 5
Government, role of
  philosophical debate over, 9
Grassroots participation. *See* Participation, grassroots

Health, right to
  as guaranteed by the state, 14
Health service delivery in the Philippines.
  *See also* Primary health care in the Philippines
  citizen participation and, 77
  primary health care and, 76
  reorganization plan of, 79

Health services in Korea
  access to, 107-110
  accessibility of 107
  availability of, 107
  community health practitioners and, 118, 123-125
  conditions for success, 124
  contextual variables in, 119-124
  criteria for evaluation of, 124
  deficiencies in, 117
  distribution of, 106
  health care stations, 117-118
  at local level, 113
  minimum intervention strategy and, 124-125
  network of, 114
  policy implications, 124
  problems of, 116-117
  regional distribution of, 106
  rural health delivery system of, 104, 112-119
  Saemaul Undong and, 118, 125
  satisfaction with, 110-111
  socio-economic factors and demand for, 119, 123
  utilization of, 123
Houses
  size of in Japan, 169
  size of in Korea, 169
Housing. *See also* Shelter
  affordability of in Korea, 173-174
  emerging problems of in Korea, 169
  and necessity for participation of the target group, 142
  as a process, 141, 142
  as a serious public issue, 158
Housing agencies, public
  tend to grossly overstate actual capacity, 143
Housing, apartment. *See* Housing, high-rise
Housing construction
  recommended investment in, 161
Housing construction in Korea
  concentration of, 165
  fundamental problems of, 169
  lack on administrative coordination, 168-169
  as a percentage of GNP, 161

role of the Korea Housing Bank in, 168
role of the Korea National Housing Corporation in, 165-168
Housing costs
  necessity for drastic reduction in, 142
Housing estates
  success of in Singapore resulting in transportation problems, 180
Housing, high-rise
  failure of, 140-141
  should not be dismissed outright, 152
Housing in Korea
  causal factors for shortages of, 160-161
  low priority of, 161
  major sources of, 170
  numbers constructed, 161
  situation of, 159
  supply ratio of, 158
Housing, low cost. *See also* Sites-and-services projects; slum upgrading
  affected by difficulties of land acquisition, 149
  conflicts with the economic rationale of cost recovery, 152
  as an important component of social policies, 152
  low affordability of, 144-145
  no panacea and no universally applicable model for, 147
  problems of are more than just technical or financial, 148
  strategies pertaining to, 137, 142
Housing, lower income
  high density of in Korea, 159
Housing policies, future
  two preconditions influencing, 148
Housing problems
  as addressed in Singapore, 179-180
  development of the Master Plan for Singapore as a result of, 179
  inseparable from the urbanization process, 150
  a major precondition for alleviation of, 150
  in primate cities, 158
  as a problem of land use, 305
  as a structural problem of peripheral capitalism, 147
Housing projects
  in the nineteen fifties and nineteen sixties, 139-140
  and causes of social segregation, 145
  and maintenance problems of, 146
Housing, public
  and administrative costs, 145
  and problems of public health and sanitation, 13
Housing, self-help. *See also* Self-help
  advantages of, 146
Housing services
  factors for effective delivery of, 141

Ideals, Athenian, 7
Implementation
  of public service delivery, 308
Industrialization
  and the growth of social services, 14
  in Korea, 160
Insecurity
  over land tenure, 145
Institutional credit in India
  growth of, 59
Institutional performance in Thailand, 36
Institutions, agricultural credit
  in India, 63
Institutions, public sector. *See* Public sector institutions
Insurance, health, 12
Insurance, social
  emergence of in the 1880s, 12
Insurance, unemployment, 12
Integrated rural development programs
  are aimed at correcting regional imbalances in development in Sri Lanka, 281
  constitute a popular development strategy at district level in Sri Lanka, 281
Integrated rural development projects
  constitute a multi-sectoral approach to

development in Nepal, 225
Intercourse, social
  and the concept of reciprocity, 5
Interdependencies
  and greater complexity in program implementation, 301
Intervention, government
  theoretical justification for, 16
Intervention, state
  necessity for, 16

King, the. *See also* Ruler
  in Confucian school of thought, 5
  ideal-type of in India, 4
  obligations of in the *Dharma-sastra*, 4
  primary function of in the *Mahabharata*, 4
  role of according to Manu, 4
  virtues of in Buddhism, 4
Kingship
  Buddhist precepts of, 5
  legitimate, 5

Labor surplus in poor households
  smaller than anticipated, 147
Land acquisition
  difficulties of, 149
Land banking
  defined, 150
  savings from in Thailand, 150
Land banks
  necessity for, 150
Land ownership
  concentration of, 150
  as a highly sensitive issue, 149
Land tenure
  persistent insecurity over, 145
Land use in Singapore
  examination of through the Concept Plan, 180-181
Law, enforcement of
  a weak point in Thailand and the Philippines, 150
Law, rule of
  Aristotelian, 8

Leaders, informal
  multi-functional role of in India, 68
Leaders, project
  critical role of in the Philippines, 92
Leadership, local
  critical to program success, 297
Legal theory
  Aristotelian influence on, 8
  Roman, 8
Liberty
  according to Machiavelli, 9
Life, right to
  as guaranteed by the state, 14
Local authorities, semi-autonomous
  in Thailand, 32-33
Local government in Malaysia
  characteristics of before restructuring, 209-210
  characteristics after restructuring, 210-211
  constraints on, 207-208
  control over finance and personnel, 212
  defined, 202
  effects of restructuring, 202
  history of, 203-204
  and the importance of grants, 208
  the present system of, 203
  problems of, 209-215
  restructuring into municipal councils and district councils, 204
  role of the National Council for Local Government, 203
  strategies for improving, 212-215
Local governments, weak
  adverse effects on primary health care in the Philippines as a result of, 93-94

*Mahabharata*, the, 3
Mass transit systems
  necessity for, 152
Master Plan, the
  as a guideline for town planning in Singapore, 179-181

Medical insurance scheme
  in Korea, 106
Mencian school of thought
  contrast with Confucian teaching, 5
Metropolitanization, trend of
  reinforced by relocation, 136
Migration, rural-urban
  in Korea, 160
Ministry of Agriculture and Cooperatives, Thailand
  breakdown by departments, 33
  central and provincial interface, 38-39
  domination by central departments, 38-39
  emphasis of ministry services, 38
  major service areas of, 36
  responsibilities of departments, 33
  service delivery channels of, 38
  state enterprises in, 33
  summary of service delivery system of, 39
Ministry of Construction
  role of in Korean national housing policy formulation, 164
Mixed economy, 21
Mobilization, horizontal
  barriers against, 139
Monitoring
  ineffectiveness of, 93
Municipal councils
  classification of in Malaysia, 205

National development, 1
Nationalism
  and colonialism, 15
Nationalism, Japanese
  basis of, 6
Norms, societal
  philosophical basis for, 3

Panchayat, district
  functions of in Nepal, 228
Panchayat, village
  functions of in Nepal, 228
Participation, grassroots, 2. See also Strategies
  as a function of the political system, 304

not an administrative solution, 304
Participation, mechanisms for
  in public housing projects, 153
Participation, people's
  in the debate over a mass rapid transit system for Singapore, 189-190
  in the delivery of health services in Korea, 127
  to ensure 'user-oriented' housing services, 142
  not provided for in India, 70
Participation, pseudo-community
  effects of in Sri Lanka, 288
Peripheral services, 23
Philosophers, later Roman, 8
Philosophies, Eastern
  and emphasis on kingly virtues, 17
  and moral obligations of the state, 16-17
Philosophies, Western
  and emphasis on scope of action of the state, 17
  and moral obligations of the state, 16-17
  as surface overlay, 3
Policies
  to benefit the underprivileged in India, 65
  that require active participation on the part of intended beneficiaries, 306
Policies, industrialization
  and concentration on primate cities, 150
Policies, interventionist, 149. See also Policies, redistributive; Policies, social; Policies, welfare.
Policies, redistributive
  must focus on land issues when considering low-cost housing, 149
Policies, social
  may lead to an increase of purchasing power among low income households, 149
Policies, welfare
  are not a luxury for developing countries, 149
Policy framework
  lack of in India, 69
Policy options
  and side effects, 305

Political system, partyless
    strengthening the local planning process is an ideological prerequisite of, 232
Political will
    necessity for in rectifying structural deficiencies in the distributive system, 148
Poor relief
    as first form of social service performed by the state, 10
    as method of pauperization, 10-11
Poor, the
    necessity for acceptance of, 153
Poor, urban
    as a political threat, 138
    divided along ethnic lines, 137, 139
    fragmented social structure of, 151
    priorities of, 139
Poverty, rural. See Rural poverty
Poverty, vicious circle of
    factors contributing to, 53
Power, redistribution of
    and decentralization, 303
Primary health care in the Philippines
    adversely affected by non-health concerns taking precedence over health concerns, 91-92, 98, 101
    adversely affected by weak local governments, 93-94
    at barangay level, 87-88
    case study of structural arrangements for, 83-84
    characteristic of, 78
    committee composition of, 78
    conceptualization of, 72
    and the difficulty of harnessing inter-agency collaboration, 91, 100-101
    at district level, 85
    effect of contextual variables on, 92-98
    extent of implementation, 89
    implementation of, 80-83
    levels of, 77, 89-90
    major structural defect in, 90-92, 100-101
    at municipal level, 85-86
    at provincial level, 84-85
    significant feature of reorganization plan of, 79
Primary health care approach in the Philippines, 76-77
    chief characteristic of, 76
    eight essential elements of, 82
    major emphasis of, 80
Primate cities
    housing problems in, 158
    and industrialization policies, 150
    as an outcome of the colonialist economic system, 15
Principles, humanitarian
    were not the reason for colonial rulers undertaking public works and social service programs, 15
Priorities of the urban poor
    focus on a more stable and secure environment to live, 139
Private sector, the
    assumed to manage more efficiently than public agencies, 1
Privatization of public enterprises
    constitutes a response to management problems, 1
Problem solving
    and the necessity for a congruence of interests among political and bureaucratic elites, 191
    and the need for administrative flexibility, 191
Procedural deficiencies
    in India, 70-71
Production, agricultural
    required inputs of, 51
Productivity, high
    when undesirable, 40
Programs, agricultural
    conditions for success, 53
Programs, housing
    of the 1950s and 1960s, 139-140
Programs, regionalization
    to divert population and economic growth from metropolitan areas to regional

centers in the hinterland, 150
Projects, development
　not for purely welfare purposes, 20
Provincial administration in Thailand, 32
　proposed improvements in, 43
Prussia. *See* Germany
Public administration
　absence in Sri Lanka of a well-established control mechanism, 286
　and public service delivery in developing countries, 294
　as the management of complexity, 299
Public administration system
　in Thailand, 30-33
Public agencies
　assumed to be less efficient than private sector organizations, 1
　role of in Thailand, 23
Public assistance program
　in Korea, 106
Public finance
　supremacy of Parliament in Sri Lanka with regard to, 274
Public funds
　mismanagement of in Sri Lanka, 286-287
Public institutions
　in Thailand, 30-33
　and Thai agriculture, 33-35
Public personnel administration
　defined, 238
Public sector, the
　in developing countries, 1
　and national development, 1
Public service, concept of
　in Asia, 6
　in city-states, 6
　in the West, 6
Public service delivery. *See also* Public services
　to achieve economic and social development goals, 1
　agents responsible for, 23
　available options for, 307
　concept of, 3
　conceptual basis of in India, 3-5
　as a consequence of the Industrial Revolution, 3
　as a consequence of urbanization, 3
　in developing countries, 294
　handling of, 307
　historical antecedents, 3
　implementation a critical issue of, 308
　importance of citizen participation in, 77
　improvements and extensions in Sri Lanka of, 280-281
　normative aspect of, 2
　objectives of in Korea, 171
　objectives of in traditional societies, 3
　oriental philosophies of, 3-6
　origins of the term, 3
　overextension by government of, 307
　prerequisites for successful implementation of, 308
　relevant contextualities pertaining to, 307
　role of the District Political Authority in Sri Lanka in, 280
　Western philosophies of, 6-10
Public services. *See also* Public service delivery
　conditions for growth of, 17
　delivery of, 1
　delivery problems in India of, 51-54
　differences in between East and West, 14
　difficulty of access to in Sri Lanka, 287
　historical antecedents
　　in India, 3-5
　　in China, 5
　　in Japan, 6
　　in Athens, 6
　　in the Roman Empire, 8
　　in the Middle Ages, 9
　　in Western Europe, 10-4
　　in Asia, 14-16
　historical developments in, 10-16
　importance of public education in, 13
　improving access to in Sri Lanka of, 291
　in the modernized commercial sector, 25
　scope and nature of, 2
　in subsistence rural areas, 25

Public services, growth of, 10-16
  beneficiaries of, 15
  due to incapacity of existing social systems, 17
  and influence in Asia of Western value orientations, 16
  not paralleling historical thought, 10
  as an outcome of the Industrial Revolution, 10
  as an outcome of urbanization, 10
  reasons for in the East, 15-16
  reasons for in the West, 15
  as resultant upon sufficient capital formation, 17
  three distinct periods in Western Europe of, 10
  differences between the first and second periods in, 12
  the third period and the emergence of social insurance in, 12
Public services, provision of
  philosophical base for societal norms governing, 3
  role and duties of government, 2
Public works
  economic reasons for under colonialism, 15
Pyung
  square feet equivalent of, 174n.10

Raffles, Sir Stamford
  suggested that Singapore be based on a grid pattern, 177-178
Reblocking
  and slum upgrading, 142-143
Recruitment, realistic, 250-251
Recruitment, traditional, 250-251
Redistribution, economic
  necessity for future housing policies of, 148
Relocation
  as a measure to cope with rapid urban growth, 138
  minimization of to conserve housing stock, 142
  as a slum clearance policy, 135, 152-153
  undesirable socio-economic effects of, 135-137
Relocation, threat of
  causes politicization of the urban poor, 139
Representation, authoritative
  of the poor, 153
Representation of interests
  new channels of communication in Singapore and, 199
Resettlement. *See* Relocation
Restructuring of local government
  minimal effects of in Malaysia, 207
Revolt, right to, 6
Role, governmental
  in the rural agricultural sector, 25
Roman Empire, the
  legacy of, 8
Ruler
  chief task of, 9
  duty of, 9
  as steward of God, 9
Rural agricultural sector. *See* Agricultural sector, rural
Rural development
  characterized by, 104
  defined, 104
  the Integrated Rural Development Project as an effective instrument of in Nepal, 224
  in Korea, 104
  prerequisite of, 51
Rural development schemes
  to reduce poverty and promote economic prosperity in India, 52
Rural poverty
  causes of in India, 53
  strategies for combating in India, 64-65

Saemaul Undong
  impact of in Korea, 123
Segregation, social
  as a result of housing projects, 145

Self-help
　and decentralization, 146
　democratizing potentials of, 146
　disadvantages of, 146
　and legalization of Korean squatter settlements, 172-173
　as 'overexploitation', 146
　potential for, 146
　role of in low-cost housing policies, 153
　role of in low-cost housing projects, 142
　warning against, 147
Service center
　advantages of in Nepal, 225-227, 229-232
　defined, 225
　recommendations to facilitate the smooth functioning of in Nepal, 233
Service delivery
　basic pattern of, 22
Service delivery, public. *See* Public service delivery
Service delivery in Thailand
　and the central administration, 36
　macro-level considerations, 37
　service-based considerations, 36
　objectives of, 39-41
　recommendations for, 41-44
Service delivery system
　basic pattern of, 22
　concept of, 21
　processes of in Thailand, 33
Service delivery system, agricultural
　core services in, 23
　peripheral services in, 23
Service delivery system of Thai agriculture, the
　public institutions involved in, 35
　structural elements fundamental to system viability, 39-41
　structural-functional framework of, 26-30
Services, delivery of
　and absence of links with attitudes which are supportive of the regions, 50
Shelter. *See also* Housing
　as an important indicator of welfare, 158
Sites-and-services projects
　constituting new types of low-cost housing programs, 142
　cost recovery as an integral part of, 143
　too expensive for low-income families, 144-145
　target populations of, 152
　two-fold function of, 143
Slaves
　function of in city-states, 6-7
Slum dwellers
　refutation of stereotypes of, 141-142
Slum improvement
　and the role of international organization, 142
Slum settlements
　disparities in, 147
Slum upgrading
　'as is where is' approach to, 144
　and reblocking, 142-143
　cost recovery as an integral part of, 143
　defined, 142
　too expensive for low-income families, 144-145
Slums
　as concomitants of socio-economic change, 147
　defined, 132
　variables affecting, 148
Slums of hope, 139
Social overhead projects
　as the first casualties of budget cuts, 285
Social service delivery. *See* Public service delivery; Public services
　in Europe, 14
Social services. *See* Public service delivery; Public services
　economic reasons for under colonialism, 15
　growth of as a direct outcome of industrialization and urbanization in the West, 14
Socratic view
　that government by the many is unjust, 7
Solidarization, horizontal
　barriers against, 139
Solutions
　arrived at through experimentation, 309

first procedural step in search for, 308-309
    precise character of, 309
Solutions, appropriate. *See* Strategies
Squatter settlements
    as concomitants of socio-economic change, 147
    defined, 132
    desire for legalization of in Korea, 171-172
    disparities in, 147
    variables affecting, 148
Squatter units
    in Korea, 161
    in Seoul, 159
Squatters
    problems of in Korea, 171-173
    refutation of stereotypes of, 141-142
    and social stability in Korea, 161
Squatting
    views on, 134
State, the
    according to Machiavelli, 9
    Aristotelian rule of law of, 7-8
    Athenian democratic ideals of, 7-8
    education and, 7, 13
    first form of social service performed by, 10
    function of, 6
    primary function of according to Augustine, 8
    Greek ideas of, 7
    role of, 1
    role of according to Bentham, 10
    role of according to Hobbes, 10
    ultimate purpose of according to Bodin, 10
    virtue and, 7
State, the capitalist
    interests represented by, 149
    not an impediment to low-cost housing services, 149
State, the perfect
    Socratic and Platonic views of, 7
Steering committees
    role of in Sri Lanka, 282

Strategies
    cautions against uniform imposition of, 302
    contracting out tasks, 1
    and correct problem specification, 304-305
    decentralization, 2
    effect of external influences on, 305-306
    as a function of contextual imperatives, 304
    general guidelines in selection of, 304
    grassroots participation, 2
    privatization of public enterprises, 1
Strategies, complementary, 302
    necessary for delivery of low-cost housing services, 148
Strategy, regionalization, 150
Structure, strong administrative
    necessity for, 69
Structures, centralized administrative, 303
Structures, old
    and administrative flexibility, 306
    and new functions, 306
Subsidization
    as a housing policy, 151-152
Subsistence, decent standards of
    as guaranteed by the state, 14
Support systems
    necessity for in Sri Lanka, 290

Targets, planning
    major reason for non-achievement of in ASEAN countries, 149
Tensions, social
    as a result of governmental neglect, 304
Thai agriculture
    dualism of, 29
    and fragmented public services, 41
    functional departmentalization in, 40
    institutional framework of, 41
    overall sectoral structure of, 41
    problems of, 40-41
    progressive sub-sector goals in, 38
    recommendations for, 41-44
    service delivery in Thailand and, 29
    subsistence sub-sector goals in, 40

Index of Subjects    333

Traffic management measures
   introduced in Singapore, 187
Transport planning
   a basic contradiction in, 191-192
   four groups of measures associated with, 183-184
Transportation
   and the distance/time ratio, 175
Transportation in Singapore
   and social obligations, 185
   strategies management role of the government in, 184-185
   subsumed under the Master Plan, 179
Transportation network
   grid pattern of in Singapore, 177-178
Transportation policy
   not a simple logistics exercise, 175
Transportation problems
   role of policy makers in, 176-177
Transportation problems in Nepal
   effect on national development as a result of, 221-222
Transportation problems in Singapore
   addressed, 178-179
   aggravated by the success of housing estates, 180
   compounded by underutilization of taxis, 191-197
   in the nineteenth century, 178
   overridden by housing problems, 179

Unity
   desirability of according to Bodin, 9-10
Urban bias
   consequences of in Sri Lanka, 285
Urbanization
   and the growth of social services, 14
   in Korea, 160
Urbanization policy, national
   to alleviate housing problems, 150

Urbanization, problems of
   initial impulses for in-depth study of, 131
Urbanization process, the
   contrast between developing and developed countries, 130
   inseparable from housing problems, 150
Utility maximization
   in the context of Thai agriculture, 40

Variables, administrative system, 299-301
Variables, contextual
   as a common denoninator in the external environment of public service delivery systems, 295-299
   defined, 295
   and delivery systems, 105
   interrelationships among, 298
   and Korean health service delivery, 119-124
   and the Primary Health Care approach in the Philippines, 92-98
Variables, political system. *See also* Variables, contextual
   four major classes of that affect public service delivery, 296-297
Variables, sociocultural, 297-298. *See also* Variables, contextual
Variables, socioeconomic, 297. *See also* Variables, contextual
Vicious circle
   of eviction, relocation, and re-migration, 136
Vicious circle of poverty
   factors contributing to, 53
Virtue, 10

Welfare
   shelter as an indicator of, 158
Welfare, economic
   in city-states, 6, 10
Welfare state, 9